Mosaic 2

GRAMMAR

Patricia K. Werner

John P. Nelson

Mosaic 2 Grammar, Silver Edition

ISBN 13: 978-0-07-325850-8
ISBN 10: 0-07-325850-4
1 2 3 4 5 6 7 8 9 10 VNH 11 10 09 08 07 06

Editorial director: Erik Gundersen
Series editor: Valerie Kelemen
Developmental editor: Susannah MacKay, Mary Ann Maynard
Production manager: Juanita Thompson
Production coordinator: Lakshmi Balasubramanian
Cover designer: Robin Locke Monda
Interior designer: Nesbitt Graphics, Inc.
Photo researcher: Photoquick Research

Cover photo: Jeffrey Becom / Lonely Planet

McGraw-Hill

The **McGraw·Hill** Companies

A Special Thank You

The Interactions/Mosaic Silver Edition team wishes to thank our extended team: teachers, students, administrators, and teacher trainers, all of whom contributed invaluably to the making of this edition.

Macarena Aguilar, **North Harris College**, Houston, Texas ▪ Mohamad Al-Alam, **Imam Mohammad University**, Riyadh, Saudi Arabia ▪ Faisal M. Al Mohanna Abaalkhail, **King Saud University**, Riyadh, Saudi Arabia; Amal Al-Toaimy, **Women's College, Prince Sultan University**, Riyadh, Saudi Arabia ▪ Douglas Arroliga, **Ave Maria University**, Managua, Nicaragua ▪ Fairlie Atkinson, **Sungkyunkwan University**, Seoul, Korea ▪ Jose R. Bahamonde, **Miami-Dade Community College**, Miami, Florida ▪ John Ball, **Universidad de las Americas**, Mexico City, Mexico ▪ Steven Bell, **Universidad la Salle**, Mexico City, Mexico ▪ Damian Benstead, **Sungkyunkwan University**, Seoul, Korea ▪ Paul Cameron, **National Chengchi University**, Taipei, Taiwan R.O.C. ▪ Sun Chang, **Soongsil University**, Seoul, Korea ▪ Grace Chao, **Soochow University**, Taipei, Taiwan R.O.C. ▪ Chien Ping Chen, **Hua Fan University**, Taipei, Taiwan R.O.C. ▪ Selma Chen, **Chihlee Institute of Technology**, Taipei, Taiwan R.O.C. ▪ Sylvia Chiu, **Soochow University**, Taipei, Taiwan R.O.C. ▪ Mary Colonna, **Columbia University**, New York, New York ▪ Lee Culver, **Miami-Dade Community College,** Miami, Florida ▪ Joy Durighello, **City College of San Francisco**, San Francisco, California ▪ Isabel Del Valle, **ULATINA**, San Jose, Costa Rica ▪ Linda Emerson, **Sogang University**, Seoul, Korea ▪ Esther Entin, **Miami-Dade Community College**, Miami, Florida ▪ Glenn Farrier, **Gakushuin Women's College**, Tokyo, Japan ▪ Su Wei Feng, Taipei, Taiwan R.O.C. ▪ Judith Garcia, **Miami-Dade Community College**, Miami, Florida ▪ Maxine Gillway, **United Arab Emirates University**, Al Ain, United Arab Emirates ▪ Colin Gullberg, **Soochow University**, Taipei, Taiwan R.O.C. ▪ Natasha Haugnes, **Academy of Art University**, San Francisco, California ▪ Barbara Hockman, **City College of San Francisco**, San Francisco, California ▪ Jinyoung Hong, **Sogang University**, Seoul, Korea ▪ Sherry Hsieh, **Christ's College**, Taipei, Taiwan R.O.C. ▪ Yu-shen Hsu, **Soochow University**, Taipei, Taiwan R.O.C. ▪ Cheung Kai-Chong, **Shih-Shin University**, Taipei, Taiwan R.O.C. ▪ Leslie Kanberg, **City College of San Francisco**, San Francisco, California ▪ Gregory Keech, **City College of San Francisco**, San Francisco, California ▪ Susan Kelly, **Sogang University**, Seoul, Korea ▪ Myoungsuk Kim, **Soongsil University**, Seoul, Korea ▪ Youngsuk Kim, **Soongsil University**, Seoul, Korea ▪ Roy Langdon, **Sungkyunkwan University**, Seoul, Korea ▪ Rocio Lara, **University of Costa Rica**, San Jose, Costa Rica ▪ Insung Lee, **Soongsil University**, Seoul, Korea ▪ Andy Leung, **National Tsing Hua University**, Taipei, Taiwan R.O.C. ▪ Elisa Li Chan, **University of Costa Rica**, San Jose, Costa Rica ▪ Elizabeth Lorenzo, **Universidad Internacional de las Americas**, San Jose, Costa Rica ▪

Cheryl Magnant, **Sungkyunkwan University**, Seoul, Korea ▪ Narciso Maldonado Iuit, **Escuela Tecnica Electricista**, Mexico City, Mexico ▪ Shaun Manning, **Hankuk University of Foreign Studies**, Seoul, Korea ▪ Yoshiko Matsubayashi, **Tokyo International University**, Saitama, Japan ▪ Scott Miles, **Sogang University**, Seoul, Korea ▪ William Mooney, **Chinese Culture University**, Taipei, Taiwan R.O.C. ▪ Jeff Moore, **Sungkyunkwan University**, Seoul, Korea ▪ Mavelin de Moreno, **Lehnsen Roosevelt School**, Guatemala City, Guatemala ▪ Ahmed Motala, **University of Sharjah**, Sharjah, United Arab Emirates ▪ Carlos Navarro, **University of Costa Rica**, San Jose, Costa Rica ▪ Dan Neal, **Chih Chien University**, Taipei, Taiwan R.O.C. ▪ Margarita Novo, **University of Costa Rica**, San Jose, Costa Rica ▪ Karen O'Neill, **San Jose State University**, San Jose, California ▪ Linda O'Roke, **City College of San Francisco**, San Francisco, California ▪ Martha Padilla, **Colegio de Bachilleres de Sinaloa,** Culiacan, Mexico ▪ Allen Quesada, **University of Costa Rica**, San Jose, Costa Rica ▪ Jim Rogge, **Broward Community College**, Ft. Lauderdale, Florida ▪ Marge Ryder, **City College of San Francisco**, San Francisco, California ▪ Gerardo Salas, **University of Costa Rica**, San Jose, Costa Rica ▪ Shigeo Sato, **Tamagawa University**, Tokyo, Japan ▪ Lynn Schneider, **City College of San Francisco**, San Francisco, California ▪ Devan Scoble, **Sungkyunkwan University**, Seoul, Korea ▪ Maryjane Scott, **Soongsil University**, Seoul, Korea ▪ Ghaida Shaban, **Makassed Philanthropic School**, Beirut, Lebanon ▪ Maha Shalok, **Makassed Philanthropic School**, Beirut, Lebanon ▪ John Shannon, **University of Sharjah**, Sharjah, United Arab Emirates ▪ Elsa Sheng, **National Technology College of Taipei**, Taipei, Taiwan R.O.C. ▪ Ye-Wei Sheng, **National Taipei College of Business**, Taipei, Taiwan R.O.C. ▪ Emilia Sobaja, **University of Costa Rica**, San Jose, Costa Rica ▪ You-Souk Yoon, **Sungkyunkwan University**, Seoul, Korea ▪ Shanda Stromfield, **San Jose State University**, San Jose, California ▪ Richard Swingle, **Kansai Gaidai College**, Osaka, Japan ▪ Carol Sung, **Christ's College**, Taipei, Taiwan R.O.C. ▪ Jeng-Yih Tim Hsu, **National Kaohsiung First University of Science and Technology**, Kaohsiung, Taiwan R.O.C. ▪ Shinichiro Torikai, **Rikkyo University**, Tokyo, Japan ▪ Sungsoon Wang, **Sogang University**, Seoul, Korea ▪ Kathleen Wolf, **City College of San Francisco**, San Francisco, California ▪ Sean Wray, **Waseda University International**, Tokyo, Japan ▪ Belinda Yanda, **Academy of Art University**, San Francisco, California ▪ Su Huei Yang, **National Taipei College of Business**, Taipei, Taiwan R.O.C. ▪ Tzu Yun Yu, **Chungyu Institute of Technology**, Taipei, Taiwan R.O.C.

Table of Contents

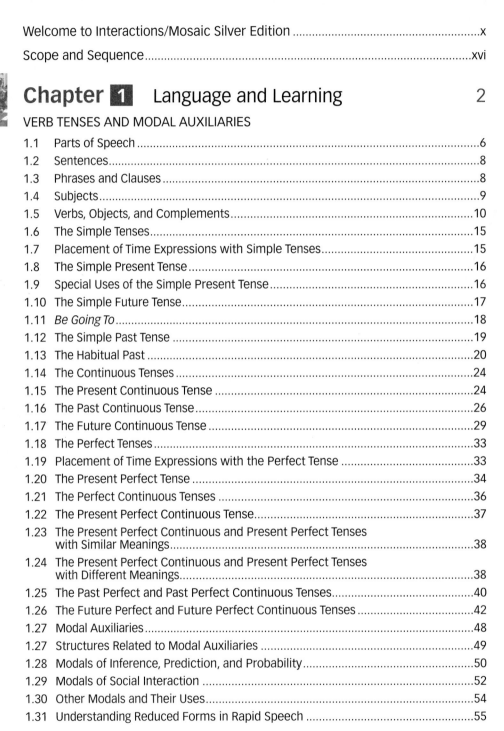

Chapter 1   Language and Learning   2

VERB TENSES AND MODAL AUXILIARIES

Chapter 2 Danger and Daring 64

NOUNS, PRONOUNS, AND MODIFIERS

Chapter 3 Gender and Relationships 114

SENTENCE TYPES AND SENTENCE PROBLEMS

Chapter 4   Beauty and Aesthetics   152

ADJECTIVE CLAUSES AND RELATED STRUCTURES

Chapter 5   Transitions   198

ADVERB CLAUSES OF CAUSE, RESULT, AND TIME

Chapter 6 The Mind 248

ADVERB CLAUSES OF COMPARISON, CONTRAST, PURPOSE, AND RESULT

Chapter 7 Working 292

NOUN CLAUSES AND RELATED STRUCTURES

Chapter 10 Conflict and Reconciliation 426

HOPE, WISH, AND CONDITIONAL SENTENCES

Appendix 1 474

Irregular Verbs

Appendix 2 476

Spelling Rules and Irregular Noun Plurals

Appendix 3 478

The with Proper Nouns

Appendix 4 480

Verbs not Normally Used in the Continuous Tense

Appendix 5 481

Modal Auxiliaries and Related Structures

Appendix 6 483

Summary of Gerunds and Infinitives

Skills Index 486

Welcome to Interactions/Mosaic Silver Edition

Interactions/Mosaic **Silver Edition** is a fully-integrated, 18-book academic skills series. Language proficiencies are articulated from the beginning through advanced levels <u>within</u> each of the four language skill strands. Chapter themes articulate <u>across</u> the four skill strands to systematically recycle content, vocabulary, and grammar.

NEW to the Silver Edition of Interactions/Mosaic Grammar:

- **World's most popular and comprehensive academic skills series**—thoroughly updated for today's global learners
- **Redesigned grammar charts**—numbered sequentially, formatted consistently, and indexed systematically—provide lifelong reference value
- **Carefully refined scope and sequence** responds to teacher recommendations for building the most logical continuum of grammar topics within and across books
- **Enhanced focus on global content** honors the diversity of *Interactions/Mosaic* students from each region of the world
- **New Self-Assessment Logs** encourage students to evaluate their learning
- **New "Best Practices" approach** promotes excellence in language teaching

Interactions/Mosaic
Best Practices

Our Interactions/Mosaic Silver Edition team has produced an edition that focuses on Best Practices, principles that contribute to excellent language teaching and learning. Our team of writers, editors, and teacher consultants has identified the following six interconnected Best Practices:

Making Use of Academic Content

Materials and tasks based on academic content and experiences give learning real purpose. Students explore real world issues, discuss academic topics, and study content-based and thematic materials.

Organizing Information

Students learn to organize thoughts and notes through a variety of graphic organizers that accommodate diverse learning and thinking styles.

Scaffolding Instruction

A scaffold is a physical structure that facilitates construction of a building. Similarly, scaffolding instruction is a tool used to facilitate language learning in the form of predictable and flexible tasks. Some examples include oral or written modeling by the teacher or students, placing information in a larger framework, and reinterpretation.

Activating Prior Knowledge

Students can better understand new spoken or written material when they connect to the content. Activating prior knowledge allows students to tap into what they already know, building on this knowledge and stirring a curiosity for more knowledge.

Interacting with Others

Activities that promote human interaction in pair work, small group work, and whole class activities present opportunities for real world contact and real world use of language.

Cultivating Critical Thinking

Strategies for critical thinking are taught explicitly. Students learn tools that promote critical thinking skills crucial to success in the academic world.

Highlights of Mosaic 2 Grammar

Compelling instructional photos strengthen the educational experience.

Activating Prior Knowledge
Questions and topical quotes stimulate interest, activate prior knowledge, and launch the topic of the unit.

Chapter 5

Transitions

Connecting to the Topic

1. What do you know about some of the major changes that have taken place in human history?
2. What are some important changes that are taking place now?
3. How do you feel about these changes?

In This Chapter

Adverb Clauses of Cause, Result, and Time

Part 1 Clauses and Related Structures of Time: Future Time
Part 2 Clauses and Related Structures of Time: Present and Unspecified Time
Part 3 Clauses and Related Structures of Cause and Result
Part 4 Clauses and Related Structures of Time: Past Time
Part 5 Review of Chapters 1–5

❝Life belongs to the living, and he who lives must be prepared for changes.❞ — Johann Wolfgang von Goethe

Interacting with Others
Group and pair work create situations for students to use the grammar they are learning.

Making Use of Academic Content
Academic topics provide context for the grammar.

Introduction

In this chapter, you will study some of the forms and uses of infinitives and gerunds. As you study, pay close attention to which verbs are followed by infinitives and which are followed by gerunds. Also, note any difference in meaning when both an infinitive and a gerund may be used.

Reading Read the following passage. It introduces the chapter theme "Art and Entertainment" and raises some of the topics and issues you will cover in the chapter.

What Is Art?

Trying to define art is almost impossible because each individual has an opinion on what is or is not art. For some, art is only certain types of music or painting or sculpture, while for others, art includes any creative act. The best way, then, to define art may be to consider what it does rather than what it is.

For most people, the function of art is to be pleasing to the eye or ear. In fact, art has served as decoration since prehistoric times. Yet, does something have to be beautiful to be art? Can a disturbing or distasteful piece be considered art? Does the definition of art as beauty exclude works like Picasso's *Guernica*, shown on page 381, which portrays the destruction of an entire town?

According to some critics, art goes beyond beauty. It involves making the world understandable by bringing order to the chaos of human experience. But can this definition be appropriate when one considers the chaos in works such as Michelangelo's *Last Judgment* or Erik Satie's *Through the Looking Glass*?

Perhaps we can define art only by giving a more general explanation of its function. Art historian John Canaday expresses this idea by saying that art is meant to clarify, intensify, or otherwise enlarge our experience of life.

Discussing Ideas Discuss the questions with a partner.

How many types of art can you name? Do you believe all creative work qualifies as art?

Cultural Note

Arts in America
The arts in America—music, dance, architecture, the visual arts, and literature—have had two strong sources of inspiration: European sophistication and U.S. originality. Great artists have managed to combine these forces in strikingly creative ways. The past century alone brought these creative geniuses, along with many more: composers George Gershwin (1898–1937) and Aaron Copland (1900–1990), dancer and choreographer Martha Graham (1893–1991), architects Louis Sullivan (1856–1924) and Frank Lloyd Wright (1869–1959), painters Georgia O'Keeffe (1887–1986), Jackson Pollock (1912–1956), Willem de Kooning (1904–1997), and Mark Rothko (1903–1970), and writers F. Scott Fitzgerald (1896–1940), Ernest Hemingway (1899–1961), Eugene O'Neill (1888–1953), and Tennessee Williams (1911–1983). Many attribute the vibrance and energy of the arts in the United States to the freedom of personal expression guaranteed in the U.S. Constitution.

Source: http://www.guggenheim.org/the_building.html

Part 1 Gerunds

Setting the Context

Previewing the Passage Discuss the questions with a group.

Many people say that jazz is the only truly American art form. What do you know about jazz? Do you like jazz music?

Reading Read the passage.

Jazz

Jazz musicians are unique as creative artists. Many poets, painters, and novelists are accustomed to working alone, but this is often impossible for jazz musicians. Because of the nature of jazz, most of their playing and practicing must be with other musicians. They need each other's sounds and impulses to become inspired.

To develop their own styles, jazz musicians must be ingenious and versatile. Playing jazz involves remembering hundreds of musical phrases and improvising on them during a solo. Each musician's personal style develops through various ways of improvising.

Some jazz musicians are so skillful at improvising that they can even impro-

Redesigned grammar charts—numbered sequentially, formatted consistently, and indexed systematically—provide lifelong reference value.

5.7 Time Clauses and Phrases with the Simple Past and Past Perfect Tenses

Connecting Words	Explanations	Examples
With Clauses		
Before	*Before, by the time (that),* and *until* + the simple past are used with the later event.	**Before** the war began, American colonists had already been rebelling for several years.
By the time (that)	Adverbs such as *already, just, hardly, recently,* and *scarcely* are frequently used with the past perfect tense.	**By the time (that)** the British brought more troops to the colonies, the rebellion had already spread.
Until		**Until** the British instituted these taxes, most colonists had been loyal to England.
After	*After* + the past perfect is used with the earlier event.	Fights broke out **after** the British had passed a series of taxes.
When	In some cases, **when** can be used with either the earlier or later event. In sentences with the past perfect and simple past tenses, **when** + the simple past is usually used with the later event.	The rebellion had already started **when** the British passed new taxes.
With Phrases		
By	Remember that phrases do not include a subject / verb combination.	**By** 1776, colonists had already been rebelling for several years.
Up to		**Up to** 1776, they had not officially declared war.
within		**Within** seven years, the Americans had gained independence.

B. Time Clauses and Phrases with the Simple Past and Past Continuous Tenses

Clauses and phrases can be used to relate actions or situations that happened at approximately the same time.

5.8 Time Clauses and Phrases with the Simple Past and Past Continuous Tenses

Connecting Words	Explanations	Examples
With Clauses with the Simple Past		
When (whenever)	*When* and *as soon as* express a direct connection in the time of occurrence of the two events.	Fighting began **when** the British tried to collect more taxes.
As soon as	*Whenever* may be used to describe habitual occurrences.	**As soon as** colonists learned of the fighting, rebellion spread rapidly.
With Clauses with the Past Continuous (and Simple Past)		
As While	The past continuous is often used with *while* or *as* to describe past actions in progress. *When* may be used with a clause in the simple past to describe an event that occurred while another event was in progress.	**While (As)** colonists in Boston were fighting the British, colonists in the South were organizing an army.
When		Colonists in Virginia were planning their own revolt **when** they received news of the fighting in Boston.
With Phrases		
During	*During* is used with phrases. Remember that phrases do not include a subject / verb combination.	They received news of the fighting in Boston **during** a meeting of anti-British colonists.

1 **Review** Complete the following sentences by using the simple past, past continuous, or past perfect forms of the verbs in parentheses.

Example In 1620, after they ____*had spent*____ (spend) five months on the Atlantic Ocean, 143 British colonists, or "Pilgrims," ____*landed*____ (land) in Massachusetts.

1. While these Pilgrims _____ (settle) in Massachusetts, they _____ (face) many problems.

2. There _____ (be) unfriendly Indians; the winter _____ (be) severe; there _____ (not be) enough food.

3. During the first year, many of the Pilgrims _____ (die).

4. However, before the year _____ (be) over, the Pilgrims

6 **Practice** Make at least three sets of sentences similar to those in Exercise 5. You may write about animals, places, people, or things. You may use adjectives of your own or choose from the following list:

beautiful	impressive
boring	reckless
careful	striking
enervating	strong
healthy	tiring

Example *Houston isn't as beautiful as Austin. In fact, Austin is much more beautiful. Many people consider Austin to be the most beautiful city in Texas.*

7 **Error Analysis** Each of the following sentences contains an error. Find the error and correct it.

Example The cat that you have as a pet is, in some ways, similar ~~than~~ _to_ a lion.

1. Humans are not more stronger than most other animals the same size.
2. We cannot run as quick as dogs or deer can.
3. We seem to be more clumsily than most creatures.
4. Horses are herbivores, likewise, cows eat only vegetation.
5. Many animals are less cleverer than chimpanzees.
6. Orangutans eat a mixed diet of seeds, nuts, fruit, and a little meat. Similarly, tigers are carnivores.
7. To some people, the coat of a leopard looks the same than the coat of a tiger.
8. Both sheep and deer provides meat to predators, including humans.

▲ In the U.S., wind power has increased an average of over 25% per year since 1990.

Using What You've Learned

9 **Describing Processes and Giving Recommendations** In small groups, talk about a practice in a field with which you are familiar—for example, engineering, construction, cooking, teaching chemistry (English, etc.). First, give a careful description of how the practice is currently done. Then give your opinion on ways this practice could be improved. State your recommendations on what *must, has to, should,* or *ought to* be done.

10 **Describing Problems and Giving Possible Solutions** In pairs, examine a problem your country or the world is facing today. Examples include inflation, unemployment, foreign debt, pollution, crime, and drug use. After you have described the problem, examine its roots and discuss what exactly caused this problem. Then offer your opinions on what *could, should,* or *ought to* have been done five, ten, or 20 years ago to avoid the current situation. Finally, tell your group what you believe *should, ought to,* or *must* be done now.

Scope and Sequence

Chapter	Grammar Structures	Context
1 Language and Learning **Verb Tenses and Modal Auxiliaries** 	• The Sentence and Its Parts • The Simple Tenses • The Continuous Tenses • The Perfect and Perfect Continuous Tenses and Verb Tense Review • Modal Auxiliaries and Related Structures	• Language similarities • Human versus animal language • Learning a new language • Learning multiple languages • Language and politeness
2 Danger and Daring **Nouns, Pronouns, and Modifiers** 	• Review of Nouns, Pronouns, and Possessive Adjectives • Indefinite Articles and Quantifiers • The Definite Article with Count and Noncount Nouns • The Definite Article with Proper Nouns • More on Nouns and Modifiers	• Marco Polo's journeys • Polynesian explorers • Explorations in the New World • Explorations of the polar regions • Mt. Everest
3 Gender and Relationships **Sentence Types and Sentence Problems** 	• Commands and Exclamations • Compound Sentences • Transitions • Complex Sentences • Sentence Problems	• Gender similarities and differences in children • Gender similarities and differences in adults • Biology and gender • Language and gender • Marriage

Scope and Sequence

Chapter	Grammar Structures	Context
4 **Beauty and Aesthetics** **Adjective Clauses and Related Structures** 	• Adjective Clauses: Restrictive Versus Nonrestrictive • Adjective Clauses: Replacement of Subjects • Adjective Clauses: Replacement of Objects • Other Adjective Clause Constructions • Adjective Clause to Phrase Reduction	• The wonders of ancient Egypt • Mayan architecture and civilization • The wonders of ancient Greece • The statues of Easter Island • Beautiful places around the world
5 **Transitions** **Adverb Clauses of Cause, Result, and Time** 	• Clauses and Related Structures of Time: Future Time • Clauses and Related Structures of Time: Present and Unspecified Time • Clauses and Related Structures of Cause and Result • Clauses and Related Structures of Time: Past Time • Review of Chapters 1-5	• Personal growth and change • Growth and change in society • The role of leadership in change • Revolutions • Changes of the last 100 years
6 **The Mind** **Adverb Clauses of Comparison, Contrast, Purpose, and Result**	• Clauses and Related Structures of Contrast: Concession • Clauses and Related Structures of Contrast: Opposition • Clauses and Phrases of Purpose • Clauses and Related Structures of Comparison • Clauses of Result	• The central nervous system • The two hemispheres of the brain • Memory and forgetting • Humans versus animals • Mysteries of the mind

Chapter	Grammar Structures	Context
7 **Working** **Noun Clauses and Related Structures** 	• Clauses with *That*; Reported Speech • Clauses with Embedded Questions • Statements and Requests of Urgency • Clauses as Subjects of Sentences • Reduction of Noun Clauses to Infinitive Phrases	• The U.S. workforce • Job interviews • Types of jobs • Working conditions • Job stress
8 **Breakthroughs** **The Passive Voice and Related Structures** 	• The Simple Tenses • The Perfect Tenses • The Continuous Tenses • The Modal Auxiliaries • Other Verbal Constructions	• Breakthrough technologies • Medicine • Agriculture • Energy • Aging
9 **Art and Entertainment** **Gerunds, Infinitives, and Related Structures** 	• Gerunds • Infinitives • Verbs Followed by Either Infinitives or Gerunds • Continuous and Perfect Forms • Gerunds and Infinitives As Subjects and Complements; Parallelism	• Jazz • Gold- and silver-smithing • Impressionist art • Gardens of East Asia • African art
10 **Conflict and Reconciliation** ***Hope*, *Wish*, and Conditional Sentences** 	• *Hope* versus *Wish* • Imaginary Conditions: Present and Unspecified Time • Perfect Modal Auxiliaries • Imaginary Conditions: Past and Present Time • Review of Chapters 6-10	• Major environmental concerns • Model societies • Current environmental problems • The impact of new technologies • Protecting our future

Author Acknowledgements

Warm thanks to Mary McVey Gill for her caring and support over all these years. Without Mary, this project would never have come to fruition.

Language and Learning

"To have another language is to possess a second soul.**"**

—Charlemagne

Connecting to the Topic

1 What do you know about the languages of the world?

2 How do children learn their first language?

3 How can people best learn a second language?

Introduction

In this chapter, you will review key terminology and the uses of all the verb tenses and the modal auxiliaries. This chapter is review. The terminology and structures reappear throughout the text. While you are reviewing the tenses, pay close attention to the time expressions used with each. Also, notice the shifts from one tense to another.

Reading Read the following passage. It introduces the chapter theme "Language and Learning" and raises some of the topics and issues you will cover in the chapter.

Language

Language is the most important development in human history. The arts, sciences, laws, economic systems, and religions of the world could not exist without language. Humans have not changed biologically for some 40,000 years. However, our ability to communicate has led us from the cave all the way to the moon. 5

Little is known about the birth of language. Written records that are more than 4,000 years old have been found, but anthropologists agree that humans were speaking thousands of years before that.

Today, most of us learn to talk by the age of three, and for the rest of our lives we rarely stop. Even while we are reading or just thinking, we are 10 in a sense "talking," if only to ourselves. Language is so much a part of human existence that we will be talking as long as we inhabit the Earth. As linguist David Thompson notes, "When language dies, so will man."

 Discussing Ideas Discuss the questions with a group.

How important is language to humans? Could we think the same way without language? Do you have thoughts that do not take the form of words?

Part 1   The Sentence and Its Parts

Setting the Context

Previewing the Passage Discuss the questions with a group.

How many languages do you think there are in the world? What similarities does your first language share with English? Do you know of any similarities that all languages share?

Reading Read the passage.

Language Similarities

In all, there are at least 1,500 different human languages. Although each has a distinct set of words and grammar, they all have similar parts of speech. For example, all languages have certain elements that function as nouns (Jack, tennis, house) and others that act as verbs (play, love, sing). In addition, every language uses one class of words to modify nouns (slow, red, beautiful) and another to modify verbs (slowly, beautifully). All languages have rules that can convert verbs either into nouns (sing, singer) or into adjectives (interest, interesting). Finally, all use both proper nouns (Sonia Lizano, San Jose) and pronouns (she, it).

  5

Discussing Ideas Discuss the questions with a partner.

The passage indicates that there are 1,500 languages. What do you think the difference is between a language and a dialect? Talk about your first language. Are there different dialects? If so, how do they differ from each other?

Grammar Structures and Practice

A. Parts of Speech

Parts of speech are the smallest grammatical units: *adjective, adverb, article, conjunction, interjection, noun, preposition, pronoun,* and *verb*.

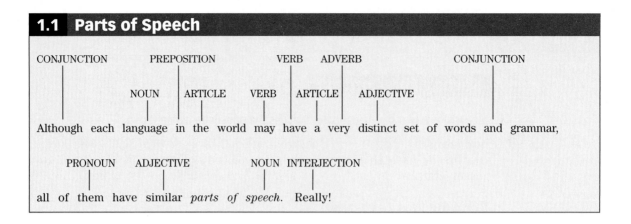

CONJUNCTION   PREPOSITION   VERB   ADVERB   CONJUNCTION

NOUN | ARTICLE   VERB | ARTICLE   ADJECTIVE

Although each language in the world may have a very distinct set of words and grammar,

PRONOUN   ADJECTIVE   NOUN   INTERJECTION

all of them have similar *parts of speech.* Really!

B.C.

By permission of Johnny Hart and Creators Syndicate, Inc.

1 **Practice** Identify the part of speech (noun, pronoun, verb, adjective, adverb, article, preposition, conjunction, interjection) of each italicized word.

article   preposition   adjective   noun

Example *A* growing number *of* people are *fluent* in several *languages.*

1. *The* most common first language in the *world* is *Mandarin* Chinese, *but it* is widely spoken only *inside* China.

2. *Wow,* there *are* over a billion Mandarin Chinese *speakers.*

3. Almost half of the world's *population* speaks one of the *Indo-European* languages.

4. *English* is the most *popular in* this group, *and its popularity* is growing.

5. *If* second-language speakers *are included,* English is the most common language in the world—*really*!

6. English is *most likely* to remain *very* important *in* the future, *but the* number *of people* who speak English *as their native* language *will decline.*

7. In the *United* States *today, approximately* 20 percent of the *population* speaks *a* language other *than* English.

8. In the future, *being* multilingual will be *common, and* being monolingual will be *rare.*

Cultural Note

Languages in the U.S.

As of 2004, over 30 million people in the United States were foreign born, and approximately ten percent of children enrolled in U.S. public schools—over 5.5 million students—had limited English proficiency. That marked an increase of over more than 65 percent during a ten-year period. Nationwide, these students bring approximately 425 native languages to the classroom. It's not unusual to find classrooms with 80 percent or more of the students learning English as their second language.

English as a Native Language Slipping

The share of people in the world who are native English speakers has been declining since 1950. Hindi-Urdu is projected to surpass English by 2050.

Percent Change of Total Population Speaking Native Language

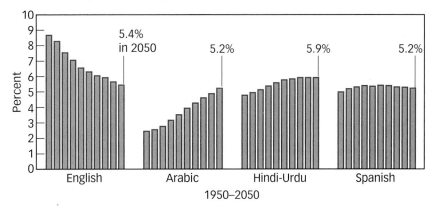

Note: Each language bar represents five years.
Source: The English Company

B. Sentences, Phrases, and Clauses

A sentence is a group of words that expresses a complete idea.

- Every sentence includes at least one subject and verb.
- The verb may be followed by an object or a complement.
- There are four basic types of sentences:

1.2 Sentences

Structures	Explanations	Examples
Statement	A statement gives information or an opinion.	English is a wonderful language. I just bought my books.
Question	A question asks for information.	What is your native language? Have you found a roommate yet?
Exclamation	An exclamation expresses surprise, pleasure, or another emotion.	What a pretty red dress you have! How handsome you are!
Command	A command tells what to do. The subject *you* is understood.	(you) Stop that train! (you) Be quiet, please.

Phrases and clauses are basic components of sentences.

1.3 Phrases and Clauses

Structures	Explanations	Examples
Phrase	A phrase is a group of two or more words. English has several types of phrases: noun phrases, verb phrases, prepositional phrases, and so on.	Linguists have identified **over four thousand languages**. Many languages are spoken **in Europe**.
Clause	A clause is a group of words that includes both a subject and a verb. One clause can form a sentence. Clauses can also be joined by conjunctions such as *but, although, because,* or *when* or by pronouns such as *that* or *which*.	**Many languages are spoken here.** **Many languages are spoken,** but **they are not written.** **Arabic is a language** that **I would like to learn.**

2 Practice Read the following sentences. Then identify the underlined part of the sentence as a phrase or a clause.

Example <u>Although some societies are technologically underdeveloped</u>, their languages are quite complex. _____ _clause_ _____

1. The Aranda people, <u>who live in the Australian desert</u>, lead simple lives.

_____

2. Still, <u>their language</u> is incredibly complicated. _____

3. While the English verb system is considered complex, <u>it is much simpler than the Arandan system</u>. _____

4. <u>The Arandan verb system</u> is particularly difficult to use. _____

5. Every Arandan verb can take <u>about a thousand different endings</u>, and each ending changes the meaning of the verb. _____

6. <u>When the verb ending changes</u>, the meaning of the verb changes.

_____

7. It is as if <u>English verbs like *run* had one thousand different forms</u>.

_____

8. Nobody knows <u>why the Arandan verb system is so complex</u>. _____

C. Subjects, Verbs, Objects, and Complements

The subject is normally the most important person, place, thing, or idea in the sentence. Subjects commonly take four forms:

1.4 Subjects

Structures	Explanations	Examples
Noun	A noun is a person, place, thing, or idea.	**Tony** just arrived from Italy.
Pronoun	A pronoun is used in place of a noun.	**He** has studied English for three years.
Phrase	A phrase is a group of related words.	**Several Italian students** study here. **To study in this country** is popular.
Clause	A clause is a group of related words with a subject and a verb.	**Why he left Italy** is a mystery.

Verbs, objects, and complements are other important parts of a sentence.

Some verbs tell what the subject does.
- In general, these verbs can be grouped as transitive or intransitive.
- Intransitive verbs do not have objects, but a transitive verb *must* have an object.

Other verbs tell what the subject is, feels, etc. This type of verb is called a linking verb because it connects the subject to the complement.
- A complement is a noun, pronoun, adjective, verb form, phrase, or clause that describes the subject.
- Common linking verbs include *be, appear, become, feel, get* (when it means *become*), *look, seem, smell, sound,* and *taste.*

1.5 Verbs, Objects, and Complements

Structures	Explanations	Examples
Intransitive Verbs	An intransitive verb is complete without an object.	Martin **arrived** (on Thursday).
Transitive Verbs and Objects	A transitive verb *must* have an object. It is incomplete without one.	He **found** a nice place to live.
Direct Objects **Indirect Objects**	Direct objects answer the questions *who(m)* or *what?* Indirect objects answer the questions *to/for who(m)* or *what?*	He brought **some gifts.** He gave **us** the gifts.
Linking Verbs and Complements	Linking verbs are followed by complements—information that describes the subject. Adverbs cannot be used as complements after these verbs.	Sam **is** a dentist. He **appears** quite intelligent. He **looks** rather tired, and he **sounds** upset.

3 **Practice** Underline the subjects once and the verbs twice. Circle the object(s) or complement(s) in sentences that have them.

Example: Humans have been using (language) for at least 40,000 years.

1. Linguists have identified over 4,000 languages.

2. Some languages are relatively new in human history.

3. Others were used for thousands of years and then mysteriously disappeared.

4. Over 4,000 languages and dialects are currently being used.

5. Many have no written form.

6. Linguists have given writing systems to some of these languages.

7. Many languages are spoken but not written.

8. With some ancient languages like Latin, people still write them, but they don't speak them anymore.

D. Verbs and the Tense System

English has 12 verb tenses, 11 modal auxiliaries, and a variety of verb expressions. The tenses are divided according to time (past, present, future) and aspect (simple, continuous, perfect). This chapter reviews the tenses and modal auxiliaries. Later chapters cover verbs, modal auxiliaries, and related forms in a variety of phrase and sentence types.

4 **Practice** The following sentences contain all the tenses of English. At this point, before completing a review, how many of the verb tenses can you identify? Underline the verbs.

simple present tense   *simple present tense*

Example Animals <u>communicate</u> through sounds, but only human beings <u>are</u> able to speak.

▲ The Rosetta Stone, ancient writings in three languages

1. How long have people been using language?
2. We don't know the exact date, but written language probably began in Sumeria.
3. Today, linguists are studying the ancient written language of Sumeria.
4. The Sumerians were writing at least 8,000 years ago.
5. However, people had learned to speak long before this.
6. In fact, humans had been speaking for thousands of years before starting to write.
7. Languages are so complex that pages of diagrams are necessary to explain a short simple sentence.
8. Yet, children have always learned their language simply by hearing it spoken.
9. When a child learns his native tongue, his life will change forever.
10. Soon, he will be talking incessantly.
11. Before long, he will have begun to look at the world through his language.
12. However, he will have been speaking for several years before he learns to read and write well.

Using What You've Learned

5 **Learning About Your Classmates** Learning a second language can be frustrating, yet it can also be one of the most rewarding experiences of a lifetime. A second language may be important for your education or profession. But beyond this, it is a pass key that allows you to explore the world and its people in a way that no monolingual person can. In small groups, use English, *your* second language, to learn about the lives of your new classmates. Use the following words to form questions. Then add any additional questions that you may think of.

1. name
2. age
3. native country and language
4. length of time in the United States or Canada
5. reason for studying English
6. number of years of English study
7. major or job
8. family (single, married, children)
9. hobbies, interests, travels
10. other

After you've finished, take turns telling the class about each other.

6 **Learning About Other Languages** Find out more about the structure of your classmates' languages. Or, find out about another language your classmates have studied or have knowledge of. In pairs, ask and answer questions about the following. Then using the same questions, compare your languages to English.

1. parts of speech
2. verb tense system (Does your language have a future tense? A past tense? Other tenses?)
3. the word order in sentences (How do you form questions? Would you say *house white* or *white house*?)
4. the use of special forms with certain groups of people (with older people, strangers, etc.)

7 **Researching Another Language** Research the grammar of another language. Check your library or check the Internet. Find out information similar to that in Activity 6, and add any other interesting information you can find. Prepare a brief talk for your classmates.

8 **English Trivia** What curious facts do you know about languages? Test your knowledge. Work in small groups and see if you know the answers to the following questions. Then, as a class, compare answers. Your teacher will verify them.

1. How many languages can one individual learn to speak fluently?

2. If varieties of English worldwide are combined, the language has more than 610,000 vocabulary words with an additional 400,000 technical terms. How many words can the average native speaker with 16 years of education understand?

3. For native English speakers, how many words does someone with 16 years of schooling actually use in day-to-day conversation? In written language?

4. How many different vocabulary words did Shakespeare use in his works?

5. What is the oldest unchanged letter in the English alphabet?

6. What are the newest letters?

7. What are the most frequently used words in English?

8. Which word in English has the greatest number of different meanings?

Setting the Context

 Previewing the Passage Discuss the questions with a group.

How do animals communicate with each other, and what do they communicate about? How is this different from human speech?

Reading Read the passage.

Humans Versus Animals

Several animals can stand upright like humans. Some use their hands in a similar way. A few know how to make and use tools. But only humans are able to speak.

When lions roar or monkeys hoot, they are indeed communicating, but only simple ideas and emotions such as *food* or *fear*. A chimpanzee that 5 happens upon a mango tree can use a call to alert his companions to his good luck. However, no chimpanzee (or any other animal) is able to discuss what he ate yesterday or what he will have tomorrow.

Human languages, on the other hand, allow us to talk about anything we think of. We can draw lessons from the distant past or speculate on the 10 distant future; we can create mythical beings that have never existed; we can lie and deceive . . . all because of language.

 Discussing Ideas Discuss the following with a partner.

The passage seems to indicate that the greatest difference between humans and animals is language ability. Do you agree? Why or why not?

Grammar Structures and Practice

A. The Simple Tenses: An Overview

The simple present, past, and future are the most often used of the tenses and generally the easiest to understand. However, they can sometimes be employed in unusual ways.

1.6 The Simple Tenses

Tenses	Examples	Time Frames
Simple Present Simple Past Simple Future	Dezen **studies** every day. She **studied** for three hours yesterday. She **will** probably **study** another three hours tomorrow.	extended present past future

Adverbs of frequency and other time expressions are often used with the simple tenses.

1.7 Placement of Time Expressions with Simple Tenses

Explanations	Tenses	Examples
Adverbs of frequency normally precede the main verb and follow auxiliary verbs or *be* as a main verb.	Simple Present	Ozden **often works** in the evening. **As a rule**, she **works** in the evening. Ozden **is usually** at work in the evening. She **can occasionally work** on weekends.
Longer time expressions usually come at the beginning or end of the sentence.	Simple Past	She was occasionally late **last semester**.
	Simple Future	She will take classes twice a week **next year**. **Next year,** she will try to be on time for her classes.

B. The Simple Present Tense

The usual time frame of the simple present tense is the extended present. The tense is used in these ways:

- To describe habits or routines
- To make general statements of fact
- To express opinions

1.8 The Simple Present Tense

Uses	Examples	Time Expressions	
Habits or Routines **Facts or Opinions**	I **study** English three hours a day. I frequently **go** to the library in the evening. I **am** rarely in my dorm room. Learning English **is** not easy. I usually **enjoy** my classes very much.	*always* *usually* *frequently* *generally* *often* *sometimes* *seldom* *rarely* *hardly ever* *never*	*from time to time* *in general* *now and then* *once in a while*

Note: See Appendix 2 for spelling rules.

There are also some special uses of the simple present tense.

1.9 Special Uses of the Simple Present Tense

Special Uses	Explanations	Examples
Reference to the Future	The simple present tense can be used for specific future events, particularly when a schedule, itinerary, or travel plans are being discussed. Verbs often used with this meaning include *arrive, leave, come, go,* and *travel*.	I **leave** Canada in two weeks. I **go** to Cairo for a month. Then I **travel** to Beirut.
Reference to the Past	In informal situations, the simple present tense may be used to tell stories in the past.	Yesterday, Jack **walks** into the office and **tells** me he's quitting. So I **say** to him that if he **quits**, I **quit**.
Nonaction Verbs	The simple present is also used with nonaction verbs—verbs that express feelings, thoughts, perceptions, or possession.	The ocean **looks** very cold today. The waves **seem** higher than normal. I **love** the sound of the waves. This beach **belongs to** the city.

1 **Practice** What is your daily routine like? What do you do on weekends? First, complete the following chart and then work with a partner. Take turns telling about your schedules. Use complete sentences and include the appropriate adverbs of frequency.

Example *I always brush my teeth in the morning.*

	Something You Always Do	Something You Rarely Do	Something You Do from Time to Time	Something You Never Do
Weekdays A.M. P.M. Weekends Saturday Sunday	*brush my teeth*			

 2 **Practice** Work in pairs. Use the present tense to tell each other your plans for this weekend or for another day in the near future.

Example *Next month, I go to Paris. I arrive at the airport at 10:00 A.M. The plane leaves at 11:30.*

 3 **Practice** Work with a partner. Add at least five sentences in the present tense to finish the story that follows.

Two months ago, after a long day at work, I arrive home at my usual time, about 8:00 P.M. I say, "I'm home, Honey," but no one answers. Anyway, I get a bottle of soda and start walking to the TV. That's when I see the note taped to the kitchen table. It says. . . .

C. The Simple Future Tense and *Be Going To*

The simple future tense and *be going to* are used for several specific meanings.
- *Will* is often used to express the future in written English. In spoken English, it is frequently used with predictions, promises, offers, and requests.
- *Be going to* is also used in conversational English. It often involves actions that have been planned before the moment of speaking.
- Both *will* and *be going to* are followed by the simple form of a verb.

1.10 The Simple Future Tense

Meanings	Examples	Time Expressions	
Offers	You look cold. **I'll get** you a sweater.	*after a while*	*later*
Predictions	The weather **will be** better tomorrow.	*before long*	*sometime*
Promises	**I'll buy** you a new jacket soon.	*in a few minutes*	*soon*
Requests	It's raining. **Will** you **give** me a ride?	*in a (little) while*	*sooner or later*

1.11 Be Going To

Uses	Examples	Time Expressions	
Actions Planned for the Future	Kunio **is going to take** his placement test tomorrow. We**'re going to meet** him after the test.	*in ten minutes* *in an hour* *next week (month)*	*this afternoon (weekend)* *tomorrow* *tonight*

4 **Practice** Complete the following dialogue with *will* or *be going to*. In some cases, either is possible.

Example A: _____Will_____ you _____have_____ lunch with me
tomorrow?   (have)

B: Sorry, I ___*'m not going to be*___ in town tomorrow.
                        (not be)

Stan: I _____ a dinner party on Monday.
                    1 (have)

_____ you _____?
        2   3 (come)

Tess: You know, I'm kind of shy. Who else _____?
                                                    4 (come)

Stan: Actually, you are the only person that I _____.
                                                        5 (invite)

Tess: Really? Then I'd be happy to come! Can I bring something?

Stan: How about a salad?

Tess: Sure, I _____ a salad . . . and I _____
                    6 (bring)   7 (come)

early and help if you like.

Stan: I'd love for you to come early, but I've already decided on a meal, so I

_____ much help.
        8 (not need)

 5 **Practice** Look at Activity 2 again. With a different partner, tell what you plan to do this weekend or another day in the near future. However, this time, use *will* and *be going to*.

Example *Next month, I'm going to go to Paris. I'll arrive at the airport about 10:00 A.M. . . .*

D. The Simple Past Tense

The simple past tense describes actions or situations that began and ended in the past.

1.12	The Simple Past Tense	
Uses	**Examples**	**Time Expressions**
Actions or Situations Completed in the Past	Joe **came** to Canada three months ago. On August 20, he **entered** the English program. He **was** a good student. Later he **began** to study at a university.	*ago* *later* *last week (month, year)* *first* *finally* *from . . . to* *then* *last*

Note: See Appendices 2 and 3 for spelling rules and pronunciation guidelines for *-ed* endings. See Appendix 1 for a list of irregular past forms.

6 **Practice** Helen Keller was a remarkable person who learned to communicate in several languages despite being completely deaf and blind. Complete the following sentences about her with the simple past form of the verbs in parentheses. Include adverbs when indicated, and pay close attention to the spelling of the past forms and the pronunciation of any *-ed* endings.

Example At birth, Helen Keller _____*was*_____ (be) able to hear.

1. Helen Keller _____ (be) born a healthy child.

2. As a baby, she _____ (like) to play.

3. Helen _____ (develop) a fever at 19 months old.

4. This fever _____ (leave) Helen permanently deaf and blind.

5. As a result, Helen _____ (not learn) language as other

   children _____ (do).

6. Helen _____ (be) difficult.

7. She _____ (ignore) everyone for hours at a time.

8. Helen _____ (get / often) frustrated and

   _____ (refuse) to cooperate.

9. Helen _____ (have) a dog, and she _____

   (sit) for hours with her dog and _____ (stare) into space.

10. She _____ (refuse / frequently) to eat and

    _____ (throw / sometimes) her food on the floor.

11. Her family _____ (think) that Helen was going to grow up to be like an animal.

12. They _____ (worry) that nothing could help her.

E. The Habitual Past: *Would* + Simple Form and *Used To* + Simple Form

Both *would* and *used to* may be used to describe actions in the past that were repeated on a regular basis.

- *Used to* may also refer to past situations, opinions, and general states of being that were continuous, not repetitive.
- *Would* does not give this continuous meaning. Notice the complete difference in meaning: ***I used to like*** *coffee.* ***I would like*** *coffee.*

1.13	The Habitual Past	
Uses	**Explanations**	**Examples**
Repeated Past Actions	Both *used to* and *would* can describe a repeated past action. Note the position of adverbs with these constructions.	As a child, Helen Keller **used to (would) spend** all day with her tutor. They **would frequently take** walks. They frequently **used to take** walks.
Past Situations	*Used to*, not *would*, can describe situations that were continuous, not repetitive.	Helen **used to love** to study languages. She **used to** study at a university.

7 Practice Reread your sentences from Activity 6. Which sentences refer to the habitual past? Which sentences can use *used to*? Which sentences can use *would*? Which sentences cannot use either? Rewrite the sentences that can be changed and pay attention to the placement of adverbs in your new sentences.

Examples Helen was born a healthy child.
This sentence cannot use would *or* used to.
As a baby, Helen liked to play.
Helen used to like to play. Would *is not possible.*

8 Practice Fill in the blanks with *used to* or *would* + verb. If neither *would* nor *used to* is possible, use the simple past form of the verbs in parentheses. Remember not to "overuse" either *would* or *used to*.

Example Alexander Graham Bell _____*advised*_____ Helen's father to hire

(advise)
Anne Sullivan as a tutor.

The "Miracle Worker"

Anne Sullivan first _____ Helen when Helen _____

1 (meet)   2 (be)

seven years old. Sullivan _____ into the Keller house, and for

3 (move)

the next several years, she _____ (spend) long hours working

4 (spend)

▲ Helen Keller

with Helen almost every day. At first, Helen _____ to communicate with her tutor by using

5 (try)
gestures and meaningless sounds. When Sullivan couldn't understand Helen, Helen _____ furious.

6 (become / often)

Sullivan _____ to teach Helen the finger

7 (decide)
patterns[1] of the alphabet. During their lessons, Sullivan _____ Helen's hand on different objects such as

8 (put)
a chair or a plate. Then, she _____ the name

9 (spell)
of the object in Helen's hand. The great breakthrough for
Helen _____ one morning when Anne _____

10 (come)   11 (hold)
Helen's hand under some water and _____ w-a-t-e-r using

12 (spell)
the hand signals. Helen later _____ that at that moment,

13 (write)
"Somehow the mystery of language _____ revealed to me. I

14 (be)
_____ that w-a-t-e-r _____ the wonderful cool

15 (know)   16 (be)
something flowing over my hand."

From then on, a new world _____ to Helen. She

17 (open)
_____ fascinated with language and _____

18 (become)   19 (work / eagerly)
with Sullivan for long periods of time. Eventually, Keller _____

20 (go)
on to attend Radcliffe College, where she _____ with honors.

21 (graduate)
Before she _____, she had learned six languages and had written 11 books.

22 (die)

---

[1]*finger patterns* System of spelling, developed for the blind, in which the fingers form the letters.

9 **Error Analysis** Each of the following sentences has an error in verb form or usage or in adverb placement. Find and correct the errors.

Example Language learning never is easy, but it can be rewarding.
Correction:
Language learning is never easy, but it can be rewarding.

1. I having a friend named Jack, who used to live a few houses away.

2. When I met him, Jack is determined to learn Spanish.

3. He was used to buy lots of language tapes.

4. He would live in Colombia.

5. Unfortunately, he practiced never speaking and listening to Spanish.

6. Now he reads and write Spanish well, but he isn't able to converse in it.

7. He will be going speak Spanish well one day.

8. He is knowing lots of people from Spanish-speaking countries.

9. Jack didn't gave up on learning Spanish.

10. He studied last year Spanish in Mexico.

11. He says that he will study also Portuguese.

12. Jack want to go to Brazil to travel and study.

13. Portuguese is seeming harder to understand than Spanish.

14. Portuguese in Brazil and Portuguese in Portugal is very different.

15. Jack will going to Rio de Janeiro next year.

Using What You've Learned

10 **Telling Stories from Childhood** Were you a difficult child? Or were you always obedient and cooperative? Of course, even the most cooperative children occasionally cause their parents problems. Use *would, used to,* and the simple past tense as you share memories about this aspect of your childhood. You can tell your stories first and then write them, or vice versa. Work in small groups when you tell (not read) your stories.

Part 3 | The Continuous Tenses

Setting the Context

Previewing the Passage Discuss the questions with a group.

What is grammar? Why is it important?

Reading Read the passage.

Creatively Speaking

The sentence you are reading now, the one you were reading a minute ago, and the one you will be reading in a moment may be completely original. Each may never have been written or spoken before. How is this possible? People do not learn language by memorizing millions of sentences. Instead, they learn to attach meaning to particular words. Then they begin to acquire a grammar, which can generate an infinite number of new sentences.   5

When people talk, they aren't just repeating sentences that they have already learned; they are organizing words into grammatical sentences. They are creating sentences, many of which they have never heard before.   10

Thus, when you understand the grammar of a language and you know enough vocabulary, you will be able to "say" the same thing in any number of ways—many of them quite original.

Discussing Ideas When you speak, you often make sentences that you have never heard before and that have perhaps never been said by anyone. Talk with a partner. Use your own words to explain how knowledge of the grammar of a language makes that possible.

Grammar Structures and Practice

A. The Continuous Tenses: An Overview

The continuous tenses generally describe actions that are in progress during another time or event.

- The time or event must be given or (especially in the case of the present continuous) implied.
- Verbs that show no action (*be, want, like, seem,* and so on) are not used in the continuous tenses.

1.14 The Continuous Tenses

Tenses	Examples	Time Frame
Present Continuous	Jane **is driving** to work now.	in progress now
Past Continuous	Jane **was driving** to work at 8:00 A.M.	in progress at 8:00 A.M.
Future Continuous	Jane **will be driving** home at 6:00 P.M.	in progress at 6:00 P.M.

1 **Practice** Quickly reread the passage "Creatively Speaking" on page 23. Which verb tenses are used in the first sentence? Give the tense and time frame of each.

B. The Present Continuous Tense

The present continuous tense is often used for activities or situations that are temporary rather than permanent. The usual time frames of this tense are as follows:
- The moment of speaking
- A specific period of time including the present
- Reference to the future

1.15 The Present Continuous Tense

Uses	Examples	Time Expressions
At the Moment of Speaking	Martha **is studying** for her final exam in French now.	*now, right now, at the moment,* and so on
Over a Specific Period of Time	She **is studying** French this quarter.	*today, this morning, this quarter, this year,* and so on
Reference to the Future	She **is taking** a literature class next quarter.	*in a few minutes, at 9:00, tomorrow,* and so on

Note: See Appendix 2 for spelling rules for *-ing* endings and Appendix 4 for a list of verbs not normally used in the continuous tenses.

 2 **Practice** Think of someone that you know well in your home country or in another country. Working with a partner, discuss what he or she is doing. Try to include all three time frames of the present continuous tense.

Example It's 3:00 P.M. in Egypt, so my sister is probably in the chemistry lab. (moment of speaking)
She's studying a lot this month. (a specific period of time)
She is taking exams in about six weeks. (reference to the future)

3 **Practice** Complete the following with either the simple present or the present continuous tense. In some cases, both tenses are possible, but be ready to explain any differences in meaning that may occur.

▲ International students at a university

Living in the U.S.A.

Hi! My name _____is_____ Mohsen. I _____ from
     (be)   1 (be)

Egypt, but three weeks ago, I said good-bye to my family and got on a plane to

the United States. Now I _____ at Cornell University in New
                              2 (study)

York, and I _____ in the dorms.
               3 (live)

How _____ dorm life? It _____ noisy and
        4 (be)   5 (be)

crowded, but it _____ also a lot of fun. I _____
                   6 (be)   7 (meet)

new people every day. It _____ a funny thing. Everyone
                             8 (be)

_____ to ask me the same question: How _____
     9 (want)   10

you _____ it here? Well, it's not that I _____
        11 (like)   12 (not appreciate)

(not appreciate) the opportunity coming to the United States represents. It's

just that a lot of things _____ strange to me. For example, the
                              13 (seem)

language _____ different from the English I learned at home.
            14 (sound)

And everybody _____ so fast. Sometimes I _____
                  15 (talk)   16 (become)

nervous and I _____ everything that people say to me. Worse,
                 17 (not understand)

people _____ to understand me. I _____ repeat
         18 (seem / never)   19 (have to / always)

myself two or three times. Now, I _____ on my pronunciation
                                            20 (work)

to improve the situation, and I _____ that it _____
                                       21 (believe)   22 (begin)

to get better. But, to be truthful, at times, I get terribly embarrassed.

But it's not only the language that seems so different. There's much more.

For instance, . . .

4 **Practice** Imagine that you are Mohsen. Complete the passage by adding one or
two additional examples and as many details as you can to explain what you mean. You
can talk about the food, the weather, the people, or anything you can think of. Pay
particular attention to the use of the present tense and the present continuous, but
don't limit yourself to these two tenses.

Example *For instance, friendships seem very different. People become*
friends very quickly, but sometimes they don't stay friends very
long. . . .

C. The Past Continuous Tense

The past continuous tense describes actions in progress in the past.
- This tense is often used to "set the scene" in speaking or in writing by telling what
  was happening, what people were doing, wearing, and so on, at a given time in the
  past.
- The "given" time may be in the recent past or it may be in the more distant past; in either case, the time is normally specified.

1.16 The Past Continuous Tense

Uses	Examples	Time Expressions
In the Recent Past	That truck almost hit me! I **was looking** at the traffic signal but not the traffic. Kurt **was sleeping** at 10:00.	*A moment (hour, week) ago, just,* and so on
At a Point of Time in the Past	He **was sleeping** when the phone rang. While he **was sleeping,** the phone rang. The phone rang as he **was sleeping.** We **were studying** while he **was sleeping.**	*At* + specific time *When* + simple past tense *As / while* + past continuous tense

Note: See Appendix 2 for spelling rules for *-ing* endings and Appendix 4 for a list of verbs not normally used in
the continuous tenses. See Chapter 5 for more information on *when* and *while.*

5 Practice Mohsen had a difficult first day at Cornell University. Complete the following exercise about Mohsen's experience. Use the simple past and past continuous tenses.

The First Day

Mohsen's first day at the university _____*was*_____ less than perfect.
(be)

While he _____ to his chemistry lecture, he _____
1 (walk)   2 (realize)

that the walk _____ longer than he _____ it
3 (take)   4 (think)

would. In fact, he _____ to the classroom just as the teacher
5 (get)

_____ himself. This _____ Mohsen a lot. He
6 (introduce)   7 (upset)

_____ into the room and _____ to find a place
8 (tiptoe)   9 (try)

to sit.

While he _____ around, the professor _____
10 (look)   11 (start)

to talk to him. Mohsen could not understand what the professor

_____, but he _____ too embarrassed to tell
12 (say)   13 (be)

the professor that he _____, so the professor continued speak-
14 (not understand)

ing. The professor _____ to help him find a seat. Finally, the
15 (try)

professor _____ to an empty chair. Mohsen _____
16 (point)   17 (understand)

this form of communication and _____ down quickly.
18 (sit)

6 Practice Read the following story and complete it by adding the verb in simple past or past continuous form as appropriate. (*Note:* You may find that one or two sentences can take the simple present tense as well.)

A Late Night Surprise

One night around 10:00 P.M., Charlie Scruggs _____*was reading*_____ his
(read)

newspaper in his favorite armchair. Everyone _____ asleep ex-
1 (be)

cept for Charlie. Suddenly, there _____ a knock at the door.
2 (be)

"Who _____ it at this hour of the night?" he
3 (be)

_____ himself. Charlie _____ and
    4 (ask)   5 (get up)
_____ to the front door. As he _____ the door,
    6 (walk)   7 (open)
he _____ someone running away from his house. He
        8 (see)
_____ to run after the person when he _____
    9 (be about)   10 (feel)
something at his feet. While _____ to get a closer look, the
                                11 (bend down)
thing at his feet _____ a tiny cry. "My goodness!"
                        12 (let out)
_____ Charlie, "What _____ this?" Charlie
    13 (think)   14 (be)
_____ to get very close. Whatever it _____
    15 (kneel down)   16 (be)
was wrapped in a blanket. Charlie _____ the blanket. He
                                        17 (uncover)
_____ what he _____. It _____ a
    18 (cannot believe)   19 (see)   20 (be)
baby!

7 **Practice** Pretend you are a detective who has come to Charlie Scruggs's home after Charlie reported finding a baby on his doorstep. You want to know exactly what happened, so you make a list of questions to ask Charlie. Work with a partner to make a list of ten questions to ask Charlie. Then find another pair of students. Make a new pair with one student. Your partner can make a new pair with the other student. Take turns playing Charlie and the detective. When you are the detective, write down Charlie's answers to your questions. After you have finished the role play, write the answers into a report about the incident.

8 **Practice** The following passage relates a funny story. Fill in the blanks with either the simple past or the past continuous form of the verb. In some cases, either is possible, but be ready to explain any differences in meaning that may occur.

An "Embarrassing" Moment

About ten years ago, my boyfriend and I _were vacationing_ in Mexico
                                            (vacation)
when we suddenly _____ to get married, right then and there!
                        1 (decide)
Neither of us _____ much Spanish, but a hotel receptionist
                    2 (can speak)
_____ a meeting with a priest for 1:00 P.M. Unfortunately, we
    3 (set up)
_____ caught in traffic, so we _____ an hour late
    4 (get)   5 (be)

for our meeting. When we _____, the priest 6 (arrive)

_____ patiently. Of course, I _____ embar-
7 (wait / still)   8 (be)

rassed and _____ to apologize for being late. While the priest
9 (want)

_____ himself, I _____ my sentence from Eng-
10 (introduce)   11 (translate / silently)

lish to Spanish. After a pause, I finally said, "Lo siento mucho . . . Estoy em-

barazada." Later that night, I _____ why the priest had sud-
12 (learn)

denly turned red and left the meeting without a word. *Embarazada* doesn't

mean "embarrassed"; it means "pregnant"!

D. The Future Continuous Tense

The future continuous tense refers to actions that will be in progress in the future. It is
commonly used within one of two time frames: at a point in time in the future or during
a period of time in the future.

In some cases, both the simple future and the future continuous may be appropriate, but there is a difference in tone between the two tenses. Generally, the future
continuous is friendlier and more conversational in tone. Compare: *When will you be going to Chicago?* (more conversational) with *When will you go to Chicago?* (more formal).

1.17 The Future Continuous Tense

Uses	Examples	Time Expressions
A Point in Time in the Future	What **will** Howard **be doing** at 3:00? He**'ll be resting** then.	*at 3:00 (4:00), by (at) that time, next Monday, tomorrow night,* and so on
A Period of Time in the Future	What **will** he **be doing** between 5:00 and 7:00? He**'ll be eating** dinner with friends.	*during the afternoon (evening), from 5:00 to 7:00, next week (month),* and so on

Note: See Appendix 2 for spelling rules for *-ing* endings and Appendix 4 for a list of verbs not normally used in
the continuous tenses.

9 **Practice** You are a reporter trying to get an interview with the president. Your
partner is the president's aide and has the schedule of the president's activities. This
schedule is confidential and only he or she may look at it. Ask your partner at least ten
questions about when you will be able to see the president. Your partner will answer
your questions by referring to the schedule. Use the future continuous or the simple

future in your questions and answers. In some cases, either tense is possible; however, be ready to explain any differences in meaning that might occur.

Example Reporter: *Will he be available at 8:00 A.M.?*
     Aide: *Sorry, he'll be eating at 8:00.*

The President's Schedule

8:00–9:00	eat breakfast
9:00–9:30	read newspapers and mail
9:30–10:00	do exercises
10:00–10:30	swim
10:30–12:00	take nap
12:00–1:00	eat lunch
1:00–5:00	go horseback riding
5:00–7:00	attend cocktail party
7:00–8:00	prepare for speech
8:00–9:00	give speech

10 Practice What does the future hold for you? Use the following time expressions to make statements about your future. Make at least one statement using *will* or *be going to,* one using the future continuous, and one using the present continuous for each time expression.

Examples soon
     I'm going to return to my country soon.
     Noriko will be arriving soon.
     David is leaving for South America soon.

1. tomorrow
2. tomorrow at 3:00 P.M.
3. before long
4. a month from now
5. next year
6. in 2020

11 Error Analysis Most of the following sentences have one or more errors in the use of verbs. Find the errors and correct them. If a sentence has no error, make no changes.

Example Mark is coming from the United States, but now he studies in Florence this year.
Correction: Mark comes from the United States, but he is studying in Florence this year.

1. Mark is trying to learn Italian, but it isn't easy.

2. When he was arriving in Florence, he immediately enrolled in a language school.

3. It has been three months, but when people are speaking to him, he still isn't understanding them.

4. Yesterday Mark was going to the language lab.

5. When the class was over, Mark was waving *good-bye* to his teacher.

6. At the same time, she beginning to motion for him to come to the front of the class.

7. When Mark got to the front of the class, his teacher was still waving, but she looking confused.

8. She said that she was simply waved *good-bye* to Mark.

9. Mark suddenly realizes that the Italian *good-bye* gesture is very similar to the American *come here* gesture.

10. Mark will be study for the next year in Florence.

11. When Mark goes back to the United States next year, he will be speaking perfect Italian.

12. At least that is what he is wanting!

Using What You've Learned

12 Discussing Communication Problems Anyone who spends time in a new culture has some problems with miscommunication. They may involve misinterpreting language or not understanding an unfamiliar culture. In small groups, talk about experiences that you have had with miscommunication. Start with setting the scene and then describe the incident itself.

Example *The three of us arrived in the New York airport late in the afternoon. It was really busy. As we were going through customs. . . .*

Setting the Context

▲ The *Tower of Babel* by Pieter Bruegel (Elder)

Previewing the Passage Discuss the questions with a group.

Do you know a religious explanation for why the world has so many languages? What are some positive things about the existence of so many languages? What are some negative things?

Reading Read the passage.

Babel

All the world once spoke a single language, but this changed at Babel. . . .
Men had been journeying east for many months when they came upon
the land of Shinar. "Come," they said. "We have been traveling days without
end. Let us build ourselves a city and a tower with a top in the heavens, and
make a name for ourselves."[1] But the Lord came down to see the city and   5
tower which mortal men were building. And He said, "Here they are, one

people with a single language, and now they have begun to do this. After this, nothing they want to do will be beyond their reach. Come, let us go down there and confuse their speech. When we finish, they will have lost their one language and in its place there will be many." So the Lord went down to the city. And after He had done this, the city was given the name "Babel" because there the Lord had made a babble of the language of the world.

[1]*make a name for oneself* make oneself famous

 Discussing Ideas Answer the questions with a partner.

According to the story, why was the Lord angry when he saw the city? What did he do? Do you know any other explanations for why we have thousands of languages in the world?

Grammar Structures and Practice

A. The Perfect Tenses: An Overview

The perfect tenses generally refer to events that are completed before another time. The exact completion time is not stated, however.

1.18 **The Perfect Tenses**		
Tenses	**Examples**	**Time Frames**
Present Perfect	Dale **has finished** the assignment.	sometime before now
Past Perfect	He **had finished** by 6:00 yesterday.	sometime before 6:00
Future Perfect	He **will have finished** by 6:00 tomorrow.	sometime before 6:00

Adverbs and other time expressions are often used with the perfect tenses.

1.19 **Placement of Time Expressions with the Perfect Tense**		
Explanations	**Tenses**	**Examples**
Most adverbs follow auxiliary verbs and precede the main verb. Longer time expressions usually come at the beginning or end of the sentence.	**Present Perfect**	Have you **ever** studied Spanish? I've **already** taken two Spanish courses. I **still** haven't taken a writing class.
Still goes before the auxiliary verb. *Yet* goes at the end of a question. It usually goes at the end of a negative statement, but it can also follow *not*.	**Past Perfect**	**Until that time,** she hadn't visited Spain **yet**, but she'd visited South America **several times**. **Until then**, she hadn't **yet** visited Spain.
	Future Perfect	He will **already** have finished all of his courses by next June.

B. The Present Perfect Tense

The present perfect tense frequently refers to these:
- Events that happened (or did not happen) at an unstated time in the past
- Repeated past actions

Note that if the specific past time is given, the simple past tense is used. *(I have gone there. I went there yesterday.)*

1.20 The Present Perfect Tense		
Uses	**Examples**	**Time Expressions**
Events at an Unstated Time in the Past	**Have** you ever **studied** Spanish? I've already **taken** two courses. **Has** Chuck **returned** from Spain yet? No, he still **hasn't returned**.	*already* *so far* *always* *up to now* *ever* *once, twice, three (four, five) times* *just* *How many times. . . ?*
Repeated Past Actions at Unstated Times	Chuck **has visited** Spain twice so far. How many times **have** you **gone** there?	*lately* *recently* *still* *yet*

Note: See Appendix 2 for spelling rules for *-ed* endings and Appendix 1 for a list of irregular past participles.

---

1 Practice Make a TO DO list for the week or month. What have you started to do? What haven't you started yet? What have you already finished? When? Use the following ideas and add at least five of your own. Make a chart like the example on page 35, and write five original sentences for each category. Use the present perfect tense and *already, not . . . yet,* and *still,* except in sentences with specific times in the past.

buy a (birthday) present for. . . .	do laundry	organize my desk	take the garbage out
call my parents	do my homework	pay bills	vacuum
check my email	download new music	pick my room up	wash the floors
clean my computer hard drive up	go grocery shopping	send a (birthday) card to. . . .	write in my journal
	go over my finances	study vocabulary	write letters
	iron		

TO DO	Have Already Done	When?	Haven't Finished Yet	Still Haven't Started
Do last Friday's homework				I still haven't started last Friday's homework.
Take the garbage out	I've already taken the garbage out.	I took it out last night.		
Iron			I haven't finished the ironing yet.	

2 **Practice** Use the simple present, present perfect, or simple past tense to complete these short passages. It will help if you underline the time expressions first.

Example There _____*have been*_____ (be) many changes in linguistic theory in the last 50 years. For example, the idea that all languages share certain elements _____*became*_____ (become) popular in the 1960s.

1. For thousands of years, scientists _____ (wonder) how children learn languages. Recently, researchers _____ (make) a number of discoveries that help explain how language is acquired. We _____ (know / now) that all healthy children _____ (go) through the same steps while learning their native tongues. They _____. (do) this at approximately the same period no matter where they _____ (live).

2. Deaf children _____ (have / always) a difficult time learning language. However, over 100 years ago, teachers _____ (begin) using sign language with deaf children. This _____ (help) Helen Keller in the late 1800s, and it _____ (help) thousands since her time.

3. Linguist Noam Chomsky _____ (be) famous for several decades. He _____ (do) some of his greatest work in the 1960s. Since then, he _____ (continue) to make important discoveries about language.

4. Children _____ (be / always) able to learn two or three languages at the same time. Years ago, however, most linguists _____ (believe) that being monolingual—learning only one language—was better for a child's intellectual development. Since the 1960s and 70s, those ideas _____ (change). A great deal of research in the last decades _____ (show) the opposite to be true.

5. A famous research study on language learning _____ (be) conducted in Canada in the 1970s. This study _____ (demonstrate) that bilingual children _____ (have) certain advantages over monolingual children. Since then, researchers _____ (conduct) many other studies on language development and bilingualism. In almost all cases, bilingualism _____ (prove) to be beneficial.

C. The Perfect Continuous Tenses: An Overview

The perfect continuous tenses refer to actions that *begin* before and *continue* up to another time or event. The duration of the first action is often given. The second time or event is either given or (especially in the case of the present perfect continuous) understood.

1.21	The Perfect Continuous Tenses	
Tenses	**Examples**	**Time Frames**
Present Perfect Continuous	Jill **has been sleeping** for two hours.	the last two hours
Past Perfect Continuous	She **had been sleeping** for two hours by 5:00.	from 3:00 to 5:00
Future Perfect Continuous	She **will have been sleeping** for two hours by 5:00	from 3:00 to 5:00

D. The Present Perfect Continuous Tense

The present perfect continuous tense can describe actions or situations that began in the past and continue to the moment of speaking.

- The present perfect continuous tense often implies that the action or situation will continue in the future.
- This tense stresses the continuous nature of the activity; it is not normally used with expressions that indicate repeated action (*one time, two times,* and so on).

1.22	The Present Perfect Continuous Tense	
Uses	**Examples**	**Time Expressions**
A Period of Time from the Past to the Present	How long **has** Octavio **been studying** English? He **has been studying** English since 7th grade. He **has been studying** English for five years. He **has been studying** all day.	*How long . . . ?* *Since* + a point of time in the past *for* + a period of time *all* + a period of time

 3 **Practice** Answer the following questions. Then tell a partner your answers.

Example *I've been studying English since 4th grade.*

1. How long have you been studying English?

2. How long have you been studying history (computer science, Chinese, etc.)?

3. How long have you been living in your current home?

4. How long have you been playing soccer (tennis, volleyball, golf, etc.)?

5. How long have you been playing the piano (guitar, violin, drums, etc.)?

6. How long have you been working at that store (restaurant, club, etc.)?

7. How long have you been doing oil painting (gymnastics, yoga, etc.)?

8. How long have you been working on this exercise?

E. The Present Perfect Continuous and Present Perfect Tenses

Sometimes the present perfect continuous and present perfect tenses have similar meanings. In these cases, both the present perfect and the present perfect continuous tenses can have a past-to-present time frame.

- This meaning of the present perfect tense occurs most commonly with verbs such as *begin, expect, hope, live, study, teach, wait,* and *work.*
- In addition, this use of the present perfect tense occurs with verbs not normally used in the continuous tenses.
- In general, a time expression is used to give this meaning and time frame to the present perfect tense.

1.23 The Present Perfect Continuous and Present Perfect Tenses with Similar Meanings

Uses	Examples	Time Expressions
A Period of Time from the Past to the Present	Joe **has been studying** here since March. Joe **has studied** here since March.	*Since* + a point of time in the past
	He **has been living** in Ottawa for three months. He **has lived** in Ottawa for three months.	*for* + a period of time
	He **has been working** hard all day. He **has worked** hard all day.	*all* + a period of time

In many cases, however, the present perfect and the present perfect continuous tenses have different meanings.

- The present perfect continuous tense stresses actions or situations that began in the past and continue to the present, while the present perfect tense usually describes actions or situations that began and ended at an unspecified time in the past.
- The present perfect continuous tense stresses the continuous nature of an event or situation, while the present perfect tense is normally used with expressions that indicate repeated action (*one time, two times,* and so on).

1.24 The Present Perfect Continuous and Present Perfect Tenses with Different Meanings

Uses	Examples	Meaning
A Period of Time from the Past to the Present	The sun **has been setting** for the last 5 minutes. I **have been learning** Japanese.	The sun is still setting. I am still learning Japanese.
An Unspecified Time in the Past	The sun **has set**. I **have learned** Japanese.	The sun is down. I know Japanese now.

Note: See Appendix 2 for spelling rules for *-ing* and *-ed* endings, Appendix 1 for irregular past participles, and Appendix 4 for verbs not normally used in the continuous tenses. See Chapter 5 for more information on *since.*

4 **Practice** Complete the following with either the present perfect continuous or the present perfect form of the verb. In some cases, both forms are possible, but be ready to explain any difference in meaning that may occur.

Example Deaf people _have communicated_ (communicate) with American Sign Language (ASL) for over a century.

1. But not only people _____ (learn) to use this sign language to exchange ideas.

2. Researchers _____ (teach) ASL to chimpanzees since the 1960s.

3. The most famous of these chimps, Washoe, _____ (learn) to understand and use over 150 different signs.

4. One of Washoe's first trainers, Beatrice Gardner, _____ (die).

5. However, other researchers _____ (continue) Washoe's "education."

6. For the past several years, Washoe _____ (live) at the Chimpanzee and Human Communication Institute (CHCI) at Central Washington University.

7. At CHCI, Washoe _____ (share) her living space with four other chimps.

8. Washoe _____ (teach / also) her four roommates many of the ASL signs that she knows.

9. She and the other chimps _____ (use) ASL to communicate with themselves and with humans for several years.

10. Washoe, perhaps the most famous chimpanzee in the world, _____ (celebrate / recently) her 42nd birthday.

F. The Past Perfect and Past Perfect Continuous Tenses

Both the past perfect and past perfect continuous tenses refer to activities or situations that had ended *before* another event or time in the past. The second event or time must be either mentioned or implied.

- The past perfect tense stresses the completion of the earlier activity, while the past perfect continuous tense stresses the duration.
- These tenses are somewhat formal and appear more often in written English than in spoken English.

- Both tenses are frequently used in complex sentences using more than one time in the past. See Chapter 5 for more examples of complex sentences.

1.25 The Past Perfect and Past Perfect Continuous Tenses

Tenses	Examples	Time Expressions
Past Perfect	Joy **had finished** the article by 8:00 P.M. She **had** never **read** that author before last night. I tried to call her, but she **had** already **left**. After I **had phoned**, I went to a movie. When I phoned, she **had** just **left** for the theater.	adverbs such as *already, just, never, still,* and *yet* *before* or *by* + point in time *after, before, until, when,* **by the time** *that* + clause
Past Perfect Continuous	By midnight, Claudia **had** already **been working** for 12 hours. After she **had been working** for 16 hours, she fell asleep.	*for* + period of time *since* + point in time

Note: See Appendix 2 for spelling rules for *-ed* and *-ing* endings, Appendix 1 for a list of irregular past participles, and Appendix 4 for a list of verbs not normally used in the continuous tenses.

---

5 **Practice** Fill in the following blanks with the correct form of the verbs in parentheses. Use the past perfect continuous wherever possible. Where this is not possible, use the past perfect.

Example Claudia starts her day early. By 7:00 A.M. this morning, she had ___already gotten up___ (get up / already).

1. At 6:45, after she _____ (sleep) for eight hours, Claudia _____ (get up).

2. She _____ (finish) breakfast before the newspaper _____ (arrive).

3. By 8:00, she _____ (shower) and _____ (eat) breakfast.

4. At 8:15, she left the house. After she _____ (close) and _____ (lock) the door, she began walking to the bus stop.

5. On the way, she noticed that a man _____ (follow) her for several blocks.

6. When she reached the bus stop, she sat down. The man sat next to her. They _____ (sit) together for about five minutes when the bus arrived.

7. Claudia climbed on the bus and took a seat, but she _____ (begin / just) to relax when she realized her purse was missing.

8. She was sure that she _____ (not forget) to bring her purse that morning.

9. When she looked out the window, she saw that the man who _____ (follow) her was running down the street with her purse.

10. When Claudia went to the police station later that day, someone _____ (turn in / already) her purse; unfortunately, all the money _____ (be) removed.

6 **Practice** Use either the simple past or the past perfect tense to complete the following passage.

Rip van Winkle

In the 18th century, Washington Irving wrote a famous tale about a man named Rip van Winkle. In the story, Rip drank a secret potion given to him by a wizard. Soon, Rip fell asleep under a tree and didn't awake for 20 years.

Example When Rip finally woke up, everything _____*seemed*_____ (seem) different. In fact, many things _____*had changed*_____ (change).

1. His gun _____ (be / still) next to him, but it _____ (rust / completely).

2. He _____ (find) his house, but it _____ (be) empty because his wife _____ (pass away / already).

3. Rip _____ (walk) to the center of his village, but no one

_____ (recognize) him. That is partly because nobody

_____ (see) him for over 20 years, and most of his friends

_____ (die) or _____ (move) away from his

village.

4. In addition, he _____ (look) quite different. His hair

_____ (be) much longer and very dirty. His beard

_____ (grow) more than a foot. Also, his clothes _____

(disintegrate / almost).

5. Luckily, Rip _____ (find) his daughter, who was now an adult,

and he _____ (move) in with her family.

7 **Practice** Imagine that you, too, drank the secret potion. Last year you woke up
from your 20-year nap. Make at least six sentences (three with the past tense and three
with the past perfect) describing the situation that you *found* and the changes that *had
occurred*.

G. The Future Perfect and Future Perfect Continuous Tenses

These tenses refer to actions or situations that will have occurred before another event
or time in the future. The second event or time must be either mentioned or implied.
- The future perfect emphasizes the completion of an activity.
- As with other continuous tenses, the future perfect continuous emphasizes an activity
  in progress.

1.26 The Future Perfect and Future Perfect Continuous Tenses		
Tense	**Examples**	**Time Expressions**
Future Perfect	By next year, my daughter **will have started** elementary school. Also, she **will have begun** tennis lessons. She **will** already **have won** her first tournament when you see her.	*before* or *by* + point in time adverbs such as *already*, *just*, *recently*, and *yet*
Future Perfect Continuous	She **will have been talking** for three years by her fifth birthday. She **will have been going** to school for 18 years by graduation day.	*for* + period of time *since* + beginning time

Note: See Appendix 2 for spelling rules for *-ed* and *-ing* endings, Appendix 1 for a list of irregular past participles,
and Appendix 4 for a list of verbs not normally used in the continuous tenses.

8 **Practice** Rap (Rip van Winkle's grandson) has just been given a magic potion that will make him sleep for 20 years, also. Use either the simple future or the future perfect to talk about how things will be different when he wakes up.

Example When Rap wakes up, everything _____*will seem*_____ (seem) different. In fact, many things __*will have changed*__ (change).

1. His gun _____ (be / still) next to him, but it _____ (rust / completely).

2. He _____ (find) his house, but it _____ (be) empty because his wife _____ (pass away / already).

3. Rap _____ (walk) to the center of his village, but no one _____ (recognize) him. That is partly because nobody _____ (see) him for over 20 years, and most of his friends _____ (die) or _____ (move) away from his village.

4. In addition, he _____ (look) quite different. His hair _____ (be) much longer and very dirty. His beard _____ (grow) more than a foot. Also, his clothes _____ (disintegrate / almost).

5. Luckily, Rap _____ (find) his daughter, who _____ (be / now) an adult, and he _____ (move) in with her family.

9 **Review** Fill in the blanks with the verb *discuss*. Choose from all tenses. In many cases, more than one tense may be appropriate. However, be ready to describe any differences in meaning that might result.

Example We _____*discussed*_____ this problem last year.

1. They _____ the problem since 10:00 A.M.

2. Some students _____ the problem when we came to class.

3. They _____ (probably) the problem when class ends.

4. We _____ it a number of times in the past.

5. I never _____ this problem last year.

6. We _____ this problem for two hours by the time he arrives.

7. College students _____ this issue quite often these days.

8. Marion and Vittorio _____ the problem right now.

9. After they _____ it for three hours, they reached a decision.

10. They _____ (never) this issue again.

10 **Review** Create sentences using the following time expressions. Use as many different tenses as you can with each time expression, but be ready to explain the differences in meaning that may result.

1. for two hours last Thursday

2. for the past 15 minutes

3. when I saw the fire

4. in 2004

5. when we meet in 2020

6. tomorrow

7. every morning at 6:00

8. at the moment

9. when I was a child

10. since we last met

11 **Error Analysis** Each of the following sentences contains an error related to verb tense. Identify the errors and correct them.

think
Example I ~~am thinking~~ that English is impossible to learn.

1. Before I had studied English, I thought it was an easy language.

2. Now I am knowing that it isn't easy.

3. My language has had only a little slang.

4. I am studying English since April, and I only begin to learn some of the common slang words.

5. I have been tried to learn more of these words every day.

6. Last night, for example, I have studied from 9:00 P.M. to midnight.

7. I was studying for three hours when I finally quit.

8. I had gone to my teacher last Monday and she was telling me to see her after class.

9. But when I went to her classroom after school, she already left.

10. It's now May 15; by the middle of June, I will be studying English for three months.

11. On June 23, I am studying the tenses in English.

12. On June 30, I will be studying the verb tenses for one week.

12 Practice Go back to the passage "Babel" on page 32 and underline the uses of the present perfect (*have* + past participle) and perfect continuous (*have* + *been* + present participle) tenses. Then answer the following questions.

1. How do the following sentences differ in meaning?
   Now they have begun to do this.
   Now they are beginning to do this.

2. What is the difference between the following sentences?
   When we finish, they will have lost their one language.
   When we finish, they will lose their one language.

3. Was the city given the name Babel before or after *the Lord had made a babble of the language of the world*? Which verb tense indicates which action came first?

13 Review Fill in the blanks with appropriate forms of the verbs in parentheses. In some cases, more than one verb form may be appropriate. However, be ready to explain any differences in meaning that may occur.

Esperanto at a Glance

The grammar is based on 16 fundamental rules, which have no exceptions. For example, all adjectives end in -*a,* all nouns end in -*o,* and the simple verb has only six inflections:

Infinitive	Present	Past	Future	Conditional	Imperative
I	As	Is	Os	Us	U
Esti	Estas	Estis	Estos	Estus	Estu
Studi	Studas	Studis	Studos	Studus	Studu
Helpi	Helpas	Helpis	Helpos	Helpus	Helpu

Esperanto

The idea of a universal language ___has interested___ people since the
(interest)

time of Babel. In the 1870s, a Polish teenager named Ludwik

Zamenhof _____ to develop such a language. He
1 (begin)

_____ his new language Esperanto, which
2 (call)

_____ "hope." At that time, he _____ in a Pol-
3 (mean)   4 (live)

ish town where Poles, Russians, Germans, and Jews all _____
5 (speak)

their own languages. Zamenhof _____ that language differences
6 (believe)

_____ the major cause of difficulties among different ethnic
7 (be)

groups. By 1890, he _____ his first book on Esperanto, and
8 (publish)

within a short time, thousands of people _____ this new
9 (learn)

language.

Esperanto _____ simple to learn and use. The grammar
10 (be)

_____ based on 16 fundamental rules. There
11 (be)

_____ no exceptions and no irregularities. In addition, the ac-
12 (be)

cent or stress always _____ on the last syllable of a word, and
13 (fall)

every letter _____ one and only one sound.
14 (have)

At first, Esperanto _____ a great success. Within a few
15 (be)

years, hundreds of thousands of people _____ Esperanto. (In
16 (speak)

fact, people _____ over 10,000 books in Esperanto since 1900.)
17 (write)

However, after a few decades, interest in the language _____.
18 (decline)

Today, it _____ still popular among thousands of people, but
19 (be)

few _____ that Esperanto _____ a universal
20 (think)   21 (become)

language.

This _____, however, that there _____ a
22 (not mean)   23 (be / never)

universal tongue. In fact, English _____ to become just such a
24 (be / likely)

language. Unlike Esperanto, English _____ thousands of ex-
25 (have)

ceptions and irregularities. But it _____ the greatest number of
26 (have / also)

speakers, and this number _____. Today, there
27 (grow / rapidly)

_____ close to a billion speakers of English. By the year 2020,
28 (be)

well over a billion and a half people _____ English. Some ex-
29 (speak)

perts _____ that by 2100, English _____ the
30 (predict)   31 (become)

first truly universal language.

Using What You've Learned

14 **Practice** The last 100 years have seen more change than any other period in the history of mankind. With a partner, make at least five sentences for each of the following:

1. changes that had taken place before you were born
2. changes that have taken place since you were born
3. changes that will have taken place before you die

Example *Before I was born, humans had landed on the moon.*
Since I was born, computers have become very popular.
Before I die, we will have explored another solar system.

Part 5 Modal Auxiliaries and Related Structures

Setting the Context

Previewing the Passage Discuss the questions with a group.

In your language, how would you ask a close friend to lend you a book? Would you use different words to ask your boss the same thing?

Reading Read the passage.

Language and Politeness

Every language has certain forms that are used to show respect or politeness. For example, in English, "Would you please open the door?" is normally a more polite request than "Open the door, would you?" or simply "Open the door." Moreover, "You might see a doctor" is usually a more polite suggestion to someone who is sick than "You should (must) see a doctor." 5

In Japan, politeness is extremely important, and the Japanese language has many polite forms. In an informal situation, a Japanese person can talk about another person's return to his house by simply saying, "He came home." However, a more formal situation may produce the sentence, "The fact of his return happened." And if local politicians are announcing the return of their leader, they might say softly, "He has become visible." 10

 Discussing Ideas Discuss the questions with a group.

Compared to English, does your language have many polite forms? How is politeness expressed in your language?

Grammar Structures and Practice

A. Introduction to Modal Auxiliaries

Modal auxiliaries form a special group because they have only one form for all persons of the verb and because they can have several meanings, depending on their context.

1.27 Modal Auxiliaries		
Structures	**Formation**	**Examples**
Simple	modal + verb	He **should arrive** at any moment.
Continuous	modal + *be* + present participle	He **may be arriving** soon.
Perfect	modal + *have* + past participle	He **must have had** a problem.
Perfect Continuous	modal + *have been* + present participle	He **might have been driving** that old car.

Note: In Chapters 8 and 10, you will study further uses of these auxiliaries.

A variety of phrases and expressions have meanings similar to modal auxiliaries.

1.28 Structures Related to Modal Auxiliaries

Modal Auxiliary	Related Structure	Modal Auxiliary	Related Structure
can, could, can, may, might must	be able to be allowed to have to, have got to	ought to, should shall, will	be supposed to, had better, need to be going to, be about to

1 Practice Read the following sentences. Find another way to express the same idea.

Example I may go tomorrow.

I might go tomorrow.

1. Deb can't go out because she must study for the test.
2. I am able to translate from Korean to English.
3. They should keep their promise.
4. You are going to enjoy that movie.
5. We weren't able to help her.
6. He has to take ten courses in Spanish in order to major in it.
7. I don't feel good; I might be getting a cold.
8. I had better study more, or I am not going to do well in this class.
9. She was allowed to go to the movie, but she wasn't allowed to stay out late.
10. We are supposed to review this chapter for the test.
11. You have got to study more.
12. They shall arrive at 8:00 P.M.

B. Modals of Inference, Prediction, and Probability

Certain modal auxiliaries and related structures are often used to express logical conclusions about an event or situation. Adverbial expressions such as *possibly, probably,* or *most likely* can also be used with inferences and predictions.

1.29 Modals of Inference, Prediction, and Probability

Uses	Words and Phrases	Examples	Meaning
Present or Future Inference	must has to may might could	There is a dog barking outside. ■ That **must (has to)** be Marty's dog. ■ That **may (might)** be Marty's dog. ■ That **could be** Marty's dog.	more certain ↓ less certain
Past Inference	must have may have might have could have	There was a dog barking outside last night. ■ That **must have been** Marty's dog. ■ That **may (might, could) have been** Marty's dog.	more certain ↓ less certain
Affirmative Predictions	will should could may might	How will the court rule? ■ They **will decide** against the union. ■ They **should decide** against the union. ■ They **could decide** against the union. ■ They **may decide** against the union. ■ They **might decide** against the union.	more certain ↓ less certain
Negative Predictions	will not should not cannot could not may not might not	How will the court rule? ■ They **won't decide** against the union. ■ They **shouldn't decide** against the union. ■ They **can't (couldn't) decide** against the union. ■ They **may not decide** against the union. ■ They **might not decide** against the union.	more certain ↓ less certain

*Note: Can is not used in making a positive inference. In negative inferences, *should* and *must* are not used.*

---

2 Practice Give at least two reactions to each of the following statements with *could, may, might,* or *must.*

Example There's a light on in the house.

Somebody must be home. Someone must have forgotten to turn it off.

1. I hear a scratching noise.

2. The traffic is moving very slowly.

3. Jack didn't go home for Christmas.

4. Paula has gained weight all of a sudden.

5. The Browns aren't having their holiday party this year.

6. I didn't do well on the final exam.

7. He had only known her for two months before he proposed.

8. Ann has been looking for a job for several weeks, but she hasn't gotten one yet.

9. Thomas and his wife have not been at any of our meetings lately.

10. Jack is having problems with his roommate.

3 **Practice** Read each of the following predictions of the famous astrologer and palm reader Madame DePriest. Then make an appropriate comment with a positive or negative modal.

Example In 2020, we will discover little green men living under the Earth.
That can't be possible.

1. The United States will revert to an English colony in 25 years.

2. In ten years, the CD will vanish like the vinyl record has.

3. Madonna will undergo plastic surgery that keeps her a constant 40 years old.

4. People will talk to their computers instead of using a keyboard.

5. The world will run out of drinkable water in our lifetime.

6. There will be a high-speed ship linking the Far East to the West Coast of the United States.

7. The nations of the world will do away with passports because all people on the Earth will be entered into a worldwide computer network as soon as they are born.

8. In 100 years, there will be no paper or metal money.

9. Some sports stars will become rich enough to buy their own countries.

10. It will rain tomorrow.

C. Modals of Social Interaction

Modals of social interaction include *can, could, might, ought to, should, will,* and *would.* The choice of modal auxiliary depends on the need for politeness or formality and on the relationship between the speaker and the person he / she is addressing.

1.30 Modals of Social Interaction

Uses	Explanations	Examples	Meaning
Making Requests	*Would* is a softer request than *will*, and *could* is softer than *can*. In general, formality is shown by using *would* and *could* rather than *can* and *will*.	**Would** you mind helping me? **Would** you help me? **Could** you help me? **Can** you help me? **Will** you help me?	more formal ↓ less formal
Asking for Permission	*May* and *might* are more formal than *can* and *could*.	**Might** I speak with Bruce? **May** I speak with Bruce? **Could** I speak with Bruce? **Can** I speak with Bruce?	more formal ↓ less formal
Giving Advice and Making Suggestions	While *must* has the feeling of a requirement or very strong advice, *might* and *could* make the advice seem more like a suggestion than a required action.	You **must** arrive on time. You **should** arrive on time. You **ought to** arrive on time. You **might** arrive on time. You **could** arrive on time.	stronger ↓ weaker

4 Practice In English, commands and requests show varying degrees of politeness or formality. A list of commands follows. Suppose that you are speaking to each of these people. Change the commands to appropriate requests.

> a classmate   your best friend   your students
> the president of your school   your son or daughter   your teacher

Example   Open the door.
Speaking to the president of the university, you should use very formal language. It would be appropriate to say, for example:
Would you mind opening the door for me?
Speaking to your son or daughter, you could say:
Open the door, please.

1. Pass the salt.

2. Give me the homework assignment.

3. Help me with this problem.

4. Don't talk so much.

5. Stop talking and listen to me.

6. Turn off the lights before you leave.

7. Lend me some money.

8. Wash the dishes.

9. Tell me the time.

10. Don't make noise.

11. Wait a minute.

12. Don't do that.

5 Practice First, complete the items in this activity with appropriate modal auxiliaries. After each, indicate whether your sentence is formal or informal. Then compare your choices in a group and discuss the level of formality of each item.

Example _____Will_____ you pass the mashed potatoes, please?

Informal (for example, as a request to a family member at the _
dinner table). _

1. You _____ see a doctor. That lump looks suspicious.

_____

2. _____ I shut the window? It's really cold in here.

_____

3. _____ Billy come with us to the movie this afternoon?

_____

4. Every citizen _____ vote in a presidential election.

_____

5. You _____ try meditating to lower your blood pressure.

_____

6. I just loved San Francisco. You really _____ go there if you have the chance.

_____

7. _____ I have this dance?

_____

8. Mr. President, _____ I be permitted to say a few words?

_____

9. If you don't like the color, you _____ always bring it back for another. _____

10. Reverend Weir, _____ you give me permission to ask for your daughter's hand in marriage?

_____

D. Other Modals and Their Uses

Modal auxiliaries and related structures can be used with ability, preference, need, and lack of need.

1.31 Other Modals and Their Uses

Uses	Explanations	Examples
Expressing Abilities	*Can* is often used to express an ability that we have. When we use *could* to express ability, it refers to an ability we no longer have.	I **can count** to ten in five languages: English, Spanish, Italian, Korean, and Japanese. When I was a boy, I **could spend** hours with my baseball card collection.
Showing Preference	*Would rather* is used to show a preference. We can also use *would prefer* to show preference, but it sounds more formal.	I **would rather spend** time in the mountains than at the seashore. I **would prefer** to have an aisle seat.
Expressing Urgent Need	*Must, must not, have to,* and *have got to* are used for situations or actions that are important and necessary.	I **have to stop** smoking, or I'll have serious problems. You **must not smoke** in here.
Expressing Lack of Need	The negative, *not have to*, has a very different meaning. It shows that something is not necessary or important.	We **don't have to leave** until 10:30. She **didn't have to do** any homework last night.

6 Practice Complete the following sentences with *must not* or *doesn't / don't have to*.

Example A student ___*doesn't have to*___ do extra credit work if he chooses not to.

1. You _____ use electrical appliances while you are in the bathtub.

2. This homework is optional; you _____ do it.

3. Students _____ go on the field trip to the art museum; they can go to the language lab instead.

4. You _____ make a left turn if there are cars coming from the opposite direction.

5. You _____ use a pen on standardized tests such as the TOEFL® test.

6. If you drop a class, you _____ wait until late in the semester.

7. A student _____ buy a gift for the teacher at the end of the course.

8. Students _____ attend graduation, but most do.

7 Practice In the United States, rules of politeness are strictest within certain institutions. A good example is the military. Restate the following sentences, using the affirmative or negative forms of these expressions of necessity: *must, have to, have got to, had to.*

Example It is forbidden for a common soldier to yell at a superior.
A common soldier must not yell at a superior.

1. It's necessary for soldiers to call officers "sir."
2. It's not necessary for officers to call soldiers "sir."
3. It's forbidden to call officers by their first names.
4. It's not necessary to bow to officers.
5. It's necessary to salute officers.
6. Many years ago, it was necessary for soldiers to treat officers almost like gods.
7. Many years ago, it wasn't necessary for officers to give soldiers any rights at all.
8. Today, it is necessary for soldiers to respect their officers, but it isn't necessary for them to be afraid of their officers.

E. Understanding Reduced Forms in Rapid Speech

In rapid speech, many structures with modal auxiliaries are not always pronounced clearly. Some are often reduced in predictable ways.

1.32 Understanding Reduced Forms in Rapid Speech

Can	/kin/	Could we?	/kudwi/	Shouldn't you?	/shudincha/
Can you?	/kinya/	Could have	/kudda/	Should he?	/shudi/
Can't you?	/kancha/	You had better	/ya bedder/	Shouldn't he?	/shudinti/
Can he?	/keni/	Have to	/hafta/	Should have	/shudduv/
Can't he?	/kanti/	Has to	/hasta/	Won't you?	/woncha/
Could you?	/kudja/	Ought to	/otta/	Would you?	/wudja/
Couldn't you?	/kudincha/	Ought to have	/ottuv/	Would he?	/wudi/
Could he?	/kudi/	Should you?	/shudja/	Would have	/wudduv/

8 Practice Listen as your teacher reads the following sentences rapidly. Circle the word(s) that you hear.

Example Could (he / we / you) go to the movie?

1. Can (he / we / you) go to the movie?
2. (Can / Can't) you go to the movie?
3. (Won't / Would) you go to the movie?
4. (Should / Shouldn't) you study?

5. Shouldn't (he / we / you) study?

6. (He / You) had better study.

7. I (can / can't) work tonight.

8. (Can / Can't) he work tonight?

9. Shouldn't (he / we) work tonight?

10. He (could / could have) come here.

11. He (would / would have) come here.

12. He (can / can't) come here.

13. (Would / Wouldn't) you help?

14. Could (he / we / you) help?

15. Couldn't (he / we / you) help?

9 **Review** Read the following sentences. Then answer these questions for each:

• Did an action occur?

• Who did it?

• When did it occur?

• Was it completed?

Rephrase each sentence to explain the meaning.

Example Jack may write the letter.
No action yet—It is possible that Jack will write it in the future.

The letter was written.
Action completed—Someone already wrote it in the past.

1. Jack is writing the letter.

2. Jack has been writing the letter.

3. Jack should write the letter.

4. The letter has been written.

5. The letter will be written.

6. Jack should have written the letter.

7. Jack will be writing the letter.

8. Jack must write the letter.

9. Jack will have written the letter.

10. Jack may have written the letter.

11. Jack wrote the letter.

12. Jack could write the letter.

13. Jack had written the letter.

14. Jack had been writing the letter.

15. Jack had better write the letter.

10 **Review** First read this passage for meaning. Fill in the blanks with appropriate forms of the verbs in parentheses. Add negatives, adverbs, and modal auxiliaries when indicated. In some cases, more than one verb form may be appropriate. However, be ready to explain any differences in meaning that may occur.

Learning Another Language[1]

Several stages _____*seem*_____ to exist in language learning, and most
             (seem)

people _____ all these stages while they _____
        1 (go through / generally)   2 (learn)

another language. Some differences _____ because every human
                                    3 (modal / occur)

_____ different and _____ his or her own inter-
   4 (be)   5 (have)

ests and experiences. However, in general, these _____ the stages
                                                   6 (be)

that _____ to proficiency in another language.
      7 (lead)

The Silent Stage

The silent stage _____ a few hours or a few months. Students
                  8 (modal / last)

_____ about 500 words. They _____ these
9 (know / often)   10 (modal / understand)

words, but they _____ very comfortable using them. As a result,
                 11 (modal / not feel)

students _____ at all, or they _____ very little
          12 (modal / not speak)   13 (modal / speak)

during this time.

The Early Production Stage

The early production stage _____ six more months. By this
                            14 (modal / last)

time, students _____ a vocabulary of about 1,000 words that they
                15 (develop / already)

_____ and _____. During this stage, students
16 (modal / understand)   17 (modal / use)

_____ in one- or two-word phrases or short sentences.
18 (speak /often)

The Speech Emergence Stage

This stage _____ for another year. By this time, the student's
            19 (modal / continue)

vocabulary _____ to about 3,000 words. You _____
       20 (grow / usually)   21 (modal / notice)

that students _____ simple sentences easily and
                    22 (use)

_____ to create longer, more complicated sentences. They
       23 (begin)

_____ many grammatical errors, but their speech
     24 (make / probably)

_____ more sophisticated.
      25 (become)

The Intermediate Language Stage

It _____ another year after speech _____ to
     26 (modal / take)   27 (emerge)

reach the intermediate stage. By the intermediate stage, students

_____ about 6,000 words. They _____ to share
     28 (learn / generally)   29 (begin / already)

their thoughts and opinions at greater length. They _____ to use
                                                          30 (begin / also)

more complex language, and they _____ willing to experiment
                                        31 (be)

with new expressions and structures.

The Advanced Proficiency Stage

To reach the advanced stage in another language, students

_____ a broad vocabulary. When students _____
     32 (modal / develop)   33 (reach)

this level, they _____ fully in the world around them. Basically,
                    34 (modal / participate)

they _____ in the same way as a native speaker. These language
        35 (modal / interact)

learners _____ and _____ at
         36 (modal / speak / understand / read)   37 (write)

about the same level as a native speaker who _____ their age and
                                                    38 (be)

_____ their level of education. In total, it _____
     39 (have)   40 (modal / take)

up to eight years to reach advanced proficiency. Of course, this

_____ several questions. For example, _____
     41 (depend on)   42

the students _____ continuously over eight years?
                  43 (study)

_____ they _____ the new language on a regu-
     44 (modal)   45 (use)

lar basis during that time? Or, _____ they _____
                                      46 (modal)   47 (interrupt)

their work in the new language? _____ they _____
                                      48 (modal)   49 (leave)

the second language environment and _____ to their native lan-
50 (return)

guage environment? In addition to the language itself, many other factors

_____ the process of becoming proficient.
51 (modal / affect)

_____

[1]Information adapted from *Overview of Second Language Acquisition Theory,* NW
Regional Educational Laboratory, May 2003

Using What You've Learned

 11 **Making Requests** With a partner, role-play the following short situations. Take turns making requests and either granting or denying them. Use language that is appropriate to the relationship between the two speakers.

1. You want to borrow your classmate's dictionary.

2. You want to use your friend's car.

3. You want to make a long-distance phone call on your neighbor's phone.

4. You want to meet your professor in his office at 1:00 P.M. today.

5. You want to borrow $1,000 from your father.

6. You want to borrow some lecture notes from a classmate whom you know casually.

7. You want your boss's permission to leave work early because you need to go to the dentist.

12 **Playing a Guessing Game** Nonverbal communication, which includes body movements and gestures, can be just as expressive as verbal language. Your teacher will give each of you a card with an occupation or activity on it. Use body language as you take turns pantomiming these occupations in front of the class. As each student performs, try to guess what he or she is doing by using modals of probability or possibility. When someone guesses correctly, the pantomime can stop. While pantomiming, you may make sounds but don't use words.

Example   Plumber
He couldn't be a dentist.
He may be a repairman.
He might be working in the bathroom.
He could be fixing the sink.
He must be a plumber.

13 Discussing Language Language is very complex, and although most people learn their first language easily, few people find learning a second language as easy. In small groups, use the following questions to discuss the process of learning another language. After you've finished, choose one member of the group to give a brief summary of your discussion to the entire class.

1. Why is it difficult to learn a second language?

2. How can people best learn another language? Give some specific suggestions or advice that has been helpful for you.

3. What roles do / might computers play in language learning? In communicating across cultures and language groups?

4. Linguists talk about interference (the problem caused by trying to apply the ideas or rules of your first language to the second language). What problems do you have because of interference?

5. How important is grammatical correctness? When is it most important? What about pronunciation? Is it possible to "lose" an accent?

6. Reread Exercise 10 in Part 5, and then do a self-assessment or assessments of each other. Where do you stand in terms of your mastery of English? You can look at English as a whole, or you can discuss one or more skills: listening, speaking, reading, writing, pronunciation, or spelling, for example.

Introduction to Focus on Testing

Each chapter in this book includes a short practice exam that is similar to standardized tests you would take for placement. With these, you will also find reminders about common problems with the structures covered in that chapter. Most of the tests focus on the structures of the particular chapter. Chapters 5 and 10 have practice exams that include a variety of structures covered in the book. Use the various exams to help you clarify any areas that you don't understand well and to learn which structures you need to study more.

Verbs, Modal Auxiliaries, and Related Structures

Problem areas with verb tenses and modal auxiliaries always appear on standardized tests of English proficiency. Check your understanding of these structures by completing the sample items.

Remember that . . .

✓ Verb tenses can have a variety of uses. For example, the simple present tense is sometimes used for past or future situations.

✓ The continuous tenses are used for actions in progress at a certain time.

✓ The perfect tenses are used for actions completed before another point in time.

✓ Modal auxiliaries do not change form, but their meanings usually depend on the context.

Part 1 Circle the best completion for the following.

Example   By 9:00, Ned _____ his breakfast.

    (A) has finished   (B) finishing

    (C) had finished   (D) had been finishing

1. When she was an adolescent, Kate _____ in a small state in the northern Midwest.

    (A) used to live   (B) would live

    (C) has lived   (D) living

2. I still _____ my job, but I wouldn't mind an extended vacation in a tropical paradise.

    (A) am loving   (B) have been loving

    (C) love   (D) have loved

3. Anyone who has a library card _____ take materials out of the library for two weeks.

- (A) should
- (B) must
- (C) may
- (D) had better

4. Has she _____ in London?

- (A) ever live
- (B) been live
- (C) lived ever
- (D) ever lived

5. While Emily _____ on her master's degree, her husband took care of their two daughters.

- (A) was working
- (B) is working
- (C) has worked
- (D) has been working

Part 2 Each sentence has one error. Circle the letter below the word(s) containing the error.

Example Joe <u>goes</u> to Paris next week, but when I <u>saw</u> him, he <u>hasn't</u> <u>bought</u> his
  　　　　　A　　　　　　　　　　　　　　　　　B　　　　Ⓒ　　　　D
ticket yet.

1. I <u>am sure</u> that she <u>is having</u> a rewarding experience, but I <u>am wanting</u> her
  　　A　　　　　　　　B　　　　　　　　　　　　　　　　　　C
<u>to return</u> home by tomorrow at noon.
  　D

2. Their guide suggested that the hikers <u>must</u> <u>to start</u> <u>walking</u> back to camp
  　　　　　　　　　　　　　　　　　　　　　A　　B　　　C
before it <u>became</u> too dark and windy.
  　　　　　D

3. In retrospect, he <u>realizes</u> that he should <u>have not</u> <u>voiced</u> his opinion before
  　　　　　　　　A　　　　　　　　　　　B　　　C
<u>verifying</u> all the facts.
  D

4. Until last year, we <u>hadn't been</u> camping there since we <u>used to</u> <u>going</u> <u>as</u>
  　　　　　　　　　　A　　　　　　　　　　　　　B　　　C　　D
small children.

5. Dr. Gutiérrez <u>has</u> <u>already</u> finished writing his report <u>when</u> Professor Oswald
  　　　　　　　　A　　B　　　　　　　　　　　　　　　C
<u>contacted</u> him about errors in the lab results.
  D

Self-Assessment Log

Check the things you did in this chapter. How well can you do each one?

	Not Very Well	Fairly Well	Very Well
I understand parts of speech and basic sentence structure.	❏	❏	❏
I can use present and future verb tenses appropriately.	❏	❏	❏
I can use a variety of past tenses appropriately.	❏	❏	❏
I can use present perfect and perfect continuous tenses appropriately.	❏	❏	❏
I can use past and future perfect tenses appropriately.	❏	❏	❏
I can use a variety of modal auxiliaries appropriately.	❏	❏	❏
I can take a test about verb forms and tenses, modal auxiliaries, and related structures.	❏	❏	❏
I understand new information about language and language learning, and I can use new structures and vocabulary to talk and write about related topics.	❏	❏	❏

Danger and Daring

❝The more danger, the more honor.**❞** —English Proverb

Connecting to the Topic

1 What do you know about the great explorers of the past 500 years?

2 What qualities or characteristics do you think these people had?

3 Who is the explorer you admire the most? Why?

In this chapter, you will review singular and plural forms of nouns, uses of articles and adjectives, and subject / verb agreement.

Reading Read the following passage. It introduces the chapter theme "Danger and Daring" and raises some of the topics and issues you will cover in the chapter.

The Challenge of Exploration

In the summer of 1275, Marco Polo reached Shangtu, China. It was the end of a grueling[1] three-year journey. During the journey, Marco Polo came close to losing his life several times. Yet he persisted and finally succeeded in reaching his goal: the kingdom of Kublai Khan.

At about the same time, Polynesians were exploring the thousands of islands of the South Pacific Ocean. Despite the great dangers of sailing long distances in open canoes, the Polynesians managed to explore and populate all the major islands within the triangle formed by Hawaii, Easter Island, and New Zealand.

About 200 years later, on August 3, 1492, Christopher Columbus left Europe to explore the unknown reaches of the Atlantic Ocean. Believing the Earth to be flat, many feared that Columbus would fall off the edge of the world. Yet Columbus persevered. He did not reach his goal, Asia. Instead, he opened up a vast new world, the Americas.

Every explorer needs a vision, a goal. What drives explorers to leave the security of the known world and to face the dangers of the unknown? For many, it is a restless spirit. For a few, it is purely the love of adventure. Perhaps a paraphrase from George Mallory expressed this best; when asked why he wanted to climb Mt. Everest, Mallory's answer boiled down to[2] "because it is there."

---

[1]*grueling* extremely difficult physically or psychologically
[2]*boiled down to* had the basic meaning of

Discussing Ideas Discuss the following with a group.

For some people, the unknown is something to fear. For others, however, the unknown holds a tremendous attraction. Why do you think people throughout history have been willing to risk their lives exploring the unknown?

Setting the Context

Previewing the Passage Discuss the questions with a group.

When you hear the name Marco Polo, what comes to mind? Where was he from? Where did he travel? Why is he important?

Reading Read the passage.

Marco Polo

In 1271, 17-year-old Marco Polo left Venice to begin one of the most amazing odysseys of all time. Marco, along with his father Nicolo and his uncle Maffeo, was about to enter Asia, a land completely unknown to Europe. The mysteries that Marco Polo saw and reported changed not only his life but also the lives of Europeans in general.   5

Marco Polo was amazed by the wonders and riches that he saw. The sophistication of the Orient made Europe seem primitive. While the weavers of Venice were just learning to work with silk, Oriental weavers had been producing exquisite brocade[1] for centuries. In making porcelain,[2] Oriental craftsmen had long used techniques that were unknown in the West.   10 Throughout the empire of Kublai Khan, money made of paper was used for business transactions, something unheard of in Europe. In all, Marco Polo spent 24 years exploring the Eastern world from Venice to Cathay. The diary of his travels remains a remarkable tale of adventure as well as a record of the Orient of the 13th century.   15

---

[1]*brocade* silk woven in complicated patterns of flowers and so forth
[2]*porcelain* "china"; finely made ceramic dishes and figures

Discussing Ideas Discuss the questions with a partner.

After reading "Marco Polo," can you answer the previewing questions? Can you add any other information about Marco Polo or his journeys?

Grammar Structures and Practice

A. Introduction to Nouns

A noun may be a person, a place, an object, an activity, an idea or emotion, or a quantity. A noun may be concrete (physical or tangible) or abstract (nonphysical or intangible). Both abstract and concrete nouns can be classified into two types: count nouns and noncount nouns.

2.1 Introduction to Nouns

Concrete		Abstract	
Count	**Noncount**	**Count**	**Noncount**
a diary	money	a mystery	anger
an uncle	porcelain	problems	justice
weavers	silk	a transaction	knowledge

B. Count Nouns

Count nouns are nouns that can be counted: *cars, ideas, people, trucks.*
- Count nouns have two forms: singular (one item) and plural (more than one item).
- Most count nouns are concrete (tangible): they can be seen, heard, felt, and so on.
- Some count nouns are abstract, however: *emotions, ideas.*

2.2 Count Nouns

	Explanations	Examples
Singular	A singular count noun *must* be preceded by an article (*a, an,* or *the*) or by an adjective (*his, my, one, three,* etc.).	I have **a car**. **The car** is small but comfortable. I bought **my car** in 1998.
Plural	Most plural nouns are not preceded by an article. Adjectives (*many, most, some*) can precede plural count nouns. *The* is used only when the noun is specifically known or identified (*the car that Jack bought*). For more on the use of *the,* see Part 3.	**Bicycles** are usually much less expensive than **cars**. **Some bicycles** are made for racing. **The bicycles that they bought for the race** were very expensive.

1 **Practice** Give the plural of the following words. See Appendix 2 for spelling rules and a list of irregular plural nouns.

Example woman *women*
party *parties*

1. valley
2. mouse
3. index
4. table
5. church
6. child
7. deer
8. baby
9. crisis
10. curriculum
11. hero

12. analysis
13. belief
14. alumnus
15. mosquito
16. stimulus
17. series
18. play
19. tooth
20. knife
21. tomato
22. monarch

2 **Practice** On his journey to the empire of Kublai Khan, Marco Polo encountered many exotic customs. Complete these sentences about his experiences. Write the plural forms of the nouns in parentheses. Then practice the pronunciation of each. Pay special attention to the pronunciation of the *-s* ending.

Example *The* _____*travels*_____ (travel) *of Marco Polo* is the English name
for Marco Polo's four _____*volumes*_____ (volume) about his
_____*journeys*_____ (journey).

1. In India, Marco Polo found _____ (woman) who padded their
_____ (hip) and who wore magnificent
_____ (ruby).

2. The _____ (person) of the _____
(highland) of Kashmir hunted and herded giant _____
(sheep) still known today as "Marco Polo _____ (sheep)."

3. Before reaching the _____ (desert) of western China, Marco
Polo found green _____ (oasis) and beautiful river
_____ (valley) filled with _____ (gem) and
_____ (mineral).

4. On the steppes of central Asia, Marco met the Tartars, nomadic

_____ (horseman) who traveled constantly across the

_____ (plain).

5. _____ (family) lived in _____ (yurt),

wooden "_____" (tent) that had round

_____ (roof) and that were easy to move.

6. The Tartar _____ (wife) decorated their

_____ (home) with colorful _____

(tapestry¹), hanging _____ (shelf), and beautiful

_____ (dish).

7. Nomads whose _____ (journey) never ended, the Tartars

used oxen to pull _____ (wagon) filled with their

_____ (possession).

8. They carried their _____ (possession) from place to place in

waterproof _____ (box).

_____

¹*tapestry* woven fabric for wall hangings or rugs

▲ Modern Day yurts in Mongolia

C. Noncount Nouns

Noncount nouns are usually mass nouns (*butter, furniture, oil, water*—categories or items that we usually measure) or abstract nouns (*honesty, love*—concepts that are difficult to quantify). Noncount nouns are always singular. Compare:

- noncount mass noun: traffic
- count nouns: cars, buses, taxis

- noncount abstract noun: dishonesty
- count noun: lies

2.3 Noncount Nouns

Types	Explanations	Examples
Mass Nouns	Mass nouns are categories or items that we usually measure. *A* and *an* are never used with noncount nouns. *The* may be used in specific cases (see p. 89). Units of measurement such as *gallon* and *pound* are often used with mass nouns (see p. 80).	**Food, clothing,** and **shelter** are basic needs for all people. How much **water** do you drink daily? Humans need at least **a gallon of water** daily. **Air** is essential for most living things.
Abstract Nouns	Adjectives (*any, our, some*) and other quantifiers (*a lot of, plenty of*) may be used with noncount nouns.	Everyone hopes for some **happiness**. We all need **a little love** and **consideration**. We appreciated **your consideration**. We also appreciated **your help** with **our math homework**.
Activities and Studies	Most activities and studies are noncount nouns, even though some end in *-s*. Gerunds (the *-ing* form of verbs) function as noncount nouns. (See Chapter 9 for more information on gerunds.)	**Mathematics** is a difficult subject. **Economics** is hard, too. **Studying** math is hard for me. **Your helping** me was very considerate.

D. Nouns That Are Both Count and Noncount

Some nouns can be count or noncount, depending on the context. Compare:

2.4 Nouns That are Both Count and Noncount

	Examples	Meanings
Noncount Noun	**Experience** is a good **teacher.**	*experience* = an idea with no specific limits
Count Noun	She's had many good **experiences** and some bad ones.	*experiences* = specific events or situations
Noncount Noun	I had **turkey** for lunch.	*turkey* = a type of food
Count Noun	Have you ever seen a wild **turkey**?	*a turkey* = a bird

3 Practice For each sentence, indicate whether the noun(s) in italics are count or noncount.

Example __N__ His *work* is restoring old paintings.

__C__ He restores *works* of art.

1. _____ We've traveled to Italy many *times*.

2. _____ I had a wonderful *experience* on my last trip.

3. _____ Do you have *time* to tell us about your trip to Rome?

4. _____ What are your *thoughts* about a trip to Venice?

5. _____ I have to consider my *finances* before planning a trip.

6. _____ Current *thought* holds that many Europeans traveled to China both before and after Marco Polo.

7. _____ At the time of Marco Polo, Venice was a center of *business* for all of Europe.

8. _____ Venice is a city surrounded by *water*.

9. _____ The *waters* of several rivers flow toward Venice.

10. _____ In Marco Polo's time, a wide variety of *businesses* flourished in Venice.

11. _____ Venice was a center of *finance*.

12. _____ Venice was also the center of ship *building* in Europe.

13. _____ In today's Venice, few *buildings* remain from pre-medieval times.

14. _____ Venice was and still is a center for the *arts*.

15. _____ Students from all over the world study *art* in Venice.

16. _____ Venice is famous for artwork made of *glass*.

17. _____ For centuries, artisans in Venice have crafted beautiful *glasses* and *bowls*.

18. _____ It takes many years of *experience* to become a master glassblower.

19. _____ Glassblowing is hard *work*.

20. _____ That glassblower produces amazing *artwork*.

4 Practice Quickly reread the passage "Marco Polo" on page 67. Then underline all the common nouns in the second paragraph (not the proper names). Indicate which are noncount and which are count. Then use these nouns to complete the following chart. For the count nouns, if the noun is singular, also give the plural form. If the noun is plural, also give the singular form.

Count Nouns				Noncount Nouns
Singular	Plural	Singular	Plural	
wonder	wonders			

5 **Practice** Form complete sentences from the following cues. Make all count nouns plural. Use *was* or *were* + *being* + the past participle, as in the example.

The Orient of the 13th century was much more advanced than the medieval cultures Marco Polo had left in Europe. His diary serves as a record of all the amazing things he encountered. He wrote that. . . .

Examples

ruby / being mined throughout Asia
Rubies were being mined throughout Asia.
Oil / being used for heating and lighting in Persia
Oil was being used for heating and lighting in Persia.

1. milk / being dehydrated into powder

2. jewel / being traded throughout Asia

3. sophisticated city / being constructed

4. canal / being built

5. weather / being studied

6. star / being charted

7. paper money / being used throughout the empire

8. eyeglasses / being developed

9. ice cream / being perfected

10. spaghetti / being made

11. silk / being woven into beautiful brocade

12. gunpowder / being used

13. highway / being built

14. plumbing system / being developed

15. astrology / being practiced

E. Personal Pronouns and Possessive Adjectives

Pronouns take the place of nouns. Possessive adjectives come before nouns or noun forms such as gerunds. (For more on gerunds, see Chapter 9.)

2.5 Personal Pronouns and Possessive Adjectives							
	Singular					**Plural**	
Subject	I	you	he	she	it	we	they	
Object	me	you	him	her	it	us	them	
Possessive Adjective	my	your	his	her	its	our	their	
Possessive Pronoun	mine	yours	his	hers	its	ours	theirs	
Reflexive	myself	yourself	himself	herself	itself	ourselves	themselves	yourselves

6 Practice Fill in each blank with an appropriate pronoun. Use arrows to indicate which noun each pronoun refers to.

Example Marco Polo traveled with _____*his*_____ father and _____*his*_____ uncle.

1. Marco, Nicolo, and Maffeo Polo left Venice in 1271. This was the beginning of _____ famous journey to Asia.

2. The three Polos financed the trip _____.

3. The Polos left _____ home in Venice, Italy.

4. In 1275, the Polos ended _____ journey when _____ reached Shangtu.

5. The great Chinese emperor Kublai Khan had built _____ summer palace in Shangtu.

6. The summer palace was magnificent with _____ walls of marble and _____ 16 square miles of parks.

7. Soon after the Polos' arrival, Marco was added to the Khan's household, and during _____ 17 years of service, _____ became very close to the Khan.

8. Marco Polo was appointed by the Khan as _____ "official personal representative" throughout the empire.

9. We owe much of _____ knowledge of 13th-century China to Marco Polo.

10. The diary of Marco Polo, with _____ tales of danger and daring, is fascinating to read even today.

11. I have a copy of the diary, which _____ brother gave _____ last year.

12. I wish that Marco Polo _____ could have signed this diary.

Using What You've Learned

7 **Describing a Special Place** Many people dream of traveling to exotic places in search of unusual experiences. Others can find the unusual close to home. What unusual experiences have you had? What unusual sights have you seen? Prepare a five-minute presentation, describing one particularly unusual place that you have visited. Try to mention as many of the different things that you saw as possible and tell about experiences that you had. Then give your presentation to a small group.

Setting the Context

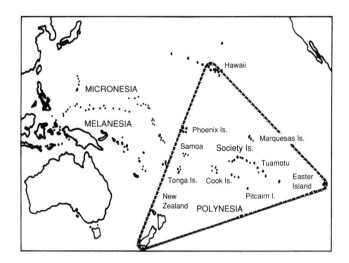

 Previewing the Passage Discuss the questions with a group.

Where is Polynesia? How large is the area that it includes? Have you visited Polynesia?

Reading Read the passage.

The Polynesians

The people of Oceania were an extremely adventurous group. As a distinct population with common origins, the Polynesians were the most widely spread people on Earth before 1500 C.E. Few other groups in history have traveled so much while taking so few material possessions with them. The Polynesians settled the islands of the vast triangle formed by the   5
Hawaiian Islands, Easter Island, and New Zealand. With sides approximately 6,500 kilometers in length, this triangle covers almost twice the area of the United States. The Polynesians began their expansion through the South Pacific around 2000 B.C.E., and by the time of Marco Polo's visit to China, they had settled all of its major islands.   10

 Discussing Ideas Discuss the questions with a partner.

What do you know about the ancient Polynesians? How were they able to navigate the large distances between the islands?

Grammar Structures and Practice

A. Indefinite Articles

A singular count noun always takes an article (*a, an,* or *the*) or an adjective *(one, another)*.

- The indefinite article may mean *one,* or it may mean an unspecified person or thing.
- Note that *a* or *an* is not used with a noncount noun or with a plural count noun.

2.6	Indefinite Articles	
	Explanations	**Examples**
a	*A* is used before a singular count noun that begins with a consonant sound.	**a** sailor **a** house **a** European
an	*An* is used before a singular count noun that begins with a vowel sound.	**an** island **an** hour

1 **Practice** Complete the following passage by using *a, an,* or *X* for no article.

Voyages to the Unknown

    <u> X </u> Polynesian travelers experienced ___1___ hardships that are difficult for ___2___ modern person to imagine. The 4,000 kilometer voyage from the Society Islands to the Hawaiian Islands may cover only inches on ___3___ map, but in ___4___ open canoe loaded with ___5___ men, ___6___ women, ___7___ children, ___8___ animals, and ___9___ precious seed plants, the voyage must surely have been ___10___ incredible ordeal. ___11___ trip like that would seem impossible today. Still, the Polynesians reached virtually every island within the huge Polynesian triangle—___12___ amazing accomplishment!

▲ Modern-day Polynesians in their canoes

2 **Practice** Try to imagine what the first voyage to Hawaii was like. Complete the following passage by using *a, an,* or *X* (to indicate that no article is necessary).

On the High Seas

For __X__ centuries, the people of the Marquesas Islands had noticed that _____ birds flew north from the islands in the fall and returned in the spring.
₁
The islanders knew that the birds must be flying to _____ piece of land where
₂
they spent the winter.

Finally, in about 500 C.E., _____ young chief decided to search for the land
₃
to the north. He recruited both _____ men and _____ women for the journey.
₄ ₅
He also recruited _____ experienced navigator who knew how to follow _____
₆ ₇
steady course even though the Polynesians didn't have _____ compasses or
₈
_____ other equipment. For _____ centuries, _____ Polynesian navigators had
₉ ₁₀ ₁₁
been using _____ birds, _____ cloud formations, _____ stars, _____ wave pat-
₁₂ ₁₃ ₁₄ ₁₅
terns, and the sun to guide them in their ocean voyages.

As the explorers made _____ preparations for this voyage northward, _____
₁₆ ₁₇
food and _____ water were _____ major problems. They knew that they would
₁₈ ₁₉
be able to catch _____ fish along the way. But they would need _____ fresh wa-
₂₀ ₂₁
ter supply that would last throughout the trip. In addition, they prepared _____
₂₂
dried bananas, _____ coconut, _____ fish, _____ large bag of taro root,[1] and
₂₃ ₂₄ ₂₅
_____ cooked breadfruit[1] for each canoe.
₂₆

Finally, _____ dozens of _____ double canoes were packed and ready to be-
₂₇ ₂₈
gin this voyage. After at least _____ month on the open ocean, these explorers
₂₉
spotted _____ land birds, _____ signal to any navigator that _____ island or
₃₀ ₃₁ ₃₂
other landmass was near. They had completed _____ voyage of over 1,500
₃₃
miles and had discovered the Hawaiian Islands.

---

[1]*taro root, breadfruit* Polynesian staple foods

3 Practice Change the words in italics from singular to plural or from plural to singular. Add or delete *a* or *an* when appropriate, and make all necessary changes in verbs or pronouns.

Example Polynesian *navigators* had to be very skillful.
   A Polynesian navigator had to be very skillful.

1. *Navigators* had to notice and understand particular movements of waves.

2. An ocean *wave* near an *island* has a particular appearance and "feeling" from the inside of a canoe.

3. A good *navigator* could tell the difference between one type of wave and another.

4. Polynesian *navigators* could also use *stars* to guide them during *voyages*.

5. A *navigator* watched a *star* that rose or set over a particular *island*.

6. *He* would only use a *star* that was near the horizon.

7. To plan the course or direction, *they* would use zenith *stars*.

8. Zenith *stars* point down to specific *islands*, and they helped *navigators* determine location.

9. By the mid 1700s, a *sextant* was generally used to determine the location of a *ship*.

10. *Sextants* can determine latitude and longitude.

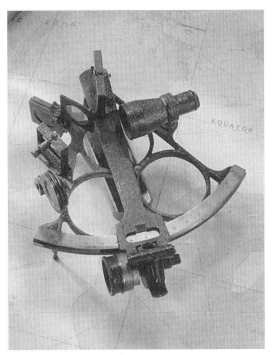

▲ Sextants were used for navigation.

B. Units of Measurement

Units of measurement are used with both count and noncount nouns. With noncount nouns, they allow us to count or measure quantities (*rice / one cup of rice, gas / one gallon of gas*).

2.7 Units of Measurement

Common Units of Measurement			Explanations	Examples
bag	carton	loaf	Units of measurement are commonly used in this pattern: number or percent + unit + *of* + name of item. *Dozen* does not follow this pattern, however.	I'd like **a box of cookies**.
bottle	dozen	piece		Please get **a gallon of milk**.
box	gallon, etc.	tube		Could you also get **two pounds of Swiss cheese**?
bunch	pound, etc.	roll		
head	package	six-pack		We need **three dozen eggs**, too.
can	jar	twelve-pack		Get **three loaves** of bread.

4 **Practice** Look at the picture. Then use units of measurement to complete the following list of provisions.

1. *three loaves of* bread
2. _____ oranges
3. _____ jam
4. _____ water
5. _____ soap
6. _____ bananas

7. _____ eggs
8. _____ rice
9. _____ toothpaste
10. _____ soda pop
11. _____ potato chips
12. _____ paper towels

C. Indefinite Adjectives and Pronouns

Indefinite expressions of quantity such as *some, many,* and *little* can be used as adjectives or pronouns in relation to other nouns.

- These expressions act as adjectives when they are combined with nouns. (Do you want *some coffee*?)
- They act as pronouns when they replace nouns. (No, I've already had *some*.)
- The type of noun (count or noncount) determines which adjective or pronoun may be used.

2.8 Indefinite Adjectives and Pronouns

	Explanations	Examples
Noncount Nouns	*Much, quite a little, a little, only a little, not much, little, very little, less,* and *the least* are used as adjectives with noncount nouns. They also may be used without the noun.	How **much** (time) do you have? How **much** (time) do you have? I have **only a little** (time). I have **very little** (time). I have **less** (time) than I'd thought.
Count Nouns	*Many, quite a few, several, a couple (of), a few, only a few, not many, few, fewer,* and *the fewest* are used with count nouns. They may also be used without the noun.	How **many** (trips) do you have to take this year? I have to take **several (a few, a couple)** (trips).
Both Count and Noncount Nouns	*(The) most, a lot (of), lots (of), plenty (of), some,* and *no* are used with both count and noncount nouns. *None* is a singular pronoun. *Any* is used in questions and negatives with both count and noncount nouns.	Do you have **some** money? Do you have **some** one-dollar bills? Do you have **any** money? Do you have **any** one-dollar bills? I have **lots of** money, but I have **no** one-dollar bills. I have **none**.

Note: A few and *a little* mean "some." *Few* and *little* mean "almost no." Example: *I have **a few** (some) friends. I have **few** (almost no) friends.*

---

5 **Practice** Work in a chain. One student begins by making a question with *some* or *any* from the first item. A classmate will answer it using *not much* or *not many*. He or she will then make a question. Another classmate will answer that question using *not much* or *not many,* and then ask the next question.

Example money

    A: Do you have any money?

    B: I don't have much money.

    one-dollar bills

    B: Do you have some one-dollar bills?

    C: I don't have many one-dollar bills.

1. free time
2. homework
3. email messages to send
4. quarters
5. good food at home
6. snacks with you
7. homework assignments
8. blank paper
9. good magazines
10. gas in your car
11. change
12. good advice for me
13. news from home
14. information about good Web sites
15. time for a cup of coffee

6 Practice Repeat Activity 5, this time giving answers with *a little* or *a few*.

Example money

> A: Do you have any money?
> B: Sure, I have a little money.

> one-dollar bills

> B: Do you have some one-dollar bills?
> C: Sure, I have a few one-dollar bills.

 7 Practice Imagine that you are about to leave for a four-week sailing trip. You will be on the open ocean for almost a month, so you need to plan which supplies to take very carefully. In pairs, ask and answer questions from the following cues. Use *how much* or *how many* in the questions and indefinite pronouns or adjectives in the answers. When you finish with the cues, add some of your own.

Example fruit

> A: How much fruit should we bring?
> B: I love fruit! Let's buy a lot.

> A: How many mangoes should we buy?
> B: Let's buy only a few mangoes. They spoil easily.

1. meat (hot dogs, steak, etc.)

2. dairy products (milk, yogurt, etc.)

3. water

4. vegetables (carrots, potatoes, lettuce, etc.)

5. staples (flour, rice, corn, beans, etc.)

8 **Practice** You are nearing the end of the four-week sailing trip. It has been three weeks since you last saw land, and supplies are beginning to run short. Complete the following conversations with *(only a) few, a few, only (a) little,* and *a little*.

Example A: Could I have _____*a little*_____ coffee with breakfast?

B: There's _____*only a little*_____ coffee left, but you can have it.

1. A: I'd like to have _____ sugar with my coffee.

   B: There is some sugar, but we have _____ fresh water. Maybe you should forget about the coffee.

2. A: What are we going to eat for dinner?

   B: We still have _____ rice left. Let's have that.

3. A: I'm tired of rice. Let's eat _____ hamburgers instead.

   B: Sorry, there is _____ hamburger meat left. But we do have _____ hot dogs. Shall we try those?

4. A: This trip is boring. Do you want to play _____ poker?

   B: Sure, but I should warn you that _____ cards are missing.

5. A: I hope we reach land soon. Then we can have _____ fun.

   B: There'll be _____ time for fun when we reach shore. We'll be too busy eating.

Using What You've Learned

9 **Talking About Groceries** Have you gone grocery shopping lately? Will you go soon? In pairs, take turns telling what you bought or what you are going to buy. Be sure to use specific units of measurement.

Example *I'm going to the store tonight, and I need to buy a lot of things. I need two or three bars of soap, a bottle of dishwashing soap, a bottle of shampoo. . . .*

10 **Planning a Journey** In small groups, imagine that you are making plans for a space voyage to a distant planet. There may or may not be fresh water and / or food available when you arrive. Also, the chances are that you will never be able to return to Earth. Make a chart listing of items for each of the following categories. Then choose a total of ten things that you will take. Don't choose more than three items from one category, and be sure to specify how much or how many of each item you are planning to take. Your spaceship is quite small, so space and weight are important considerations. When you have finished, report your selections to the class. Be ready to give explanations for your choices.

Foods	Plants	Animals	Tools	Weapons	Liquids	Educational Materials

11 **Describing Equipment** In pairs or small groups, test your knowledge of the equipment used in different occupations. Ask and answer questions from the following cues. Then add some more of your own.

Example a pilot
 A: What equipment does a pilot use?
 B: A pilot uses a compass.

1. scientist

2. secretary

3. gardener

4. cowboy

5. hunter

Setting the Context

▲ Replicas of Christopher Columbus's three ships: the *Niña,* the *Pinta,* and the *Santa Maria*

Previewing the Passage Discuss the questions with a group.

What period was called the "Age of Discovery"? What were Europeans searching for? How did this lead to the discovery of the Americas?

Reading Read the passage.

Trade Routes to the East

By the first part of the 15th century, Europe was beginning the most dramatic period of change in its history. Economics, together with politics and religion, was changing the societies of Europe. The recent, tremendous growth in the population of Europe had brought the cultivation of new land, the demand for new products, and a new class of merchants to trade   5
in these products. The merchants were interested in trading in Asia. However, Asia was still a mystery to them, for most of their knowledge of the East was based on Marco Polo's hundred-year-old diary. Its tales were fresh and enticing enough, though, to spark the search for new sea routes to Asia. The European search for new trade markets and products led to dis-   10
coveries that radically changed the course of history. This search eventually led to the discovery of the "New World."

Discussing Ideas Discuss the questions with a partner.

What was happening in Europe at the beginning of the 1400s? Why were
Europeans so interested in trading with Asia?

Grammar Structures and Practice

A. The Definite Article with Count Nouns

The is frequently used before a singular or plural count noun in these cases:
- When that noun is specifically identified: *They bought a boat, but **the** boat sank.*
- When the identity of the noun is already understood: ***the** beautiful new boat that Nick bought*
- When a noun is identified by a prepositional phrase or an adjective clause: ***the** man in the hallway;* ***the** man who came to dinner*

2.9	The Definite Article with Count Nouns	
	Explanations	**Examples**
Nonspecific	When plural nouns are used in a general (nonspecific) way, *the* is **not** used. *A* or *an* is used with nonspecific singular nouns.	**Merchants** had been interested in a new trade route for years. **A merchant** always needs new markets.
Specific	The prepositional phrase tells *which* merchants. *Note: The* + noun + *of* is a frequent combination in English. The adjective clause tells *which merchants.* Note that no commas are used with this clause. See Chapter 4 for more information on clauses. *The* is almost always used with superlatives.	**The merchants** of Spain were particularly interested in a new route. **The merchants** that paid for explorations wanted to become rich. **The most dramatic period** of change in the history of Europe was beginning.

B. The Definite Article with Noncount Nouns

Articles are not normally used with noncount nouns. However, noncount nouns, like
count nouns, may be preceded by *the* when the noun is *specifically* identified.

2.10 The Definite Article with Noncount Nouns

	Explanations	Examples
Nonspecific	No articles are used with unspecified noncount nouns.	**Pepper** was very important to Europeans.
Specific	*The* is often used with a noncount noun when the noun is identified by a phrase or clause. *The* is almost always used with superlatives.	**The pepper** from India was treasured. **The pepper** that was sold in European markets was often more valuable than gold. At that time, India produced **the most pepper** in the world.

1 Practice Quickly reread the passage "Trade Routes to the East" on page 85. Then do the following:

1. Underline all examples of identifying phrases that follow this pattern: *the* + noun 1 + *of* + noun 2. Then identify each noun as count or noncount.

2. Now underline any other examples of identifying phrases that follow this pattern: *the* + noun 1 + preposition + noun 2. Then identify each noun 1 as count or noncount.

3. Look at the phrase *a new class of merchants* in Line 5. *The* is not used here, and *a* is used instead. Explain why.

2 Practice Work in a chain and add identifying phrases or clauses to the following count nouns. Choose any noun on the list or add some count nouns of your own.

Example A: book
             B: the book on the table
             B: boat
             C: the boat that I want to buy

1. apple	**5.** camera	**9.** computer	**13.** month	**17.** stereo
2. boat	**6.** car	**10.** egg	**14.** painting	**18.** sweater
3. book	**7.** class	**11.** exam	**15.** party	**19.** vacation
4. business person	**8.** clothes	**12.** house	**16.** problem	**20.** yacht

3 Practice Now, do the same with noncount nouns. Work in a chain and add identifying phrases or clauses to the following noncount nouns. Choose any noun on the list or add some of your own.

Example   A: sugar
              B: the sugar in the sugar bowl.

              B: oil
              C: the oil that Kuwait exports

1. advice	**5.** energy	**9.** jewelry	**13.** oil	**17.** tea
2. anger	**6.** fish	**10.** love	**14.** studying	**18.** time
3. chicken	**7.** furniture	**11.** money	**15.** sugar	**19.** traffic
4. coffee	**8.** gas	**12.** news	**16.** sunlight	**20.** water

4 Practice Complete the following by using *the* or *X* (to indicate that no article is necessary). In some cases, either may be appropriate. Be prepared to explain your choices.

▲ A caravan makes its way across the desert.

Example   Fifteenth-century Europe needed __X__ precious metals.

1. Europeans wanted _____ metals so that they could make _____ coins for use in trading.

2. Of course, _____ most valuable metal was _____ gold.

3. _____ Europeans wanted to control _____ gold that _____ Arab traders were bringing from the East.

4. _____ Arab merchants in the Middle East were also dealing in _____ emeralds, _____ rubies, _____ sapphires, and _____ silk.

5. _____ silk from China was far superior to _____ silk from Europe.

6. Above all, _____ Europe wanted _____ spices.

7. _____ Europeans used these spices from Asia to preserve and season _____ meat.

8. _____ pepper grew far away in India and Sumatra, and it was outrageously expensive.

9. _____ pepper from one ship could make a merchant very rich.

10. _____ pepper merchants of London formed a special group, _____ Guild of Pepperers.

C. *The* with Quantifiers

Quantifiers such as *all, most, some,* and *enough* can be used as pronouns followed by prepositional phrases. When the quantifier is used as an adjective, *the* is omitted in most cases.

2.11	*The* with Quantifiers	
	With *the* (pronoun quantifier + phrase)	**Without *the*** (adjective quantifier)
Count Nouns	**All of the passengers** are on board.	**All passengers** are on board.
Noncount Nouns	**Most of the luggage** is now on board.	**Most luggage** is now on board.

Note: In conversational English, *the* is sometimes used after *all*. Compare: *All of the passengers are on board. All passengers are on board. All the passengers are on board.*

5 **Error Analysis** Many of the following sentences have errors in the use of *the* with expressions of quantity. Find and correct each error.

Example   All of money for Columbus's voyage came from Spain.
Correction: *All money for Columbus's voyage came from Spain.*
All of the money for Columbus's voyage came from Spain.

1. Some of world's greatest explorers lived during the 15th century.

2. All of these explorers were hoping to find a short route to "the Indies."

3. Some explorers were financed by merchants.

4. Many of explorers were financed by monarchs of different European kingdoms.

5. Most of exploring was in search of faster routes to bring pepper and other spices to Europe.

6. Most of the exploration was to search for shorter and faster routes to import spices.

7. Enough pepper eventually reached Europe that ways of cooking and preserving meat actually changed because of this exotic spice.

8. The most of pepper came from India.

9. Some of other spices valuable in 15th-century Europe were anise, cinnamon, coriander, and marjoram.

10. One of spices that Columbus found in the West Indies was allspice.

D. Quantifiers and Subject / Verb Agreement

Many pronoun quantifiers can be followed by phrases with either count or noncount nouns. The noun in the prepositional phrase determines whether the verb is singular or plural.

- When count nouns are used, plural verbs follow.
- When noncount nouns are used, singular verbs follow.

2.12	Quantifiers
	Quantifier + Prepositional Phrase + Verb
Singular	All of the money was from Spain.
Plural	All of the people were from Spain.

2.13 Quantifiers and Subject / Verb Agreement

Explanations	Expressions	Phrases with Noncount Nouns + Singular Verbs	Phrases with Count Nouns + Plural Verbs
A variety of quantifiers may be used as pronouns and followed by *of the* (or *of* + a demonstrative or possessive) + noun. They may also be used as adjectives with either count or noncount nouns *(all money, enough people)*. A singular verb follows a noncount noun, and a plural verb follows a count noun.	**all, most, some, enough** **fractions and percentages**	**All** of the **money was** lost. **Half** of the **food has** been eaten. **Fifty percent** of the **food has** been eaten. **The rest** of the **food has** spoiled. **The majority** of the population **was** very young.	**Most** of that man's **ideas were** wrong. **Half** of the **sandwiches have** been eaten. **Fifty percent** of the **sandwiches have** been eaten. **The rest** of the **sandwiches are** in the kitchen. **The majority** of the people **were** very young.
In formal English, *none* is always followed by a singular verb. In conversational English, a plural verb is often used.	**none**	**None** of the **information was** correct.	**None** of the **sailors was** experienced. (formal) **None** of the **people were** happy. (informal)

---

6 Practice Complete the sentences by using the singular or plural forms of the nouns and verbs in parentheses. Use the past tense.

Example All of the great 15th-century European ___*explorers were*___ (explorer / be) trying to find a short route to "the Indies."

1. All of their early _____ (exploration / be) directed toward eastward routes.

2. At that time, most _____ (person / be) convinced that the Earth was flat and that a westward voyage would be impossible.

3. In the late 1400s, some of the important _____ (ruler) of Europe _____ (be) interested in trying a westward route.

4. Two of these _____ (leader / be) told of a young man named Christopher Columbus.

5. Most of Columbus's _____ (knowledge) of the Earth _____ (be) based on incorrect theories.

6. Many of his _____ (calculation) of distance _____ (be) wrong.

7. Enough of his _____ (guess / be) correct, however, and he accurately calculated the 2,500-mile width of the Atlantic Ocean.

8. At first, none of the _____ (monarch) of Europe _____ (be) interested in financing Columbus.

9. Finally, enough of the necessary _____ (money / be) gathered for Columbus to set sail on August 3, 1492.

10. The majority of the _____ (crew) with Columbus _____ (be) trustworthy.

11. Many of the _____ (sailor) _____ (be) ready to turn back at times during the long and arduous voyage, but eventually they reached land— "the New World"—on October 12, 1492.

12. Because of Columbus's voyage, all of the existing _____ (idea) about the shape and size of the Earth _____ (be) eventually proven wrong. Unfortunately, however, Columbus never knew the incredible impact of his explorations.

E. *The Number Of* versus *A Number Of*: Subject / Verb Agreement

Both *a number of* and *the number of* are followed by plural nouns. However, the use of *a* or *the* affects both the meaning of the phrase and the form of the verb that follows.

2.14	*The Number Of* versus *A Number Of*	
	Explanations	**Examples**
a number of **the number of**	*A number of* means "many." The verb must be plural. *The number of* refers to a specific quantity. It must be followed by a singular verb.	**A number of** ships **were** built. **The number of** ships **was** quite high.

7 Practice Choose the correct verb form to complete these sentences.

Example A number of countries (was /(were)) recruiting explorers.

1. By the mid-1400s, a number of European monarchs (was / were) paying for explorations in search of a new route to India.

2. A number of unsuccessful attempts to circle Africa (was / were) financed by the Portuguese king, Manuel I.

3. In 1497, Manuel I chose Vasco da Gama to make another attempt to circle Africa. The number of sailors (was / were) determined by da Gama.

4. A number of his sailors (was / were) veterans of many voyages.

5. Three long months on the open ocean passed before a number of land birds (was / were) spotted.

6. Because of da Gama's "fearfully violent" character, the number of attempted mutinies on the voyage (was / were) low.

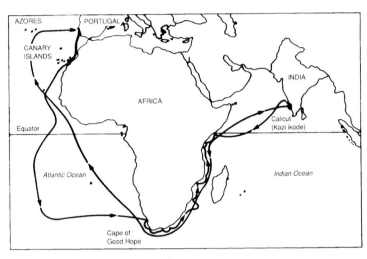

▲ Vasco da Gama's voyage to India

F. Two-Part Subjects: Subject / Verb Agreement

When there is more than one noun before the verb, there may be confusion about whether the verb should be singular or plural.

2.15 Two-Part Subjects: Subject / Verb Agreement		
Structures	**Explanations**	**Examples**
both . . . and	A plural verb always follows subjects with *both . . . and*.	**Both** the sailors **and** Columbus **were** considered mad.
either . . . or **neither . . . nor** **not only . . . but also**	With these expressions, the verb is singular or plural, depending on the subject closest to the verb.	**Neither** Columbus **nor** his aides **were** Spanish. **Neither** his aides **nor** Columbus **was** Spanish.
along with **as well as** **in addition to** **together with**	The nouns that follow these expressions do not affect the verb. The subject alone determines whether the verb is singular or plural. *Note:* Phrases with these expressions are normally set off by commas.	**Columbus, together with** his men, **was** ready to set sail on August 3, 1492. **The sailors, as well as** their captain, **were** on the open seas a few days later.

8 Practice First read each sentence for meaning. Underline the word or words that determine whether the verb is singular or plural. Finally, choose the appropriate verb form in parentheses.

Example As young boys, not only Ferdinand Magellan but also <u>his brother and his cousin</u> (was /(were)) pages in the Portuguese court.

1. Both the loyalty and ability of the Portuguese sailor Ferdinand Magellan (was / were) well known by King Manuel I.

2. However, neither King Manuel I nor his advisers (was / were) interested in Magellan's plan to reach the East by sailing west.

3. Neither his pleas for money nor his request for a ship (was / were) granted by the Portuguese king.

4. However, King Carlos I of Spain, as well as several rich and influential Spaniards, (was / were) willing to pay for Magellan's new voyage.

5. Magellan's flagship *The Trinidad,* along with four other ships, (was / were) ready to sail for "the Indies" by September 1519.

6. Not only Spaniards and Portuguese but also one Englishman (was / were) in Magellan's crew.

7. Magellan set sail with 250 sailors, but either battles or sickness (was / were) going to kill 232 of the crew.

8. On September 8, 1522, Juan Sebastian del Cano—who commanded after Magellan's death—along with 18 survivors, (was / were) welcomed back to the Spanish harbor of Seville.

9. Neither Magellan nor many of his crew members (was / were) able to survive.

10. The survivors, as well as their dead captain, (was / were) heroes, for they had participated in the first trip around the world.

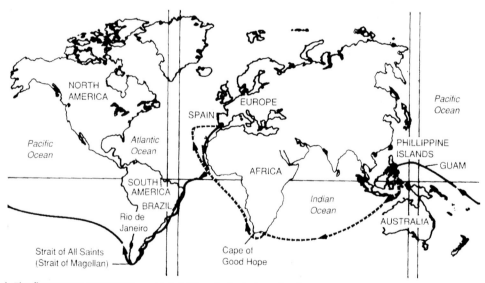

▲ The first voyage around the world. Solid lines indicate Magellan in command; dotted lines indicate del Cano in command.

Using What You've Learned

9 **Making Generalizations and Giving Examples** Natural resources are an essential part of every economy. Different countries have resources such as oil, minerals, water, and good soil. What are the primary resources in your area or native country? Work in small groups, and take turns telling about resources. Make a general statement about one of these resources. Then follow this with a more specific remark.

Example   Oil is one of our most important natural resources.

Most of the oil is in the northwestern part of the country.
OR
The oil from the southern part is very heavy.

10 **Playing a Trivia Game** Use your knowledge of products and resources worldwide to organize a trivia game. Separate into two groups and prepare a brief list of ten to 15 products or resources to use in the game. Then write at least two questions for each item. Products can include watches, golf clubs, cars, chocolate, etc. Resources can include oil, diamonds, uranium, etc. The questions may ask for any type of information, but someone on your team must know the answer. Write the answers to give to your teacher.

Example   Question: *Which country produces most of the world's diamonds?*
Answer: *South Africa.*

To play the game, take turns asking and answering each other's questions about the different items. A different student must answer each item until everyone on the team has participated. Score five points for acceptable answers; your teacher will be the judge of the answers.

11 **Keeping a Journal** Use your imagination. Pretend that you were one of the crew with Vasco da Gama, Christopher Columbus, or Ferdinand Magellan. Write one or more "journal entries" about your journey. Tell about your commander and your ship, the supplies on board, the food for the journey, and so on. Describe your hopes, your fears, and your encounters with new places.

Part 4 | The Definite Article with Proper Nouns

Setting the Context

Previewing the Passage Discuss the questions with a group.

What is the Arctic? Where is it? When did Europeans begin to explore this region?

Reading Read the passage.

The Polar Regions

In the 16th century, Spain and Portugal controlled the only known sea routes to Asia. As a result, the northern nations of Europe began to explore the Arctic for a passage to China. Their voyages took them to the icy edges of Siberia and into the unknown northern tip of North America. During the following two centuries, Britain and Russia in particular sent numerous expeditions into the North Atlantic and the North Pacific Oceans. 5

The 18th century's greatest explorer, the British commander James Cook, traveled far into both the frigid north and the icy south. In 1773, Cook made the first known crossing of the Antarctic Circle, and in 1778, he sailed through the Bering Strait. Cook was looking for an ice-free passage 10 east or west, but he failed to find one.

Discussing Ideas Discuss the questions with a partner.

According to the reading, what was the purpose of exploring the Arctic? Why were Britain and Russia so interested in finding a "Northwest Passage"?

Grammar Structures and Practice

A. *The* with Proper Nouns and Other Expressions

The is frequently used with proper nouns, especially with geographical locations and other landmarks. This is because proper nouns identify specific places. *The* is also used with nouns and with adjectives used as nouns when they identify specific groups of people, periods of time, and so on. For a detailed summary of these special uses of *the* with certain grouping of nouns and adjectives, see Appendix 3.

1 Practice Quickly reread the passage "The Polar Regions" and underline the proper nouns in the passage. Then answer the following questions.

1. Which proper nouns are preceded by *the* and which are not?
2. Are names of countries usually preceded by *the*? Can you give any examples?
3. Are names of oceans and seas usually preceded by *the*?

2 Practice Complete the following by using *the* or *X* (to indicate that no article is necessary).

Example ___the___ Suez Canal

___X___ Mt. Everest

1. _____ Africa
2. _____ continent of Africa
3. _____ Santa Barbara
4. _____ Park Avenue
5. _____ Hawaiian Islands
6. _____ Madagascar
7. _____ Lake Tahoe
8. _____ Sahara Desert
9. _____ Black Sea
10. _____ England

11. _____ Panama Canal
12. _____ Stanford University
13. _____ University of Connecticut
14. _____ Washington Monument
15. _____ General de Gaulle
16. _____ Dr. Strangelove
17. _____ president
18. _____ April 27th
19. _____ 1600s
20. _____ queen of England

3 Practice The following exercise concerns the voyages of Captain James Cook. Fill in the blanks with *the* or *X* (to indicate that no article is necessary).

Example Since ___the___ time of ___the___ ancient Greeks, ___X___ some geographers had believed that a great unknown southern continent was balancing ___the___ land masses of ___the___ Northern Hemisphere.

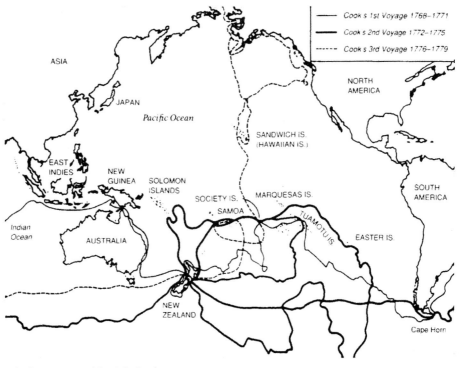

▲ The voyages of Captain Cook

1. In 1768, the British Navy commissioned _____ Captain James Cook to explore _____ South Pacific in search of this unknown continent.

2. On _____ August 25, 1768, _____ Captain Cook's ship, _____ *Endeavor*, set sail, leaving _____ English Channel to cross _____ Atlantic Ocean.

3. After a brief stop in _____ Madeira Islands, Cook headed _____ south to _____ South America, _____ Pacific Ocean, and up to _____ Tahiti.

4. After a stay on _____ island of _____ Tahiti, which is part of _____ Society Islands, Cook sailed to _____ New Zealand.

5. Cook then crossed _____ Tasman Sea, and on April 28, 1770, he came to _____ Australia, docking in _____ Botany Bay (which he named for _____ great number of _____ new plants he found there).

6. Cook claimed all of _____ east coast of _____ Australia for _____ British, naming it _____ New South Wales.

7. On his return to _____ England, Cook continued westward, following _____ treacherous Great Barrier Reef, stopping in _____ Indonesia, crossing _____ Indian Ocean, and finally _____ reaching home on _____ 31st of _____ July, 1771.

8. On his second voyage, Cook left _____ Great Britain on July _____ 13, 1772, to attempt an exploration of _____ Antarctica.

9. On January 17, 1773, his ship, _____ *Resolution,* became _____ first ship in _____ history to enter _____ Antarctic Circle.

10. On this voyage, Cook continued eastward, still searching for _____ unknown southern continent, and finally arrived at _____ Spitshead, England, on July 30, 1775, having covered a total distance of 70,000 miles (equal to almost three full navigations around the Earth).

11. Cook left for his third and final voyage in _____ 1776 to explore _____ Northern Hemisphere in search of the "Northwest Passage," a mythical northern link between _____ Atlantic and Pacific Oceans.

12. Sailing _____ north from _____ New Zealand, Cook and his crew became _____ first _____ Europeans to visit _____ Hawaiian Islands (Cook called them _____ Sandwich Islands).

13. Stepping ashore on _____ island of Kauai, Cook found himself being honored as a god by _____ native Hawaiians.

14. From _____ Hawaii, Cook went northward, sailing along _____ coast of _____ Alaska, crossing _____ Bering Strait, and even entering _____ Arctic Circle, until he was finally stopped by _____ walls of _____ ice.

15. He returned to _____ Hawaii, where he was killed on February _____ 14, 1779.

4 **Practice** Complete the following by using *a, an, the,* or *X* (to indicate that no article is necessary).

Example   ___The___ Arctic is ___the___ northernmost ocean.

1. _____ two-thirds of _____ Arctic Ocean is covered by _____ ice.

2. _____ outer limits of _____ Arctic are surrounded by _____ coasts of _____ northern continents.

3. _____ Antarctica, in contrast, is _____ continent larger than _____ Australia.

4. In _____ years after _____ Cook's voyages, only _____ few ships attempted to explore _____ northern and _____ southern extremes of _____ Earth.

5. It wasn't until _____ late 1800s that _____ explorers were successful in reaching _____ polar regions.

6. In _____ 1893, Norwegian Fridtjof Nansen, with _____ crew of 13 sailors and scientists, headed for _____ Arctic Ocean.

7. _____ Norwegians turned back before they reached _____ pole. However, they had come _____ closest in _____ history: 224 miles from _____ pole.

8. _____ years later, in 1909, after _____ number of _____ attempts, _____ American explorer, Robert Peary, reached _____ northernmost point of _____ world, _____ North Pole.

9. In _____ 1911, _____ expedition led by _____ Norwegian Roald Amundsen and _____ expedition led by _____ Briton Robert Scott began _____ exploration of _____ Antarctica at approximately _____ same time.

10. _____ Scott's expedition came to _____ tragic end, but _____ Amundsen's expedition became _____ first in _____ history to reach _____ South Pole.

Cultural Note

Antartica

The Antarctic Treaty is an international ownership treaty[1] signed by 12 nations in 1959. The Antarctic Treaty established a legal framework for the governing of Antarctica, the only uninhabited continent on Earth. According to the treaty, this continent is to be used for scientific investigation and all military activity is banned. The U.S. runs the Scott-Amundsen Station at the South Pole. It can be reached at www.quest.arc.nasa.gov/antarctica/.

---

[1] Other international ownership treaties include the Law of the Sea, the Outer Space Treaty, the Moon Treaty, and the Extra-terrestrial Real Estate Treaty.

5 **Practice** Complete the following by using *a, an, the,* or *X* (to indicate that no article is necessary).

Shackleton's Incredible Voyage

The story of _X_ Ernest Shackleton and _____ crews of
                                                 1

_____ British ships _____ *Endurance* and _____ *Aurora* is one of
2   3   4

_____ most remarkable stories of _____ adventure, _____ courage,
5   6   7

_____ endurance, _____ heartbreak, and _____ stamina ever recorded.
8   9   10

_____ goal of _____ Shackleton expedition was to cross _____ Antarc-
11   12   13

tica on _____ foot and _____ dogsled. Their goal was never reached, but
14   15

their story is perhaps _____ greatest adventure story ever told.
16

In _____ December 1914, Shackleton and _____ his crew left _____
17   18   19

island of _____ South Georgia on board _____ ship _____ *Endurance.*
20   21   22

_____ another ship, _____ *Aurora*, left _____ port of _____ Sydney,
23   24   25   26

Australia. _____ *Endurance* would head for _____ Weddell Sea, in _____
27   28   29

Western Hemisphere, and the *Aurora* would head for _____ Ross Sea, on
30

_____ other side of _____ continent. _____ winter of 1915 _____ was
31   32   33   34

an early winter. _____ both ships encountered _____ high winds and
35   36

_____ heavy ice much sooner than expected. Despite horrific conditions,
37

_____ crew of _____ *Aurora* completed _____ its duty of leaving food
38   39   40

supplies for _____ Shackleton's expedition. Shackleton's overland expedi-
41

tion never took place, however. _____ ice of _____ Weddell Sea trapped
42   43

_____ boat. _____ ice damaged and then crushed _____ *Endurance.*
44   45   46

Eventually, _____ both ships were lost, as _____ *Aurora* was destroyed by
47   48

_____ fierce storm. _____ both parties had to face _____ tremendous
49   50   51

hardships in order to survive. _____ entire crew of _____ *Endurance* sur-
52   53

vived, but _____ three members of _____ crew of _____ *Aurora* died. All
54   55   56

of these men, those who died and those who lived, will be remembered in

_____ history for their incredible bravery and fortitude.
57

▲ Shackleton's ship, the *Endurance*, was destroyed by ice.

Using What You've Learned

6 **Describing a Special Place** Everyone has one special place where he or she feels most comfortable. For some, this is a city; for others, a park. Still others find that one room or even one particular chair provides an atmosphere that allows them to relax. At the end of a long and difficult day, where do you most like to go? Prepare a brief presentation describing a place that is special for you. Tell why it is special and why it helps you relax. Give your presentation to a group. Paint a verbal portrait, giving enough detail that other students will be able to picture your special place and to share in its serenity.

Part 5 More on Nouns, Verbs, and Modifiers

Setting the Context

▲ Mt. Everest, 29,035 ft (8850m)

Previewing the Passage Discuss the questions with a group.

What is the highest mountain on Earth? Where is it located? Have you climbed any high mountains? Are there any mountains you would like to climb?

Reading Read the passage.

Mt. Everest

Other mountains share with Everest a history of adventure, glory, and tragedy, but Everest is unique in that it is the highest mountain on Earth. More than two-thirds of the Earth's atmosphere lies below its summit, and for an unacclimatized[1] person without oxygen, the top of the mountain is endurable for only two or three minutes. The primitive, often brutal, struggle to reach the top is an irresistible challenge to the human need for adventure. But more than this, Everest has become, since the first attempt to climb it, a universal symbol of human courage and endurance.

---

[1]*unacclimatized* not accustomed, physically, to high altitudes

Discussing Ideas Discuss the questions with a partner.

What do you know about attempts to climb Mt. Everest? Why do you think so many people have attempted this dangerous feat?

Grammar Structures and Practice

A. Word Order with Noun Modifiers

When a noun has several modifiers, the modifiers are generally used in a set order. Note that descriptive words can include these five categories: 1) changing qualities or characteristics, 2) date, 3) shape or size, 4) color, and 5) unchanging qualities or characteristics.

2.16 Word Order with Noun Modifiers						
Articles, Demonstratives, Possessives	Numbers	Descriptive Words*	Other Nouns	Noun	Phrases, Clauses, Appositives	Predicate
The		long, winding		path	to the house	was very dark.
These	two	red	paper	clips		are from Japan.
His father's		beautiful 1990		Porsche,	which is outside,	has a dent in it.
That		nice new		student,	Kunio,	is coming for dinner.

1 Practice Complete the following sentences by adding the information in parentheses. Pay careful attention to word order as you complete each. Add punctuation where necessary. Some sentences may have more than one possible answer.

Example In 1852, calculations revealed data. (exciting / routine / of the Himalaya Mountains / new)

In 1852, routine calculations of the Himalaya Mountains revealed exciting new data.

1. The Himalayas are the highest range. (in the world / of mountains)

2. According to a clerk, Peak XV was the mountain. (highest / at the Trigonometric Survey of India / in the world)

3. This peak, Peak XV, was the highest peak. (that had ever been recorded)

4. A check confirmed his claim. (of his calculations / careful)

5. The elevation was set at 29,002 feet. (of Peak XV / of the top)

6. Observations established an elevation. (later / of 29,028 feet / careful / more)

7. Early surveyors did not know that Tibetans had long ago recognized Peak XV. (as the mountain / greatest / world's)

8. For centuries, the Tibetans had called it Chomolongma. (which means mother goddess of the world / many)

9. Peak XV was named after Sir George Everest. (who was the British surveyor-general of India / in 1865)

10. Calculations determined Mt. Everest's elevation to be 29,035 feet (8850m). (new / using GPS[1] technology / completed in 1999)

_____

[1] Trimble Global Positioning System, a satellite-based technology

B. Collective Nouns: Agreement with Verbs and Pronouns

Collective nouns are nouns that refer to a group of people, animals, things, and so on *as a unit*.

- Collective nouns can use either singular or plural verbs, depending on the context.
- In American English, collective nouns generally use singular verbs; however, British English uses plural verbs more frequently.
- In American English, both singular and plural pronouns are used to refer to the nouns, although singular pronouns are preferred in standard written English.

2.17 Collective Nouns: Agreement with Verbs and Pronouns

	Examples	Common Collective Nouns		
Singular	The **team** of climbers **hasn't arrived** yet. **It is** expected soon.	army	data	group
		audience	department	jury
Plural	The **team** of climbers **haven't arrived** yet. (more common in British English)	class	expedition	majority
		committee	family	pair
	They are expected soon. (common in spoken American English)	community	food	population
		company	furniture	public
		couple	gang	staff
		crew	generation	team
		crowd	government	union

2 **Practice** In each of the following sentences, choose the form(s) that would be most acceptable in written American English.

1. The Tibetan government (was / were) unwilling to give permission for explorers to visit the Himalayas. (It / They) did not allow foreigners to enter the mountain range until 1921.

2. In 1921, after years of negotiation, the British government (was / were) given permission to enter Tibet, and the first British climbing expedition (was / were) organized.

3. The first group explored various climbing routes on Mt. Everest, but (it / they) did not even come close to the summit.

4. In 1922, an exploratory team located the northeast route up Mt. Everest, but (it / they) (was / were) unable to reach the summit.

5. The third Everest expedition (was / were) to have a tragic ending, as (its / their) most famous member, George Mallory, would disappear while trying to reach the summit.

6. After Mallory disappeared in 1924, a number of expeditions (was / were) launched from Tibet in the attempt to climb the northeast route.

7. In 1949, the government of Nepal finally gave (its / their) permission for foreigners to enter the territory, and several teams tried to climb the mountain from the south.

8. In 1953, a British team (was / were) successful in (its / their) attempt.

9. The 1953 group (was / were) composed of ten climbers, including Edmund Hillary (age 33), a beekeeper from New Zealand, and Tenzing Norkay (age 39), a Sherpa guide from India.

10. At 11:30 on May 29, 1953, this pair of climbers—Edmund Hillary and Tenzing Norkay—(was / were) standing on the highest place in the world, the summit of Everest.

▲ Tenzing Norkay (left) and Edmund Hillary celebrate the day after they reached the summit of Mt. Everest.

C. Subject / Verb Word Order with "Negative" Adverbs

When a "negative" adverb precedes the subject of a sentence, the auxiliary verb or the verb *be* is placed before the subject, just as it is in most questions. When these adverbs occur after the subject, no inversion takes place.

2.18 Subject / Verb Word Order with Negative Adverbs		
Adverbs	**Standard Word Order**	**Inverted Word Order**
barely **no sooner** **hardly** **rarely** **hardly ever** **seldom** **never**	He was **scarcely** able to breathe. He **never** considered quitting. He had **no sooner** reached the top when a storm began.	**Scarcely was he** able to breathe. **Never did he consider** quitting. **No sooner had he reached** the top when a storm began.

3 Practice Restate each of the sentences in italics in two ways. First, add the adverb in parentheses to the beginning of the sentence; second, add it to the middle of the sentence. Make all necessary changes.

Example In 1953, a group of climbers was organized for another attempt at Mt. Everest. *The climbers had been chosen when they left for Nepal.* (scarcely)

Scarcely had the climbers been chosen when they left for Nepal.
The climbers had scarcely been chosen when they left for Nepal.

1. *A man had succeeded in reaching the summit.* (never)

2. Ten climbers were chosen, including a doctor. *Men had climbed to such heights without needing medical assistance.* (seldom)

3. On May 29th, the day of Hillary and Norkay's final climb, the wind was calm. *There are calm days on Mt. Everest.* (rarely)

4. After several hours of extremely dangerous climbing, Hillary and Norkay arrived at the top of the world. *They had reached the summit when they embraced and Hillary took Norkay's picture.* (barely)

5. *Humans had stood on the top of Mt. Everest.* (never before)

6. *Human beings endure so much hardship and yet succeed.* (rarely)

D. Parallel Structure with Nouns and Noun Modifiers

When a noun has two or more modifiers, parallel structures should be used. Parallel structure means that the same grammatical form (words, phrases, or clauses) should be used whenever possible. While a sentence with mixed forms may be grammatically correct, the mixed forms are considered incorrect usage.

2.19 Parallel Structure with Nouns and Noun Modifiers

Explanations	Correct Usage	Incorrect Usage
Parallel forms should be used in series of words, phrases, and clauses. Parallel forms must also be used with these connectors: *and, but, or, both . . . and, not only . . . but also, either . . . or,* and *neither . . . nor.* See Chapter 3 for more information on these structures.	The **cold, tired climbers** returned to their camp. Both **Swiss** and **British climbers** reached the top of the mountain.	*The tired climbers, who were also cold, returned to their camp. *Both Swiss climbers and climbers from Britain reached the top.

4 Error Analysis Study the following sentences. Then correct those that have errors in parallelism. If a sentence contains no error, write *correct* after it.

Example By the time the Americans arrived, both a British expedition and an expedition that was Swiss had already climbed Mt. Everest.
Correction: By the time the Americans arrived, both a British (expedition) and a Swiss expedition had already climbed Mt. Everest.

1. After 1953, different climbing teams established routes on the northeast ridge and the ridge on the south side of Mt. Everest.

2. None of these expeditions attempted the west ridge, which was considered to be an extremely difficult route, and it was dangerous.

3. Between 1953 and 1963, only a British expedition and a Swiss expedition succeeded in reaching the summit of Mt. Everest.

4. In 1963, an American group planned to climb Everest from not only the south ridge but also the west ridge.

5. The south ridge of the mountain was quite well known to the climbers, but the west ridge of the mountain was something that was completely unknown.

6. On February 20, 1963, an army of a thousand, including Sherpas, porters, and people who climbed, began the 185-mile hike to Mt. Everest.

7. On May 1, James Whittaker, an American from Washington, and Nawang Gombu, a nephew of Tenzing Norkay, reached the summit of Everest.

8. Three weeks later, on May 22, Luther Jerstad and Barry Bishop, climbing the south ridge, and Thomas Hornbein and William Unsoeld, who were climbing the west ridge, reached the top of Mt. Everest.

Using What You've Learned

5 **Discussing Qualities and Characteristics** George Mallory was the most famous of the early climbers who attempted to reach the summit of Mt. Everest. His death was a tragedy to all who knew him. Yet like many before and after him, Mallory died attempting to attain a personal goal.

In small groups, read the following quotation from Mallory. Consider Mallory's goal and his outlook on life. Then discuss other occupations or hobbies that require the bravery, determination, and drive that Mallory had. As a group, try to answer the question that Mallory was so often asked: "Why?"

> The first question which you will ask and which I must try to answer is this, "What is the use of climbing Mount Everest?" and my answer must at once be, "It is no use." There is not the slightest prospect of any gain whatsoever. Oh, we may learn a little about the behavior of the human body at high altitude, where there is only a third of an atmosphere, and possibly medical men may turn our observation to some account for the purposes of aviation. But otherwise nothing will come of it. We shall not bring back a single bit of gold or silver, not a gem, nor any coal or iron. We shall not find a foot of earth that can be planted with crops to raise food. It's no use. So, if you cannot understand that there is something in man that responds to the challenge of this mountain and goes out to meet it, that the struggle is the struggle of life itself upward and forever upward, then you won't see why we go. What we get from this adventure is just sheer joy. And joy is, after all, the end of life. We do not live to eat and make money. We eat and make money to be able to enjoy life. That is what life means and what life is for.

George Leigh Mallory, Lt. Col. C. K. Howard-Bury's *Mount Everest, the Reconnaisance,* 1921, Longmans, Green, and Company

Noun and Article Usage

Problem areas with nouns and articles are frequently tested on standardized English proficiency exams. Check your understanding of these structures by completing the sample items that follow.

Remember that . . .

✔ A singular noun takes a singular verb, while plural nouns take plural verbs.

✔ An article or adjective is always used before a singular count noun.

✔ *The* is used with proper nouns, names of landmarks, superlatives, and many expressions of quantity.

✔ Modifiers of nouns have a set word order.

✔ Collective nouns are generally singular in formal American English, and singular pronouns are used to refer to them.

✔ Subjects and verbs are inverted when "negative" adverbs are used at the beginning of sentences.

✔ Parallel structures should be used with groups of nouns and noun modifiers.

Part 1 Circle the best completion for the following.

Example   By 9:00, Ned _____ his breakfast.

    (A) has finished   (B) finishing

    (C) had finished   (D) had been finishing

1. He enjoys traveling on _____.

    (A) airplane   (B) airplanes

    (C) an airplanes   (D) a airplane

2. Brocade is _____ fabric with raised designs.

    (A) an Oriental rich silk   (B) an Oriental silk rich

    (C) a rich silk Oriental   (D) a rich Oriental silk

3. _____ when the phone rang.

    (A) Scarcely I had walked in the door

    (B) Scarcely had I walked in the door

    (C) I had walked scarcely in the door

    (D) I had walked in the door scarcely

4. _____ most beautiful pre-Columbian artwork can be seen in Bogotá's Gold Museum.

    (A) Much of the   (B) Much of

    (C) Many of   (D) Many of the

5. At the grocery store, we bought _____.

- (A) a dozen of eggs
- (B) dozen of eggs
- (C) a dozen eggs
- (D) a dozen of egg

Part 2 Each sentence has one error. Circle the letter below the word(s) containing the error.

Example   By the time the American <u>arrived</u>, <u>both</u> a British and a Swiss
                                   A   B

expedition <u>already had</u> <u>climbed</u> Mt. Everest.
            Ⓒ   D

1. The <u>Norwegian</u> spent many months <u>assembling</u> <u>its team</u>, which included
       A   B   C

a <u>number of</u> scientists.
     D

2. The <u>Arctic</u> is a frozen ocean surrounded by land, while <u>Antarctica</u> is a
       A   B

landmass <u>that is frozen</u> <u>surrounded by</u> ocean.
              C   D

3. In the 1400s, a number of <u>unsuccessful</u> voyages <u>around</u> the horn of Africa
                                 A   B

<u>was financed</u> <u>by the</u> king of Portugal, Manuel I.
       C   D

4. <u>Highest mountain</u> in the world, Mt. Everest was named <u>after</u> George Everest,
             A   B

<u>the first</u> surveyor-general of <u>India</u>.
      C   D

5. <u>Linguists</u> are not certain of <u>the</u> exact date, but <u>written language</u> probably
           A   B   C

began in <u>region</u> of Sumeria over 8,000 years ago.
              D

Self-Assessment Log

Check the things you did in this chapter. How well can you do each one?

	Not Very Well	Fairly Well	Very Well
I understand use of nouns, pronouns, and possessive adjectives.	❏	❏	❏
I can use indefinite articles appropriately.	❏	❏	❏
I can use the definite article appropriately.	❏	❏	❏
I can use a variety of quantifiers and units of measurement appropriately.	❏	❏	❏
I can use singular and plural verb forms appropriately.	❏	❏	❏
I can use appropriate word order with noun and verb modifiers.	❏	❏	❏
I can take a test about nouns, adjectives, articles, pronouns, and parallel structure.	❏	❏	❏
I understand new information about explorers and their explorations, and I can use new structures and vocabulary to talk and write about related topics.	❏	❏	❏

Gender and Relationships

“In a variety of different contexts, gender refers to the masculinity or femininity of words, persons, characteristics, or non-human organisms.”

—Wikipedia

Connecting to the Topic

1. What differences have you noticed between males and females, if any?

2. Do you think they differ in different parts of the world?

3. Do you think there are situations that males are better suited for and situations that females are better suited for? Explain.

Introduction

In this chapter, you will review the various types of sentences in English, and you will study problems with incorrect punctuation or sentence structure.

Reading Read the following passage. It introduces the chapter theme "Gender and Relationships" and raises some of the topics and issues you will cover in the chapter.

The Sexes

How different we all are from each other! Take a moment to study the people around you, and you'll undoubtedly be struck with this fact. Features such as height, weight, skin color, and hair texture vary markedly from individual to individual and from race to race.

These characteristics, however, are not what we notice first about any other human being. Regardless of how tall, dark, or heavy another person is, it is his or her gender that first catches our attention. In fact, no matter how different two people are, we view them as fundamentally similar if they are of the same sex. Thus, the most basic division among human beings is that between male and female.

Because of this division, special roles for each sex have developed. Obviously, males and females perform different functions in reproduction, but the distinction goes far beyond that. In fact, it enters into every area of our lives.

 Discussing Ideas Discuss the questions with a group.

In your opinion, are there differences between the way males and females act in the workplace? At home? At sporting events? Give specific examples.

Setting the Context

Previewing the Passage Discuss the questions with a group.

Do you think that parents treat boys differently than they treat girls? If so, why do they do this? What effect can this have on children as they grow up?

A Traditional Nursery Rhyme
What are little girls made of?
Sugar and spice and everything nice—
That's what little girls are made of.
What are little boys made of?
Snakes and snails and puppy dog tails—
That's what little boys are made of.

Reading Read the passage.

Conditioning

Society "teaches" children to act like males or females at a young age. In fact, the lifelong process of conditioning a person to fit his or her sex role begins at birth. Pink or blue clothing is purchased, a name is chosen from the appropriate category, and the pronoun *he* or *she* is used. Even before the child can talk, he or she is told such things as, "What a handsome boy you are!" or "How pretty you look!" Later come the constant reminders from parents, relatives, and teachers: "Be a brave boy; don't cry," or "Be a nice girl and help Mother with the dishes." 5

Discussing Ideas Discuss the questions with a partner.

In your opinion, how much of male and female behavior is natural or innate and how much is learned? Give reasons or examples to support your opinion.

Grammar Structures and Practice

A. Commands

Commands are the simplest complete sentences in English.

3.1 Commands		
Explanations	**Examples**	
	Affirmative	**Negative**
Commands in the second person consist of the simple form of the verb with or without modifiers. The subject *you* is not stated.	**Wait** a minute. **Stop** it! **Listen** to me. Please **be** quiet.	Please **don't go**. **Don't do** that! **Don't talk** so much. **Don't raise** your voice.

1 Practice Quickly reread the passage "Conditioning." Then underline the commands at the end of the passage. What is the verb for each of these commands? What is the subject?

2 Practice Make the following six statements and requests into commands. In your opinion, would any of these commands more often be given to a girl? Are any more likely to be given to a boy? Explain your answers to your classmates.

Example You can cry if it makes you feel better.
　　　　　Cry if it makes you feel better.

1. You need to get some exercise.

2. You should go on a diet.

3. You should eat more so you can be strong.

4. You shouldn't go around with those types of people.

5. You need to think about your reputation.

6. You should have a good time before you're too old.

3 Practice Fill in the blanks with affirmative or negative commands. Some answers may vary.

Example _____*Don't go*_____ to the show before your homework is done.

1. _____ so much or you'll get fat.

2. _____ your hair. You look like a girl!

3. _____ your hair. It's a mess.

4. _____ this perfume. It will drive men crazy.

5. _____ this cologne. No woman will be able to resist you.

6. _____ your hands. They're filthy!

B. Exclamations

Exclamations are used for emphasis and in emotional statements.

- *How* or *what* often begins the exclamation, and the subject and verb follow in normal word order.
- In conversational English, the subject and verb are often omitted.

3.2 Exclamations

Types	Explanations	Examples
Adjectives and Adverbs	Adjectives and adverbs follow *how*.	**How** quickly he works! **How** kind that was! **How** kind!
Nouns	Nouns follow *what* or *what a(n)*.	**What** a terrible job he is doing! **What** a terrible job!

4 **Practice** Look at the passage "Conditioning" on page 117 once again. This time, underline the exclamations that compliment the appearance of a boy or a girl. Why is *what* used in the first case and *how* used in the second?

5 **Practice** Form exclamations from these statements. Use either *how* or *what*.

Examples

Jane's baby is cute.
    How cute Jane's baby is!
    Jane has a cute baby.
    What a cute baby Jane has!

1. Bill looks tired.

2. Bill has a tired expression.

3. Pinocchio had a large nose.

4. Pinocchio's nose was large.

5. Mary has a warm smile.

6. Mary is smiling warmly.

7. Tim is incredibly rich.

8. Tim has an awful lot of money.

Using What You've Learned

6 Role-playing Work in pairs for a role-play. Pretend you are talking to your 12-year-old son or daughter. Tell your "child" what to do and what not to do. Make at least three affirmative commands and three negative commands.

7 Playing a Guessing Game Work in a group. Give a short description of another member of your class without giving his or her name. Use exclamations when possible. When you are finished, the other members in the group will try to guess whom you were describing.

Examples How beautiful her hair is! What lovely brown eyes she has! But what terrible handwriting she has!

What bushy eyebrows he has! What curly hair he has! How warm his smile is!

What a lazy student he is! How little work he does! But what good grades he gets!

8 Giving Compliments Are you or is anyone in your class a good actress or actor? Imagine yourselves acting in a melodramatic soap opera, and pretend you and your partner are boyfriend and girlfriend. Gaze into each other's eyes and exchange compliments (or insults) using exclamations! As this is melodrama, be sure to exaggerate! (And please avoid doing this in real life.)

Example **Jack:** What beautiful brown eyes you have!
Jill: How charming you are!

9 Reading a Fairy Tale Read the fairy tale "Little Red Riding Hood" and then in groups, prepare a skit of the story. As you act out the skit, be sure to emphasize Little Red Riding Hood's exclamations, "What big ears you have! What big eyes you have! What big teeth you have!"

Setting the Context

Previewing the Passage Discuss the questions with a group.

Do you believe there are differences in intelligence between women and men? If so, explain. Are there differences in achievement levels? Give examples to support your opinion.

Reading Read the passage.

Wasted Potential?

In neither primitive nor modern societies do the achievements of women even approach those of men. Yet the reason for this gap apparently has little to do with natural ability. It is obvious that women are at least as intelligent as men, for girls consistently perform better on IQ tests than boys do. Still, studies of gifted children of both sexes have shown that boys with high IQ scores normally achieve success as adults but high-scoring girls often do not.

5

Discussing Ideas Discuss the questions with a partner.

Why do you think that women have traditionally tested as well as or better than men but have not achieved as much? Is this changing? What is your definition of achievement?

Grammar Structures and Practice

A. Coordinating Conjunctions with Clauses

Coordinating conjunctions (*and, but, for, or, so, yet,* and *nor*) are used to join two independent clauses of roughly equal importance into one *compound sentence.*

3.3 And, But, For, Or, So, Yet

Explanations	Examples		Meanings
Each conjunction shows the logical relationship between the clauses. When a coordinating conjunction joins two clauses, it is normally preceded by a comma. However, with two short clauses, the comma can be omitted.	Fred is antisocial,	**and** he can be quite rude. **but** he has a few friends. **for** he is very insecure. **or** at least he seems that way. **so** many people don't like him. **yet** he loves to go to parties.	*and* = addition *but* = contrast *for* = reason *or* = choice *so* = result *yet* = contrast

3.4 Nor

Explanation	Simple Sentences	Compound Sentences
Nor is used to join two negative clauses. When *nor* begins the second clause, the auxiliary or the verb *be* is placed before the subject and the negative in the second clause is omitted.	Fred is not very sociable. He is not very polite.	Fred is not very sociable, **nor is he** very polite.
	Patty doesn't stay out late. She doesn't gamble.	Patty doesn't stay out late, **nor does she** gamble.
	May hasn't read the chapter. She hasn't written her essay.	May hasn't read the chapter, **nor has she** written her essay.

1 Practice Quickly reread the passage "Wasted Potential?" Underline the connecting words *for* and *but*. What type of relationship does each express? Are the sentences punctuated in the same way?

2 Practice Combine these sentences with coordinating conjunctions, making necessary changes in punctuation and capitalization. Use each conjunction once.

Example   In rural areas of developing nations, women are often underfed. They are also overworked.

In rural areas of developing nations, women are often underfed, and they are also overworked.

1. Men are more muscular than women. Women often do the hardest physical labor.

2. Male infants receive better treatment in many countries. They are more highly prized than female babies.

3. Often, baby girls are not fed as much as their brothers. The girls don't get as much attention.

4. In rural Guatemala, female infants are less valued than males. Female babies are breast-fed for a much shorter period than male babies.

5. In very poor regions, girls often suffer from severe malnutrition. Their brothers do not.

6. Female babies may be treated better in the future. Their situation may worsen.

3 **Practice** Complete the following sentences with a clause. Use the names of people you know or of students in your class for the subjects.

Example _____*Francesca*_____ loves to dance, but. . . .
Francesca loves to dance, but she rarely goes out at night.

1. Last Friday, _____ asked me to go to a movie, but. . . .

2. _____ is very wealthy, so. . . .

3. _____ may never be wealthy, for. . . .

4. _____ will never be wealthy, nor. . . .

5. _____ is in love with one of his / her teachers, yet. . . .

6. _____ doesn't have a new car, nor. . . .

7. _____ has several boyfriends, and. . . .

8. After dinner, _____ does the dishes, or. . . .

9. _____ has never taken the TOEFL® iBT test, nor. . . .

10. _____ is going to visit Las Vegas next weekend, so. . . .

4 **Practice** Some people have strong opinions about the roles of men and women, but other people are more flexible. Choose the word that best expresses your own opinion and then finish each sentence by adding a complete clause. Use the connecting words that are provided. Finally, discuss your answers in small groups. You may choose to discuss your opinions in groups of all women and all men.

Example Men are mentally (stronger) / weaker than women, so *men should make all the decisions.*
Men are mentally (stronger) / weaker than women, but *women are more intelligent.*

1. Men are mentally stronger / weaker than women, yet. . . .
Men are mentally stronger / weaker than women, so. . . .

2. Women / Men should never have to do any housework, nor. . . .
Women / Men should never have to do any housework, but. . . .

3. A woman's / man's place is at home with the children, yet. . . .
A woman's / man's place is at home with the children, or. . . .

4. Men / Women are more important in the world, so. . . .
Men / Women are more important in the world, and. . . .

B. Coordinating Conjunctions with Words and Phrases

Some coordinating conjunctions can be used to join clauses. Other coordinating conjunctions are used to join phrases.

- *So* and *for* can join clauses only.
- *Nor* usually joins clauses.
- *And, but, yet,* and *or* are often used to join units smaller than clauses. Of course, the structures on both sides of the conjunction must be parallel (noun . . . noun, adjective . . . adjective, verb . . . verb, adverb . . . adverb, phrase . . . phrase).

3.5 Coordinating Conjunctions with Words and Phrases	
Structures	**Examples**
Nouns	**Khalil** and **Tasir** met us at the airport.
Adjectives	We were **tired** but **happy**.
Verb Phrases	They **took** us to the hotel and **arranged** for a room.
Adverbs	The clerk spoke **rapidly** yet **clearly**.
Prepositional Phrases	We will return **in August** or **at the end of the year**.

5 **Practice** Combine each group of sentences that follow into one sentence, using *and, or, nor, for, so, but,* or *yet.* Don't use the same connecting word more than once within each set. Make these sentences as short as possible by omitting all unnecessary words.

Julie

Some women have decided that their place is not at home, even if they have children. This is the story of such a woman, Julie.

Example In class, Julie's eyes are always sparkling with attention.
In class, Julie's eyes are always sparkling with joy.
In class, Julie's eyes hold a deep sadness.
In class, Julie's eyes are always sparkling with attention and joy, but they hold a deep sadness.

1. Julie's face seemed, at times, childlike.
   Her face on closer inspection was wizened.[1]
   She had been through a lot in her life.

2. Julie was born in the Philippines.
   She grew up in China during the ten-year Cultural Revolution.
   She was no stranger to hard times.

3. Some of her family starved during the Cultural Revolution.
   There was no food to buy.
   There was no food to borrow.

4. Julie was able to stay alive by moving to a communal farm.
   She became ill with hepatitis[2] there.
   She almost died.

5. Eventually, the situation in China improved.
   Julie moved back to the city.
   She got married.

6. She had a husband.
   She had a child.
   She had a relatively well-paying job.
   She left them all to come to the United States.

7. She worked in Santa Barbara, California.
   She studied in Santa Barbara.
   She didn't see her son for several years.
   She didn't see her husband for several years.

8. Leaving China was a big sacrifice for her.
   Leaving China was a big sacrifice for her family.
   It was an opportunity that comes once in a lifetime.

9. Julie finally left California for China.
   She wanted to see her son.
   She wanted to see her husband.
   She planned to return to Santa Barbara someday to finish her degree.

10. Life gave Julie an opportunity.
    The opportunity was very special.
    Life also forced Julie to make choices.
    The choices were difficult.
    The choices were between family and education.

---

[1]*wizened* wrinkled, with lines in the skin
[2]*hepatitis* a disease of the liver

C. Correlative Conjunctions

Correlatives are conjunctions that have two parts:

- *either . . . or*
- *neither . . . nor*
- *not only . . . but (also)*
- *both . . . and*

They can connect either clauses or smaller grammatical units, but the structures must always be parallel. For example, if a clause follows *either,* a clause must follow *or;* if a noun follows *either,* a noun must follow *or.*

3.6 Correlative Conjunctions

Correlative Conjunctions	Structures	Examples	Meanings
either . . . or	Clauses	**Either** we should give Ann a raise, **or** we should give her a vacation.	*Either . . . or* = choice
	Nouns	We should give her **either** a raise **or** a vacation. (Incorrect: *Either we should give Ann a raise or a vacation.)	
not only . . . but (also)	Clauses	**Not only** is her boss dishonest, **but (also)** he is temperamental.	*Not only . . . but (also)* = addition
	Adjectives	Her boss is **not only** dishonest **but (also)** temperamental. (Incorrect: *Not only is her boss dishonest but also temperamental. Her boss is not only dishonest, but also he is temperamental.)	When *not only . . . but (also)* joins two clauses, the auxiliary is placed before the subject in the first clause only.
either . . . nor	Verb Phrases	She **neither** got a raise **nor** took a vacation.	*Neither . . . nor* = negative addition
	Nouns	She got **neither** a raise **nor** a vacation. (Incorrect: *She neither got a raise nor did she take a vacation. Neither did she get a raise nor a vacation.)	*Neither . . . nor* is often used to join smaller units. It is usually not used to join clauses.
both . . . and	Adverbs	He works **both** quickly **and** carelessly.	*Both . . . and* = addition
	Nouns	**Both** Ann **and** her boss are stubborn. (Incorrect: *He works both quickly, and he works carelessly. Both Ann is stubborn, and her boss is stubborn.)	*Both . . . and* is not used to join clauses.

Note: In writing, it is considered better style to combine the smallest possible grammatical units with correlative conjunctions. Thus, while the first sentence below is perfectly grammatical, the second sentence is preferred.

Not only have I written the president, but I have also talked to my congressman. I have not only written the president but also talked to my congressman.

6 **Practice** Combine the following sentences using correlative conjunctions. In 1 and 2, combine the sentences in two ways. Combine the two clauses; then remove all repetition. In 3 and 4, remove all repetition.

Jassem

Jassem Al Khadher learned that his company in Kuwait was willing to sponsor him to do graduate study in the United States.

Example He could study in the United States. He could stay at his present job in Kuwait. (either . . . or)
  a. Either he could study in the United States, or he could stay at his present job in Kuwait.
  b. He could either study in the United States or stay at his present job in Kuwait.

1. Jassem loved the idea of studying in the United States.
   He wanted a break from his job. (not only . . . but also)
   a.
   b.

2. He could study at Columbia University.
   He could study at Michigan State University. (either . . . or)
   a.
   b.

3. His colleagues encouraged him to go.
   His family encouraged him to go. (both . . . and)
   a.

4. However, his wife couldn't accompany him. She couldn't visit him for at least six months. (neither . . . nor)
   a.

7 **Practice** Underline the repetitive parts within the following sets of sentences. Then combine each of the sets, using an appropriate correlative conjunction. Remove all repetition.

Example After arriving in New York, Jassem was impressed. He was frightened.
  After arriving in New York, Jassem was both impressed and frightened.

1. He had never been far away from his family. He had never been outside of Kuwait.

2. The language was new to him. The food, climate, and culture were new to him.

3. His fellow students couldn't help him. His friends from Kuwait couldn't help him.

4. In the following months, Jassem's homesickness grew. His telephone bill grew. (It was $1,000 one month.)

5. He would call his wife every morning and afternoon. She would think that something was wrong. (If he didn't call his wife, she would think something was wrong.)

6. Tonight, he could do his homework. Tonight, he could call his wife.

8 **Practice** After a few months, Jassem went to his consulate to complain. Complete the following sentences.

Example I will either stay in the United States. . . .

I will either stay in the United States or return to Kuwait.

1. I want to see both my wife. . . .

2. Either send my family to the United States. . . .

3. I am not only bored. . . .

4. Living alone is neither convenient. . . .

5. I wish I knew someone who was both rich. . . .

6. Neither my son. . . .

7. Not only are my children intelligent. . . .

8. Either my children will study at Berkeley. . . .

9. Both my daughter. . . .

10. Today, I spoke to neither my wife. . . .

Unfortunately for the phone company, Jassem's wife and children joined him after six months.

9 **Error Analysis** Most of the following sentences have errors. Find each error and correct it. If the sentence is correct, do not change it.

both
Example Julie ~~Both~~ was sick and hungry.

1. Julie not only survived the Cultural Revolution but also life without her mother and father.

2. She didn't stop neither working nor studying.

3. Both Julie and her husband hoped she would graduate soon.

4. Not only Julie missed her family, but also she missed her country.

5. Either Jassem had to pay the phone bill or lose his phone.

6. Not only was Jassem unhappy, but also was his wife unhappy.

7. Studying in another country was both a joy, and it was a hardship for Julie and Jassem.

8. Neither Jassem nor Julie still live in Santa Barbara.

9. Jassem will return to his country, so he is tired of living away from home.

10. Julie is studying very hard, for she will receive good grades.

Using What You've Learned

10 **Describing Traditional Customs** Marriage customs differ from one culture to another. Think about marriage customs in a culture you know, or research marriage customs in a culture of your choice. Does the married couple usually live alone, or do relatives live with them? Do both the husband and wife work outside the home? Which person does which household chores?

In a five-minute presentation, discuss these and any other points about marriage customs in the culture you chose. You may give your presentation individually or in groups.

Setting the Context

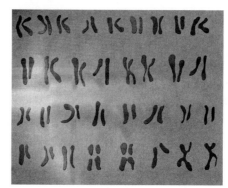

▲ Human chromosomes. Each human cell
has 23 pairs of chromosomes.

Previewing the Passage Discuss the questions with a group.

What are genes? What are chromosomes? Does the mother or the father determine
the sex of a child?

Reading Read the passage.

Biological Differences

The sex of a child is determined at conception through the parents'
chromosomes. Each human cell contains 23 chromosome pairs. (One in
each pair is from the mother and one is from the father.) However, the sex
of the child is determined by only one of these chromosome pairs, the so-
called sex chromosomes. There are two types of sex chromosomes: X and   5
Y. The mother always contributes an X. The father, on the other hand, may
contribute either an X or a Y. Therefore, when united, the chromosomes
from the mother and father form one of two patterns: an XX—a baby girl,
or an XY—a baby boy. Interestingly, the XY combination is more likely. In
fact, some 20 percent more males than females are conceived. Nature soon   10
changes this ratio, however. Many more males die during pregnancy; moreover, more baby boys die at birth. As a result, only four percent more males
are born than females.

Discussing Ideas Discuss the questions with a partner.

According to the passage, which chromosome combination is more probable? Does
the ratio of XX to XY change during pregnancy or birth? How?

Cultural Note

CULTURE NOTE The Human Genome Project

Formally begun in 1990, the Human Genome Project is a U.S. initiative coordinated by the U.S. Department of Energy and the National Institutes of Health to map DNA. Human genome work is giving us a tremendous amount of new information about human genetics, heredity versus environment, and health. For example, some personality traits, such as shyness, seem to be inherited. In the future, many human differences and similarities—in personality or in gender, for example—will hopefully be explored. In the end, we may gain the most information from proteins, because they make up the majority of the cell structure. Studies to explore proteins will be the focus of much research for decades to come and will help us understand both health and disease.

Grammar Structures and Practice

A. Transitions

Transitions are words or phrases that link two related ideas.
- Transitions may be used in a series of simple sentences, or they may be used with a conjunction or semicolon to join two sentences.
- Transitions are particularly common in formal situations and in writing.

3.7 Transitions

	Explanations	Examples
A Series of Sentences	Transitions may begin sentences; they are normally followed by commas.	The dinner was delicious. **Nevertheless**, we felt that it was overpriced.
Compound Sentences	In written English, a semicolon and a transition are often used to form compound sentences.	The main course was superb; **however**, none of us liked the dessert. The meal was expensive; **as a result**, we decided not to return there.
	Some transitions (particularly *however*) may be used at various points within a sentence. In these cases, commas precede and / or follow the transition.	**However,** we enjoyed ourselves very much. The Smiths, **however,** enjoyed themselves very much. The Smiths enjoyed themselves very much, **however**.

Common transitions include the following:

3.8 Common Transitions			
To Give Additional Information	*also, furthermore, in addition, moreover*	**To Express a Negative Condition**	*otherwise*
To Show Contrast	*however, nevertheless*	**To Add Comments Clarification**	*as a matter of fact, in fact*
To Show Result	*as a result, consequently, hence, therefore, thus*		

1 Practice Link the following sentences with the transitions indicated. Add all necessary punctuation. The transitions within each group are interchangeable.

Additional Information *also, furthermore, in addition, moreover*

Example More baby boys die in childbirth. More males die in each succeeding year of life.

More baby boys die in childbirth; moreover, more males die in each succeeding year of life.

Additional Information *also, furthermore, in addition, moreover*

1. At birth, boys are, on average, one-half inch taller than girls. Boys weigh slightly more.

2. Girls develop faster physically than boys. Girls mature more quickly intellectually.

3. Female babies suffer from fewer birth defects. As they mature, women contract fewer diseases.

4. Later in life, men are more prone to hepatitis. They are more susceptible to heart disease, tuberculosis, and asthma.

Contrast *however, nevertheless*

5. The Y chromosome brings more males into the world. It does not make things easier for them when they arrive.

6. By the age of 20, the number of surviving males and females is about equal. By the age of 30, women are clearly ahead.

7. A great number of diseases are more likely to trouble men. Only genital cancer and diabetes more often strike women.

8. Women have a higher rate of genital cancer. When all types of cancer are included, men suffer in greater numbers.

Result *as a result, consequently, hence, therefore, thus*

9. Men's bodies are generally bigger than women's. Men have heavier brains and hearts.

10. A man's lungs are larger than a woman's. He takes four to six fewer breaths per minute.

11. Women's hips are larger than men's. When women walk, their hips sway, and they run more slowly.

12. Women have less water in their bodies. Women become drunk more quickly.

Negative Condition *otherwise*

13. Scientists have done a great deal of genetic research. We wouldn't know the role of genes and chromosomes in reproduction and illness.

14. The Y chromosome weakens males. Men would live as long as women.

15. Men have more water in their bodies. They would get drunk just as easily as women.

16. Women have larger hips. They might be able to run faster than men.

Added Comment or Clarification *as a matter of fact, in fact*

17. Women are stronger than most people think. A woman can often lift and carry a larger percentage of her body weight than a man can of his.

18. Women float in water more easily than men. Women are on average 10 percent more buoyant.

19. Women often have a great endurance for extremely low temperatures. They can survive in very cold conditions much longer than men can.

20. Men tend to have a lower percentage of fat than women. Adult males average 20 percent fat, whereas adult women commonly have over 25 percent.

2 Practice The following paragraphs are missing necessary capital letters and punctuation. Read the paragraphs carefully. Then with a partner, underline all transitions and make changes in punctuation and capitalization. Finally, suggest one or more alternatives for as many of the transitions as you can.

Male or Female?

The sex of a child is determined at conception however no differences begin to show in the fetus[1] until six to eight weeks later. At that point, androgens, the male hormones, come into play. Interestingly, these male hormones (or their absence) affect both sexes. Androgens are produced within the XY fetus as a result a boy   5
begins to develop. These androgens are absent in the XX fetus thus the latter starts to take on female characteristics.

How important are these androgens to the development of the male child? As a matter of fact they are essential. For the boy to develop, the male hormones must be present otherwise "he" will be   10
born with the anatomy of a girl.

_____
[1]*fetus* unborn child

3 Practice Read the following paragraphs carefully. Then fill in the blanks with the transition that best shows the logical relationship between the sentences. Don't use any transition more than one time in each paragraph. Be sure to add all necessary punctuation.

- Men are bigger and stronger than women. _____*Thus*_____, they tend to do better in athletics. In 1911, a British magazine found that men were about 50 percent better in sports than women _____ 1
in recent years, the gap has been shrinking. For example, in javelin, the men's record is only about 25 meters ahead of the women's record.

- Women are still slower than men in some long-distance swimming events _____ they are swimming faster today than many of the 2
men's champions of the past. In the 1924 Olympics, Johnny Weissmuller, who later played Tarzan in movies, gained world fame by winning the 400-meter freestyle event _____ today there are thousands of 3
women who have beaten Weissmuller's Olympic time.

_____ if a world-class female swimmer could be trans-4
ported back to 1924, she would beat Weissmuller by an embarrassing 80 meters!

- Women can be much stronger than they appear _____ under certain circumstances women have shown incredible strength. Florence Rogers of Tampa, Florida, provides a good example. When a jack[1] collapsed, pinning her son under the car, she knew she had to lift the car _____ he would die. This, of course, seems impossible even for a man _____ in the desperation of the moment, Florence raised one end of the 3,600-pound car _____ her son was able to escape.

_____

[1]*jack* device used to lift a car when, for example, a tire is being changed

4 **Practice** Complete the following sentences using all of the transitions provided. Add appropriate punctuation.

Example Women are smaller than men; furthermore, *they weigh less even at birth.*

1. Women are smaller than men (nevertheless)
2. In the past, women rarely exercised (consequently)
3. Women suffer from fewer diseases (as a result)
4. Men have historically dominated women (in fact)
5. Boys were believed to be better at math (however)
6. We should finish this exercise (otherwise)

Using What You've Learned

 5 **Summarizing** Close your book and work in pairs to summarize (in your own words) the major ideas in Exercise 2. Refer back to the book only if really necessary. When you are finished, write your summary, adding transitions where appropriate.

 6 **Debating** What was the strongest position that you took in Activity 4? Could you defend that position? Choose a partner of the opposite sex. Find one issue from Activity 4 about which you are in total disagreement. Then take turns explaining your position and summarizing your partner's. Begin by stating your opinion in no more than two minutes. Your partner must then summarize what you have said to your satisfaction. Only then can your partner state his or her opinion. Continue this process for several rounds or until you and your partner understand each other's positions completely.

Setting the Context

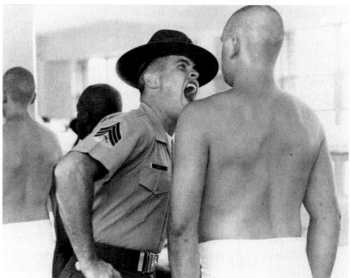

Previewing the Passage Discuss the questions with a group.

Are the differences between men and women reflected in their speech? How do men and women talk differently?

Language Differences

Throughout history, the most important distinction between human beings has been their sex. Linguists have found that this distinction between males and females even affects people's speech.

Among some peoples, differences in the way men and women speak are aparent in pronunciation. In the Chukchi society of Siberia, men pronounce the word that means "people" *ramkichnin*. Women, on the other hand, pronounce it *tsamkitstsin*. Women of the Yana tribe in California say *au* ("fire") and *ya* ("people"), whereas men say *auna* and *yana*.

In many other cultures, certain words are used by one sex but not the other. In Madagascar, women use more direct language and harsher words. If a confrontation between males is necessary, the men often have their female relatives say the harsh words for them. Later, the men patch up any hurt feelings that may have resulted.

 Discussing Ideas Discuss the questions with a partner.

What differences in men's and women's speech exist in your culture? Do men pronounce certain words differently than women do? Do men and women use different vocabulary?

Grammar Structures and Practice

A. Complex Sentences: An Overview

A complex sentence joins two or more clauses of unequal importance. Each complex sentence includes at least one *main (independent) clause* and one *dependent clause*. The most important idea is generally placed in the independent clause. A variety of connecting words may be used to join the clauses. There are three basic types of dependent clauses:

- Adjective
- Adverb
- Noun

3.9 Adjective Clauses

MAIN CLAUSE   DEPENDENT CLAUSE

We are working on a project that is very difficult.

Connecting Words Used in Adjective Clauses (Relative Pronouns)

	Examples
Animals and Things	which, that
People	who, whom, that
Place	where
Possessives	whose
Reason	why, that
Time	when

3.10 Adverb Clauses

DEPENDENT CLAUSE   MAIN CLAUSE

After we have finished the project, we'll take a long vacation.

Common Connecting Words Used in Adverb Clauses (Subordinating Conjunctions)

	Examples
Comparison	more (less, -er . . . than, as . . . as)
Condition	if, unless, as long as, provided that, whether or not
Contrast: Concession	although, even though, though, despite (in spite of) the fact that
Contrast: Opposition	while, where, whereas
Manner	as, as if, as though
Place	where, wherever
Purpose	so that, in order that
Reason	so . . . that, such . . . that
Result	as, because, since
Time	after, as long as, as soon as, before, once, since, until, when, whenever, while

3.11 Noun Clauses

MAIN CLAUSE   DEPENDENT CLAUSE

Phil said that we should all go to a movie.

Common Connecting Words Used in Noun Clauses (Subordinating Conjunctions)

	Examples
Reported Speech	that (or no conjunction)
Embedded Questions	how, if, what, when, whether, why, and all other question words

1 **Practice** Quickly reread the passage "Language Differences." Then look at the sentences in lines 2 to 3, 11 to 12, and 12 to 13, and answer these questions for each sentence.

1. How many clauses are there in the sentence?
2. What connecting word is used?
3. Which is the main clause?
4. Which is the dependent clause?
5. Where does the dependent clause come in relation to the main clause?
6. What punctuation (if any) is used?

2 **Practice** Underline the dependent clauses and circle the connecting words in each of these sentences. Identify the type of dependent clause: adverb, adjective, or noun. In some cases, there may be more than one dependent clause; in others, there may be none.

Example In Madagascar, women use more direct language than men (because) women are in charge of situations of confrontation. _adverb clause_

1. Researchers in Madagascar have found that the most aggressive buyers and sellers are women. _____

2. Although women often bargain in the marketplace, men only buy and sell goods that have a fixed price. _____

3. Social scientists who have studied Madagascar aren't sure why the women dominate confrontations. _____

4. In most other cultures, the men control situations of confrontation. _____

5. Any Japanese speaker can add _yo_ at the end of a sentence, but the meaning changes somewhat, depending on the sex of the speaker. _____

6. When a male uses *yo,* it means something similar to, "You had better believe me!" _____

7. If a female says *yo,* it often has a softer meaning. _____

8. Sex differences in the English language were much greater in the past because men and women socialized together very little. _____

9. In Victorian England (1837-1901), the difference between male and female language was so great that women couldn't use or listen to a large number of "male" words. _____

10. For example, *leg* was considered such an offensive word that it was never used in the presence of a woman. _____

11. Even the legs of furniture were covered so that women would not be shocked. _____

▲ The majority of people in this marketplace are women.

3 **Practice** Fill in each blank with a connecting word from the category in parentheses. Then underline the dependent clause(s).

Example The reason _____*that / why*_____ (adjective clause) men don't use "refined" English is _____*that*_____ (noun clause) they admire the rougher qualities of the working class.

1. _____ (adverb clause: time) Victoria ruled Britain, the language of males and females had become quite similar.

2. Linguists have proved _____ (noun clause) differences still exist in the way men and women speak English.

3. The differences _____ (adjective clause) remain are more subtle, however.

4. _____ (adverb clause: contrast) some "offensive words" are more common among males, women are using these words more and more.

5. Still, women tend to speak a more refined form of the language than men _____ (adjective clause) are in the same social class.

6. In most languages, the voice quality of males and females is so different _____ (adverb clause: reason) the sex of a speaker is recognized immediately.

7. In fact, there is such a big difference _____ (adverb clause: reason) one sex has trouble imitating the other.

8. _____ (adverb clause: time) an American woman imitates a man, she separates the syllables more clearly and lowers the pitch.

9. However, _____ (adverb clause: condition) an American male wants to sound like a female, he uses more "breathiness" in his voice, blends the stressed syllables, and raises the pitch.

10. By contrast, a male Mohave Indian needs only to use words typical of a woman _____ (adverb clause: purpose) he can sound like one.

B. Complex Sentences: Focus

In a complex sentence (a sentence with both a main clause and a dependent clause), the information that the speaker or writer wants to emphasize is usually placed within the main clause.

- The main clause is the focus of most complex sentences; it gives the topic or "main" idea.
- In contrast, clauses in compound sentences (sentences with two independent clauses) generally have equal importance. Compare:

3.12 Complex Sentences: Focus

Sentence Types	Examples	Focus
Complex Sentences	In England, sex differences in language were greater in the past because men and women rarely socialized together.	Sex differences in language were greater in the past.
	In England's past, men and women rarely socialized together, which created greater sex differences in language than exist today.	In the past, men and women in England rarely socialized together.
	During England's past, men and women had so little social contact that sex differences in language developed.	In the past, men and women had very little social contact.
Compound Sentences	During England's past, men and women had very little social contact; as a result, sex differences in language developed.	In the past, men and women did not socialize. Because of this, sex differences in language developed.

4 **Practice** Work with a partner. Study the following sets of sentences and underline the main clause in each. Discuss the differences in focus in each set. In some cases, there may be only main clauses.

Example The word *matriarchy*, which appears in all dictionaries, <u>is usually defined as a society dominated by females</u>.
<u>The word *matriarchy* appears in all dictionaries</u>, where it is usually defined as a society dominated by females.

In sentence 1, the focus is on the meaning of the word matriarchy. The clause which appears in all dictionaries is extra information; it doesn't give information necessary to the main idea of the sentence.
In sentence 2, the focus is on dictionaries and the fact that matriarchy appears in them. The clause where it is usually defined as a society dominated by females gives additional information. It reinforces the main idea of the main clause: dictionary definitions.

1. The Iroquois Indians, who probably came as close to having a matriarchal society as any people, lived in North America.
The Iroquois Indians, who lived in North America, probably came as close to having a matriarchal society as any people.

2. In this society, even though the women played a central role in the election of new leaders, these leaders were always men.
In this society, even though the leaders were always men, women played a central role in the elections of these leaders.

3. In the last century, Great Britain and the Philippines each gave the highest governmental position to a woman; thus, these might at first glance appear to have been matriarchal societies.
Because Great Britain and the Philippines each gave the highest governmental position to a woman, they might appear at first glance to have been matriarchal societies.

4. While the leaders of both countries were female, the governments actually were dominated by males.
The leaders of both countries were female in spite of the fact that the governments actually were dominated by males.[1]

5. Margaret Thatcher became Prime Minister of Great Britain when her Conservative Party defeated the Labor Party in 1979.
When Margaret Thatcher became Prime Minister of Great Britain in 1979, it was due to the victory of the Conservative Party over the Labor Party.

6. It was a revolution in 1985 that brought Corazon Aquino to power in the Philippines.
Corazon Aquino came to power in the Philippines because of the revolution that broke out in 1985.

---

[1]In Great Britain, in the late 1980s, for example, every one of Prime Minister Margaret Thatcher's ministers was male.

5 **Practice** Work with a partner. Reread the sentences in Activity 4 and then try to create a third possibility for each set. Do this by omitting the connecting word and replacing it with either a transition (*however, therefore,* and so forth) or a coordinating conjunction (*and, or,* and so forth). You may also need to add or change words. Finally, discuss the difference in focus between the old and new sentences.

Example *The word matriarchy is usually defined as a society dominated by females; as a matter of fact, this definition appears in all dictionaries.*
Women played a strong role among the Iroquois Indians in North America; in fact, the Iroquois Indians came as close to having a matriarchal society as any people.

Using What You've Learned

6 **Sharing Opinions** Beyond physical differences, how do men and women differ? Should men and women share household duties? Should both have equal opportunities in the business world? Should boys and girls be raised in the same way? Discuss these and other questions you may have in small groups. You may want to form a variety of groups, if possible: all males, all females, all members from the same culture, all members from different cultures, younger groups, older groups, and so on.

7 **Conducting an Interview** The roles of men and women differ from culture to culture. Interview a classmate from a different cultural background than yours and learn his or her opinions about gender roles. Ask the preceding questions and others that you may think of. Then write a short summary of your partner's opinions, using as many connecting words as possible.

Setting the Context

Previewing the Passage Discuss the questions with a group.

In your culture, do fathers often stay at home and raise the children while mothers work outside the home? Why or why not?

Variations on a Theme

Karen and Bob Maness. They were married about 15 years ago; she was 16 and he was 21. Eventually, one of them became a police officer; the other got a part-time job and took care of the house and the children. Even though this family seems quite ordinary, it was not. It was Karen who was the police officer and Bob who raised the couple's two daughters. 5

The couple seemed quite satisfied with the unconventional marriage. "I could never go back to doing all the housework," Karen told an interviewer while Bob nodded his head in agreement. Unfortunately (some might say inevitably), the strains of this lifestyle were greater than the couple was willing to admit. Karen and Bob filed for divorce only one month after their 10 interview.

—Peter Swerdloff

Discussing Ideas Discuss the questions with a partner.

What do you think happened to Bob and Karen's marriage?

Grammar Structures and Practice

A. Comma Splices and Run-On Sentences

There are three ways to join two clauses correctly.

3.13	Examples of Correct Sentences
Coordinating Conjunction	Bob got married in June, **but** he was divorced by July.
Semicolon	Bob got married in June; he was divorced by July.
Subordinating Conjunction or Relative Pronoun	**Although** Bob got married in June, he was divorced by July. Bob, **who** had gotten married in June, was divorced by July.

Two clauses cannot be joined correctly without one of the preceding. Therefore, the following sentences are incorrect:

3.14	Examples of Incorrect Sentences
Comma Splice	*Bob got married in June, he was divorced by July.
Run-On	*Bob got married in June he was divorced by July.

1 **Error Analysis** Identify the run-on sentences in the following exercise. Then correct them by adding a connecting word, a semicolon, or a period. Make all necessary changes in punctuation and capitalization. If a sentence has no mistake, do not change it.

Example A number of couples have changed their husband / wife roles⊙
Many
(many) have been more successful than Karen and Bob Maness.

1. They live in a traditional society Jean and Françoise have a "modern marriage."

2. Jean is a well-known political cartoonist and works at home his wife, on the other hand, teaches linguistics at a university and spends most of her day on campus.

3. Since Jean is at home more, he does more of the housework and helps care for the children, Françoise does the rest of the cleaning and all of the sewing.

4. Whereas Françoise fills out the tax forms, Jean does the shopping and most of the cooking the relationship is not perfect but it works.

5. They are delighted to have three daughters each of the marriage partners disciplines the children, but Jean is more successful at it.

6. The whole family spends as much time together as possible, for they want their modern family to have old-fashioned love and warmth.

B. Fragments

Fragments are incomplete sentences. They are also incorrect. There are two common types of fragments:
- Incomplete clauses
- Dependent clauses

3.15 Incomplete Clauses

Explanations	Fragments	Problems	Corrections
Every clause must have at least one subject and one verb.	*Helen, Harry, and the rest of the family.	**No verb**	Helen, Harry, and the rest of the family are in China.
	*In the middle of July began work.	**No subject**	In the middle of July, Ellen began work.

3.16 Dependent Clauses

Explanations	Fragments	Problems	Corrections
A dependent clause cannot be a sentence by itself. It must be accompanied by a complete main clause.	*Although they had been married for years.	**No main clause**	Although they had been married for years, they were quite unhappy.
	*The couple that lived next to us.	**No verb in the main clause**	The couple that lived next to us had a perfect marriage.

2 **Error Analysis** Underline the fragments in the following sentences. Identify the problem in each, then correct the problem.

Example   Monogamy[1] is practiced by a majority of people in all societies. <u>Thus, making it the most popular form of marriages.</u>
Correction: Thus, it is the most popular form of marriage.

1. Many other types of marriage have been tried in different cultures. For example, polygamy.[2]

2. Polygamy, which is another marital variation. It involves the marriage of several women to one man.

3. Polygamy is still practiced in several societies. Particularly where there are large numbers of Muslims.

4. Although most Muslims have monogamous marriages. The Koran, the holy book of Islam, allows a man to be married to four wives at one time.

5. Ibn Saud, who founded the Kingdom of Saudi Arabia, had hundreds of wives in his lifetime. But never more than four at one time.

6. Historically, Mormons[3] also practiced polygamy. Which they called "plural" or "celestial marriage."

7. When the U.S. government made it illegal, the leadership of the Mormon Church outlawed plural marriage, however a splinter group left the Church because they believed that it was God's will to continue this practice.

8. In some small towns in Utah, Arizona, and Southern Canada. Plural marriage is still practiced even though it is illegal.

9. The marriage of several men to one woman. This is called polyandry.

10. Polyandry is uncommon today. Despite the fact that it was once practiced in India, Ceylon, Tibet, and the South Pacific.

---

[1]*monogamy* the practice of having only one husband or wife at one time
[2]*polygamy* the practice of having more than one wife at one time
[3]*Mormons* members of the Church of Jesus Christ of Latter-day Saints

3 **Error Analysis** Find the fragments and run-on sentences in the following paragraph. Then make necessary corrections.

The Oneida Community

The marriage of one group of males to another group of females is not practiced today, however, "group marriage" has been tried at different times in the past. The Oneida community in upstate New York was the most successful of these efforts. Oneida, which was founded in 1848 with some 58 adults and their children. It was perhaps the most radical social experiment in the history of the United States.

Oneidans believed that romantic love produced selfishness and jealousy, in its place, the members adopted a policy of "free love." Under this policy, all adults were considered married to all adults of the opposite sex. Any male could mate with any female. Though both parties had to agree. Later, in 1869, Oneida began the world's first large-scale experiments in eugenics.[1] At that time, a special committee selected certain males and females to be mates. So that the strongest and most intelligent children would be born.

---

[1]*eugenics* the science of improving the inherited traits of human beings

4 Discussing and Analyzing Poetry Poets try to express a great deal in as few words as possible, often ignoring many of the rules of grammar. In small groups, read and discuss the following poem. Then try to find all the rules of grammar and punctuation the author has broken. Finally, change the lines of this poem into grammatical sentences, adding subjects, verbs, conjunctions, and punctuation.

She

Mischievous eyes peeping from tiny windows
Sweet smiles flowing from rosy lips
Peaceful expression rendering endless affection
Long black eye-lashes in a continuous dance
5 Resembling a frail shining hummingbird
Not only is she beautiful but shy,
She wanders about the most splendid gardens
Darting between green leaf and silver blossom
Whenever you are down and needing warmth
10 Lie on your garden and raise your eyes
Search among the flowers, scan the clouds,
She will be there, she is part of the sky

—John Benites

Compound and Complex Sentences

Problem areas with compound and complex sentences are frequently tested on standardized English proficiency exams. Check your understanding of these structures by completing the sample items that follow.

Remember that . . .

✔ Every sentence must have at least one subject-verb combination.

✔ Compound sentences are formed by joining sentences with a comma and a coordinating conjunction, with a semicolon, or with a semicolon and a transition.

✔ Compound sentences with *nor* use special word order.

✔ Correlative conjunctions such as *either . . . or* connect parallel structures.

✔ Complex sentences are formed by joining sentences with a subordinating conjunction.

Part 1 Circle the best completion for the following.

Example Although people are similar, _____ are still divided by their sex.

    (A) always   (B) but

    (C) they   (D) we

1. The child appears healthy; _____, it's a good idea for her to have a checkup soon.

    (A) otherwise   (B) therefore

    (C) nevertheless   (D) always

2. We had wanted to go for a walk, _____ it was raining.

    (A) furthermore   (B) but

    (C) but however   (D) so

3. To lead a peaceful life, women should not try to do too much, nor _____ do too little.

    (A) should they   (B) they

    (C) women should   (D) they should

4. Human beings are divided by sex; _____ we view all people as fundamentally similar.

    (A) on the contrary,   (B) however,

    (C) moreover,   (D) but,

5. Either Jack or his friends _____ clean out the garage this weekend.

    (A) are going to   (B) going to

    (C) is going to   (D) are going

Part 2 Each sentence has one error. Circle the letter below the word(s) containing the error.

Example   During England's past, men and women <u>had</u> very little contact; <u>but,</u>
                                                  A   (B)

        sex differences in <u>the language</u> <u>developed</u>.
                            C   D

1. <u>Sometimes</u> a man takes care of the children <u>because</u> his wife has a job
       A   B
outside the home; <u>but</u> <u>however</u>, this arrangement may not work well for
                  C   D
every couple.

2. <u>Even though</u> the men were the leaders in <u>the</u> society; <u>nevertheless</u>, within
       A   B   C
the family, they were <u>subordinate</u> to the women.
                  D

3. In Madagascar, the women are <u>such</u> aggressive buyers and sellers <u>so</u> <u>that</u>
                           A   B   C
they dominate <u>the</u> marketplace.
            D

4. <u>Although</u> the Weikers live in a <u>relatively</u> traditional society, <u>and</u> the couple <u>has</u>
      A   B   C   D
a modern marriage.

5. <u>As</u> Prime Minister, Margaret Thatcher headed the government of Great Britain
    A
in the <u>1980s</u> all <u>of</u> her ministers <u>were</u> male.
        B   C   D

Self-Assessment Log

Check the things you did in this chapter. How well can you do each one?

	Not Very Well	Fairly Well	Very Well
I understand sentence types.	❏	❏	❏
I can use commands appropriately.	❏	❏	❏
I can use coordinating conjunctions to form compound sentences.	❏	❏	❏
I can use correlative conjunctions appropriately.	❏	❏	❏
I can use a variety of transitions appropriately.	❏	❏	❏
I can identify a variety of complex sentences.	❏	❏	❏
I can identify sentence focus in compound and complex sentences.	❏	❏	❏
I can identify and correct fragments, comma splices, and run-on sentences.	❏	❏	❏
I can take a test about compound and complex sentences.	❏	❏	❏
I learned new information about males and females, and I can use new structures and vocabulary to talk and write about related topics.	❏	❏	❏

Beauty and Aesthetics

In This Chapter

Adjective Clauses and Related Structures

> **❝** In every man's heart there is a secret nerve that answers to the vibrations of beauty. **❞**
>
> —Christopher Morley

Connecting to the Topic

1. What do you know about the world's antiquities—its ancient monuments, temples, and relics?

2. Have you ever visited any of these?

3. Are there any interesting historical or archaelogical sites near the place where you live?

Introduction

In this chapter, you will study a variety of adjective clauses and phrases. As you study, pay careful attention to the use of commas.

Reading Read the following passag. It introduces the chapter theme "Beauty and Aesthetics" and raises some of the topics and issues that you will cover in the chapter.

World Treasures

Perhaps the greatest treasures we have in the world today are those that have been given to us by ancient cultures. Some of the art and architecture that was created by our distant ancestors and that still survives today has astounding beauty. Equally astounding, these beautiful creations were produced by artisans whose primitive tools and supplies were made of bits of wood, stone, minerals, and metal. 5

We see the grandeur of their productions, yet what do we know about the people who created them? Our knowledge of many of these ancient civilizations, some of which existed up to one hundred thousand years ago, is quite limited. In fact, written history reaches back only a few thousand of years. Even in Egypt, where the documents go back the furthest, we have only the vaguest ideas of history before 1600 B.C.E. Despite our lack of concrete knowledge concerning many of these cultures, the wonders left to us hold clues about those who made them. 10

Something that we know for certain is that even the ancients were fascinated by ideas of beauty. In fact, the study of "aesthetics," the study of beauty and taste in art and architecture, has its roots in Greek philosophy. The Greek philosophers, Plato and Aristotle, both attempted to describe the nature of beauty—what is beautiful and why. 15

 Discussing Ideas Discuss the questions with a group.

Can you name several ancient societies? Have you ever visited areas where these peoples lived? Have you visited museums where art or artifacts from them are exhibited?

Setting the Context

▲ Egyptian ruins

Previewing the Passage Discuss the questions with a group.

What do you know about the Egyptian pyramids? What is the name of the largest?

Reading Read the passage.

The Wonders of Ancient Egypt

The Great Pyramid of Cheops, which is the last remaining of the Seven Wonders of the World, is among the most important historical structures on Earth. It is a structure that has captivated people for centuries. Though the pyramid has been damaged over the centuries, it still has a beauty and magnificence that inspires and awes visitors.

This magnificent pyramid was built for Cheops, who was pharaoh around 2585 B.C. Cheops, whose name comes to us from Greek, was actually known as the Pharaoh Khufu. He reigned for less than 25 years, and most of these years may have been spent in the construction of this grand pyramid.

Discussing Ideas Discuss the questions with a partner.

Approximately when was the Great Pyramid built? Why do you think it was built? What else do you know about it?

▲ The Great Pyramid of Cheops, which is located on the plateau of Giza

Grammar Structures and Practice

A. Introduction to Adjective Clauses

An adjective (or relative) clause is one type of dependent clause.
- An adjective clause modifies a noun or pronoun or occasionally a whole sentence.
- An adjective clause usually comes immediately after the word(s) that it modifies.
- In some cases, a prepositional phrase may come between a (pro)noun and an adjective clause.
- There are several types, as shown below.

4.1 | Adjective Clauses

Types of Clauses	Relative Pronouns	Examples
Subject	*that, which, who*	Archaeology is a subject **that is very interesting**.
Object	*that, which, who(m)*	It is a subject **which I would like to study**.
Possessive	*whose*	Dr. Jenkins, **whose class meets today**, is an expert.
Time and Place	*when, where*	Does the class meet at a time **when you can attend**?
Quantity	quantity + *of* + *which* or *whom*	I saw three classes, **one of which was boring**.

B. Restrictive Versus Nonrestrictive Adjective Clauses

Adjective clauses are divided into two basic types: restrictive and nonrestrictive. The type of adjective clause determines whether or not commas are used.
- No commas are used in restrictive clauses.
- Commas are used with nonrestrictive clauses.

4.2 Restrictive Versus Nonrestrictive Adjective Clauses

Structures	Explanations	Examples
Restrictive Clauses	A restrictive adjective clause explains *which* people, places, things, or ideas: not everyone or everything. It limits the (pro)noun that it modifies to only what is described in the clause. No commas are used.	The students **who passed the class** will take the next level. There is only one museum **that is open on Sundays**.
Nonrestrictive Clauses	Nonrestrictive clauses do *not* define or identify the word(s) they describe. A nonrestrictive adjective clause adds interesting information about a (pro)noun. It does *not* explain *which* people, places, or things. Nonrestrictive clauses generally include adjective clauses that modify proper names (John, etc.), nouns that are unique (the sun, etc.), and nouns preceded by demonstratives (*this*, *these*, etc.). Commas are used to set off these clauses. *That* cannot be used.	Imhotep, **who built Joser's Pyramid**, was worshipped after his death. We visited this pyramid, **which is located near Cairo**. The moon, **which appears in many ancient drawings**, was an ancient symbol of fertility.

In some cases, a particular adjective clause can be either restrictive or nonrestrictive. It can either identify or give extra information.

- The type of clause depends on the speaker's / writer's point of view.
- Commas (with nonrestrictive clauses) and no commas (with restrictive clauses) also help indicate the type of clause.

Compare the following sentences:

4.3 Clauses with Multiple Meanings

Types of Clauses	Explanations	Examples	Meanings
Restrictive Clause	This adjective clause identifies *which* sister (the one in Bishop) I am talking about. No commas are used. In spoken English there is no pause before or after the clause.	My sister **who lives in Bishop** teaches in a high school.	I have more than one sister. However, I'm talking about one sister in particular.
Nonrestrictive Clause	This adjective clause gives extra information about my sister (she lives in Bishop). Commas are used. In spoken English, pauses are likely before and after the clause.	My sister, **who lives in Bishop**, teaches in a high school.	I have only one sister; by the way, she lives in Bishop.

1 **Practice** Underline the adjective clauses in the sentences below and circle the nouns that they modify. Add commas where necessary.

Example Ten miles west of Cairo stands the manmade (plateau of Giza,) which overlooks the Nile Valley from a height of 130 feet.

1. In all, ten pyramids of varying sizes stand on Giza, but the one which archaeologists have studied the most is the Great Pyramid.

2. This pyramid was named after the pharaoh Cheops who supposedly ordered it to be built.

3. The Great Pyramid which is as tall as a 40-story modern skyscraper is made up of more than two and a half million blocks of limestone and granite.

4. These blocks which came from an area about 20 miles to the east weigh from two to 20 tons a piece.

5. The Great Pyramid contains more stone than all the cathedrals, churches, and chapels that have been built in England since the time of Jesus.

6. The Great Pyramid's base which is perhaps the most impressive feature would cover 13 acres or seven blocks in New York City.

7. The huge piece of land on which the pyramid sits was made level to within a fraction of an inch.

8. Modern engineers who have studied the structure are astounded by the problems which were involved in building the pyramid.

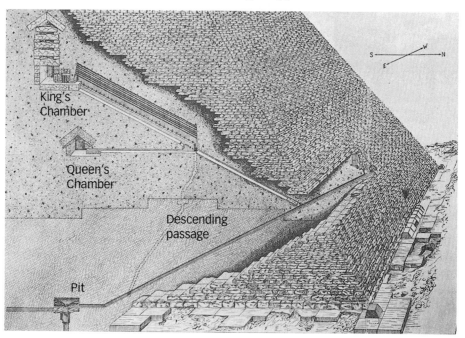

▲ The Great Pyramid

Cultural Note

Pyramid Power

In 1973, Patrick Flanagan, a respected researcher and inventor, claimed that the Great Pyramid of Giza had supernatural powers. According to Flanagan, the Great Pyramid and any other pyramid structure with the exact relative dimensions could act as electronic antennas that focused unseen energy. Food placed under a pyramid frame was supposed to develop increased nutrition; knives put under a pyramid were said to become sharper. Over 1.5 million copies of Flanagan's book were sold, and soon people in many parts of the world began using pyramids around the house. Some even started wearing pyramid hats, believing that this sharpened their mental powers. Today, pyramid power is thought to be nonsense.

2 **Practice** Add the adjective clause to each sentence that follows. If the clause is nonrestrictive (only gives extra information), add punctuation. If the clause is restrictive (defines or identifies the noun it follows), do not add punctuation.

Example which are located near Cairo

There are thousands of pyramids in the world, but the pyramids _which are located near Cairo_ are perhaps the most famous monuments in the world.

The pyramids of Giza, _which are located near Cairo_, are perhaps the most famous monuments in the world.

1. where the pyramid stands

The place _____ is almost perfectly level.

The plateau of Giza _____ is almost perfectly level.

2. who majored in Egyptian architecture in college

My brother _____ visited Giza in 1985. (I have only one brother.)

My brother _____ visited Giza in 1985. (I have three brothers.)

3. whose ancient name was Thebes

The famous Temple of Karnak is located near a town _____.

The famous Temple of Karnak is located in Luxor _____.

4. who was to become the world's most famous archaeologist

In 1922, Howard Carter _____ uncovered the tomb of Tutankhamen across the Nile from Karnak.

In 1922, the man _____ uncovered the tomb of Tutankhamen across the Nile from Karnak.

5. which warned "Death will slay with his wings anyone disturbing the pharaoh"

While Carter and his men were opening this tomb, they came upon a curse

_____ .

While Carter and his men were opening this tomb, they came upon the curse of Tutankhamen _____ .

6. who were present at the tomb's opening

Not one of Carter's 20 men _____ believed that his life was in danger.[1]

Carter's 20 men _____ believed that his life was in danger.

_____

[1] Within five years, 13 of these men, none of whom was over 50 years old, had died suddenly of either an unidentified virus or heart failure.

▲ King Tutankhamen's death mask

3 **Practice** The following passage has many adjective clauses, but it does not include commas with the nonrestrictive clauses. First, read the passage silently. Underline the adjective clauses. Add commas around adjective clauses when you feel they are necessary.

Then read the passage aloud or listen as your teacher reads it aloud. Does the oral reading of the passage match your punctuation of it? Remember that in spoken English, a pause is likely before (and after) a nonrestrictive clause. The first adjective clause is done as an example.

The Wonders of King Tutankhamen

What do kings and queens "take with them" at death? What are these powerful people, <u>who have possessed incredible riches on Earth,</u> buried with? What are some of the riches that have been found in their tombs?

Of the tombs that have been found in Egypt, the tomb of King Tutankhamen has been our greatest source both of knowledge and treasure. What was buried with King Tut who had one of the richest graves that has ever been found? Who was this king?

King Tut who probably reigned only nine or ten years was a little known pharaoh. His tomb which had been covered over by the tomb of another pharaoh remained hidden for centuries. Only once or twice had the tomb been robbed. The robbers of King Tut's grave who had made small tunnels into the tomb left thousands of objects behind. When Tutankhamen's tomb was found in 1922, it was probably still filled with most of the objects which had been placed there at the time that the young king's funeral was held around 1300 B.C.E.

In the tomb were artifacts that included art, jewelry, statues, furniture, and even a chariot! The burial chamber housed much more than just King Tut's coffin which was actually four coffins one inside the other. There were hundreds of gold objects, and some of these were covered with precious stones that had been carefully inlaid. One of the most beautiful objects was a type of crown that is also called a diadem. This diadem which was on the head of the mummified king was probably worn by King Tut while he was alive, too. Perhaps the most famous object that was found in the tomb was King Tut's death mask which still covered the mummy. In all, thousands of artifacts accompanied this young pharaoh in death.

Using What You've Learned

4 **Discussing Superstitions** Do you believe that the Egyptian curse could have caused the death of the men who opened the tomb of King Tutankhamen? Do you have any superstitious beliefs? (For instance, in the United States and Canada, many people believe that black cats can cause bad luck.) What are some of the superstitious beliefs in your culture? In small groups, share information about things in your culture that are associated with good and bad luck. Be sure to include information about colors, numbers, and animals. After you've finished your discussion, choose one member of the group to give a summary to the entire class.

Setting the Context

Previewing the Passage Discuss the questions with a group.

What do you know about the Mayans of the past? Of today's Mayans?

Reading Read the passage.

Wonders of Central America

Who were the Mayans, the people who built complex cities and majestic temples in Central America? What happened to this amazing civilization, whose total collapse came suddenly around 900 C.E.?

Earliest evidence of the Mayan civilization dates to over 4,000 years ago. The Mayan culture developed in independent but loosely linked city-states that were located over much of Central America, from the Yucatan to modern Honduras. The culture flourished during its Classic Period, which spanned about 700 years. The Classic Period was the glory period of the Mayans, whose accomplishments included a highly complex writing system, advanced mathematics with the concept of zero, astrological calendars of astonishing accuracy, and massive constructions of astonishing beauty.

Then came the collapse. Around 900 C.E., the southern Mayans abandoned their cities. The northern Mayans were absorbed by another society, the Toltec, by C.E. 1200, and the Mayan dynasty ended, although some outlying city-states continued until the Spanish Conquest in the 1500s.

The Mayan empire no longer exists, but the Mayan people still populate areas where they once ruled. Today, over one million Mayans live in Chiapas, which is a state in southern Mexico. In total, about five million Mayans are spread throughout Mexico and Central America.

 Discussing Ideas Discuss the questions with a partner.

Civilizations seem to go in cycles of growth and development and then disintegration and decline. Can you name other great civilizations that eventually collapsed? What caused their collapse?

Grammar Structures and Practice

A. Clauses with *Who, Which,* or *That*

The relative pronouns *who, which,* and *that* may replace the subject of a simple sentence in order to form an adjective clause.

- In restrictive clauses, *who* or *that* can refer to people, but *who* is preferred. *Which* or *that* can refer to animals or things, but *that* is preferred.
- In nonrestrictive clauses, only *who* or *which* can be used. *That* is not possible.

4.4	Clauses with *Who, Which,* or *That*: Replacement of Subjects	
Structures		**Examples**
Restrictive *who* or *that* *that* or *which*	**Simple Sentences**	**The man** was named Stephens. **He** found the ruins.
	Complex Sentence	The man **who (that) found the ruins** was named Stephens.
	Simple Sentences	The **pyramid** is El Castillo. **It** is the most famous.
	Complex Sentence	The pyramid **that (which) is the most famous** is El Castillo.
Nonrestrictive *who* *which*	**Simple Sentences**	I read about **Stephens. He** was a very interesting character.
	Complex Sentence	I read about Stephens, **who was a very interesting character**.
	Simple Sentences	We visited **El Castillo. It** is at Chichén Itzá.
	Complex Sentence	We visited El Castillo, **which is at Chichén Itzá**.

1 Practice Make the second sentence in each pair of sentences into an adjective clause using *who, that,* or *which* to combine it with the first. Add commas where necessary.

Example Mayan ruins can be found from southern Mexico to Honduras. These Mayan ruins range from crumbling walls to full cities.
Mayan ruins that (which) range from crumbling walls to full cities can be found from southern Mexico to Honduras. (no commas)

1. John Lloyd Stephens was from the U.S. He discovered Mayan ruins in the 1840s.

2. The man was an American lawyer and explorer. He discovered Mayan ruins in the 1840s.

3. The famous Pyramid of Kukulcan is located at Chichén Itzá. Chichén Itzá was the capital of the Mayas of the Yucatan.

4. The Pyramid of Kukulcan is a magnificent structure. The Pyramid of Kukulcan is also known as *El Castillo*.

5. Tikal is located in the Tikal National Park. This park is a 575 sq. km. preserve with thousands of ruins.

6. The central city of Tikal had about 3,000 buildings. Tikal was about 16 sq. km.

7. Tikal was first explored in 1881 by Alfred Maudslay. Maudslay was an English archaeologist.

8. Tulum was a fortress-like port. The port was established by the Maya for its vast trading network.

9. The temple at Tulum has a small arch. The arch frames the rising sun at dawn on the winter solstice[1].

10. Copan has the best-preserved of the ancient ball courts. Copan was one of the largest Mayan cities.

11. Copan has amazing examples of Mayan hieroglyphs. The hieroglyphs include the longest stone inscription in the western hemisphere.

12. The museum has amazing examples of hieroglyphs. The hieroglyphs came from many central American sites.

---

[1] *winter solstice* in the Northern Hemisphere, usually December 22, which has the shortest day and the longest night

▲ The ruins at Tikal

B. Clauses with *Whose*

Whose may replace a possessive noun, pronoun, or adjective in the subject of a simple sentence in order to form an adjective clause.

- *Whose* may be used to refer to people, animals, or things.
- *Whose* may be used in both restrictive and nonrestrictive clauses.

4.5 Clauses with *Whose*: Replacement of Subjects

Structures		Examples
Restrictive *whose*	**Simple Sentences**	Kings employed **priests. Their** job was to keep written records.
	Complex Sentence	Kings employed priests **whose** job was to keep written records.
Nonrestrictive *whose*	**Simple Sentences**	We read about **John Stephens. His** book on the ruins became famous.
	Complex Sentence	We read about John Stephens, **whose** book on the ruins **became famous.**

2 **Practice** Make the second sentence into an adjective clause and use *whose* to combine it with the first. Add commas when necessary.

Example   The Mayan writing was in the form of hieroglyphs. Their inscriptions were made on stone and wood.

The Mayan writing was in the form of hieroglyphs whose inscriptions were made on stone and wood.

1. Many Mayan pyramids are still covered by the jungle. The jungle's humid climate continues to damage the ruins.

2. Archaeologists have explored many sites. Their ruins have deteriorated.

3. At some sites, archaeologists found books. The books' pages were filled with hieroglyphics.

4. A great accomplishment of the Mayans was their writing system. Its inscriptions were in hieroglyphics.

5. The Mayans were ruled by kings. The stories of the kings were written in manuscript books called *codexes*.

6. The bark of fig trees was used to make these books. Their pages were inscribed and then folded together and placed in royal tombs.

7. The Mayans had a well-organized society. The Mayans' kings had absolute power.

8. The Mayans had developed a complex system of books. Their books' primary purpose was to record the transition of power from king to king.

3 **Practice** Central America is a beautiful land filled with exotic birds, animals, and plants. Use the cues below to describe some of them. Use *whose, that,* or *which* to make adjective clauses from the sentences in the column on the right. Combine these with the cues from the column on the left to form new sentences.

Example: *1. The boa constrictor is a snake whose size and ability to crush its prey make it a dangerous predator.*

Animal / Plant	Cues
1. boa constrictor / snake	Its size and ability to crush its prey make it a dangerous predator.
2. coral snake / snake	It is small and highly poisonous.
3. mangroves / salt-water loving trees	They grow tightly intertwined at the edge of the sea.
4. jaguar / spotted feline	Its size and ferocity make it feared throughout the region.
5. ocelot / spotted leopard-like cat	Its snout is flexible.
6. ceiba / large tree	It is home to many species of plants such as orchids and reptiles such as iguanas.
7. orchids / plants	These plants don't have roots and live on the branches and trunks of trees.
8. iguana / large reptile	It is found throughout Central and South America.
9. tapir / large, stout mammal	Its habitat extends from Texas through South America.
10. black howler / monkey	It is one of the largest primates in the Americas.
11. spider monkey / golden brown monkey	Its tail is often longer than its body.
12. agouti / rodent	It is short-haired, short-eared, and similar to a rabbit.
13. caiman / fierce crocodile	It lives in tropical areas in the Americas.
14. quetzal / large tropical bird	Its bright red, green, and white feathers gave Mexico its national colors.
15. toucan / bird	It has a gigantic but lightweight bill.

▲ An ocelot

▲ A spider monkey

▲ A toucan

C. Anticipatory *It* with Adjective Clauses

Anticipatory *it* is often used with adjectives to place more emphasis on the word or phrase modified by the adjective clause.

4.6	Anticipatory *It* with Adjective Clauses	
Explanation	**Examples**	
	Simple Sentences	**Anticipatory *it* + Adjective Clauses**
The verb in the adjective clause is singular or plural depending on the complement of the main clause.	Hernando Cortez led the Spanish conquest of Central America.	**It** was Hernando Cortez **who led the Spanish conquest of Central America.** **It** was Hernando Cortez **who was leading the Spanish conquest of Central America.**
	Did an environmental disaster cause the end of the Mayan empire?	Was **it** an environmental disaster **that caused the end of the Mayan empire?**

4 **Practice** Rephrase the following sentences to begin with *It* and to include adjective clauses.

Example Cortez conquered much of Central America.
It was Cortez who conquered much of Central America.

1. European diseases killed thousands of Mayans.

2. Catholic missionaries burned all but four of the sacred Mayan bark-paper books.

3. John Lloyd Stephens wrote about his travels in Central America.

4. Stephens published *Incidents of Travel in Central America, Chiapas, and Yucatan* in 1841.

5. The English artist Frederick Catherwood drew amazing pictures of the ruins covered by jungle growth.

6. The Mayans created the Sun Stone, an elaborate calendar.

7. The Mayans invented the concept of zero.

8. Mayan geometric architecture amazed archaeologists.

9. The Great Ball Court at Chichén Itzá has amazing acoustics.[1]

10. The famous conductor Leopold Stokowski spent four days trying to understand the acoustics of the Great Ball Court at Chichén Itzá.

---

[1] *acoustics* ability to carry sound

Chichén Itzá

The Yucatan is a peninsula. It juts into the western Caribbean Sea. The Yucatan is the site of many impressive Mayan ruins. Many of the ruins are amazing, but it is Chichén Itzá. Chichén Itzá is perhaps the most amazing. Chichén Itzá was the most important city in the peninsula from the 10th to 12th centuries. 5

Chichén Itzá is filled with structures. These structures are beautiful and awe-inspiring. For example, at Chichén Itzá there is an impressive ball court. Its acoustics are phenomenal. In fact, the acoustics of the Ball Court still baffle[1] scientists and musicians. Scientists and musicians have spent long hours analyzing its construction. Dominating the ruins is the famous 98-foot-tall El Castillo pyramid. El Castillo is the most impressive monument in Chichén Itzá. El Castillo is a masterpiece of Toltec-Maya architectural design and genius. 10

---

[1]*baffle* bewilder, be very difficult for a person to understand

5 **Practice** Rewrite the passage above by changing some sentences into adjective clauses and combining them with other sentences. Do not try to combine every sentence. Sometimes more than one adjective clause can be added to one sentence. Add all necessary punctuation.

▲ El Castillo

▲ The Ball Court at Chichén Itzá, whose acoustics are astounding. A whisper from one end can be heard clearly at the other end 500 feet away. The sound waves are unaffected by wind direction or time of day.

Using What You've Learned

6 **Writing Definitions** With a partner, write definitions for three or more of the following terms. Then add three more interesting words and write definitions for them. Make the definitions as clear and thorough as possible. Finally, write a couple of your best definitions (not the words) on the board. See if the class can guess which words you are defining.

Example   pyramid *a four-sided figure whose sides slope upward and meet at their uppermost point*

architecture	predator
art	prey
astrologer	priest
astronomer	rectangle
habitat	ruins
justice	solstice
knowledge	square

▲ The Parthenon

Previewing the Passage Discuss the questions with a group.

This picture shows one of the world's most famous ruins. Where are these ruins located? When did this civilization flourish? Can you name another great ancient civilization?

Reading Read the passage.

The Legacy of Ancient Greece

The ancient Greeks were some of the most adventurous and creative people who have lived on Earth. In ancient times, their civilization spread far beyond the small country we call Greece today. In the late fourth century B.C.E., Alexander the Great and his armies conquered territory from Egypt in the west to India in the east.

Ancient Greece was a collection of independent communities or "city-states." The city-state of Athens, which we usually think of first, was the largest, but it was not "the capital." There was no capital and no central government in ancient Greece.

5

The independence that ancient Greeks enjoyed helped to shape the way that they lived and thought. The ideas that these people developed eventually spread widely. For example, it was the Greeks who taught the Romans to write, paint, build, and even organize government.

10

Even today we can see the profound effect that Greek people and Greek ideas have had. Drama, athletics, philosophy, and democracy are not only named from words that stem from Greek; they are concepts and activities that the ancient Greeks developed.

15

 Discussing Ideas Discuss the questions with a partner.

What else do you know about the ancient Greeks? Have you studied classic literature or concepts of art and architecture? Have you studied philosophy? Share your experiences with your classmates.

Grammar Structures and Practice

A. Clauses with *Whom, Which,* or *That* (1): Replacement of Objects

The relative pronouns *whom, which,* or *that* may replace the object of a simple sentence in order to form an adjective clause.

- In restrictive clauses that refer to people, *who(m)* or *that* can be used, or the relative pronoun can be omitted. *Whom* is preferred in formal English, however.
- In restrictive clauses that refer to animals or things, *which* or *that* can be used, or the relative pronoun can be omitted.
- In nonrestrictive clauses, only *who(m)* or *which* are possible, and they cannot be omitted. The examples are in order of most to least formal.

4.7 Clauses with *Whom, Which,* or *That*: Replacement of Objects

Structures		Examples
Restrictive *whom* or *that*	Simple Sentences	The artists lived centuries ago. Historians credit them for the statues.
	Complex Sentences	The artists **whom historians credit for the statues** lived centuries ago. (formal) The artists **who historians credit for the statues** lived centuries ago. The artists **that historians credit for the statues** lived centuries ago. The artists **historians credit for the statues** lived centuries ago.
that or *which*	Simple Sentences Complex Sentences	The figure is of a horse. I like this figure the most. The figure **which I like the most** is of a horse. The figure **that I like the most** is of a horse. The figure **I like the most** is of a horse.
Non-restrictive *whom*	Simple Sentences	Plato was born in Athens around 427 B.C.E. We recognize Plato as one of history's greatest thinkers.
	Complex Sentence	Plato, **whom we recognize as one of history's greatest thinkers,** was born in Athens around 427 B.C.E.
which	Simple Sentences	The Parthenon must be protected. Tourists visit it daily.
	Complex Sentence	The Parthenon, **which tourists visit daily,** must be protected.

---

1 **Practice** In these sentences, change the italicized word(s) to *who(m), which,* or *that*. Then make the second sentence into an adjective clause and combine it with the first. Give all possible combinations and add commas when necessary. Finally, indicate any sentence in which the relative pronoun may be omitted.

Example What inspired the sculptures? Greek artists created these *sculptures* several thousand years ago.

What inspired the sculptures that Greek artists created several thousand years ago?

The relative pronoun can also be omitted: What inspired the sculptures Greek artists created several thousand years ago?

1. The Acropolis was called the "high city." Athenians chose *the Acropolis* for their most important temple to Athena.

2. The place had beautiful views. The Athenians selected *this place* for Athena's temple.

3. Athena was the protector of Athens. The ancient Greeks honored *Athena* as the goddess of wisdom and war.

4. The god was Athena. The Athenians saw *this god* as their protector.

5. The Parthenon was the largest building. The Athenians built *the building* on the Acropolis.

6. The Parthenon is very different from the Parthenon of ancient times. We see *the Parthenon* today.

7. In ancient times, the freshly cut stone would have been brilliant white. Artisans used *the stone* to build the Parthenon.

8. Inside the Parthenon was a gigantic statue of Athena. Artisans made *this statue* out of gold and ivory.

9. Much of the work on the Parthenon was directed by Pheidias. We recognize *Pheidias* as one of the greatest artists in history.

10. The marble friezes[1] showed scenes honoring Athena. Pheidias and his sculptors carved *the friezes* along the four sides of the Parthenon's interior.

---

[1] *frieze* A decorative horizontal band

B. Clauses with *Whom, Which,* or *That* (2): Replacement of Objects of Prepositions

The relative pronouns *whom, which,* or *that* may replace the object of a preposition in a simple sentence in order to form an adjective clause.

- In formal English, the preposition is sometimes placed before the relative pronoun. In this case, only *whom* or *which* can be used.
- If the preposition is placed at the end of a restrictive clause, *that* can also be used, or the relative pronoun can be omitted. This construction is frequently used in conversational English, but it is not preferred in formal written English.
- In nonrestrictive clauses, *whom* or *which* must be used.

The following examples are in order of most to least formal.

4.8 Clauses with *Whom, Which,* or *That*: Replacement of Objects of Prepositions		
Structures		**Examples**
who(m)* or *that	Simple Sentences	The gods are depicted in the statues. The Greeks believed in them.
	Complex Sentences	The gods **in whom the Greeks believed** are depicted in the statues. The gods **whom the Greeks believed in** are depicted in the statues. The gods **who the Greeks believed in** are depicted in the statues. The gods **that the Greeks believed in** are depicted in the statues. The gods **the Greeks believed in** are depicted in the statues.
which* or *that	Simple Sentences	The museum has many Greek artifacts. I bought some books at the museum.
	Complex Sentences	The museum **at which I bought some books** has many Greek artifacts. The museum **which I bought some books at** has many Greek artifacts. The museum **that I bought some books at** has many Greek artifacts. The museum **I bought some books at** has many Greek artifacts.

2 **Practice** In these sentences, change the italicized word(s) to *who(m), which,* or *that.* Then make the second sentence into an adjective clause and combine it with the first. Give all possible combinations and add commas when necessary. Indicate any sentence in which the relative pronoun may be omitted. Finally, tell which possibility is most formal.

Example The Acropolis is a rocky hill. Athenians built the Parthenon on *it.*
The Acropolis is a rocky hill on which Athenians built the Parthenon. (most formal)
The Acropolis is a rocky hill that Athenians built the Parthenon on.
The Acropolis is a rocky hill which Athenians built the Parthenon on. (not preferred)
The Acropolis is a rocky hill Athenians built the Parthenon on. (The relative pronoun can also be omitted.)

1. The hill is the highest place in Athens. The Acropolis is located on *this hill.*

2. The Acropolis was the site. The people of Athens built some of their finest temples on *this site.*

3. The Greek gods were thought to reside on Mt. Olympus, to the north. The Athenians built temples for *these gods.*

4. Like the gods, the early Greek rulers also chose to live in high places. The temples were built by *them.*

5. There were three kinds of columns: Doric, Ionic, and Corinthian. Greek architects worked with *these columns.*

6. A good example of Doric columns is the Parthenon. The Greeks used this type of column around *the Parthenon.*

7. Some of what we know about life in ancient Athens comes from pottery. Greek artisans painted beautiful pictures and scenes of everyday life on *pottery.*

8. Ancient craftsmen made and painted this pottery. Little is known about *these craftsmen.*

▲ Doric columns

C. Clauses with *Whose*

The relative pronoun *whose* may replace a possessive in the object or the object of a preposition in a simple sentence in order to form an adjective clause.

4.9 Clauses with *Whose*: Replacement of Objects		
Explanations	**Structures**	**Examples**
Whose may be used to refer to people, animals, or things in both restrictive and nonrestrictive clauses. *Whose* may not be omitted.	**Simple Sentences**	One of Greece's greatest philosophers was Socrates. Plato put Socrates' ideas in writing.
	Complex Sentence with *whose*	One of Greece's greatest philosophers was Socrates, **whose ideas Plato put in writing**.

3 Practice Change the italicized words to *whose*. Then change the second sentence into an adjective clause and combine it with the first. Add all necessary punctuation.

Example Much of the art at the Parthenon was created by Pheidias. Art historians admire *his* sculptures.

Much of the art at the Parthenon was created by Pheidias, whose sculptures art historians admire.

1. Greece is located between Europe and the Middle East. Archaeologists have studied *Greece's* ancient art for hundreds of years.

2. The most famous area in Athens is the Acropolis. Fifth-century Greeks completed *its* buildings in just 40 years.

3. Pleides was in charge of the artistic program at the Acropolis. Scholars know little about *his* life.

4. After 267 B.C.E., a series of invaders conquered Athens. They often stole *its* treasures.

5. The Parthenon was largely destroyed in 1687 during a war between Venice and the Turks. No building has ever equaled *its* precision and beauty.

6. Today millions of tourists visit the Acropolis. Greece has restored *its* buildings.

7. Ancient ruins are scattered in many parts of Greece. Thousands of tourists visit *its* countryside every year.

8. I had a tour book about Greek ruins. I can't remember *the book's* name.

D. Superlatives and Adjective Clauses

Restrictive adjective clauses often follow superlative constructions.

4.10 Superlatives and Adjective Clauses	
Explanations	**Examples**
Adjective clauses can be used to identify superlatives. *The* is generally used with the noun(s) being modified.	Several of **the greatest statues that were originally in the Parthenon** are now in London. Fifty of **the most important statues that were removed** were sold to the British Museum. Some of **the most beautiful statues that we have ever seen** are in the British Museum.

4 **Practice** Using your own ideas, create sentences from the following cues. In your new sentences, be sure to use superlative adjectives and adjective clauses with a perfect tense.

Example   beautiful place / visit

The most beautiful place that I have ever visited is the coast of southern Chile.

1. good book / read
2. amazing artwork / see
3. scary movie / see
4. delicious meal / eat
5. bad meal / eat
6. bad experience / have

7. frightening experience / go through
8. long trip / take
9. pretty painting / see
10. interesting museum / visit
11. boring class / attend

Using What You've Learned

5 **Researching an Ancient City** Ancient cities have fascinated historians and archaeologists for hundreds of years. Choose one of the cities listed below (or any other that you are interested in) as the subject for some library research. Use the Internet, encyclopedias, or other sources to gather information. Then in a one-page paper, summarize what you have found.

- Ankor Wat
- Babylon
- Persepolis
- Tikal
- Troy

Setting the Context

Previewing the Passage Discuss the questions with a group.

Where is Easter Island? What is it famous for? Would you like to go there? Why or why not?

Easter Island

Easter Island is one of hundreds of Pacific islands that were formed from volcanic eruptions thousands of years ago. It is, however, the only one of these islands that carries its own mystique. First, it is isolated: It lies 2,000 miles from the South American coast and 1,400 miles from the nearest inhabited islands. But more importantly, it is a place where a mysterious civilization once flour- 5 ished, leaving behind more than a thousand huge stone statues as testimony to its greatness.

The first Europeans came to the island in 1722, when three Dutch ships landed on Easter Sunday. Since that time, thousands of archaeologists have come to Easter Island to study the great stone statues, some of which weigh 10 over one hundred tons. The archaeologists' work has yielded many answers, but we may never understand all of the history behind these haunting stone faces. Even after a century of study, the written language found on the island has not been deciphered. In addition, no one knows for certain how the stone statues were transported or even why they were built. 15

Discussing Ideas Discuss the questions with a group.

To create and transport these statues must have been extremely expensive in terms of workers and planning. What could lead people to make such a tremendous effort to produce statues? In modern society, are we willing to make such efforts? Can you give any examples?

Grammar Structures and Practice

A. Clauses with *When* and *Where*

When and *where* may be used to form adjective clauses. A variety of possibilities exist.
- In nonrestrictive clauses, only *when, where,* or *which* + preposition is possible.
- In restrictive clauses, *that* or *that* + preposition can also be used. Or, the relative pronoun can be omitted.

4.11 Clauses with *When* and *Where*

Structures		Examples
Restrictive *when* or *that*	**Simple Sentences**	**At the time**, the statues were still standing. The Dutch arrived **then**.
	Complex Sentences	At the time **when (that) the Dutch arrived**, the statues were still standing. At the time **the Dutch arrived**, the statues were still standing.
Nonrestrictive *when*	**Simple Sentences**	**In 1722**, the statues were still standing. The Dutch arrived **then**.
	Complex Sentence	In 1722, **when the Dutch arrived**, the statues were still standing.
Restrictive *where, which,* or *that*	**Simple Sentences**	This is **an island**. An advanced society had flourished **here**.
	Complex Sentences	This is an island **where an advanced society had flourished**. This is an island **on which an advanced society had flourished**. This is an island **which an advanced society had flourished on**. This is an island **that an advanced society had flourished on**. This is an island **an advanced society had flourished on**.
Nonrestrictive *where* or *which*	**Simple Sentences**	This is **Easter Island**. An advanced society had flourished **here**.
	Complex Sentences	This is Easter Island, **where an advanced society had flourished**. This is Easter Island, **on which an advanced society had flourished**. This is Easter Island, **which an advanced society had flourished on**.

1 **Practice** Make the second sentence into an adjective clause and combine it with the first. Use *when* or *where* and add commas when necessary.

Example The statues were built at a time. A mysterious society ruled the island then.

The statues were built at a time when a mysterious society ruled the island.

The relative pronoun can also be omitted: The statues were built at a time a mysterious society ruled the island.

1. Easter Island is a place. A sophisticated society lived there hundreds of years ago.

2. Easter Island is dominated by the volcano, Rano Raraku. Over 600 giant statues were carved in quarries[1] in this volcano.

3. The statues were built during the 16th and 17th centuries. A mysterious society ruled the island then.

4. By 1722, the society that made the statues had vanished. The Dutch visited the island in 1722.

5. On this island, there were only 4,000 inhabitants. The Dutch had gone there in search of supplies.

6. The Dutch left a few days later, recording that the island was a place. Tremendous stone figures stood facing the ocean there.

7. Fifty years later, all the statues were lying face down. Captain James Cook visited Easter Island at this time.

8. Recently, archaeologists have gone to Easter Island. They have used modern machinery there to stand some of the statues upright.

---

[1]*quarry* a place where large pieces of rock can be cut from the earth

B. Nonrestrictive Adjective Clauses and Expressions of Quantity

Expressions such as *one of, all of, none of, the rest of, either of,* and *neither of* may be used to begin nonrestrictive adjective clauses.

4.12 Nonrestrictive Adjective Clauses and Expressions of Quantity		
Explanations	**Structures**	**Examples**
These clauses must include *whom* or *which*, depending on whether an object or person is being described.	**Simple Sentences**	Sailors attacked **the islanders.**
		Three of the islanders were killed.
	Complex Sentence	Sailors attacked the islanders, **three of whom** were killed.
These clauses must be preceded and / or followed by commas.	**Simple Sentences**	**These statues** are world famous.
		Many of them weigh over 20 tons.
	Complex Sentence	These statues, **many of which** weigh over 20 tons, are world famous.
	Simple Sentences	They sailed **two ships.**
		Neither of the ships (neither ship) was safe.
	Complex Sentence	They sailed **two ships, neither of which** was safe.

2 Practice In these sentences, change the italicized words to *whom* or *which*. Then change the second sentence into an adjective clause and add it to the first. Add all necessary punctuation.

Example No one knows for certain how the islanders transported the statues. Most of *them* are located miles from the quarry.

No one knows for certain how the islanders transported the statues, most of which are located miles from the quarry.

1. These huge stones certainly could not have been carried. Several of *them* weigh 20 tons or more.

2. At the peak of production, island engineers were able to create enormous statues. A few of *them* were up to 40 feet tall.

3. A few sculptures were left in the rock quarry. One of these *sculptures* was over 70 feet long.

4. It seems unlikely that the statues were dragged over the land. Much of *the land* is extremely rough.

5. Some archaeologists think that the islanders used huge wooden platforms. They have never found the remains of *these platforms*.

6. The wood for these platforms would have had to come from large forests. None of *these forests* exist on the island today.

7. A number of authors suggest that extraterrestrials moved the statues. Archaeologists totally disregard most of *these authors*.

8. According to the islanders, the finished statues were transported by the island's kings. All of *the kings* had magical powers.

C. Adjective Clauses and Subject / Verb Agreement

In adjective clauses where the subject has been replaced, the form of the verb depends on the noun(s) being modified.

4.13	Adjective Clauses and Subject / Verb Agreement		
	Explanations	**Structures**	**Examples**
Nouns	Use a singular verb in an adjective clause that modifies a singular noun. Use a plural verb in an adjective clause that modifies a plural noun.	**Singular** **Plural**	The **islander** who **was** kidnapped later died. The **islanders** who **were** kidnapped later died.
the only one	Use a singular verb with *the only one* (even though a plural noun follows in the prepositional phrase).	**Singular**	It was **the only one** of the islands that **was** formed by volcanoes.
one of the + plural noun	Use plural verbs with adjective clauses that follow *one of the* + plural noun. The clause modifies the plural noun in the prepositional phrase. In conversational English, a singular verb may sometimes be used.	**Plural**	It is **one of the islands** that **were** formed by volcanoes.

3 **Practice** Select the singular or plural form of the verbs in parentheses. Use formal, written English.

Example The famous Norwegian, Thor Heyerdahl, is one of the many archaeologists who (has/have) studied Easter Island.

1. Thor Heyerdahl was one of the first archaeologists who (was / were) convinced that the people on Easter Island came from South America.

2. He was the only one of his colleagues who (was / were) willing to make the 4,000-mile journey from Peru to Easter Island on a primitive raft.

3. In the 1940s, Heyerdahl was the only scientist who (was / were) able to complete such a voyage.

4. Erich von Daniken is one of the scientists who (has / have) proposed theories about Easter Island's statues.

5. Von Daniken's book *Chariots of the Gods* is one of a few books that (suggest / suggests) that extraterrestrials built the statues.

6. *Chariots of the Gods* is the only one of these books that (has / have) sold over a million copies.

4 **Practice** In the following passage, select the correct form of the verbs in parentheses. Use formal, written English.

The Tablets from Easter Island

Written languages originate only in large, complex societies that (has / (have)) a great deal of information that (need / needs) to be stored. Even the Incas, who
1
(was / were) very advanced, never developed a writing system. It is, therefore,
2
astounding that wooden tablets that (contain / contains) writing (was / were)
3   4
discovered on tiny Easter Island in the 19th century. The writing was in hieroglyphics, and among the characters (was / were) figures of animals which
5
(was / were) unknown on the island.
6

For over one hundred years, scientists worldwide (has / have) tried to decipher
7
the writing. However, any hope of doing this (was / were) probably lost in 1862,
8
when one-fifth of the island's population (was / were) carried off to slavery in Peru.
9
Among the unlucky (was / were) King Mauratu, along with his family, who
10
(was / were) the last of the learned[1] on Easter Island.
11

Political pressure, which (was / were) supplied by France and England,
12
eventually brought the release of the captives. Unfortunately, by that time, over 80 percent (was / were) dead. And the survivors who (was / were) returned to the
13   14
island brought smallpox, which ravaged the natives. Thus, by 1875, the population, which in 1860 (was / were) about 5,000, had shrunk to 600.
15

Of course, these victims did not die alone. With them died knowledge of the oral history and written language that (has / have) not been and perhaps will never
16
be recovered. Today only a few of the tablets (remain / remains); the rest
17
(has / have) vanished.
18

---

[1] *learned* a person (people) having great knowledge. Note that in the adjective form, the word has two syllables and the *-ed* ending is clearly pronounced.

▲ These hieroglyphs on a wooden tablet are believed to have been used by priests on Easter Island to recite ritual chants. The only writing of the Polynesians, these tablets remain undeciphered.

5 **Review** Complete the following sentences with adjective clauses. Add commas when necessary.

Example My favorite ocean is the Pacific which. . . .
My favorite ocean is the Pacific, which <u>has some of the most beautiful islands on Earth</u> .

1. Easter Island is the place where. . . .

2. It had a small population that. . . .

3. We visited the island in the summer when. . . .

4. We arrived in a large boat which. . . .

5. We were traveling with several people most of whom. . . .

6. Our group had five children three of whom. . . .

7. I was talking with one young man whose father. . . .

8. Our group also included an archaeologist whom. . . .

9. He explained many things that. . . .

10. The island is filled with beautiful statues many of which. . . .

Using What You've Learned

6 **Writing an Extended Sentence** Including one adjective clause in a sentence may now be easy for you. But could you include ten? In pairs, test your grammatical skill and creative genius by writing a sentence with one main clause and ten or more adjective clauses. When you are finished, put your sentence on the board and read it to your classmates. Be sure to use each of the following connecting words at least once: *who, whom, that, which, on which, whose, some of whom, where, when, most of which*. Add commas where necessary.

Example *There was an old woman who lived in a house that was on a hill which. . . .*

Warning: This is a once-in-a-lifetime opportunity. Don't ever create a sentence like this again, especially not in a composition. It could jeopardize the mental health of your teacher!

7 **Playing a Memory Game** Test your memory of information from this chapter. Separate into three or four small groups and write ten to 15 questions about people, places, or things discussed in this chapter. Then exchange quizzes with another group. As a group, complete your quiz. To get "credit," your answers must include adjective clauses. Return your quiz to the original group for grading.

Examples

Who was John Stephens?

John Stephens was the American explorer who first wrote about the Mayan ruins in 1841.

Name three items that were found in King Tut's tomb.
Three items that were found in King Tut's tomb were a beautiful diadem, King Tut's death mask, and a chariot.

Setting the Context

 Previewing the Passage Discuss the questions with a group.

Do you recognize the structures shown in the pictures above? Where are they located? Have you ever visited either? Have you visited other amazing antiquities?

Reading Read the passage.

The Most Beautiful Places on Earth

Beautiful structures designed and built over the centuries exist in every corner of the world. A testament to humans' creative forces, these beautiful homes, religious buildings, museums, villages, and cities are found in every culture and every time. However, a few structures of particular splendor stand out.

One example is the Taj Mahal. Built by a grieving emperor as a symbol of   5
eternal love, the Taj Mahal is a structure of striking beauty and symmetry located outside of Agra, India.

Another is Machu Picchu. Near Cuzco in the Andes, Machu Picchu was an exquisite city providing breathtaking views of the surrounding mountains. It also provided the Incan royalty a place to hide from the Spanish Conquistadors.   10

A third example is the spectacular Borobudur temple. Located in today's Indonesia, Borobudur was a spectacular monument to Buddhism filled with sculptures.

Finally, there is the Great Wall of China. Perhaps the most impressive building project in the history of humankind, the Great Wall is the only manmade   15
structure having been seen from outer space with the naked eye.

Discussing Ideas Discuss the questions with a partner.

What buildings come to mind when you think of beauty? List a few large public buildings that you find impressive. What makes them stand out? Now, identify a private home that is particularly beautiful. What is it about this house that makes it special?

Grammar Structures and Practice

A. Introduction to Participial Phrases

A participial phrase is a phrase that includes a present or past participle.

- Participial phrases can be formed from adjective clauses if the relative pronoun is the subject of the adjective clause.
- The time frame of these phrases is determined by the verb in the independent clause or by the general context.

In adjective clauses with verbs in the active voice, eliminate the connecting word and use the present participle of the main verb.

- The present participle is used to replace verbs in a variety of tenses.
- To form the negative, use *not* at the beginning of the participial phrase.
- If the adjective clause is nonrestrictive and has commas, the phrase has commas. Otherwise, it does not.

4.14 Reduction of Adjective Clauses with Verbs in the Active Voice

Structures		Examples
Nonrestrictive	Clause	The Taj Mahal, **which sits on the Yamuna River**, is one of the architectural wonders of the world.
	Participial Phrase	The Taj Mahal, **sitting on the Yamuna River**, is one of the architectural wonders of the world.
	Clause	Shah Jahan's son, **who didn't respect Jahan**, overthrew his father and placed him in prison.
	Participial Phrase	Shah Jahan's son, **not respecting Jahan**, overthrew his father and threw him in prison.
Restrictive	Clause	The emperor **who ruled the Agra region of India at that time** was named Shah Jahan.
	Participial Phrase	The emperor **ruling the Agra region of India at that time** was named Shah Jahan.

1 **Practice** Underline the adjective clause in each sentence. Then change the clause into a participial phrase.

Example The Taj Mahal, which rises from the flat lands along the Yamuna River, is a magnificent complex of buildings.

The Taj Mahal, rising from the flat lands along the Yamuna River, is a magnificent complex of buildings.

1. The Taj Mahal, which sits on the banks of the Yamuna River in northern India, was commissioned by Shah Jahan as a tomb for his wife.

2. The Taj Mahal is a white marble building which shines like a jewel along the Yamuna River.

3. More than 60,000 people visit the Taj Mahal every day, which makes it one of the most popular tourist destinations in the world.

4. The Taj Mahal was built by thousands of craftsmen who worked day and night for 22 years.

5. Highly skilled craftsmen, who included stonecutters, bricklayers, and calligraphers, labored to create this magnificent structure.

6. Brick makers who worked extremely long hours produced thousands of bricks.

7. Elephants and oxen that pulled wagons and sleds hauled tons of marble more than 200 miles to the site.

8. Today, people who visit the Taj Mahal are struck by the beautiful symmetry of its buildings.

▲ The Taj Mahal, built by Shah Jahan in memory of his wife, Mumtaz Mahal

B. Reduction of Adjective Clauses with Verbs in the Passive Voice

Adjective clauses with verbs in the passive voice can also be reduced to participial phrases.

- In adjective clauses with verbs in the passive voice, eliminate the connecting word and *is, are, was,* or *were.*
- If the passive verb is in a continuous tense, *being* + the past participle remain.
- To form the negative, use *not* at the beginning of the participial phrase.
- If the adjective clause is nonrestrictive and has commas, the phrase has commas. Otherwise, it does not.

4.15 Reduction of Adjective Clauses with Verbs in the Passive Voice

Structures		Examples
Simple Tenses	Clause	The Taj Mahal, **which was built by Shah Jahan**, is made of white marble.
	Participial Phrase	The Taj Mahal, **built by Shah Jahan**, is made of white marble.
Continuous Tenses	Clause	The temples **that were being built during this time** had a variety of designs.
	Participial Phrase	The temples **being built during this time** had a variety of designs.
Nonrestrictive	Clause	Today tourists flock to Machu Picchu, **which was discovered by archaeologists in 1911**.
	Participial Phrase	Today tourists flock to Machu Picchu, **discovered by archaeologists in 1911**.
Restrictive	Clause	Some cities **that were not protected by walls** fell to invaders.
	Participial Phrase	Some cities **not protected by walls** fell to invaders.

2 **Practice** Underline the adjective clauses in the following sentences and then change them to participial phrases. Include any necessary punctuation.

Example The Great Wall, which was constructed entirely by hand, goes for thousands of miles across northern and north-central China.

The Great Wall, constructed entirely by hand, goes for thousands of miles across northern and north-central China.

1. The Great Wall of China, which was built for defensive purposes, was begun as early as the seventh century B.C.E.

2. It began when different states that were located in the northern part of China each built its own wall.

3. The walls that were being built by these states were supposed to provide a defense against invaders.

4. These walls probably also served as boundaries that were used to mark different territories.

5. The walls that were being constructed during this era were similar in design.

6. Today's China grew from these different states, which were unified in 221 B.C.E. by the Qin dynasty.

7. China was unified in 221 B.C.E. by the king of the state of Qin, who was called Shi Huangdi or "first emperor."

8. Shi Huangdi, who was known as a strong and ruthless leader, gave orders for the separate walls to be linked.

9. Thus, the numerous walls that were positioned along the northern borders of several Chinese states became one wall, the Great Wall of China.

10. The large numbers of arrowheads that were found near the Great Wall indicate that battles took place nearby.

▲ China's Great Wall, the only structure created by humans that can be seen from outer space with the naked eye

C. Reduction of Adjective Clauses with Verbs in Perfect Tenses

Adjective clauses with verbs in the perfect tenses may be reduced in two ways.

- The verb *have* (*have, has, had*) can be changed to *having,* and the past participle of the main verb is used. *Having* + the past participle are used to emphasize the completion of the activity.
- Or, the verb *have* can be eliminated and the main verb of the clause is changed to a present participle. This use does not stress the completion of the earlier action.
- With clauses in the passive voice, *having* + *been* + the past participle are normally used.
- *Not* (for the negative) and adverbs come at the beginning of the participial phrase.

If the adjective clause is nonrestrictive and has commas, the phrase has commas. Otherwise, it does not.

4.16 Reduction of Adjective Clauses with Verbs in Perfect Tenses	
Structures	**Examples**
Active Voice Clause	The workers, **who had finally finished the temple**, returned to their villages.
Participial Phrase	The workers, **finally having finished the temple**, returned to their villages.
Passive Voice Clause	There are new sections of the Great Wall **that have been discovered recently**.
Participial Phrase	There are new sections of the Great Wall **having been discovered recently**.
Nonrestrictive Clause	Five workers, **who had already been paid**, left for their villages.
Participial Phrase	Five workers, **already having been paid**, left for their villages.
Restrictive Clause	The workers **who had not been paid** refused to continue on the project.
Participial Phrase	The workers **not having been paid** refused to continue on the project.

---

3 **Practice** Underline the adjective clauses in the following sentences and then change them to participial phrases. Add all necessary punctuation.

Example Archaeologists, <u>who have excavated major parts of the ruins of Borobudur</u>, now worry about damage to its porous stone.
Archaeologists having excavated major parts of the ruins of Borobudur now worry about damage to its porous stone.

1. India and Indonesia, which have traded since ancient times, share similarities in history and culture.

2. Priests who had accompanied traders from India stayed in Java and Sumatra and shared Indian knowledge of Buddhism and Hinduism.

3. The rulers of Java and Sumatra, who had been eager for new knowledge and ideas, welcomed Buddhism in their realms.

4. By the end of the seventh century, Sriwijaya, which had become a rich and powerful Buddhist kingdom, built the spectacular Borobudur temple in Central Java.

5. Buddhist temples traditionally consisted of three tiers that had been determined long ago by the Buddha: a square base, a hemisphere, and a pentacle.

6. Borobudur, which had been built on and over a hill, has no inside or roof.

7. The terraces of the monument, which had been constructed in layers up the hillside, were then filled with amazing sculptures.

8. Today, Borobudur, which has been excavated and exposed to rain and heat, is in danger of crumbling.

▲ Borobudur, the stunning Buddhist monument on the island of Java, in Indonesia

D. Placement of Nonrestrictive Participial Phrases

Nonrestrictive participial phrases are reduced from nonrestrictive adjective clauses.

- When a nonrestrictive phrase modifies the subject of the main clause, it is most often placed directly after the subject. However, it can also be placed directly before the subject.

- A nonrestrictive clause is *occasionally* placed at the end of the sentence. This place-ment is used *only* if there is no confusion about which noun the phrase is modifying.

4.17 Placement of Nonrestrictive Participial Phrases

Placement	Structures	Examples
Before or After the Subject	Clause	Machu Picchu, *which is located* high in the Andes, was constructed by the Incas.
	Participial Phrases	Machu Picchu, *located* high in the Andes, was constructed by the Incas. *Located* high in the Andes, Machu Picchu was constructed by the Incas.
At the End of the Sentence	Clause	The Taj Mahal, *which shines* like a jewel on the Yamuna River, is a marble building of majestic beauty.
	Participial Phrases	The Taj Mahal, *shining* like a jewel on the Yamuna River, is a marble building of majestic beauty. *Shining* like a jewel on the Yamuna River, the Taj Mahal is a marble building of majestic beauty. The Taj Mahal is a marble building of majestic beauty, **shining like a jewel on the Yamuna River**.

4 **Practice** Underline the adjective clauses in the following sentences. Change them to participial phrases. Then show all other possibilities for placement of these phrases. Add all necessary punctuation. Finally, discuss with classmates which placement sounds the best and why.

Example India and Indonesia, <u>which have traded since ancient times</u>, share similarities in history and culture.

*India and Indonesia, **having traded since ancient times**, share similarities in history and culture.*

***Having traded since ancient times**, India and Indonesia share similarities in history and culture.*

*India and Indonesia share similarities in history and culture, **having traded since ancient times**.*

1. Shi Huangdi, who was followed out of respect and fear, ordered the building of the Great Wall of China.

2. A new 50-mile section of the wall, which was discovered in northwestern China just a few years ago, had been covered by desert sands for centuries.

3. The Taj Mahal, which shines like a jewel along the Yamuna River, dominates the landscape outside of Agra.

4. Skilled craftsmen, who were working day and night for 22 years, built the Taj Mahal.

E. Appositives

Adjective clauses with the verb *be* can be reduced to phrases by eliminating the connecting word and the verb. These are often called appositives.

- Commas are generally used with appositives.
- Word order can often be changed in appositives.

4.18	Appositives	
Placement	**Structures**	**Examples**
	Clause	Shah Jahan, **who was the fifth emperor of the Mogul Empire**, built the Taj Mahal.
After the Subject	Phrase	Shah Jahan, **the fifth emperor of the Mogul Empire**, built the Taj Mahal.
Before the Subject	Phrase	**The fifth emperor of the Mogul Empire**, Shah Jahan, built the Taj Mahal.

5 **Practice** Reread Exercises 1-3. Find at least ten items where the adjective clauses can be changed to appositives. Add punctuation when necessary, and show all possibilities for placement of the appositives.

Example   More than 60,000 people visit the Taj Mahal every day, which makes it one of the most popular tourist destinations in the world.
One of the most popular tourist destinations in the world, more than 60,000 people visit the Taj Mahal every day.
Every day, more than 60,000 people visit the Taj Mahal, one of the most popular tourist destinations in the world.

6 **Review** Make the second sentence into an adjective clause and add it to the first. Be sure to include commas where they are appropriate. Then decide if the adjective clause can be reduced. If so, give all possible reductions.

Example   South America has many areas. These areas are filled with archaeological wonders.
South America has many areas which are filled with archaeological wonders.
South America has many areas filled with archaeological wonders.

1. Machu Picchu is now very popular with tourists. It is a famous archaeological site in Peru.

2. It's a place. Its history is fascinating.

3. It's located above a river valley in the Andes Mountains. The Inca Indians fled there from the Spanish conquerors.

4. Tourist trains take most foreigners to Machu Picchu. All of these trains are rather expensive.

5. It is also possible to walk to Machu Picchu on a trail. The Incas built this trail hundreds of years ago.

6. I arrived on the train one morning. It was raining then.

7. I climbed the adjacent mountain called Huayna Picchu. Many photographers have captured its beauty.

8. The view of the ruins is spectacular. Climbers have this view of the ruins.

9. Our guide had a bachelor's degree in antiquities. We hiked with him for several hours.

10. Next to the archaeological site there used to be a hotel. We found the hotel very comfortable.

▲ Machu Picchu

Using What You've Learned

7 **Describing a Beautiful Structure** What is the most beautiful structure that you have ever seen? It could be a monument or a statue, a house or a castle, a church, a temple, or a mosque. Write a brief composition about it. Use as much descriptive language as you can. Then share your composition in small groups or as a class. Bring pictures to share, if possible.

8 **Describing a Beautiful Place** Now think about the most beautiful place that you have ever visited. It could be a spot in the mountains or along a river or a beach. Or, it could be a village or a city. Again, write a brief composition about it, using as much descriptive language as possible. Then share your composition with your classmates, again including pictures if you can.

Adjective Clauses and Phrases

Problem areas with adjective clauses and phrases are frequently tested on standardized English proficiency exams. Check your understanding of these structures by completing the sample items that follow.

Remember that . . .

✓ Adjective clauses are generally placed immediately after the word(s) they modify.

✓ Subjects and verbs must agree in number.

✓ *That* may not be used in nonrestrictive clauses.

✓ In formal English, *whom* (not *who*) must be used in object clauses.

Part 1 Circle the best completion for the following.

Example The people ——————————— scientists credit for the work lived centuries ago.

    (A) that   (B) whose

    (C) who   (D) they

1. Our friend Mary, ——————————— was recently promoted, really likes her new position.

    (A) whom   (B) who

    (C) that   (D) who she

2. The ruby-throated hummingbird, ——————————— the most common variety in North America, beats its wings about 50 times per second when flying.

    (A) who   (B) which

    (C) which is   (D) that

3. Today, the Egyptian pyramids are endangered by pollution, ——————————— may destroy them completely.

    (A) the effect of whose   (B) whose its effect

    (C) whose effect   (D) which its effect

4. Dr. Jones, ——————————— at the party, will teach History 225 next semester.

    (A) who we met her   (B) whom we met

    (C) whom we met her   (D) we met

5. It took skilled craftsmen —————————— day and night for 22 years to build the Taj Mahal.

(A) who working   (B) worked

(C) who they were working   (D) working

Part 2 Each sentence has one error. Circle the letter below the word(s) containing the error.

Example   This is Easter Island, where an advanced society had flourished here.
            A   B   C   (D)

1. A variety of economic indicators, some of which is the consumer price index,
                  A   B   C

are used to calculate the rate of inflation.
D

2. In 1923, Howard Carter, who he was to become the world's most famous
                         A   B

archaeologist, uncovered the tomb of the pharaoh Tutankhamen.
                        C   D

3. One of the strongest fibers that it exists on Earth is the silk that spiders use
   A   B   C   D

to create their webs.

4. Stonehenge, a fascinating archaeological site that located in southwestern
                A   B

England, consists of rings of stone arranged in concentric circles.
        C   D

5. Paul Cézanne was one of the painters who was part of the 1874 exhibition
                                     A   B

that would mark the beginnings of Impressionism.
C   D

Self-Assessment Log

Check the things you did in this chapter. How well can you do each one?

	Not Very Well	Fairly Well	Very Well
I can use a variety of adjective clauses appropriately.	❑	❑	❑
I can use a variety of participial phrases appropriately.	❑	❑	❑
I can use appositives appropriately.	❑	❑	❑
I can use singular and plural verb forms appropriately.	❑	❑	❑
I can use commas appropriately.	❑	❑	❑
I can take a test about adjective clauses and participial phrases.	❑	❑	❑
I understand new information about beauty and aesthetics, and I can use new structures and vocabulary to talk and write about related topics.	❑	❑	❑

Transitions

In This Chapter

Adverb Clauses of Cause, Result, and Time

❝Life belongs to the living, and he who lives must be prepared for changes.**❞** — Johann Wolfgang von Goethe

In this chapter, you will study adverb clauses and related structures that show relationships by time, cause, and result. As you study these structures, pay attention to how the focus or main idea of a sentence can change, depending on the choice of connecting word.

Reading Read the following passage. It introduces the chapter theme "Transitions" and raises some of the topics and issues you will cover in the chapter.

Transitions: Evolutionary and Revolutionary Changes

Change, movement, and transition characterize our lives as we grow and age. In addition to our own personal growth and change, we are frequently faced with global changes in technology, culture, religion, economics, and politics.

Some of these changes are radical. Occasionally, the shock waves of their impact are felt globally. This has been true of political revolution. For example, when the American colonies successfully revolted against the British, a wave of revolutions began. Shortly after the American Revolution had ended, the French Revolution erupted. Within less than 25 years, most of Latin America had begun to rebel. Later, these revolutions sparked others. 5

Not all change is dramatic, however. Many changes are more gradual and more subtle. In the same way that we don't notice ourselves aging day to day, it is difficult to notice the evolution of our societies. Yet human history has been a constant progression of development from primitive hunting tribes to sophisticated postindustrial nations. Since our ancestors first organized villages and towns, we have been developing social structures to give solidity to our lives. 10

Today's world is unique in human history because both primitive and highly developed societies live within a few hundred miles of each other. We can actually see revolution and evolution in politics and economics as different countries and cultures experiment with new forms of government, ownership, and production. Changes in family and social structures surround us. Today, change is virtually unavoidable. The world is in a state of continuous transition. 20

 Discussing Ideas Discuss the questions with a partner.

Can you give some specific examples of important changes that occurred during the 20th century? Now that we have entered the 21st century, what further changes can you imagine?

 Previewing the Passage Discuss the questions with a group.

What are some of the physical and mental changes that people go through during their lives, from infancy to old age?

Reading Read the passage.

Personal Transitions: The Stages of Life

As we live our lives, we all face changes that many social scientists consider to be natural stages. Let us take a newborn, Alex, as an example. The first few months of his life will be spent in a limited environment. In fact, he won't develop an awareness of his surroundings or truly enter the world until he's begun to walk and talk. Alex will be spending the next few years discovering the world   5
around him. Later, while he is going through adolescence, his ideas and feelings, as well as his body, will change. His outlook on the world will broaden. When he has passed through his teenage years, he'll face the choices of young adulthood: marriage, family, career. Through the 30s, his life may go smoothly, but yet another "passage" will approach near "midlife," as he reaches his 40s. At that   10
point, time will "speed up," and suddenly, he will find himself in his 60s or 70s, fast approaching the end of his life.

 Discussing Ideas Discuss the questions with a partner.

What are some specific changes that occur to all of us as we go through childhood? What is adolescence? At what age do children become adults? At what age do adults become middle-aged? Elderly?

BLOOM COUNTY   by Berke Breathed

"Bloom Country" by Berke Breathed, 1984.

Grammar Structures and Practice

A. Transitions of Sequence

Transitions of sequence relate a series of events or situations by order of occurrence.

5.1	Transitions of Sequence		
Explanations	**Common Transitions of Sequence**		**Examples**
Transitions of sequence are used to tell the order of events or situations. For example, they are commonly used in storytelling and in descriptions of processes. They may be used with any verb tense and are sometimes followed by a comma.	*first, second,* etc. *now, then, finally* *earlier, later* *afterward* *after that*	*at that time* *at that point* *at the same time* *meanwhile*	**First,** a child will start smiling at its mother. **Later,** it will learn to tell the difference between people. **After that,** the child will begin to imitate its parents' actions.

1 **Practice** The following are steps in a child's process in learning to talk. Form complete sentences from the cues and put them in order using transitions of sequence (*first, second,* etc.). Then confirm the correct order with your teacher.

Example *First, the child will respond to human voices.*

1. uses his or her first words
2. begins to use tenses
3. makes sounds such as *ma, mu, dar,* and *di*
4. understands and uses up to 50 words
5. responds to human voices
6. puts two words together
7. responds to his or her name
8. combines words into short sentences

2 **Practice** How does a child first begin to walk? How does a child learn to read? Think of these or other processes related to a child's development. Briefly describe the steps involved. Create at least six sentences for one or more of the following processes. Or, choose one or more of your own. Use transitions in your description.

1. learning to walk
2. learning to climb stairs
3. learning to eat by oneself
4. learning to read
5. learning to write
6. learning to ride a bicycle
7. learning to swim
8. learning to skip

B. Time Clauses with the Present, Present Perfect, and Future Tenses

Time clauses may be used to relate actions or situations that will occur at the same time or in a sequence in the future. In general, the focus of these sentences will be on the main clause.

5.2	Time Clauses with the Present, Present Perfect, and Future Tenses	
Connecting Words	**Explanations**	**Examples**
After	In sentences referring to the future, the verb in the dependent clause can be in the simple	**After** the baby finishes eating, we'll put her to bed.
As soon as	present or the present perfect (*not* the future). The present perfect emphasizes the completion of the first action.	I'm going to bathe her just **as soon as** she's finished eating.
Before	The verb in the main clause uses a future form (*will* or *be going to* + verb) or a modal auxiliary (*can, may, should*, etc.).	I'll give her a bath just **before** I put her to bed.
Once		**Once** she goes to bed, we may be able to relax a little.
Until	The expressions *as soon as* and *just* + conjunction (*just before, just after*) give the strongest sense of immediacy. *Once* emphasizes the idea of *not before*.	You shouldn't put her to bed **until** her hair has dried.
When		**When** her hair has dried, you can put her to bed.
As	The present continuous is often used in dependent clauses with *while* or *as*. It emphasizes an action in progress.	
While		I might read her a story **while** I am waiting for her hair to dry.

Note: See Chapter 3 for more information on sentence focus. See Chapter 9 for information on phrases using these connecting words.

C. Time Clauses with the Simple Present and Future Perfect (Continuous) Tenses

Time clauses may be used to specify a time in the future when something will be happening or will be finished. In general, the focus of these sentences will be on the main clause.

5.3 Time Clauses with the Simple Present and Future Perfect (Continuous) Tenses		
Connecting Words	Explanations	Examples
With Clauses		
By the time (that) **When**	The future perfect (continuous) is sometimes used to emphasize that an action or situation will be completed before a certain time in the future. It is most often used in sentences with *by* or *when*. In general, the focus of the sentence is on the main clause.	**By the time** she gets up, she will have slept for ten hours. **When** she wakes up, her father will already have left for work.
With Phrases		
By + time **Within + time**	The prepositions *by* and *within* are often used with the future perfect tenses. *By* is used with an ending time, and *within* is used with a period of time.	**By 9:00**, she will have been sleeping for several hours. **Within an hour**, she will have finished her breakfast.

D. Placement and Punctuation of Adverb Clauses and Phrases

Most adverb clauses and phrases come either before or after the main clause in a sentence.

5.4 Placement and Punctuation of Adverb Clauses and Phrases

Structure	Explanations	Placement
Clauses of Time	Most adverb clauses and phrases come either before or after the main clause in a sentence.	**When the baby wakes up,** we'll leave. We'll leave **when the baby wakes up**. (no comma)
Phrases of Time	Phrases can also come at different points within the sentence, depending on the meaning and the length of the phrase. Commas are generally used after introductory phrases and clauses, but in the case of short phrases, the comma is frequently omitted.	**After the baby's nap,** we'll leave. We'll leave **after the baby's nap**. (no comma)
Other Time Expressions	Other time expressions, such as adverbs of frequency, often come between a subject and verb or between verbs, but they almost never come between a verb and its direct object.	**Before the baby's nap,** we **almost always** feed him. **Before the baby takes a nap,** we **almost always** feed him. We **almost always** feed the baby **before his nap**. (no comma) We **almost always** feed the baby **before he takes his nap**. (no comma)

---

3 **Practice** Imagine that you are taking a course in child development. You are listening to a lecture about Jean Piaget. Complete the lecture by using the present continuous, simple present, present perfect, future continuous, or simple future form of the verbs in parentheses. When more than one tense is appropriate, show all possibilities.

Jean Piaget

Today's lecture is on Jean Piaget, a French-Swiss child psychologist who developed detailed theories on children's intellectual growth. I ___will begin___ (begin) by giving you a brief overview of Piaget's theories. To do so, I _____ the probable development of my newborn niece Molly.
1 (follow)
After I _____ you the overview, we _____ at
2 (give)   3 (look)
each stage in more detail.

What changes _____ 4 (do) Molly _____ 5 (go through) during the next few years? According to Piaget, Molly _____ 6 (start) to recognize and organize her environment while she _____ 7 (be / still) an infant. During her first 18 months, she _____ 8 (develop) a basic model of her world.

By the time Molly _____ 9 (be) 18 months old, she _____ 10 (begin / actively) to expand, organize, and reorganize her view of the world. She _____ 11 (do) this through play and through exploring and experimenting. However, she _____ 12 (not be) able to understand things beyond present situations until she _____ 13 (reach) age four or five. Within another year or two, a notable change _____ 14 (take) place. Molly _____ 15 (start) to understand the basic concepts of distance, length, number, speed, mass, and groupings. By the time that Molly _____ 16 (turn) seven or eight, she _____ 17 (enter) Piaget's stage of "concrete operations": Her thinking _____ 18 (develop) structured patterns. At the same time, she _____ 19 (prepare) for the final development: abstract thought. For Molly, like other children, thinking abstractly _____ 20 (involve) the ability to imagine and hypothesize. As Molly _____ 21 (go) through this stage, she _____ 22 (develop) all the basic skills for adult thinking.

▲ Child psychologist Jean Piaget

4 Practice Following are notes taken during a child development class. Use the notes to help you form sentences with the cues. Use appropriate verb tenses. You will see that articles, pronouns, and so forth are missing in the notes. Be sure to add them when necessary.

Examples   when / be born
              When a baby is born, it cannot move by itself.
              When a baby is born, it will have reflexes. . . .
              by the time / two months
              By the time the baby is two months old, it should be able to focus its eyes. . . .

1. by the time / two months
2. before / four months
3. when / 20 weeks
4. until / 24 weeks
5. before / eight months
6. by the time / eight months
7. after / ten months
8. when / 12 months

Child Development 210—Monday lecture

Physical Development, First Year

1.   At birth

 a. is immobile

 b. has reflexes like sucking, finger grasping

2.   Up to 2 months

 a. is able to focus eyes and coordinate stares

 b. begins to lift head

3.   By 4 months

 a. can raise head

 b. can turn head and eyes to speaker

4.   4–6 months

 a. 20 weeks: opens hand to grasp an object

 b. 24 weeks: grasps objects with palm and fingers but not thumb

5. *6–8 months*

    a. 7 months: sits alone without support for a short time

    b. 8 months: stands with minimum help; grasps objects using thumb and index finger

6. *10–12 months*

    a. walks with help

    b. stops putting objects in mouth

5 **Practice** Use your own knowledge and experience to follow an infant through its life. Name the child and then use *when, before, after, until,* or *by the time that* and a variety of present and future verb tenses. Write at least eight sentences describing his or her development. Be sure to include emotional, educational, and physical factors.

Example *When she's 13, she'll be entering high school. By age 16, she'll have finished two years of high school.*

1. age 6	**3.** age 16	**5.** age 40
2. age 13	**4.** age 25	**6.** age 65

Using What You've Learned

6 **Talking about the Future** Visit your resident "fortune teller." In groups, take turns role-playing a fortune teller and telling the secrets of the future to your classmates. Ask and answer questions using time clauses.

Example A: Will I be married by the time I am 25?

        B: By the time you're 25, you will have been married three times!

        A: How many children will I have?

7 **Talking and Writing about the Future** Much of our development centers on our outlook for the future and the goals that we set. Take a more serious look at your own future and your own goals. In groups, discuss your futures. Then write a short paragraph about your plans. You can use the following ideas to help you.

1. What are your immediate plans for the future (educationally, etc.)?

   a. Before I. . . .

   b. I'll . . . until. . . .

   c. Once I have. . . .

2. What are your long-term goals (lifestyle, career, etc.)?

   a. When I. . . .

   b. After I. . . .

   c. By (the time that). . . .

3. What do you think you will be like when you are 35?

   a. After I. . . .

   b. When I. . . .

   c. By (the time that). . . .

8 **Discussing the Process of Aging** Aging is a major change that will eventually affect us all. How do you view aging? Someone once said that age is a state of mind. When and how do we age? Is aging a slow, steady process that is inevitable for all of us? Or is aging a series of abrupt stages that each of us goes through? Do physical, emotional, and intellectual maturing and aging occur at the same time and at the same rate?

Separate into small groups and spend ten to 15 minutes discussing your ideas. Share stories from your life and the lives of your friends and family as well as your thoughts on the general topic of aging. Take notes as you talk. Then use your notes as the basis for a short composition on one aspect of the aging process.

Previewing the Passage Discuss the questions in a group.

What is the theory of evolution? Does it apply only to biological development, or do societies evolve just like plants and animals? Give reasons for your opinion.

Reading Read the passage.

Social Transitions: The Evolution of Societies

When we hear the word *evolution*, we usually think of the biological theory of change. Evolution is also a theory of social change. It is a theory of gradual change in societies over time. Whenever living things exist in groups, their societies tend to become more complex and specialized. This is true of some animals, and it is especially true of humans. Although some groups develop more slowly than others, all human societies follow the same basic pattern. Once a hunting society has established a permanent base in one area, its people begin to use agriculture for their food needs. When food surpluses develop, the population grows and commerce begins. As villages grow into towns and cities, technological innovation is introduced. This pattern is true of almost every time and place in history.

Discussing Ideas Discuss the question with a partner.

According to the passage, what is the basic pattern of development in human societies?

Grammar Structures and Practice

A. Time Clauses with the Simple Present, Present Continuous, and Present Perfect Tenses

Time clauses can relate situations or actions that occur at the same time or in a sequence.
- These activities may occur habitually, or they may be occurring at the moment of speaking.
- A present form of the verb is used in each clause. In general, the focus of these sentences will be on the main clause.

5.5	Time Clauses with the Simple Present, Present Continuous, and Present Perfect Tenses	
Connecting Words	**Explanations**	**Examples**
When **Whenever**	*When(ever)* means "any time." *When(ever)* joins two actions that happen one immediately after the other. *When(ever)* comes before the earlier action.	**When** people work together, they can accomplish much more. **Whenever** people work together, they can accomplish much more.
After **As soon as** **Before** **Once** **Until** **Up to the time (that)**	*After, as soon as, before, once, until*, and *up to the time* join actions that occur in sequence. Either the simple present or the present perfect may be used in the dependent clause. The present perfect emphasizes the completion of the action.	People settle in one area **before** they develop agriculture. **Once** more people have begun to farm, a food surplus often develops. There is very little commerce **until** the village has grown.
As **While**	*As* and *while* join two actions that happen at about the same time. The present continuous can be used in the dependent clause to emphasize the continuous nature of the activity. It may also be used in the main clause.	**As** the population increases, a need for technology develops. **While** villages are growing, their societies become more complex. In some societies, **while** men are hunting, women are working in the fields.
Since	*Since* joins a previous action or situation to an action or situation in progress. The main clause is in the present perfect (continuous). The dependent clause may be in the simple past or the present perfect. When both clauses are in the present perfect, both activities are still in progress.	Societies have been developing **since** the first humans walked on the Earth. Commerce has increased steadily ever **since** people have lived in communities.

1 **Practice** Complete the following by using appropriate forms of the verbs in parentheses. Choose between the simple present, simple past, and present perfect tenses or add the modal auxiliaries *can* or *must*.

The Evolution of Communities

Whenever living things ————— *work* ————— in groups, they
                                          (work)

————————————— a better chance for survival. When life forms
        1 (have)

————————————— for defense and for labor, they ————————————
        2 (cooperate)   3 (be)

much more successful than life forms working independently. In fact, since

life ————————— , it ————————————— into more and more com-
        4 (begin)   5 (develop / steadily)

plex communities. This ————————————— true of the tiniest cells as well
                                        6 (be)

as the most complicated humans.

Before living things ————————————— successfully in groups, they
                                    7 (function)

————————————— systems for communication. Interestingly, even com-
        8 (develop)

munities made up of the most primitive organisms —————————————
                                                                        9 (have)

communication systems. For example, microscopic plants and animals

————————————— by chemical signals. Insects, birds, and animals
        10 (communicate)

————————————— a variety of sounds and movements when they
        11 (use)

————————————— to communicate. However, no group —————————————
        12 (need)   13 (develop / ever)

a communication system that compares to human language.

2 **Practice** Work with a partner. Combine the following pairs of sentences using the connecting words in parentheses. Change or omit words and add punctuation when necessary. When you have finished, discuss any difference in meaning or focus in each pair of sentences.

Example Communities can develop. Living things have a form of communication. (whenever, when)

Communities can develop whenever living things have a form of communication.

Communities can develop when living things have a form of communication.

Focus: The focus of both sentences is "The development of communities."

Meaning: The meaning is basically the same, but whenever gives more emphasis to the idea of "anytime."

1. People must have a way of producing a steady supply of food. They can build settled communities. (before, after)

2. People build villages. Large marketplaces develop. (after, when)

3. Commerce expands. Cities develop. (as, as soon as)

4. The social structure of a village remains generally constant. The population reaches 500 to 1,000. (until, up to the time that)

5. Towns grow in size. Their character changes drastically. (when, once)

6. The population grows to several thousand. The impersonal nature of a city begins to develop. (after, as soon as)

3 **Practice** According to anthropologists, there is a continuum of community development ranging from the village at one extreme to the large city at the other, and certain characteristics are typical of these communities in every part of the world.

Use information from the two charts that follow to form at least eight sentences with *as, once, when,* and *whenever*. Add *more* or *less* when necessary.

Examples diversified

Whenever towns grow in size, they become more diversified.

heterogeneous
As more and more people move to a city, the city becomes more heterogeneous.

religious
When the population increases, it becomes less religious.

Characteristics of Villages and Cities

Village
isolated
homogeneous
deeply religious
tightly organized
uniform group behavior

City
mobile
heterogeneous
secular
loosely organized
individualistic lifestyles

Strength of Social Structures

- family stability maternal or paternal authority

- participation in social institutions (churches, etc.)

- respect for elders

- specific guidelines for behavior

Stronger

Weaker

Village   City

4 Practice Jacob Bronowski wrote *The Ascent of Man,* an account of human development. In his book, he emphasized the fundamental role of settled community life in the development of civilization. He said, "Settled agriculture creates a technology from which . . . all science takes off. [It began] . . . when man first harnessed a power greater than his own, the power of animals. Every machine is a kind of draft animal—even the nuclear reactor."[1]

Consider the following developments in human history. What have these inventions or discoveries led to? Use the following list and add your own information to form at least five sentences with *since*.

_____

[1]Jacob Bronowski, *The Ascent of Man* (Boston and Toronto: Little, Brown, 1973), p. 74.

Beginning Points	Further Developments
invention of lenses and mirrors	eyeglasses, contact lenses, cameras, microscopes, telescopes
invention of the steam engine	railroads, turbines, steamboats, internal combustion engine, cars, airplanes, rockets
discovery of electricity	batteries, lights, telegraphs, radios, telephones, televisions, computers
splitting of the atom	atom bomb, nuclear reactors
invention of the silicon chip	smaller micro-, mini-, and mainframe computers; handheld organizers; microelectronic devices

Example   steam engine / railroads
Since the steam engine was invented, we've developed trains and built railroads throughout the world.

1. _____

2. _____

3. _____

4. _____

5. _____

Using What You've Learned

5 Describing Effects of Social Changes Most observers agree that people living in large cities are somehow different from people in less crowded areas. From your experience, what seems to happen to people when they leave the countryside and move to the city? What happens when cities become overcrowded? Write a brief essay about population movement and growth. Write from a general standpoint, but be sure to add specific examples from your own experience, too.

6 Describing Effects of Technological Changes Look at Activity 4 again. Can you think of other landmark discoveries or inventions? Can you tell what changes or breakthroughs have occurred since that invention or discovery was made? Try to create a chart similar to the one in Activity 4, using information from your own field or from another area that interests you. Then in pairs or small groups, take turns explaining the effects and ramifications of the discoveries or inventions that you've listed.

7 Giving a Sequence of Events Rube Goldberg was an American artist who created some of the most amazing inventions possible (at least on paper!). In small groups, look at the following example of his inventiveness and follow it step by step.

FLAME FROM LAMP (A) CATCHES ON CURTAIN (B) AND FIRE DEPARTMENT SENDS STREAM OF WATER (C) THROUGH WINDOW—DWARF (D) THINKS IT IS RAINING AND REACHES FOR UMBRELLA (E), PULLING STRING (F) AND LIFTING END OF PLATFORM (G) — IRON BALL (H) FALLS AND PULLS STRING (I), CAUSING HAMMER (J) TO HIT PLATE OF GLASS (K) - CRASH OF GLASS WAKES UP PUP (L) AND MOTHER DOG (M) ROCKS HIM TO SLEEP IN CRADLE (N) CAUSING ATTACHED WOODEN HAND (O) TO MOVE UP AND DOWN ALONG YOUR BACK.

Example *After the lamp has set the curtains on fire, the firefighters arrive. . . .*

Now, as a group, try to come up with your own invention. Make a drawing of it and explain it in writing using a variety of time clauses and transitions. You might invent a machine to do your homework, wake you up in the morning, etc. Finally, present your inventions to your classmates.

Setting the Context

▲ Martin Luther King, Jr., delivers his famous speech, "I Have a Dream," Washington, D.C., 1963

Previewing the Passage Discuss the questions with a group.

What is charisma? In your opinion, who are some of the most charismatic individuals alive today? What is the source of their charisma?

Transitions: The Role of Leaders

Every movement needs a leader if it is to be truly successful. At various times and places, people have risen up to demand political, social, economic, or religious change. Yet, because of human nature, most of these movements have died as soon as a few of the demands have been met. To unite people in a long-term struggle toward a goal, charismatic leadership is necessary. Because people are usually more willing to fight or die for a leader than an idea, the success of a movement often depends on the personality of one individual.

5

 Discussing Ideas Discuss the questions with a partner.

What charismatic leaders do you know of from the past? What social, political, economic, or military movements did they lead? Were they successful?

Grammar Structures and Practice

Adverb Clauses and Related Structures of Cause and Result

Both phrases and clauses may be used to relate ideas and to show cause and result.

- Transitions may also be used to relate effects or results to their causes.
- In general, the focus of the sentence will be on the main clause(s).
- See Chapter 3 for more information on compound and complex sentences.

5.6 Adverb Clauses and Related Structures of Cause and Result

Connecting Words	Explanations	Examples
With Clauses		
Because Due to the fact (that) Since	*Because* is used in both spoken and written English. *Due to the fact (that)* is more formal, while *since* is less formal.	**Because** he was a dynamic speaker, crowds always gathered to hear Martin Luther King, Jr. Crowds always gathered to hear Martin Luther King, Jr., **due to the fact that** he was a dynamic speaker. Crowds always gathered to hear Martin Luther King, Jr., **since** he was a dynamic speaker.
With Phrases		
Because of As a Result of Owing to Due to	These expressions are followed by a noun (phrase) or a gerund. They may *not* be followed by a subject and verb (a clause).	**Because of** his dynamism, crowds always gathered to hear Martin Luther King, Jr. People still admire Dr. King **due to** his amazing accomplishments.
With Transitions		
As a Consequence As a Result Consequently Hence Therefore Thus	Like other transitions, these may begin sentences, or they may be used with a semicolon to join two clauses. In either case, a comma is used after the transition. Note that *hence* and *thus* are used primarily in formal English. The other transitions, especially *as a result*, are used in both formal and informal language.	Gandhi was respected throughout India; **as a result,** he was given the name Mahatma, meaning "Great Lord." Gandhi was respected throughout India. **Thus,** he was given the name Mahatma, meaning "Great Lord."

Note: Traditionally, *due to / due to the fact* were used only adjectivally, to refer to nouns, not actions. They were used to show cause, not reason. Today *due to / due to the fact* are widely used to show either cause or reason. Compare:

The violence at the demonstration was *due to* (caused by) the police.

The police at the demonstration started the fight *due to* (because of) their frustration.

---

1 **Practice** Quickly reread the passage "Transitions: The Role of Leaders" on page 219. Then answer these questions.

1. Look at *because of* and *because* in the passage. What follows *because of*? What follows *because*?

2. What words or phrases could be used instead of *because of* and *because*?

2 Practice Change the following sentences from compound to complex or from complex to compound. Use appropriate connecting words or transitions. Pay close attention to the punctuation. Then compare each original and new sentence. What is the focus of the original sentence? What is the focus of the new sentence?

▲ Simón Bolívar, known as "the Liberator"

Example Because Spain was taken over by France in 1808, a crisis of authority developed in Spanish lands in South America.

Spain was taken over by France in 1808; as a result, a crisis of authority developed in Spanish lands in South America.
Original focus: the crisis of authority in Spanish lands
New focus: on both the French takeover of Spain and the crisis of authority in Spanish lands

1. Because many South Americans had resented Spanish rule for years, they were prepared to revolt.

2. South America had a mixture of races and interest groups; therefore, it was difficult to unite all the people.

3. Since the various colonial groups disagreed with each other, one leader was needed to unite all of these groups.

4. Simón Bolívar ultimately became the political and military leader of the South Americans because he was able to appeal to a wide variety of people.

5. Bolívar could see beyond immediate problems and conflicts; thus, he was able to develop long-term military and political goals.

6. Bolívar directed the war for independence throughout much of South America; as a result, he is known today as "the Liberator."

7. Bolívar believed in a united South America; hence, he struggled to unite the region into one nation—"Grand Colombia."

8. Because individual groups and regions had their own interests in mind, most leaders resisted the idea of one nation in South America.

9. Even without political or cultural differences, South America would be difficult to unite since most areas are separated into distinct regions by major geographic boundaries such as the Amazon and the Andes Mountains.

10. Many geographical, political, and cultural differences exist among regions in South America; for this reason, one united country has never been achieved.

3 Practice Fill in the blanks with *because, since, because of, due to,* or *as a result of.*

Example _____*Because*_____ his brother was killed by the tsar's[1] government, Lenin decided to become a professional revolutionary.

1. _____ his personal strength and dedication, Lenin succeeded in shaping a new Russia.

2. _____ Lenin was totally dedicated, he risked his life to overthrow the tsar.

3. _____ his political position, Lenin went into exile.

4. _____ he needed a way to send information back into Russia, Lenin established the newspaper *Iskra* ("the spark").

5. _____ his power of persuasion, various groups began to support Lenin and his party, the Bolsheviks.

6. _____ Lenin believed that only violent revolution could succeed, he fought against more moderate groups.

7. _____ careful planning and the economic and political confusion in Russia, Lenin and the Bolsheviks took control of the government in October of 1917.

8. _____ his role in shaping post-tsarist Russia, Lenin still "sparks" strong feelings—both negative and positive—even 80 years after his death.

---

[1]*tsar* king, male ruler of Russia before 1917

4 Practice Rephrase each pair of sentences in italics three different ways, using the connecting words indicated. Then explain the focus of each new sentence.

Example *Some leaders are charismatic. They are able to unite large, diverse groups of people.*
therefore
Some leaders are charismatic; therefore, they are able to unite large, diverse groups of people.
Focus: equal focus on both clauses

because
Because some leaders are so charismatic, they are able to unite large, diverse groups of people.
Focus: ability to unite large, diverse groups

because of
Because of their charisma, some leaders are able to unite large, diverse groups of people.
Focus: ability to unite large, diverse groups

1. Benito Juarez spent much of his life working to unite Mexicans. He believed Mexicans should govern their own country, and he resisted attempts by Napoleon III of France to conquer Mexico.

Juarez opposed rule by foreigners. He led his people in fighting against the French invasion of Mexico in 1862.

because   because of   consequently

2. Mustafa Kemal (Ataturk) led the four-year revolution that formed Turkey in 1923. He then devoted his last 16 years to religious, economic, and educational reform.

Kemal dreamed of modernizing Turkey. He toured every part of his country to learn the conditions and needs of the people.

therefore   because   because of

3. Martin Luther King, Jr., was a black minister who fought segregation[1] through nonviolent protests.

Martin Luther King, Jr., was successful in uniting people in nonviolent protest. He attracted worldwide attention and was awarded the 1964 Nobel Peace Prize.

thus   since   as a result of

4. A missionary born in Yugoslavia, Mother Teresa devoted much of her life to helping the desperately poor in the slums of Calcutta. In later years, she extended her work to help the poor in many countries worldwide.

Mother Teresa worked tirelessly for the hungry, the homeless, and the sick. She was awarded the Nobel Peace Prize in 1979.

because   owing to   thus

---

[1]*segregation* forced separation of people based on race

5 Practice Combine each of the following sets of sentences in at least two ways. Use connecting words such as *as a result, because, because of, consequently, due to, since, that, therefore, which, who,* or any others that are appropriate. You may also reword some of your sentences to eliminate the connecting word(s). After you have finished, discuss the focus or main idea of each sentence. Explain how the focus may change when a different connecting word is used (or when it is eliminated).

Example In the early 20th century, Great Britain ruled an enormous empire. This empire included India.

In the early 20th century, Great Britain ruled an enormous empire that (which) included India.
Focus: Great Britain and its empire

In the early 20th century, India was part of an enormous empire (that was) ruled by Great Britain.
Focus: India as part of the British empire

1. Mohandas K. Gandhi was an Indian. This man worked for change through nonviolent means.

2. Gandhi believed that violence only produced more violence. Gandhi devoted his life to the idea of nonviolent resistance.

3. Gandhi developed numerous techniques for nonviolent disobedience of the British. These techniques included economic boycotts, national strikes, and refusal to pay taxes.

4. Most governments expect revolutionaries to be violent. Gandhi's nonviolent techniques confused the British.

5. Gandhi and his followers had incredible inner strength. They were able to protest nonviolently.

▲ Mohandas K. Gandhi

6. Many Indians didn't understand the idea of nonviolent resistance. These Indians found it difficult to follow Gandhi's example.

7. Nonviolent protests required tremendous self-control (which many protesters didn't have). Many large demonstrations became violent.

8. Gandhi persevered in his struggle against British rule. He became a worldwide symbol of nonviolent resistance.

Using What You've Learned

6 **Describing Leaders** What charismatic leaders have led movements in your country or culture? What movements did they lead and why? What were the results of their efforts?

Choose a leader from your culture and write a brief composition about this individual. If necessary, do some research on the Internet or at the library in order to complete your composition. As you write, try to include as many of the following connecting words as possible: *as a result, because, because of, consequently, due to, therefore,* and *thus.*

7 **Doing Public Speaking** Practice your oratory (speaking) skills. Choose a topic of interest to you, perhaps one related to a recent composition you have done, and create a speech. Try to keep your speech under five minutes. Then practice orating! Practice your speech at least ten times. You may do most of your practicing alone, but at least two practice sessions should be with an audience, with a friend or a teacher, for example. Finally, deliver your speech to your class. Your teacher may critique you or may ask classmates to critique you to help you hone your public-speaking skills.

Part 4 | Clauses and Related Structures of Time: Past Time

Setting the Context

Previewing the Passage Discuss the questions with a group.

Which occurred first, the French or the American Revolution? What were some of the causes of these revolutions?

Reading Read the passage.

Countries in Transition: Revolution

Change comes in many forms, but perhaps the most radical form is revolution. While many causes underlie revolutions, economics is a factor in virtually every one. The world's first two political revolutions, the American and the French, illustrate the role of economics in political uprisings and demands for social change.   5

In the case of the American Revolution, the main issue was taxation. In 1763, Great Britain completed a series of expensive wars against France that had lasted for 70 years. Soon after peace had been declared, the British Parliament instituted a number of taxes to make the American colonists help pay for these wars. These new taxes deeply angered the American colonists, and they   10
began protesting as soon as Britain tried to collect the taxes. By 1775, fighting had begun. On July 4, 1776, the American colonies declared independence, and by 1783, the first free nation in the New World—the United States of America— had been founded.

As the American Revolution was taking place in the 1770s, the social unrest 15
leading to the French Revolution was building. France in the 1700s was sharply divided along class lines. The wealth and power of the upper class were increasing steadily. At the same time, the middle class was paying most of the taxes,

and the large peasant population was becoming desperately poor. The economic situation worsened in the 1780s, and in 1789, revolution erupted. By the time it ended six years later, over 40,000 people had been executed, and a new social order was in place.

20

▲ March 5, 1770, "Boston Massacre": British soldiers attack an angry crowd of American colonists. One of the first to be killed was a black man named Crispus Attucks, shown in the center.

 Discussing Ideas Discuss the questions with a partner.

Since these two major revolutions, what other revolutions have taken place around the world? Have the causes always been similar?

Grammar Structures and Practice

A. Time Clauses and Phrases with the Simple Past and Past Perfect Tenses

Phrases and clauses may be used to relate an earlier time or event to a later one. The past perfect (continuous) is generally used for the earlier event; it can never be used for the later event.

- In conversational English, the simple past is often substituted for the past perfect in sentences with *before, after,* or *until.*
- In written English, writers sometimes change to the simple past after the time frame has been established by the past perfect (continuous).
- In clauses with *when,* however, the past perfect must be used if there is a distinct difference in time. Compare: *It began to rain when I went outside.* (The rain began at that time.) *It had begun to rain when I went outside.* (The rain had begun earlier.)

5.7 Time Clauses and Phrases with the Simple Past and Past Perfect Tenses

Connecting Words	Explanations	Examples
With Clauses		
Before	*Before, by the time (that)*, and *until* + the simple past are used with the later event.	**Before** the war began, American colonists had already been rebelling for several years.
By the time (that)	Adverbs such as *already, just, hardly, recently*, and *scarcely* are frequently used with the past perfect tense.	**By the time (that)** the British brought more troops to the colonies, the rebellion had already spread.
Until		**Until** the British instituted these taxes, most colonists had been loyal to England.
After	*After* + the past perfect is used with the earlier event.	Fights broke out **after** the British had passed a series of taxes.
When	In some cases, **when** can be used with either the earlier or later event. In sentences with the past perfect and simple past tenses, **when** + the simple past is usually used with the later event.	The rebellion had already started **when** the British passed new taxes.
With Phrases		
By	Remember that phrases do not include a subject / verb combination.	**By** 1776, colonists had already been rebelling for several years.
Up to within		**Up to** 1776, they had not officially declared war.
within		**Within** seven years, the Americans had gained independence.

B. Time Clauses and Phrases with the Simple Past and Past Continuous Tenses

Clauses and phrases can be used to relate actions or situations that happened at approximately the same time.

5.8 Time Clauses and Phrases with the Simple Past and Past Continuous Tenses

Connecting Words	Explanations	Examples
With Clauses with the Simple Past		
When (whenever) **As soon as**	*When* and *as soon as* express a direct connection in the time of occurrence of the two events. *Whenever* may be used to describe habitual occurrences.	Fighting began **when** the British tried to collect more taxes. **As soon as** colonists learned of the fighting, rebellion spread rapidly.
With Clauses with the Past Continuous (and Simple Past)		
As **While** **When**	The past continuous is often used with *while* or *as* to describe past actions in progress. *When* may be used with a clause in the simple past to describe an event that occurred while another event was in progress.	**While (As)** colonists in Boston were fighting the British, colonists in the South were organizing an army. Colonists in Virginia were planning their own revolt **when** they received news of the fighting in Boston.
With Phrases		
During	*During* is used with phrases. Remember that phrases do not include a subject / verb combination.	They received news of the fighting in Boston **during** a meeting of anti-British colonists.

---

1 **Review** Complete the following sentences by using the simple past, past continuous, or past perfect forms of the verbs in parentheses.

Example In 1620, after they _____*had spent*_____ (spend) five months on the Atlantic Ocean, 143 British colonists, or "Pilgrims," _____*landed*_____ (land) in Massachusetts.

1. While these Pilgrims _____ (settle) in Massachusetts, they _____ (face) many problems.

2. There _____ (be) unfriendly Indians; the winter _____ (be) severe; there _____ (not be) enough food.

3. During the first year, many of the Pilgrims _____ (die).

4. However, before the year _____ (be) over, the Pilgrims

_____ (sign) a treaty with the local Indians.

5. After a few years, they _____ (produce) more food than they could eat.

6. In the years after the Pilgrims _____ (arrive), the population _____ (grow) steadily.

7. In 1650, 52,000 colonists _____ (live) in North America.

8. By 1759, the population _____ (increase) to over one million.

9. Colonial development _____ (continue) until the revolution _____ (start).

10. When the American Revolution _____ (begin), there _____ (be) 13 colonies.

2 **Practice** The information that follows is listed in chronological order. Combine each pair of sentences using the connecting words in parentheses. Change the verb tense to the past perfect in one of the clauses in each new sentence. Note any cases where the simple past may be used instead of the past perfect without any change in meaning. Remember to omit any repetitious information.

Example The British completed a series of wars against France. The British increased taxes in the American colonies. (soon after)
Soon after the British had completed a series of wars against France, they increased taxes in the American colonies. (The simple past may also be used.)

1. Most of the colonists felt loyal to Britain. The British started taxing the colonies. (until)

2. The British Parliament increased import taxes. American merchants began to rebel. (after)

3. The British started to collect the new import taxes. The colonists began to organize a rebellion. (by the time)

4. Boston was already a center of rebellion for years. The first armed conflict occurred there in March of 1770. (by the time)

5. The fighting around Boston stopped. The British Parliament passed the Tea Act of 1773, another new set of import taxes. (soon after)

6. British soldiers started enforcing the Tea Act. Boston merchants disguised as Indians attacked a British ship. (after)

7. These merchants secretly boarded the British ship. They dumped over 300 chests of British tea into the ocean.[1] (when)

8. The British learned of the dumping of their tea. British soldiers closed Boston Harbor to all trade. (after)

9. Only a few people were killed or injured in the rebellion. The British closed Boston Harbor. (before)

10. The rebellion continued to grow. The first real battles were fought at Lexington and Concord on April 19, 1775. (until)

_____

[1]This event is known as the Boston Tea Party.

▲ The Boston Tea Party

3 **Practice** Reread the first paragraph of the passage "Countries in Transition: Revolution" on page 225 and Exercises 1 and 2. Then create a time line showing the events of the American Revolution. Use the time expressions to help you order the events chronologically. Which happened in a sequence? Which were happening at the same time?

4 **Practice** Combine the following sentences using *while* or *as*. Change at least one of the verbs in each pair to the past continuous.

Example Louis XVI ruled France. The French Revolution began.

While Louis XVI was ruling France, the French Revolution began.
or
The French Revolution began while Louis XVI was ruling France.

1. Louis XVI ruled France. He did little to help the poor.

2. France suffered an economic crisis. Louis XVI nearly bankrupted the country by sending large sums of money to the American revolutionaries.

3. French incomes fell dramatically. Prices seemed to rise daily.

4. Shortages of bread occurred regularly. The price of bread skyrocketed.[1]

5. The wealth of the upper class increased. The life of peasants became steadily worse.

6. Thousands of Parisians searched for work. Unemployed peasants looking for jobs flooded Paris.

7. His people lost their jobs and their homes. Louis XVI relaxed in his palace at Versailles, 30 miles from Paris.

8. Louis XVI stayed in Versailles. He had virtually no contact with the French people.

---

[1]*skyrocket* to go up suddenly and sharply

5 **Practice** Rephrase sentences 1, 2, 4, and 8 from Activity 4. Use *during* and the nouns from the following list. Since you will be forming a phrase, remember to omit the verb.

Example rule

During Louis XVI's rule, the French Revolution began.

1. rule

2. economic crisis

4. bread shortages

8. stay

6 **Practice** Imagine that you have a series of Parisian newspapers from 1770 to 1790. The following might have been some of the headlines. Use the information, listed in chronological order, to form at least ten sentences in the simple past tense with *when*. Because headlines often leave out words, you may have to add articles or other words in addition to changing the verbs.

Example AMERICAN COLONIES DECLARE WAR ON BRITAIN!
FRANCE'S KING LOUIS XVI SUPPORTS COLONIES!
When the American colonies declared war on Britain, France's King Louis XVI supported the colonies.

1. COST OF SUPPORTING AMERICANS IS TOO HIGH

2. LOUIS XVI MUST INSTITUTE NEW TAXES

3. UPPER CLASSES REFUSE TO PAY!

4. LOUIS XVI IS FORCED TO CALL MEETING OF ESTATES GENERAL[1]

5. MEETING BEGINS MAY 5, 1789

6. FIRST MEETING IN 174 YEARS!

7. DELEGATES OF THIRD ESTATE DEMAND DISCUSSION OF GOVERNMENT REFORM

8. FIRST AND SECOND ESTATES REFUSE TO DISCUSS CHANGES

9. THIRD ESTATE DECLARES ITSELF THE NATIONAL ASSEMBLY! [2]

10. LOUIS XVI RECEIVES NEWS OF NEW NATIONAL ASSEMBLY

11. KING FORBIDS NATIONAL ASSEMBLY TO MEET

12. NATIONAL ASSEMBLY IGNORES KING!

13. KING ORDERS TROOPS TO PARIS

14. SOLDIERS SURROUND CITY!

15. RIOTS BREAK OUT IN PARIS AND THE PROVINCES

---

[1]*Estates General* legislative body that served the king. It had three branches: The First Estate, representing the nobles; the Second Estate, representing the church; the Third Estate, representing everyone else.
[2]*National Assembly* legislative body with powers superceding the king's

7 **Practice** Complete the following paragraph with connecting words such as *after, as, by the time (that), because, because of, before, due to, since, when, while,* or any others that are appropriate. Try to use as many of the connecting words as you can.

The Storming of the Bastille

_____When_____ Louis XVI ordered troops to Paris, the working class organized protests, and the middle-class radicals formed a militia.

_____1_____ workers were protesting in the streets, intellectuals were making plans for action. _____2_____ tensions had built up for several weeks, Paris exploded on July 14, 1789, with the storming of the Bastille.

The Bastille was a 14th-century fortress and prison. _____3_____ political prisoners were usually held there, it was a symbol of royal oppression. _____4_____ Parisian crowds attacked the Bastille, only a few political prisoners were actually being held. However, _____5_____ the military also stationed soldiers at the Bastille, a large amount of gunpowder was stored there. _____6_____ the crowds gathered outside the walls of the prison on July 14, they demanded the gunpowder. _____7_____

the governor of the Bastille had refused to give up the gunpowder, the protestors forced their way into the prison. _____ the crowd entered
8

the courtyard, the governor ordered his soldiers to shoot. _____
9

the shooting stopped, 98 had been killed and 73 wounded. Finally, the governor surrendered. _____ the Bastille's importance as a revolu-
10

tionary symbol, news of its fall sped through France. Today, Bastille Day, July

14, is an important French holiday.

8 Practice Write a paragraph from the information that follows. Combine the
sentences, using connecting words and transitions and omitting repetitious information.
You may want to include some additional information covered in the previous exercises.
Try not to use the same connecting word or phrase twice.

Example May 5, 1789: The Estates General met. It was their first meeting in
over a century. France was near financial disaster.

*When the Estates General met on May 5, 1789, it was the first
meeting in over a century, and France was near financial
disaster. Two months later. . . .*

July 12, 1789: Riots broke out throughout Paris. Louis XVI ordered new troops to
Paris.

July 14, 1789: Angry crowds stormed the Bastille.

October 5, 1789: Over 10,000 Parisians marched to the Palace of Versailles. The
crowds demanded bread. The crowds forced the royal family to return to Paris with
them.

June 20, 1791: King Louis XVI and his family tried to escape to Germany. King
Louis XVI and his family were captured at Varennes. The king and queen were
forced to return to Paris.

April 20, 1792: France declared war on Austria. Austria declared war on France.
Prussia declared war on France.

August 17, 1792: Parisians marched to the Tuileries. Louis XVI lived in the Tuileries then. The Tuileries was the royal palace in Paris. Parisians believed Louis XVI
was a traitor. Louis's wife, Marie Antoinette, was Austrian. Parisians believed Louis
was helping the Austrians in the war.

August 19, 1792: The revolutionary government took control.

September 20, 1792: The National Convention was formed to replace the Assembly.

September 21, 1792: The monarchy was abolished.

January 21, 1793: King Louis XVI was executed.

October 16, 1793: Queen Marie Antoinette was executed.

9 Practice Think of an important time of change in your country or culture. You may choose a time of political change or a period of social, religious, cultural, or economic change. Answer the following questions about that particular time and the events that occurred then.

1. What had the general situation been before the period of change? Give a two- to three-sentence description.

2. What particular events led to the change?

3. What changes took place?

4. How did people react while the change was occurring?

5. How have these changes affected your area or culture since then? Give a brief (two- to three-sentence) description.

Example *American music was beginning to change in the 1950s. Elvis Presley and many others had already created rock and roll. Then, in the early 1960s, the Beatles arrived in the United States. The country went wild when they arrived, and American music has never been the same.*

Using What You've Learned

10 Describing Holidays Major political events often become national holidays. Bastille Day, July 14, is a national holiday in France. July 4 is celebrated in the United States. September 16 is celebrated in Mexico. Do you have a special holiday that commemorates a major political event in your country or culture? How do people celebrate this holiday? Are there parades? Do people wear special clothing? Is there special food or music to celebrate the day?

Individually or in small groups, prepare a brief presentation on an important holiday in your culture. Give some background information on its origins and explain how it is celebrated.

Setting the Context

Previewing the Passage Discuss the questions with a group.

How do you feel when things change in your life? Do the changes usually result in something better? Worse? Do you think these changes help you learn?

Reading Read the passage.

The Nature of Change

An old proverb says, "There is nothing permanent except change." Change is movement in space and time. The universe is in motion; our atmosphere is in motion; the cells in our bodies are in motion. Change is occurring all around us, and change always involves adaptation.

Humans long for stability and permanence, yet we are repeatedly forced to change and adapt to new circumstances. We do this because we want to survive. Moreover, we adapt so that we can improve our situation. We want not only to survive but also to thrive.

This raises a difficult question. Does adaptation always lead to progress? Is all of this movement and change for the better? Which changes have improved our quality of life? Which changes will give our children and grandchildren better lives? Only time will tell which of the current changes are beneficial for us and for our descendants and which are not.

5

10

Discussing Ideas Discuss the questions with a partner.

Think of three important changes that have taken place in your lifetime. Choose from distinct areas: education, international trade and business, physical health and well-being, political movements, the role of women in society, or technology, for example. In your opinion, how has each of these developments changed the way that we live?

Grammar Practice

1 **Review** Complete the following by using *a, an, the,* or *X* (to indicate that no article is necessary).

History and Change

What is ___X___ history? It's ___the___ story of _____ everything that
                                                            1
_____ humans have experienced. Thus, _____ history of mankind includes
   2   3
everything from _____ first cave dwellers to _____ space travelers of to-
                    4   5
day. It has seen such terrible incidents as _____ use of human beings as
                                               6
property, _____ World Wars I and II, and _____ advent of devastating dis-
            7   8
eases such as _____ Black Plague, _____ influenza of 1918, and _____
                 9   10   11
AIDS. However, history also encompasses _____ development of agricul-
                                           12
ture, _____ Renaissance, _____ emancipation of slaves in much of the
         13   14
world, and _____ ongoing revolution in medical science.
              15

_____ debate as to what lies behind _____ history has raged for more
   16   17
than _____ thousand years. Does _____ history repeat itself again and
        18   19
again as _____ ancient Greeks believed? Is it, instead, _____ result of
            20   21
broad patterns and tendencies that lead humankind on _____ relentless path
                                                        22
towards progress? Or, is _____ history simply _____ arbitrary series of
                            23   24
events over which we have only _____ little control?
                                  25

It is impossible to answer these questions with any certainty. However,
this much is clear. _____ study of history is _____ essential part of _____
                       26   27   28
good education. As _____ President Abraham Lincoln said, "We cannot es-
                      29
cape history." And as _____ famous Spanish-American philosopher and poet,
                         30
George Santayana, noted, "Those who cannot remember the past are con-
demned to repeat it.[1]"

---

[1] George Santayana, *The Life of Reason or The Phases of Human Progress: Reason in Common Sense* 284 (2nd ed., Charles Scribner's Sons, New York, New York 1924 (Appears in Chapter XII, "Flux and Constancy in Human Nature.")

2 Review Numerous political changes have occurred during the last two decades. One major change was the break-up of the former Soviet Union. This exercise examines some of these changes. Combine the following sets of sentences and then rewrite them in paragraph form. Use commas when necessary, and add other information if you wish.

Example 1989 was a year.
This year brought innumerable changes to our globe.
1989 was the year that brought innumerable changes to our globe.

1. In the fall of 1989, the Berlin Wall was torn down.
   It had stood as a physical and psychological barrier between East and West for almost 30 years.

2. A new government was elected in Poland in September 1989.
   It was the first noncommunist government since World War II.

3. The Polish people elected a new type of leader.
   Their leader had been a dedicated communist.

4. It was also in 1989.
   Hungary, the former Czechoslovakia, East Germany, and the former Soviet Union all opened their borders to the West then.

5. Many of the changes had been put in motion decades earlier.
   These changes occurred in 1989.

6. One can see the influence of history on the present.
   The events of 1989 are compared to the events of the 1870s, the 1920s, and the 1940s.

7. Many of the countries had been parts of larger empires years earlier.
   These countries gained freedom in the 1980s.

8. The new borders may remain.
   These borders were created in recent years. The new borders may change again someday soon.

3 Review Where have we humans made progress in recent years? Read the information below gathered from the United Nations and other nonprofit organizations such as the Red Cross and Red Crescent, CARE, and Heifer. Complete the passage by using appropriate forms of the verbs in parentheses. Choose the active or passive voice and add adverbs when indicated. You may also want to add modal auxiliaries. Note cases where more than one answer is possible.

Changes in the Quality of Life

What changes ___*have occured*___ in the past two decades? ___*Have*___
                        (occur)

these changes ___*always meant*___ progress? Consider the following:
                    (mean / always)

Life Expectancy

- In Sri Lanka, life expectancy _____ by 12 years in less than a

1 (increase)
  decade.

- China _____ seven years to life expectancy since 1985. This

2 (add)
  increase _____ smaller than the increase in life expectancy

3 (be)
  that China _____ between 1953 and 1962. During that time,

4 (see)
  life expectancy in China _____ by 13 years.

5 (increase)

- Some of the poorest countries _____ spectacular improve-

6 (make / also)
  ments. For example, Bangladesh and Bolivia _____ child

7 (reduce)
  mortality between 40 and 50 percent.

Hunger

- According to the Food and Agriculture Organization of the United Nations,
  efforts to reduce world hunger by one-half by the year 2002
  _____ short of what people _____ to have

8 (fall)   9 (need)
  basic nutrition. Current statistics _____ that 852 million peo-

10 (show)
  ple worldwide _____ with chronic[1] hunger.

11 (live / still)

- The vast majority of those suffering from hunger (815 million people)
  _____ in the developing world, but nine million (more than

12 (be)
  the total population of metropolitan New York City) _____

13 (live)
  in the world's richest countries.

- Six million children under the age of five _____ every year

14 (die)
  as a result of hunger.

- In any given year, five to ten percent of world hunger _____

15 (come)
  from specific events: droughts or floods, armed conflict, political, social, and
  economic disruptions.

- Good news _____ 16 (exist) , however.

- In East Asia, the number of people who _____ 17 (survive) on less than $1 / day _____ 18 (drop) by almost one-half during the 1990s.

- Brazil's Zero Hunger program _____ 19 (provide) school lunches and other food safety nets for many people.

School Enrollment

- In developing regions worldwide, more than 80 percent of children _____ 20 (attend) primary school. For example, Botswana _____ 21 (double) school enrollment rates in 15 years.

- Literacy _____ 22 (give) cause for celebration because there _____ 23 (be / now) approximately four billion literate people in the world. Many of these _____ 24 (be) children—the hope of the future—because one in six of the world's adults _____ 25 (be / still) illiterate.

- Unfortunately, three-fifths of the 115 million children not in school _____ 26 (be) girls, and two-thirds of the 876 million illiterate adults _____ 27 (be) women. However, the world _____ 28 (make) some progress in recent years. Between 1990 and 2001, the ratio of literate females to males (ages 15 to 24) in developing countries _____ 29 (increase) from 70 to 81 women per 100 men.

- In general, illiteracy and percent of population without any schooling _____ 30 (decline) during the past several decades. For example, the worldwide percent of population without any school _____ 31 (drop) from 36 percent in 1960 to 25 percent in 2000. Among developed countries, illiteracy rates _____ 32 (decrease) from six to one percent, and percent without school decreased from five to two percent.

Illiteracy rates
Population aged 15 years and over

World total	
1970	37
2000	20.3
Developing countries	
1970	52.3
2000	26.4
Developed countries and regions in transition	
1970	5.5
2000	1.4

---

[1]*chronic* continuing; lasting for a long duration

4 **Review** For parts of Asia and Africa, change came suddenly on December 26, 2004, in the form of giant deadly waves. Complete the passage by selecting the correct words in parentheses.

The Indian Ocean Tsunami[1]

Deep under (a / an / the) floor of the Indian Ocean, more than a hundred miles
1
from (a / an / the) coast of the Indonesian island of Sumatra, is the boundary between
2
two of the world's tectonic plates[2]. At this boundary lies a 745-mile trench called
(a / an / the) Andaman-Sumatran Subduction Zone. On December 26, 2004, (a / an / the)
3   4
massive earthquake, (which / whose / where) lasted approximately eight minutes,
5
struck along this trench. Among the strongest earthquakes in recorded history, this
temblor[3] (raises / has raised / raised) the level of the ocean about one centimeter
6
worldwide and even altered the rotation of the planet. More significantly, with its
unimaginable force, the earthquake suddenly thrust the ocean floor upward 65 feet
along the trench, giving birth to a series of tsunamis These deadly waves fanned
out from (a / an / the) site of the earthquake, traveling at speeds of 300 to 600 miles
7
an hour. Thirty minutes after the shaking had stopped, the first tsunami reached
the port of Banda Aceh in Sumatra. (Within / When / Before) a few moments, tens of
8

thousands of people were dead. (Therefore / Otherwise / However), the destruction
9
was only beginning. Over the next seven hours, other parts of Indonesia, Thailand,
Sri Lanka, India, and Africa (was / were / has been) severely hit. These waves,
10
(which / that / where) were only about two feet high while in deep water, reached
11
heights of up to 100 feet before hitting land. (While / Whenever / Before) the
12
destruction was over, more than 275,000 people (were / have been / had been) killed
13
in 12 different countries. 168,000 of them were from Indonesia. 1.6 million people
in all (were losing / have lost / had lost) their homes.
14

---

[1] *tsunami* an unusually large sea wave caused by an underwater earthquake or volcanic
eruption
[2] *tectonic plates* semi-rigid sections of the Earth's crust, according to current theories of the
movement of continents
[3] *temblor* shaking and vibration at the surface of the Earth resulting from underground
movement

5 **Review** Suwannee was 12 years old when the tsunami swept across her village in
Thailand. She lost her parents, her grandmother, several other relatives, and 27
classmates. In the following passage, she is speaking one year after the disaster.
Complete the passage by choosing from these connecting words: *after, and, because,
before, but, however, in addition, moreover, so, therefore, when, whenever, while*. Add
commas and / or semicolons when necessary.

I live with my grandfather in the Bang Muang Temporary Camp. I miss my
parents, _____ *but* _____ I have to go on living. At the camp I attend
school, _____ I go to an after-school center almost every day.
1
_____ I feel sad, I practice traditional dance or listen to mu-
2
sic—especially the favorite songs of my mum and dad. I'm not sad all of the
time. I enjoy talking to my grandfather _____ I like going to
3
school. _____ I am at school, I can learn new things like draw-
4
ing and painting pictures, dancing or working on the computer. Today, my life
is getting a little better.

I remember the day of the tsunami. I was standing by the sea watching my parents' boat come toward the shore just _____ the tsunami

₅

hit. The wave carried the boat to the top and then rolled the boat in it.

_____ I saw that, I thought that they might not survive. I was

₆

very frightened _____ I ran for my life. I wanted to go out to

₇

my mum _____ I couldn't _____ there was

₈ ₉

water everywhere.

Many children are now in centers such as the one Suwannee attends-centers where children find a safe place to play, a library and activities that help provide a normal rhythm to lives turned upside down.

▲ A tsunami survivor

Using What You've Learned

6 **Preparing for Disasters** Imagine that you are 12 years old and that you are experiencing or have just experienced a natural disaster. Write a brief story of the experience—through the eyes of a young child like Suwannee.

7 **Discussing Change** Reread the passage on p. 235, "The Nature of Change," along with the section "Discussing Ideas." Choose one area that you mentioned as important, and decide on one specific change during your lifetime. It might be technology such as the advent of the Internet, or societal changes such as women taking jobs outside of the home, or changes in business such as the free-trade movement. In your opinion, how has each of these developments changed the way that we live? Are these changes positive or negative? Prepare notes or a composition to speak from for a presentation for your class.

Focus on Testing

Review of Problem Areas from Chapters 1–5

A variety of problem areas are included in this test. Check your understanding by completing the sample items that follow.

Part 1 Circle the best completion for the following.

Example   By 9:00, Ned _____ his breakfast.

      (A) has finished   (B) finishing

      (C) had finished   (D) had been finishing

1. _____ the Internet was originally set up, it was for military purposes.

      (A) While   (B) When

      (C) After   (D) By the time that

2. Anne Sullivan _____ Helen Keller when Helen was about seven years old.

      (A) first met   (B) was first meeting

      (C) had first met   (D) met first

3. Before going into the meeting, he stopped to have _____ coffee.

      (A) little   (B) a little

      (C) some of   (D) a few

4. The traditional yurt is a wooden tent _____ has a round roof and is covered with animal skins.

      (A) what   (B) what it

      (C) which it   (D) that

5. A child's brain is one mass, _____ an adult's brain is separated into two hemispheres.

      (A) when   (B) while

      (C) why   (D) how

6. _____ their inability to exercise self-control, some of Ghandi's followers resorted to violence.

      (A) As a result   (B) Because

      (C) Because of   (D) Due

7. It's late. We _____ now.

    (A) should be leave   (B) should be leaving

    (C) should left   (D) should have left

8. George Mallory, _____ had been a member of the 1921 and 1922 Everest expeditions, disappeared on the mountain in 1924.

    (A) who   (B) whom

    (C) that   (D) who he

9. During the Middle Ages, spices, _____ did not grow in Europe, had to be imported from Asia.

    (A) most of   (B) most of which they

    (C) most of which   (D) most of them

10. Molly and Richard _____ lost.

    (A) looking   (B) looks

    (C) has looked   (D) look

Part 2 Each sentence has one error. Circle the letter below the word(s) containing the error.

Example Joe goes to Paris next week, but when I saw him, he hasn't bought his
           A   B   Ⓒ   D
ticket yet.

1. Marco Polo was the first European explorer to enter, live in, and write about
                     A   B
Asia, a land completely unknown to Europe in 13th century.
    C   D

2. Erika must to finish most of her work before she leaves for the evening
             A   B   C
because the report that she is working on is due in three days.
                D

3. After Martin's father was offering to loan him the money, Martin decided to
                  A   B   C
buy a used car.
     D

4. Because her tireless work with the impoverished and the sick, Mother Teresa
   A   B
was awarded the Nobel Peace Prize in 1979.
    C   D

5. Gold has been <u>one of</u> the most prized <u>metal</u> throughout <u>history</u>.
    A   B   C   D

6. Social scientists who <u>have studied</u> Madagascar <u>has found</u> that women tend
                              A   B

to be <u>the</u> most aggressive buyers and sellers in <u>marketplaces</u>.
      C   D

7. <u>Beginning</u> in Arabia in the 600s, the religion <u>we</u> now call <u>it</u> Islam spread
    A   B   C   D

quickly throughout Asia.

8. While Sputnik <u>was launched</u> by the <u>Soviets</u> in 1957, the race to space began
          A   B   C

<u>in earnest</u>.
  D

9. Ms. Jones <u>would like to</u> interview <u>the</u> woman <u>from who</u> we received a résumé
              A   B   C

<u>early</u> last week.
  D

10. English is one of the richest languages in <u>the</u> world, <u>for</u> it <u>is having</u> over
                                       A   B   C

400,000 vocabulary <u>words</u>.
                D

Self-Assessment Log

Check the things you did in this chapter. How well can you do each one?

	Not Very Well	Fairly Well	Very Well
I can use a variety of adverb clauses appropriately.	❏	❏	❏
I can use a variety of adverb phrases and transitions appropriately.	❏	❏	❏
I can use verb forms and tenses appropriately.	❏	❏	❏
I can use appropriate punctuation.	❏	❏	❏
I can take a test about nouns, verbs, modal auxiliaries, articles, conjunctions, transitions, and adjective and adverb clauses and phrases.	❏	❏	❏
I understand new information about personal, social, and global change, and I can use new structures and vocabulary to talk and write about related topics.	❏	❏	❏

The Mind

In This Chapter

> "Knowing others is intelligence; knowing yourself is true wisdom. Mastering others is strength; mastering yourself is true power."
>
> —Tao Te Ching

Connecting to the Topic

1 What does *intelligence* mean to you?

2 What does *wisdom* mean to you?

3 How can we "master" ourselves?

In this chapter, you will study adverb clauses and related structures that show contrast, purpose, and result. As you study the chapter, pay attention to all connecting wordings. Notice their meanings. Also notice what punctuation is used with each, where each can be placed in a sentence, and how the focus of a sentence can change according to the choice and placement of the connecting word.

Reading Read the following passage. It introduces the chapter theme "The Mind" and raises some of the topics and issues you will cover in the chapter.

The Mysteries of the Mind

Although the mind has always fascinated people, its workings were an almost complete mystery until recently. In the last several decades, however, researchers have been so active in this area that we understand more about the mind today than we ever imagined possible.

We now know that the brain controls the nervous system, which, in turn, directs all muscular and mental activity. In addition, we know that certain functions are carried out by specific parts of the brain. We have even come to realize that the brain must forget some pieces of information so that it can remember others.

But in spite of all the recent scientific advances, we continue to ask the most basic question: What *is* the mind? Is the mind merely an electrochemical operation, or is it much more? We are beginning to understand the complexities of the nervous system, but is the mind something that we will never completely understand?

 Discussing Ideas Discuss the questions with a partner.

What else do we currently know about the functioning of the brain? What is some of the research that is being done to learn more? What do you know about the mind?

Setting the Context

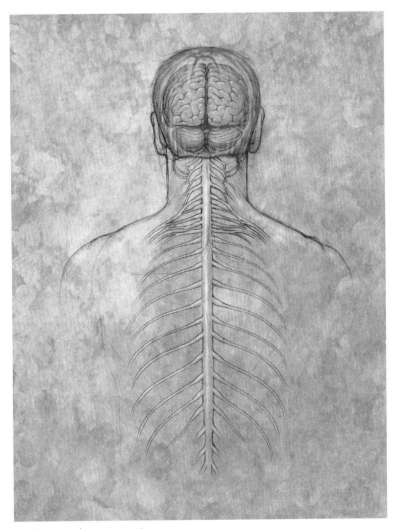

▲ The central nervous system

Previewing the Passage Discuss the questions with a group.

What is the central nervous system? Which organ controls it? What are some examples of the central nervous system at work?

Reading Read the passage.

The Central Nervous System

At the sound of a horn, a child jumps back to the safety of the sidewalk, even though he never saw the truck that almost hit him. A mother sleeps undisturbed in spite of the noise of her neighbor's television set, yet wakes immediately at the first cry from her baby in the next room. Although a businessman worries about a problem for days, the answer comes to him   5
out of the blue while he is busy thinking about something entirely different.

These are just three examples of the routine functioning of the human nervous system. A thousand examples, however, could only begin to describe the capabilities of this incredible system of nerves that leads throughout the body to the center of control, the brain.   10

 Discussing Ideas Discuss the questions with a partner.

Can you give more information about the functioning of the central nervous system? Can you explain how the brain sends and receives messages?

Grammar Structures and Practice

A. Adverb Clauses and Related Structures of Contrast: Concession

The clauses, phrases, and transitions below are used to express ideas or information that is different from our expectations.

- In a sentence with an adverb clause or phrase, the focus is on the main clause.
- If a transition is used and there are two main clauses, each clause has equal focus.
- Note that a comma normally follows introductory clauses and phrases.
- See Chapter 3 for more information on punctuation, sentence focus, and alternative positions for transitions.

6.1 Adverb Clauses and Related Structures of Contrast: Concession

Connecting Words	Explanations	Examples
With Clauses		
Although **Even though** **Though** **In spite of the fact (that)** **Despite the fact (that)**	A comma normally follows introductory clauses and phrases. Commas are also used occasionally with *although, even though, though, in spite of the fact that,* and *despite the fact that* when they appear in the middle of a sentence.	**Even though** the child hadn't seen the truck, he managed to avoid it. The child managed to avoid the truck **although** he hadn't seen it. The child managed to avoid the truck **in spite of the fact that** he hadn't seen it.
With Phrases		
Despite **In spite of** **Regardless of**	A comma normally follows introductory clauses and phrases.	**Despite** living next to a freeway, she was always able to sleep. She was able to sleep **in spite of** the noise. She always sleeps well **regardless of** the noise.
Transitions		
All the same **Even so** **However** **Nevertheless** **Still**	Transitions are normally followed by commas. These transitions are listed from more formal to less formal. All of them are used in both speaking and writing.	His doctor had warned him not to take more than two. **Nevertheless,** he took four. Steve took four pills altogether; **even so,** he didn't sleep well.

Note: Remember that transitions may be placed within a second sentence, but the punctuation changes: *The left hemisphere allows us to analyze. The right, however, provides us with our artistic ability.*

---

1 Practice Quickly reread the passage "The Central Nervous System" on page 252. Then do the following:

1. Circle the following connecting words: *even though, in spite of, but, although,* and *however.*

2. What kind of relationship do these connecting words express?

3. Underline the subject(s) and verb(s) in the sentences with these connecting words. What structures does each connect (for example, phrases, clauses)?

4. What punctuation is used with each?

2 Practice Our brains interpret our perceptions and often adjust them to our view of reality. As a result, we sometimes see, hear, or feel what we expect instead of what is really there. Change the following sentences from compound to complex or from complex to compound. Rewrite the sentence, using the connecting word in parentheses and omitting the connecting word already there. Change or add punctuation when necessary.

Example   Although the word *bear* can be written in a sentence about breweries, a person will usually misread the word as *beer*. (however)
The word bear can be written in a sentence about breweries; however, a person will usually misread the word as beer.

1. Your eye will record an image as it is; however, your brain may change the information it receives. (although)

2. Though you look at an optical illusion very carefully, your brain may "correct" the image to appear normal. (even so)

3. Even though a large and a small box may be exactly the same weight, the large box will feel heavier. (however)

4. A person wearing blue-tinted glasses sees a blue world at first; nevertheless, the blue effect soon disappears, and the world looks normal again. (although)

5. The sound of the phone does not change although the phone appears to ring much louder when we are expecting a call. (still)

6. Despite the fact that five people may witness the same accident, each person will remember the accident somewhat differently. (all the same)

7. The humidity level may be exactly the same on two different days; however, the air will seem damper on a cloudy day than on a sunny day. (even though)

8. Time seems to pass quickly on some days; nevertheless, it goes slowly on others. (even though)

9. A dog's bark seems especially loud at midnight. However, it may be just as loud during the day. (despite the fact that)

10. Even though we are tired, we have to continue working! (however)

▲ Optical illusions are visual images that are misleading or deceptive. This illusion *House of Stairs* was created by M. C. Escher (1898–1972), the famous Dutch printmaker.

3 **Practice** Use *in spite of the fact that, despite the fact that, in spite of,* or *despite* to complete the following sets of sentences.

Examples *Despite the fact that* we spend about one-third of our lives sleeping, we know relatively little about sleep.

_____*Despite*_____ spending about one-third of our lives sleeping, we know relatively little about sleep.

1. _____ years of study, no one knows for certain why humans and animals sleep.
_____ scientists have been studying sleep for years, no one knows for certain why humans and animals sleep.

2. _____ the body seems to rest during sleep, the brain remains quite active.
_____ the rest that the body gets during sleep, the brain remains quite active.

3. _____ most adults like to sleep approximately eight hours a day, some people can survive comfortably on half that much.
_____ the desire that most adults have for about eight hours of sleep a day, some people can survive comfortably on half that much.

4. Some insomniacs[1] lead happy, productive lives _____ they sleep only one or two hours a night.
Some insomniacs lead happy, productive lives _____ sleeping only one or two hours a night.

_____

[1]*insomniacs* people who have trouble falling or staying asleep

Cultural Note

The Importance of Sleep
"To sleep, perchance to dream" —*Hamlet,* by William Shakespeare

After decades of research, we know several things about sleep. Sleep has many phases from light sleep to the deepest sleep, including REM (rapid eye movement). Dreams often take place during REM. Though it is still unclear exactly why we sleep, it is obvious that sleep is important to our health. A person who does not get enough sleep is at higher risk of depression, impaired concentration, irritability, and accidents of any kind. Lack of sleep can even lead to hallucinations.

4 **Practice** Provide an appropriate connecting word of contrast in each of the blanks that follow. Include all necessary punctuation.

Example _____*Although*_____ researchers used to think the brain was similar to a telephone switchboard, they now suggest the brain is more like a computer. _____*However*_____, even a supercomputer is not nearly as complicated as the brain.

1. Memories come from the sights and sounds of the world. _____ the eye may see an image for less than one second this image can be stored for a lifetime.

2. Scientists realized years ago that memories were saved through the use of electrical impulses. _____ today they know that chemicals also play an important role.

3. How exactly does memory work? _____ the question cannot be answered this much is known: The memory image moves from the eye to the brain in electrical form. _____ this provides for only short-term memory and the image may be forgotten within moments.

4. _____ many parts of the brain are involved in memory certain types of memory are controlled by specific areas. This has been shown in the case of a young man (H.M.), who was suffering from extreme epilepsy.[1] _____ many treatments had been tried none had been successful. In 1953, H.M. came to a group of neurosurgeons.[2] These doctors removed a small part of his brain, and his epilepsy was cured. _____ this operation left him with a permanent memory disability. _____ he was able to remember things that happened before the operation he could not form a single lasting new memory. "Every day is alone in itself," H.M. said. "Whatever enjoyment I've had, whatever sorrow I've had."

---

[1]*epilepsy* disease of the brain that causes sudden uncontrolled movement and loss of consciousness
[2]*neurosurgeons* doctors who operate on the brain

5 Practice Combine the following sentences by using *although, though, even though, even so, however, nevertheless, still, despite,* or *in spite of (the fact that).* Substitute pronouns for nouns to avoid repetition. Try to use each of these connecting words at least once.

Example   The brain controls all of our body movements. The brain itself never moves.

Even though it controls all of our body movements, the brain itself never moves.

1. The adult brain uses up to 25 percent of the blood's oxygen supply. The adult brain does not perform physical work.

2. The brain comprises only two percent of the body's weight. The brain receives 20 percent of all the blood pumped from the heart.

3. All parts of the brain receive blood. Areas that control intellectual activity have the most blood vessels.

4. Blood pressure often changes in other parts of the body. Blood pressure stays relatively constant in the brain.

5. Great amounts of energy are consumed in the production of thought. The exact process is still not understood.

6. A loss of blood in a body part only causes numbness. A 15-second interruption in the blood flow to the brain results in unconsciousness.

7. In some traumatic situations, damage to the brain can occur. Blood flow is normal.

8. Blood flows normally through the body. Traumas like choking can cause brain damage.

9. The brains of humans and apes have many similarities. The human brain allows far greater abilities in language and reasoning than apes will ever have.

10. Tall people tend to have larger brains than short people. There is very little correlation between the size of the brain and intelligence.

6 Practice Use your knowledge and imagination to complete the following sentences. Be sure to add capital letters and appropriate punctuation.

Example Although I usually get eight hours of sleep, *last night I slept for only three hours.*

1. Even though time usually passes very quickly in this class
2. I have a headache today however
3. Molly couldn't get to sleep last night despite the fact that
4. Kate studied for the test all last night nevertheless
5. I stayed up until four A.M. even so
6. Jack finished all of the work despite
7. In spite of the fact that Mark has lost all of his hair
8. Jorge was fired last week in spite of
9. Although Sonia found a new job last week
10. Gary has lost 20 pounds all the same

Now go back and suggest a different connector for each of the sentences that you have created.

Example *I usually get eight hours of sleep; even so, last night I slept for only three hours.*

Using What You've Learned

7 Writing about the Brain Use information from this section to write a short paragraph on the working of the brain. Rephrase sentences to use a variety of connecting words and be sure to include both compound and complex sentences.

8 Describing Optical Illusions In normal vision, our eyes actually receive a distorted view of the world. The image on our retina is upside down and reversed left to right. Straight lines curve and colors form a fringe around the edge of the image.

The brain, however, takes over and adapts the information it receives from our eyes. It matches the new information with what it already knows about the world in order to give us a true picture.

Because the brain insists on correcting new information, it also corrects optical illusions. What we believe we see at first may not be the true image at all.

In pairs or in small groups, look carefully at the following pictures and share your first impressions. Then look more carefully and compare what you now see with what you thought you saw.

PARIS
IN THE
THE SPRING

What's wrong with this phrase?
(a)

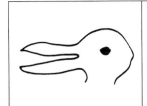

What kind of animal is this?
(b)

Who or what is this?
(c)

Is this woman young or old?
(d)

9 **Describing Personal Experiences** Think about the information mentioned in Activity 8. Then work in small groups and discuss the following. Add ideas of your own, too. Use the connecting words you have just studied.

- Think about your perception of time. When does time seem to pass quickly? When does it pass slowly?
- Think about your perception of temperature. Do clouds or sunshine affect whether you feel hotter or colder?
- Think about your hearing. When you're in a dark room, can you hear things more clearly? Do sounds seem louder? What about when you're in a strange place?

10 **Describing Personal Experiences** When you move to a new place, and especially when you live in a new culture and speak a new language, your perceptions are often much more specific than they would be in a familiar place. You may notice many things that others don't because they are completely accustomed to them, while you are not.

Think about some of your perceptions in recent months: the sights, the sounds, the smells, the textures surrounding you. Write a short paragraph describing something that has struck you in particular. This perception may involve one sense or a variety of senses.

Then work in small groups and share your observations. *Tell* about them. Don't read them!

Example *One of the most interesting things for me here has been the smells, or rather, the lack of smells, especially in the markets. In my own country, food smells are a very common part of everyday life, but here, nothing smells. Everything seems to be antiseptic!*

Clauses and Related Structures of Contrast: Opposition

Setting the Context

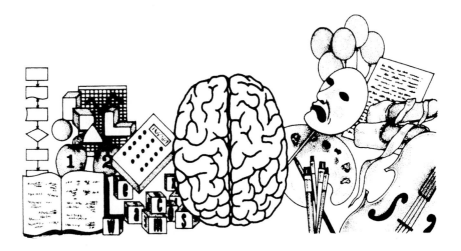

Previewing the Passage Discuss the questions with a group.

There are many questions about the brain and the way it works. One such question is: Do certain parts of the brain have certain functions, or does the entire brain function as one unit? What other questions and mysteries regarding the brain are you aware of?

Reading Read the passage.

The Two Hemispheres of the Brain

The cortex of the brain is divided into two hemispheres. The right hemisphere mainly controls the left side of the body, whereas the left hemisphere directs the body's right side.

While both hemispheres can potentially perform many of the same functions, each of the hemispheres tends to specialize. The left hemisphere 5 seems to control most analytic, logical thinking. It appears to process information in sequential order, handling logical thought, language, and mathematics. The right hemisphere, on the other hand, is limited in laguage ability, but it appears to process different kinds of information simultaneously. It specializes in spatial orientation, artistic endeavors, crafts, body 10 image, and recognition of faces. Thus, where the left hemisphere is more analytic and sequential, the right is more holistic and relational.

Discussing Ideas Discuss the questions with a partner.

This passage presents one theory that says the brain is highly specialized for certain types of tasks. Do you know of other theories that currently exist?

Grammar Structures and Practice

A. Adverb Clauses and Related Structures of Contrast: Opposition

The clauses, phrases, and transitions below are used to express opposite views about something.

- Note that a comma normally follows an introductory phrase or clause or a transition.
- Commas may also be used with *while, where,* and *whereas* when they appear in the middle of a sentence.
- See Chapter 3 for more information on punctuation and sentence focus.

6.2 Adverb Clauses and Related Structures of Contrast: Opposition

Connecting Words	Explanations	Examples
With Clauses		
Where **Whereas** **While**	*Whereas*, *where*, and *while* are often used to contrast direct opposites. *Whereas* is used in formal English.	**Whereas** the right hemisphere of the brain is much older in terms of human evolution, the left hemisphere is more highly developed.
With Phrases		
Different from **Similar to** **Like** **Unlike**	*Different from*, *unlike*, and *instead of* contrast opposites. *Similar to* and *like* compare related ideas. Noun or gerund phrases normally follow these expressions.	The right side of the brain seems quite **different from** the left side. The right side is apparently not very **similar to** the left. **Unlike** the left hemisphere, which is responsible for language, the right hemisphere specializes in body image and recognition of faces.
Instead of	*Instead of* can be followed by a variety of forms: adjectives, adverbs, noun phrases, or gerunds.	The right hemisphere tends to process a variety of information simultaneously **instead of** sequentially.
Transitions		
In contrast **On the other hand**	*In contrast* and *on the other hand* relate different points that are not necessarily directly opposite.	The left hemisphere seems to process information in sequential order; **in contrast**, the right hemisphere handles different types of data simultaneously.
On the contrary	*On the contrary* is used differently from other transitions of contrast. It indicates that the *opposite* of some idea is true. It often reinforces the negative idea in the preceding sentence or can be used to answer a question.	The right side of the brain is not primarily analytical; **on the contrary**, it is responsible for the artistic aspects of the mind. Is the right side of the brain responsible for analyzing information? **On the contrary**, it is responsible for the artistic aspects of the mind.

Note: Remember that transitions may be placed within a second sentence, but the punctuation changes: *The left hemisphere allows us to analyze. The right, however, provides us with our artistic ability.*

---

1 Practice Quickly reread the passage "The Two Hemispheres of the Brain" on page 260. Then do the following:

1. Circle the connecting words that express contrast. For each case, find the subject(s) and verb(s) of the sentence. What structures do these words connect (for example, phrases, clauses)?

2. What punctuation is used with the various connecting words? Compare this to the punctuation used with connecting words in "The Central Nervous System" on page 252. Do you notice any differences in punctuation?

3. Look again at the second sentence and the last sentence in "The Two Hemispheres of the Brain" on page 260. What is the primary focus of each sentence?

2 **Practice** Rewrite the following sentences, using the connecting word in parentheses to replace the connecting word already there. Give all possibilities. Change or add punctuation where necessary. Then tell the primary focus of both the original and the new sentences.

Example A child's brain is one mass; in contrast, the brain of an adult is separated into two hemispheres.
Focus: Both a child's brain and an adult's brain
(whereas)
Whereas a child's brain is one mass, the brain of an adult is separated into two hemispheres.
Focus: An adult's brain
or
A child's brain is one mass, whereas the brain of an adult is separated into two hemispheres.
Focus: A child's brain

1. An adult brain is more specialized; on the other hand, a child's brain has large areas that are uncommitted. (while)

2. While children can learn many things easily, adults often have a much harder time. (in contrast)

3. Few adults can learn to use a new language without mistakes or accent; on the other hand, children frequently become completely fluent in new languages. (whereas)

4. Whereas most children do not favor either hand until they are about five years old, most adults are either right-handed or left-handed. (in contrast)

5. Some functions, such as smell, are located in specific areas in the brain, while others are handled throughout the brain. (on the other hand)

6. Considerable research is being done on the "geography" of the brain; however, only a few areas have actually been "mapped." (while)

3 **Practice** Show the contrast in the following sentences by filling in *while, where, whereas, on the other hand,* or *in contrast.* Add all necessary punctuation.

Brains and Computers

The human brain is often compared with a computer. _____*While*_____ they may have a number of things in common, they are actually quite differ-ent. First, they differ physically. The brain is made up of soft tissue. A com-puter _____₁_____ is composed of electrical circuits. In addition, the difference in capabilities is immense. _____₂_____ computers are complex a brain is a million times more intricate. The brain constantly gathers information from its five sophisticated senses. The computer _____₃_____ receives its data from a keyboard. The brain can simultaneously process tremendous amounts of information; the computer _____₄_____ must proceed one step at a time. But perhaps most significant of all,

_____₅_____ a brain is conscious of its own existence a computer is not.

4 **Practice** Combine the following sets of sentences in two ways. First, use *unlike,* then use *instead of.* Add necessary punctuation.

Example   A brain has thousands of neurons. A computer is made up of circuits.
   Unlike a brain, which has thousands of neurons, a computer is made up of circuits.
   Instead of having thousands of neurons like a brain, a computer is made up of circuits.

1. A brain is capable of emotions and dreams. A computer only processes information.

2. A computer may weigh hundreds of pounds. A brain weighs only about three pounds.

3. A computer can cover a desk. A brain fits neatly into the top of the skull.

4. A brain is aware of its own existence. A computer has no such sense of "being."

5 Practice Complete the sentences that follow by using either *on the contrary* or *on the other hand*. Add punctuation when necessary.

Example Computers and human brains have many differences.
On the other hand, some similarities do exist.

1. The brain is not very much like a computer. _____ the two are quite different.

2. The brain is not very much like a computer. _____ there are a few similarities between the two.

3. Some people believe computers will soon rule our lives. _____ most think that this will never happen.

4. Some people believe computers will soon rule our lives. I don't believe it. _____ in my opinion, this could never happen.

5. A: Do you think computers will ever take control of the world?
   B: I can't say. _____ Frank is sure they will.

6. A: What about you? Do you think computers could take control of the world?
   B: _____ computers are simply machines and always will be.

6 Practice Use your own ideas to complete the following sentences.

Example Some people believe we now know virtually everything about the brain.
On the contrary, _we have only begun to understand its workings_.

1. Is there a difference between the brain and the mind?
   On the contrary, . . .

2. Children learn foreign languages with considerable ease.
   On the other hand, . . .

3. Adults rarely find it easy to learn a second language.
   On the contrary, . . .

4. Jack has had a difficult time learning Spanish.
   On the other hand, . . .

5. Artists often have trouble with analytical thinking.
   In contrast, . . .

6. Does Marina like math?
   On the contrary, . . .

7. Marina hates math, . . .
   In contrast,

8. Diane isn't a strong swimmer.
   On the contrary, . . .

9. Diane isn't a strong swimmer.
   On the other hand, . . .

10. Are we getting tired of this exercise?
    On the contrary, . . .

7 **Practice** Use your imagination to complete the following. Be sure to add capital letters if needed and appropriate punctuation. In some cases, your correction will require completing a single sentence. In other cases, it will be necessary to write two sentences.

Example Whereas some researchers believe the right and left sides of the brain have distinct functions, *others think the idea is nonsense* .

1. While Jamie loves to use computers

2. Children learn languages easily on the other hand

3. I had a fascinating dream last night in contrast

4. Where some people have no trouble sleeping

5. Unlike Molly, who sleeps 12 hours a night,

6. Whereas I take a nap every afternoon

7. A: Do you take a nap every afternoon?
   B: On the contrary,

8. My children are bilingual in contrast

9. Some parents think their children should learn foreign languages whereas

10. Gulay studies five hours every night unlike

8 **Practice** Using a variety of phrases, connecting words, and transitions of contrast, combine the following into one paragraph. You may leave out some of the information or add information of your own to make the new paragraph read smoothly. Begin the paragraph with a general statement such as, *If recent research is correct, the left and right sides of the brain differ in a number of ways.*

The Right Brain

The right hemisphere of the brain probably dates back millions of years in our evolution. All mammals have right-hemisphere thinking. Right-hemisphere thinking provides us with instinct, feeling, and intuition. The right brain appreciates music, allows for three-dimensional vision, recognizes faces, and gets jokes. In short, the right hemisphere helps us feel where we belong in the world.

The Left Brain

The left hemisphere of the brain is relatively young in terms of evolution. The development of left-hemisphere thinking within the human species accounts for the fundamental differences between human and animal thought. The left hemisphere controls rational, verbal, and analytical thinking. It specializes in language, logic, long-term memory, reading and writing, and critical thinking. The left hemisphere is the business part of our brain organizing, analyzing, and choosing.

9 **Error Analysis** Each of the following sentences contains an error concerning the connecting words from Parts 1 and 2. The error may involve the connecting word, the punctuation, or the need for a capital letter. Find and correct all errors.

Example The right side of the brain seems quite different <u>from</u> the left side.

1. Whereas the right brain processes information sequentially, on the other hand, the left brain handles information simultaneously.

2. Keesia studied left-brain functions last semester, in contrast Miki focused on the right.

3. Unlike the left brain is responsible for language, the right brain specializes in recognition of faces.

4. Where I love studying the brain, Shirley thinks it is fascinating.

5. Though I have spent nine months in China I still cannot communicate in Chinese.

6. Even though Chinese is very difficult, however, it is possible to learn it.

7. Artists tend to use the right side of the brain more. On the contrary, accountants rely more on the left.

8. Although, migraine headaches are associated with women millions of men have the same problem.

9. Despite Mary has taken four aspirin, she still has a terrible headache.

10. In spite the fact that Mary has seen several doctors, none has been able to help her.

Using What You've Learned

10 **Describing Yourself** It is probable that no one is completely "right-brained" or "left-brained." However, many people seem to be influenced by one side more than the other. What about you? Review the information in Activity 8 and other information you can find. Then write a short paragraph about yourself describing whether you are "right-brained" or "left-brained." Be sure to provide several examples to support your point of view. Finally, share your ideas with your classmates, in small groups or as a class.

Setting the Context

 Previewing the Passage Discuss the questions with a group.

Who was Dr. Alois Alzheimer? Which disease did he identify? What do you know about the disease?

Reading Read the passage.

Alzheimer's Disease

"My mother always had such a sharp mind. Then in her mid-seventies, she began to become forgetful. She would be halfway through a sentence and stop because she couldn't remember a word. Today, three years later, she can no longer carry on a conversation. Worse, most of the time, she doesn't even recognize me."   5

In 1906, Dr. Alois Alzheimer, a German doctor, decided to do an autopsy[1] on a woman who died so that he could better understand the woman's strange illness. In the woman's brain, he found many hallmarks[2] of the most common brain dysfunction in older people, Alzheimer's disease (AD).

Today we know a great deal about Alzheimer's disease. AD disrupts the   10
way we think by causing physical changes in the brain. It affects the parts of the brain that control thought, memory, and language. While younger people may have AD, the disease normally attacks the elderly.

For decades, scientists around the world have been doing research in order to find a cure for AD. Recently there have been promising develop-   15
ments. It is likely that we will find a treatment to prevent the disease or at least to soften its effects soon.

---

[1] *autopsy* examination of a body after death to determine the cause of death or the extent of changes produced by disease
[2] *hallmarks* distinguishing features, traits, or characteristics

Discussing Ideas Discuss the questions with a partner.

Do you know anyone who suffers from AD? What are some of its most obvious effects for that person?

Grammar Structures and Practice

A. Adverb Clauses and Phrases of Purpose

Clauses with *so that* and *in order that* and phrases with *in order to* show the intention or purpose of something.

- Clauses with *so that* and *in order that* do not begin sentences.
- Commas are not normally used with either.
- Commas are used with *In order to* when it begins a sentence.

6.3 Adverb Clauses and Phrases of Purpose		
Structures	**Explanations**	**Examples**
With Clauses		
In order that **So (that)**	*So (that)* and *in order that* are usually used between two clauses. A modal auxiliary (*can, will*: present / future; *could, would*: past) is normally used in the dependent clause.	Scientists are studying the brain **so (that)** they can understand more about learning.
With Phrases		
In order to	In written English, *in order to* is used more frequently than *so that*. *In order to* + verb and *to* + verb are considered better stylistically.	Scientists are studying the brain **in order to** understand more about learning.

Note: That (in *so that*) is sometimes omitted, especially in conversational English. Do not confuse *so (that)* (expressing purpose) with the conjunction *so* (expressing result). The use of a modal auxiliary in the dependent clause signals "purpose" as opposed to "result." Compare: *Result: I wanted a college education, so I enrolled at the university. Purpose: I wanted a college education so (that) I could get a good job.*

1 Practice Combine the sentences by using *so that* or *in order that*. You will need to omit some words from the second sentence and add a modal auxiliary.

Example Dr. Alzheimer conducted an autopsy. He wanted to understand an unusual mental illness.
Dr. Alzheimer conducted an autopsy so that he could understand an unusual mental illness.

1. Both university and drug company researchers are studying AD. They want to understand the disease.

2. Tests are being developed. We want to diagnose AD easily.

3. Drugs are being tested. These drugs may slow down the development of the disease.

4. Researchers are working on a vaccine. They want to eliminate the disease.

5. Mice were used in experiments. Researchers wanted to see how effective the vaccine was.

6. Information on the research is posted on Web sites. People want to know the latest developments.

7. The disease was named Alzheimer's. Everyone was able to recognize who discovered it.

8. I hope the vaccine is successful. I want Alzheimer's disease to disappear.

2 Practice Western medicine has traditionally tried to treat illnesses through drug therapy. The Eastern approach is sometimes quite different. Substitute *in order to* for *so that* in the following sentences. Include all necessary changes.

Example   Today, doctors are developing biofeedback[1] techniques so that they can teach patients to heal themselves.
Today, doctors are developing biofeedback techniques in order to teach patients to heal themselves.

▲ This yogi can control his involuntary nervous system.

1. In the 1970s, Western scientists began traveling to India so that they could study the "powers" that yogis were rumored to have.

2. The scientists used electronic instruments so that they could test yogis' ability to control "involuntary" body functions such as heartbeat and reaction to pain.

3. In one experiment, a yogi pushed a rusty needle completely through his arm so that he could demonstrate his ability to block all pain.

4. He used meditation[2] so that he could ignore this pain.

5. Yogis undergo years of training so that they can control their bodily functions through meditation.

6. Now some patients in the West are using biofeedback so that they can control their involuntary nervous systems like yogis.

7. The patients use machines so that they can "see" and "hear" a problem and then consciously solve it.

8. Other people practice Transcendental Meditation[3] so that they can control their nervous system without the help of machines.

---

[1]*biofeedback* technique of making certain bodily processes (such as the heartbeat or brain waves) perceptible to the senses in order to mentally control them

[2]*meditation* Meditation is at the heart of Eastern religions such as Hinduism and Buddhism. It is a method practiced in order to become pure consciousness, to transcend body and mind.

[3]*Transcendental Meditation* Transcendental Meditation, or TM, involves techniques that allow people to begin meditating after only a few sessions. TM seems to help improve physical and mental coordination, lower blood pressure, and reduce stress.

3 **Practice** Use your knowledge and imagination to answer the following questions. Include *so that, in order that,* or *in order to* in your answers. Try to come up with at least three answers for each question.

Example Why did you take a sleeping pill last night? *I took a sleeping pill so that I could get a good night's rest.*

1. Why do you have a physical checkup every year?

2. Why did you shave your head?

3. Why do you study so much?

4. Why didn't you go to the party last weekend?

5. Why don't you eat meat?

6. Why do you sing in the shower?

7. Why didn't you go to the movies with me last weekend?

8. Why are you studying English?

Using What You've Learned

4 **Summarizing Research** Scientists have been intrigued by the mind for thousands of years. The following is a list of scientists and a brief summary of some of their work. Choose one of these scientists (or any other that you are interested in) as the subject for some research. Use encyclopedias, the Internet, or other sources to gather information on this person and his or her work. Then, in a one-page paper, summarize what you have found. Be sure to include information on the exact focus of the scientist's research and the purpose for doing this research.

Aristotle (384–322 B.C.E.) did research on animals to learn more about anatomy and to classify similarities and differences; he also studied dreams, memory, and the senses to create a theory about thought processes.

René Descartes (1596–1650) applied concepts of mathematics to psychology in order to develop a scientific method for the study of human behavior.

Sigmund Freud (1856–1939) studied hysteria to determine psychological factors that produce physical problems and used hypnosis to probe the subconscious mind.

Carl Jung (1875–1961) worked with dreams, mythology, Buddhism, and astrology to learn about the "unconscious."

Roger Sperry (1913–1994) received the 1981 Nobel Prize in Medicine for his discoveries concerning the specialized functions of the hemispheres of the brain.

Arvid Carlsson (1923–) was a 2000 Nobel Prize winner for discoveries concerning the transmission of signals in the nervous system.

Robert Ornstein (1942–) suggested that the two halves of the brain deal with different mental functions.

Maharishi Mahesh Yogi (1911–) influenced many in the West to begin meditation.

Richard Seed (1930–) is a geneticist who has gained notoriety for pledging to clone the first human being.

Part 4 | Clauses and Related Structures of Comparison

Setting the Context

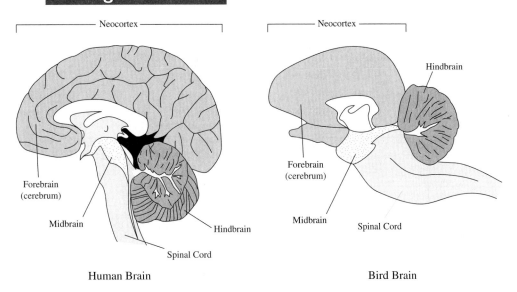

Human Brain

Bird Brain

 Previewing the Passage Discuss the questions with a group.

What are some animals that are approximately the same size as human beings? Name some physical advantages human beings have over these animals.

Reading Read the passage.

Man and Animals

    Physically speaking, humans are rather unimpressive. We are not as strong as most other animals our size. We walk much more awkwardly, for example, than cats do. We cannot run as fast as dogs or deer can. In vision, hearing, and in the sense of smell, we are inferior to many other animals. When we think in evolutionary terms of the beautiful efficiency of fish for 5 swimming or of birds for flying, we seem to be more clumsily and poorly designed than most creatures. In fact, we have come to dominate all other animals only because of one rather important specialization—our brain.

 Discussing Ideas Discuss the questions with a partner.

Use your own words to explain the first sentence in the passage. In what way(s) are human beings superior to animals?

"■ ■ ■ The Mind   273"
■ ■ ■ The Mind

Grammar Structures and Practice

A. Comparative and Superlative Forms of Adjectives and Adverbs

Comparative and superlative forms are used to describe two or more things.

- Positive forms of adjectives and adverbs are used in expressions with *(not) as . . . as (as slow as, not as slowly as)*.
- Comparative forms are used to compare two things.
- Superlative forms are used to discuss three or more things.
- *The* is normally used with superlative forms.
- Note that spelling rules for adding *-er* and *-est* are the same as for adding *-ed* (see Appendix 2).

6.4 Comparative and Superlative Forms of Adjectives and Adverbs

Structures	Explanations	Positive	Comparative	Superlative
One-Syllable Adjectives Adjectives and Adverbs That Have the Same Form	Add *-er* and *-est* to one-syllable adjectives and adverbs that have the same form. Or, use *less* and *least*.	nice young early fast hard late	nicer / less nice younger / less young earlier / less early faster / less fast harder / less hard later / less late	the nicest / the least nice the youngest / the least young the earliest / the least early the fastest / the least fast the hardest / the least hard the latest / the least late
Most Two-Syllable Adjectives	With two-syllable adjectives, add *-er* and *-est*. Or, use *more, less, the most, the least*.	clever funny shallow simple	cleverer more / less clever funnier more / less funny shallower more / less shallow simpler more / less simple	the cleverest the most / the least clever the funniest the most / the least funny the shallowest the most / the least shallow the simplest the most / the least simple
Two-Syllable Adjectives That End in *-ed, -ful, -ing, -ish, -ous, -st,* and *-x*	With two-syllable adjectives that end in *-ed, -ful, -ing, -ish, -ous,-st,* and *-x*, use *more, less, the most, the least*.	worried harmful caring selfish joyous robust complex	more / less worried more / less harmful more / less caring more / less selfish more / less joyous more / less robust more / less complex	the most / the least worried the most / the least harmful the most / the least caring the most / the least selfish the most / the least joyous the most / the least robust the most / the least complex
Longer Adjectives and Most *-ly* Adverbs	With longer adjectives and most *-ly* adverbs, use *more, less, the most, the least*.	difficult experienced interesting quickly slowly	more difficult more experienced more interesting more quickly more slowly	the most / the least difficult the most / the least experienced the most / the least interesting the most / the least quickly the most / the least slowly

Note: With words ending in *-y* and *-le*, the *-er* and *-est* forms are more common, although both forms may be used.

6.5 Irregular Adjectives and Adverbs

Adjectives	Adverbs	Comparative	Superlative
bad	badly	worse	the worst
good	-	better	the best
well	well	better	the best
far	far	farther	the farthest (distance)
		further	the furthest
little	little	less	the least
many	-	more	the most
much	much	more	the most

1 Practice Give the affirmative (+) or negative (-) comparative and superlative of the following words.

Examples (+) lazy *lazier, the laziest*
(-) bright *less bright, the least bright*

1. (+) tall	**8.** (+) good	**15.** (-) exhausted
2. (+) stocky	**9.** (-) tired	**16.** (+) boring
3. (+) quickly	**10.** (+) handsome	**17.** (+) far
4. (-) interesting	**11.** (+) fascinating	**18.** (-) angrily
5. (+) big	**12.** (-) studious	**19.** (+) well
6. (+) slowly	**13.** (+) lovely	**20.** (+) dim
7. (+) bad	**14.** (-) little	**21.** (+) deep

B. Comparisons with *Than*

Two items can be compared using clauses or phrases with *than*.

6.6 Comparisons with *Than*

Structures	Explanations	Examples
Clauses of Comparison	Clauses of comparison can be formed with comparative adjectives or adverbs and *than*. In speaking and sometimes in writing, the verb in the dependent clause is often changed to the corresponding auxiliary verb.	Susan runs fast, but Marina runs **faster than** Susan **runs**. Marina runs **faster than** Susan **does**. Susan is **slower than** Marina **is**.
Implied Comparisons	In speaking and sometimes in writing, the verb or the dependent clause itself is omitted entirely. The comparison is not stated; rather, it is implied.	Marina runs **faster than** Susan. Marina runs **faster**. Susan is **slower than** Marina. Susan is **slower**.

In formal and conversational English, different pronouns are often used with comparisons.

6.7 Formal Versus Informal Comparisons with *Than*

Explanation	Structures		Examples
In informal conversation, a subject pronoun is often replaced by an object pronoun, although it is grammatically incorrect.	**More Formal** **Conversational**	**Subject Pronouns** **Object Pronouns**	She runs faster than **I**. She runs faster than **I do**. She runs faster than **me**.

2 **Practice** Use the following model to make sentences from the words in Exercise 1. Describe your friends, roommates, or classmates.

Examples

Laura is lazier than Jane, but Nancy is the laziest person I have ever seen.

C. Comparisons with *As*

Items can also be compared using clauses or phrases with *as*.

6.8 Comparisons with *As*

Structures	Explanations	Examples
Clauses of Comparison with *as . . . as*	Positive adjectives and adverbs are used with *as . . . as*. In speaking and sometimes in writing, the verb in the dependent clause is often changed to the corresponding auxiliary verb.	We cannot run **as fast as** many animals **can run**. We cannot run **as fast as** many animals **can**.
Clauses of Comparison with *the same . . . as*	Nouns are often used with *the same . . . as*. In speaking and sometimes in writing, the verb in the dependent clause is often changed to the corresponding auxiliary verb.	A lion cannot run **the same** distance **as** a cheetah **can run** in the same time. Amazingly, that lion ran **the same** distance **as** the cheetah **did** in the same time.
Implied Comparisons	In speaking and sometimes in writing, the verb or the dependent clause itself is omitted entirely. The comparison is not stated; rather, it is implied.	We cannot run **as fast as** many animals. We cannot run **as fast**. Amazingly, that lion ran **the same** distance **as** the cheetah. Amazingly, that lion ran **the same** distance.

In formal and conversational English, different pronouns are often used with comparisons.

6.9 Formal Versus Informal Comparisons with *As*			
Explanation	**Structures**		**Examples**
In informal conversation, a subject pronoun is often replaced by an object pronoun, although it is grammatically incorrect.	**More Formal**	**Subject Pronouns**	She runs as fast as **I**. She runs as fast as **I do**.
	Conversational	**Object Pronouns**	She runs as fast as **me**.

3 **Practice** Fill in appropriate comparative or superlative forms of the adjectives and adverbs in parentheses.

Humans Versus Animals

In all animals—from the ____*least*____ vertebrates, such as fish
(- developed)

and reptiles, to humans—the brain is divided into three parts: the forebrain,

the midbrain, and the hindbrain. The forebrain, or cerebrum, becomes

_____ in _____ animals until, in human be-
1 (+ developed)   2 (+ high)

ings, the cerebrum and its covering, the neocortex, dominate brain functions.

The neocortex plays an important role even in _____ mam-
3 (+ primitive)

mals. For example, a horse's neocortex is _____ and
4 (+ small)

_____ than those in _____ mammals, but it
5 (+ smooth)   6 (+ high)

still oversees brain functioning.

In _____ mammals, the neocortex becomes so much
7 (+ advanced)

_____ than the cerebrum that it is bent into folds or "convolu-
8 (+ large)

tions." This folding makes possible the _____ complexity of
9 (+ great)

the brain of the primate—most notably that of humans.

D. Phrases Showing Comparison

A variety of transitions and other expressions can be used to express comparisons. The following are common in both spoken and written English.

6.10 Phrases Showing Comparison

Connecting Words	Explanations	Examples
With Phrases		
As well as	Phrases with *as well as* come after the noun(s) they modify. The verb in the main clause is singular or plural, depending on the subject of the sentence.	Gorillas, **as well as** people, walk on their hind legs. The gorilla, **as well as** the chimpanzee and the orangutan, walks on its hind legs.
Both . . . and	*Both . . . and* is followed by a plural verb.	**Both** chimpanzees **and** gorillas live in the jungle.
Similar to	Phrases with *similar to* can appear at different points in a sentence.	**Similar to** chimpanzees, humans are omnivores.[1] Humans are omnivores **similar to** chimpanzees. Humans, **similar to** chimpanzees, are omnivores.
Transitions		
Likewise **Similarly**	*Likewise* and *similarly* are used in both speaking and writing. In writing, they are normally followed by commas.	Lions are carnivores; **likewise,** cheetahs have a diet that consists mainly of meat. Many birds have developed extraordinary eyesight. **Similarly,** the eyesight of humans has improved greatly through the ages.

[1] *omnivores* animals that eat both meat and vegetation

---

4 Practice Circle the correct answers. Then add any appropriate punctuation and capital letters.

Example Gorillas, (as well as)/ likewise) people, walk on their hind legs.

1. Gorillas walk on their hind legs (as well as / likewise) people stand upright on two legs.

2. Gorillas don't live to (the same age as / as old as) people.

3. Elephants can live past 60 (similarly / the same) dolphins survive six decades or more.

4. (Both Anne and Harry / Anne likewise Harry) are fascinated by various types of snakes.

5. At the zoo, Anne devotes most of her time to watching snakes (the same as / likewise) Harry can spend hours at the snake exhibit.

6. A worm isn't (as developed / more developed) as a crab.

7. (Both crabs and lobsters / Likewise crabs and lobsters) are shellfish with antennae and pincers.

8. (Similarly / Similar to) crabs, lobsters have front pincers. However, the lobster's pincers are much larger and are usually called *claws*.

5 **Practice** Fill in the correct forms of the words on the left. Add any necessary words. Then try to answer the question. Confirm your answers with your teacher.

1. (fast) Lions can't run as _____ *fast* _____ as cheetahs. In fact, cheetahs

run much _____ than lions. Are cheetahs the _____

animals on Earth?

2. (far) Cheetahs can rarely run as _____ as lions. In fact, lions

can run a great deal _____ than cheetahs. Do you know

which predator can run the _____?

3. (good) Humans can't see as _____ as many birds. In fact,

birds of prey have sight many times _____ than people.

Which bird, do you think, has the _____ eyesight?

4. (tall) Elephants aren't as _____ as giraffes. In fact, an adult

giraffe is on average nine feet _____ than a mature elephant.

Is the giraffe the _____ animal on Earth?

6 **Practice** Make at least three sets of sentences similar to those in Exercise 5. You may write about animals, places, people, or things. You may use adjectives of your own or choose from the following list:

beautiful	impressive
boring	reckless
careful	striking
enervating	strong
healthy	tiring

Example *Houston isn't as beautiful as Austin. In fact, Austin is much more beautiful. Many people consider Austin to be the most beautiful city in Texas.*

7 **Error Analysis** Each of the following sentences contains an error. Find the error and correct it.

Example The cat that you have as a pet is, in some ways, similar ~~than~~ *to* a lion.

1. Humans are not more stronger than most other animals the same size.

2. We cannot run as quick as dogs or deer can.

3. We seem to be more clumsily than most creatures.

4. Horses are herbivores, likewise, cows eat only vegetation.

5. Many animals are less cleverer than chimpanzees.

6. Orangutans eat a mixed diet of seeds, nuts, fruit, and a little meat. Similarly, tigers are carnivores.

7. To some people, the coat of a leopard looks the same than the coat of a tiger.

8. Both sheep and deer provides meat to predators, including humans.

Using What You've Learned

8 **Making Comparisons** In pairs, use the following information comparing humans and various animals to write a true / false quiz for your classmates. Include at least ten statements with comparisons. Be sure to use *both . . . and, as well as, more / er than, the most / est, the same . . . as, similarly,* and *likewise* at least once. When you have finished, exchange your quiz with another pair. Then take the quiz without referring to the book. Finally, return the quiz to be graded.

Human Life Expectancies: Male and Female

Country	Male	Female	Country	Male	Female
Japan	78	84	China	70	73
Australia	77	83	Russia	62	73
United States	74	80	Pakistan	60	62
Chile	72	79	Angola	37	40

Size: Mammals

blue whale	90 feet long	rhinoceros	6 $\frac{1}{2}$ feet at shoulder
giraffe	19 feet tall (full length)	cow	5 feet at shoulder
African elephant	10 $\frac{1}{2}$ feet at shoulder	cat	9 inches at shoulder
brown bear	8 feet when standing erect	shrew	1.7 inches long
camel	7 feet to top of humps		

Life Expectancies: Animals

mayfly	1 day	owl	24 years
mouse	1-3 years	lion	25 years
trout	5-10 years	horse	30 years
sheep	10-15 years	ostrich	40 years
squirrel	11 years	African elephant	70 years
rabbit	12 years	dolphin	50 years
cat	13-17 years	tortoise	100 years

Examples Ⓣ F *An elephant lives much longer than a lion.*

T Ⓕ *Lions, as well as rabbits, live over 20 years.*

Part 5 | Clauses of Result

Setting the Context

Previewing the Passage Discuss the questions with a group.

What percentage of the things that you saw, heard, felt, tasted, or smelled yesterday do you remember today? Why do you think the brain does not remember most of these things?

Reading Read the passage.

It's Important to Forget

For decades, scientists have been interested in how the brain stores and recalls memories. In fact, this has been such an interesting topic that they have by and large ignored an area of equal importance—how the brain forgets.

Through the five senses, the brain receives the impressions from *every-* 5
thing we see, hear, touch, taste, and smell. This amounts to so much information that it is impossible for the brain to commit more than a small percentage to permanent memory. If the brain held on to everything that it received, it would have so many memories that it would soon run out of room and could accept no more. As a result, the brain filters out or forgets 10
millions of pieces of information every minute. This type of forgetting is so important that without it, the efficient use of memory would be impossible.

Discussing Ideas Discuss the questions with a partner.

When you consciously decide to remember something, are you always successful? What do you do in order to remember something new, such as an address or phone number? Give an example of something you forgot recently.

Grammar Structures and Practice

Adverb Clauses of Result

Clauses with *so* or *such . . . that* may be used with adjectives, adverbs, or nouns to show the result or effect of a situation. In informal English, *that* is sometimes omitted.

6.11 Adverb Clauses of Result

Connecting Words	Explanations	Examples
so . . . that	Adjectives and adverbs are used with *so . . . that*.	The idea was **so** complicated **that** no one could understand it.
so much . . . that **so many . . . that**	Noncount nouns are used with *so much . . . that*. Plural count nouns are used with *so many . . . that*.	The speaker gave **so much** information **that** no one could understand the talk easily. He talked about **so many** ideas **that** we became confused.
such . . . that	*Such . . . that* can be used with *a(n)* + adjective + singular count noun or adjective + plural noun *or* adjective + noncount noun.	He was **such** a poor speaker **that** we fell asleep. They were **such** good speakers **that** they influenced all of us. The speakers had **such** extensive knowledge **that** we were all impressed.

Differences exist between formal and conversational English in sentences with *so, such,* and *so many / much.*

6.12 Formal Versus Informal Adverb Clauses of Result

Explanations		Examples
In formal English, *so, such,* and *so many / much* are used in complex sentences with two or more clauses. In conversational English, they are commonly used in simple (one-clause) sentences.	**More Formal**	It's **so hot** today **that** I won't go outside. It's **such a hot day** today **that** I won't go outside.
	Conversational	It's **so hot** today. It's **such a hot day** today.

---

1 **Review** Complete the following passages by adding *much* or *many.*

1. The brain receives so _____*many*_____ perceptions that it cannot begin to store all of them in the memory. Imagine yourself, for example, at a crowded party. There is so _____ input—so _____ colors, odors, and tastes, so _____ noise, so _____ shapes and sizes—that your brain must be selective. While you are enjoying yourself, your brain is hard at work deciding what you will or will not remember.

2. All memory experts agree that you will remember _____ more if you concentrate and practice. If you pay close attention and repeat a

piece of information several times, you will remember _____
more details. In fact, _____ people have developed systems
for repeating details.

3. We constantly receive _____ more information than we can
remember, and we can remember some things _____ more
easily than others. Memories are triggered by _____ things,
including sight, sound, smell, and taste. However, there are only two basic
types of memory: short-term memory and long-term memory.

4. _____ scientists believe that short-term memory, lasting only
one-half hour or so, is only an electrical activity. Long-term memory, however,
seems to be _____ more complicated. It involves
_____ electrical and chemical processes, and it appears to
actually change the brain physically. So _____ processes are
involved that we are only beginning to understand what creates long-term
memory.

5. Currently, _____ research is being conducted on the process
of long-term storage of memories. _____ of these
experiments are being directed toward dreams and their role in the process.
Some scientists suggest that dreams are a review of _____ of
the day's activities to determine which ones are important enough to
remember. So _____ events happen during a day that
remembering everything would be impossible.

6. _____ brain research today is also focusing on the role of
repetition in remembering. Scientists are looking at how
_____ repetition is necessary. That is, how
_____ times do you need to repeat something like a phone
number in order to remember it?

2 Practice Complete each sentence by using *so, such,* or *such a(n)* and adding an
ending.

Example I was ___so___ cold that _I couldn't sleep_.
It was ___such a___ cold day _that I couldn't get my car started_.

1. The weather was _____ beautiful. . . .

It was _____ beautiful weather. . . .

2. They sang _____ wonderfully. . . .

They have _____ wonderful voices. . . .

3. It was _____ loud noise. . . .

The noise was _____ loud. . . .

4. The article was _____ interesting. . . .

It was _____ interesting article. . . .

5. She got _____ bad sunburn. . . .

She got _____ badly sunburned. . . .

6. The race was _____ exciting. . . .

It was _____ exciting race. . . .

3 **Practice** Complete the following selections by using *so, so much / many, such,* or *such a(n)* and adding an ending to each sentence. In some cases, you will need to add your own adjective.

Example **The Smell of Fresh Bread**

Fresh-baked bread has __*such a*__ wonderful smell that *it makes my* mouth water.

I put __*so much*__ butter on it that *it's very fattening* .

It tastes __*so*__ good that *I can eat a whole loaf* .

Life in a New Place

1. A new city or country has _____ new sights, sounds, tastes, and smells that. . . .

2. When I first arrived here, I had _____ difficult time adjusting that. . . .

3. The people were _____ _____ (adjective) that. . . .

4. The food was _____ _____ (adjective) that. . . .

5. There was _____ noise that. . . .

Neighbors

6. Last night, my neighbors had _____ violent arguments that . . .

7. The neighbors' voices were _____ _____ (adjective) that. . . .

8. They seem to have _____ problems that. . . .

9. They are both _____ aggressive people that. . . .

Childhood Nightmares

10. When I was younger, I used to have _____ terrible nightmares that. . . .

11. Some of them were _____ vivid that. . . .

12. In fact, one was _____ realistic nightmare that. . . .

 4 **Review** In pairs, combine the following ten sentences. Use a variety of connecting words, phrases, or transitions. These may include *that, which, when, so that, in order to, because, however, more than,* and so on. Many combinations are possible, but be prepared to discuss differences in meaning and / or focus as you try different possibilities. Omit unnecessary words.

Example   The earliest psychologists believed in magic and the supernatural. Modern psychology is a respected science. Modern psychology is based on careful research.

Although the earliest psychologists believed in magic and the supernatural, modern psychology is a respected science (which is) based on careful research.

1. Psychoanalysis involves remembering dreams. Psychoanalysis involves analyzing dreams. Psychoanalysis is a type of therapy. Psychoanalysis was developed by Sigmund Freud.

2. Freudian analysts use dreams. These analysts want to unlock the secrets of their patients' minds.

3. According to psychoanalysts, our dreams represent ideas. Our dreams represent emotions. We are trying to suppress these ideas or emotions.

4. We suppress these ideas. We suppress these emotions. Then we cannot resolve conflicts. Ideas or emotions create conflicts.

5. Many current brain researchers disagree with psychoanalysis. These researchers believe dreams have a different purpose.

6. According to them, the brain collects too much information. The brain cannot store all of this information.

7. The brain may use dreaming. In this way, it can forget incorrect information. It can forget useless information.

8. Attempting to remember dreams may not be helpful. Attempting to remember dreams may interfere with the brain's housecleaning.

9. Brain researchers and psychoanalysts do not agree. Both are attempting to unlock secrets. Our minds hold these secrets.

10. Both groups continue to search for answers. One day we may understand the mysteries of the mind.

▲ Psychoanalysts discuss memories and dreams with patients in order to unlock some of the mysteries of the mind.

5 **Error Analysis** The following sentences all have one or more errors in connecting words or comparisons. Find the errors and try to correct each sentence in at least two different ways.

Example In 1778, Franz Anton Mesmer went to Paris so that he demonstrated animal magnetism, better known today as hypnotism.

Correction: In 1778, Franz Anton Mesmer went to Paris so that he could demonstrate animal magnetism, better known today as hypnotism.
OR
In 1778, Franz Anton Mesmer went to Paris to demonstrate animal magnetism, better known today as hypnotism.

1. Despite he had been unknown in the French capital, Mesmer soon became a celebrity.

2. Thousands flocked to his salon in order that be cured of every illness imaginable.

3. In fact, many patients came for help so that Mesmer had to turn large numbers of them away.

4. Mesmer's treatment gained popularity that crowds gathered outside his salon demanding treatment.

5. At one point, the crowds became such an uncontrollable that he devised a special treatment.

6. Mesmer "magnetized" a tree and had these people hang from ropes in order cure them.

7. However, Dr. Mesmer developed a large group of supporters, others were more skepticaler of the doctor and his treatments.

8. In particular, government officials in Paris were so unimpressed by animal magnetism. In spite Mesmer's loyal followers, a French Royal Commission declared animal magnetism dangerous.

9. This was so important judgment that Mesmer was forced to leave Paris in disgrace.

10. Mesmer was discredited. Therefore, hypnotism eventually became a respected treatment.[1]

---

[1]Today, hypnotism is used in fields such as psychiatry, medicine, sports, and entertainment. As for Dr. Mesmer, he has become immortalized in language. The verb *mesmerize* and its derivatives are found in English, French, and several other European languages.

Using What You've Learned

6 **Using Descriptive Language** In groups, discuss the meanings of the following adjectives. Then try to use as many of them as possible in a two-minute conversation. You may want to discuss the weather, your apartment, a place near your home, various types of food, and so forth. Use the example as a model.

Example cold

It's so cold today that there is ice on the road.
OR
We're having such cold weather that I hate to go outside.
OR
We've had so much cold weather lately that my tan has totally faded.
OR
We've had so many cold days that the river may freeze.

acrid	exhilarating	hot	pungent	slippery
bitter	foggy	humid	repulsive	soft
bright	fragrant	icy	rough	sweet
bumpy	frightening	nauseating	salty	tart
dreary	harsh	painful	shrill	tense

Adverb Clauses and Related Structures

Problem areas with adverb clauses often appear on standardized English proficiency exams. Check your understanding of these structures by completing the sample items that follow.

Remember that . . .

✔ Connecting words must link ideas grammatically and logically.

✔ Concession and opposition express different types of contrast.

✔ *So that* indicates purpose while *so* shows result.

✔ Modal verbs generally appear in clauses with *so that* or *in order that*.

Part 1 Circle the best completion for the following.

Example   She was able to sleep _____ the noise.

    Ⓐ although   Ⓑ even though

    Ⓒ in spite of   Ⓓ however

1. Rex was exhausted and unsettled, _____.

    Ⓐ he insisted on starting a new project

    Ⓑ he slept for the remainder of the day

    Ⓒ but he insisted on starting a new project

    Ⓓ and wanted to go to bed

2. Mike seemed optimistic and well-rested even though _____.

    Ⓐ he was in the midst of an extended vacation

    Ⓑ he had been struggling with a tremendous task

    Ⓒ he had just returned from a month of vacation in Hawaii

    Ⓓ he appeared depressed and exhausted

3. The right hemisphere of the brain developed long ago _____ the left hemisphere appears to be relatively young.

    Ⓐ unlike   Ⓑ whereas

    Ⓒ on the other hand   Ⓓ as well as

4. Despite _____, the tournament officials decided against canceling the match.

    Ⓐ the impending bad weather

    Ⓑ the beautiful weather

    Ⓒ the fact that the weather was supposed to be acceptable

    Ⓓ of the bad weather which was forecast

5. Los Angeles is an enormous city. In contrast, _____.

   Ⓐ it has intractable traffic problems

   Ⓑ Monterey is rather small

   Ⓒ San Francisco

   Ⓓ I adore large cities

Part 2 Each sentence has one error. Circle the letter below the word(s) containing the error.

Example   They <u>were</u> <u>such</u> good speakers <u>so</u> they influenced <u>all of us</u>.
          A   B   Ⓒ   D

1. Jane tends to <u>dominate</u> at all meetings. <u>On the contrary</u>, George <u>prefers</u> to let
                  A   B   C

others <u>be</u> in charge.
        D

2. Many parts of the brain are involved in <u>humans'</u> ability to remember, <u>but</u>
                                          A   B

<u>although</u>, specific areas seem <u>to control</u> certain aspects of memory.
   C   D

3. Last night Jack stayed out very late and didn't get <u>much</u> sleep, <u>so</u> <u>that</u> he
                                                  A   B   C

feels <u>awful</u> today.
      D

4. The <u>keynote</u> speaker at the <u>campaign</u> luncheon was <u>such</u> good <u>that</u> almost
          A   B   C   D

the entire audience pledged to support him.

5. Robert has finally reached <u>the</u> conclusion that he <u>had better</u> give up his
                              A   B

position in order that he <u>returns</u> to school to <u>earn</u> a Ph.D.
                          C   D

Self-Assessment Log

Check the things you did in this chapter. How well can you do each one?

	Not Very Well	Fairly Well	Very Well
I can use a variety of adverb clauses appropriately.	❏	❏	❏
I can use a variety of adverb phrases and transitions appropriately.	❏	❏	❏
I can use a variety of adjectives, adverbs, and nouns to make comparisons.	❏	❏	❏
I can use verb forms and tenses appropriately.	❏	❏	❏
I can use appropriate punctuation.	❏	❏	❏
I can take a test about adverb clauses, phrases, and related structures.	❏	❏	❏
I understand new information about the brain, and I can use new structures and vocabulary to talk and write about related topics.	❏	❏	❏

Working

" The world is filled with willing people; some willing to work, the rest willing to let them. **"**   —Mark Twain

1. Have you held a job?

2. What kind of work do you hope to do in the future?

3. If you were independently wealthy, would you still choose to work?

Introduction

In this chapter, you will study ways of replacing words and phrases with noun clauses. As you study the chapter, notice any changes in emphasis when noun clauses are used. Also, pay attention to changes in verb tenses and position in noun clauses.

Reading Read the following passage. It introduces the chapter theme "Working" and raises some of the topics and issues you will cover in the chapter.

The U.S. Workforce

The U.S. census gathers much more information than simply the number of people living in the United States. The census tells us about population growth, life expectancy, housing, crime, eating and drinking habits, immigration and migration, and ethnic backgrounds of Americans. Some of the most interesting statistics, however, concern the work habits of Americans. The census gathers 5 detailed information on who is or isn't working, what kinds of jobs people hold, where they find the jobs, how much money they make, how they spend their earnings, how often they change jobs, how many people are injured on the job, and when men and women retire.

What recent census information has shown is that a definite shift in em- 10 ployment has occurred. America has moved from goods-producing industries to service-sector jobs. That Americans are better educated, healthier, and more mature by the time they enter the labor force is also significant. What the statistics do not show, unfortunately, is a significant narrowing in the gap between the earnings of men and women or between the opportunities available for 15 whites and minorities. Even more troubling, the gap between rich and poor is widening.

 Discussing Ideas Discuss the questions with a partner.

Do you think the information gathered from the census is important? What do you think about the changes shown by census information? Why do you think some things have changed? Why do you think some things haven't changed?

Setting the Context

Previewing the Passage Discuss the questions with a group.

In the United States, which occupations are growing the fastest? Which are declining? What do you think are the most interesting growing occupations?

Reading Read the passage.

The Changing U.S. Job Market

Which fields offer the best opportunities for a job? This is a question millions of people in the United States ask daily. It's particularly relevant because of all of the changes in the U.S. economy. According to a report from the Bureau of Labor Statistics (BLS), the transformation in the U.S. from a manufacturing to a service-based economy is continuing at a rapid pace. The report indicated   5
that the fastest-growing occupations were in areas such as information technology, education and health services, professional and business services, leisure and hospitality, and finances and that these trends would most likely continue. It also noted that the educational level of workers had risen dramatically and speculated that those without a college education would find it increasingly   10
difficult to find well-paying jobs. Finally, the report showed that the U.S. population is changing and the workforce is becoming more diverse. The number of Hispanic and Asian workers will continue to increase.

Discussing Ideas Discuss the questions with a partner.

How many service industries can you list? How many manufacturing industries can you list? What trend has been occurring in the U.S. economy in recent years? Is this likely to stop soon?

Grammar Structures and Practice

A. Introduction to Noun Clauses

A noun clause functions as a noun in a sentence.

- Just like nouns, noun clauses may be used as subjects, objects of verbs, objects of prepositions, and complements.
- Noun clauses are often used after these verbs:

add	*conclude*	*explain*	*illustrate*	*note*	*show*	*think*
ask	*estimate*	*find*	*indicate*	*remark*	*tell*	*wish*
believe	*exclaim*	*hope*	*mention*	*say*		

7.1 Noun Clauses

Structures	Explanations	Examples
Subject	In formal English, nouns clauses are often used as subjects. In conversational English, anticipatory *it* + noun clause is more common.[1]	**That the job market is changing** is obvious.
Complement	Complements follow linking verbs such as *be*.	A major concern is **how fast these changes are taking place**.
Object of Preposition	Noun clauses can follow prepositions.	We are concerned about **how fast these changes are taking place**.
Object of Verb	Noun clauses are often used in reporting after verbs such as *say, show, tell,* and *think*.	Statistics show **(that) white-collar jobs are increasing**.

Note: The verbs *say* and *tell* are often confusing. In general, *tell* is used when a person is referred to. Compare: *He told me he was leaving. He said he was leaving.* Not: **He said me he was leaving.*
[1]*It's obvious that the job market is changing* is an example of anticipatory *it* + noun clause.

1 Practice Use the accompanying charts of changes in employment in the United States to form sentences with noun clauses. Form five sentences for each chart. Begin your sentences with *This chart shows* (*says, tells us, indicates, illustrates,* etc.). . . . In your sentences, use adverbs (*slightly, moderately, substantially, tremendously,* etc.) or comparatives and superlatives to indicate the extent of the increase or decrease in jobs.

Example jobs in education and health services

This chart shows (indicates, tells us) that the growth of jobs in education and health services will decline moderately during the next several years.

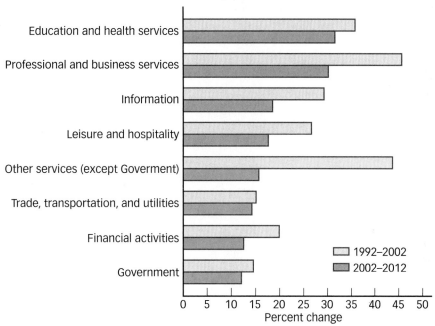

Percent Change in Wage and Salary Employment, Service-providing Industry Divisions, 1992–2002 and Projected 2002–2012

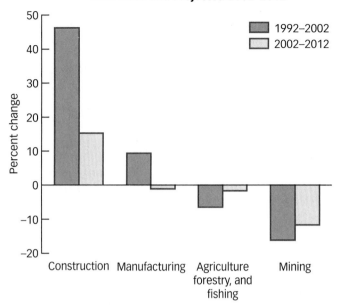

Percent Change in Wage and Salary Employment, Goods-producing Industry Divisions, 1992–2002 and Projected 2002–2012

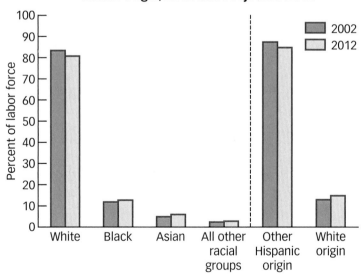

Percent of Labor Force by Race and Ethnic Origin, 2002 and Projected 2112

Source: http://stats.bls.gov

B. Quotations Versus Reported Speech

Quotations are someone's exact words, while reported speech often involves paraphrasing-keeping the idea but changing some language. Grammatically, certain changes often occur in reported speech.

7.2 Quotations Versus Reported Speech

Structures	Explanations	Examples
Quotations	Quotations are the exact words that a person has used to state something. A quotation appears within quotation marks, and a comma normally precedes or follows it.	Someone once said, "Work is what you do until you go home at night."
Reported Speech	Reported speech tells the ideas, but not necessarily the exact words, of the original speaker. Reported speech does not normally require commas or quotation marks.	Someone once said that work is (was) what we all do (did) until we go (went) home at night.

C. Changes in Verb Tense and Modals in Reported Speech

Verb tenses often change in reported speech. When the verb in the main clause (*Susan said,* etc.) is in the past, the verb in the noun clause is often shifted to one of the past tenses.

7.3 Changes in Verb Tense with Reported Speech

Explanations	Quotations	Reported Speech
In general, the verb in the main clause determines whether or not verbs shift tenses in the noun clause that follows. In some cases, the shifts can be optional, especially if the information is still true at the moment of speaking, but the changes *must* be consistent. The use of *that* is also optional in these sentences.	"Chris is at work." "Chris is finishing lunch." "He is going to stay until he finishes." "Chris hasn't finished yet." "He was working all day." "He came home very late."	Susan said that Chris **was** at work. She mentioned that Chris **was finishing** lunch. She added he **was going to stay** until he **finished**. Susan told me that Chris **hadn't finished** yet. She remarked that he **had been working** all day. She said that he **had come** home very late.

Note: When the noun clause gives "timeless" factual information, either present or past forms can be used: *Susan said that Chris always works (worked) on Saturdays.* The present is generally used when scientific or technical information is given: *The professor stated that water freezes at 32 degrees Fahrenheit.*

In reported speech, some of the modal auxiliaries also shift to past forms.

7.4 Changes in Modal Auxiliaries with Reported Speech

Explanations	Quotations with Modal Auxiliaries	Reported Speech
Can, may, must (referring to need), and *will* shift to past forms.	"Ann can help Chris." "John may help, too." "We all must help Chris." "Jami will also help."	Susan said that Ann **could help** Chris. She added John **might help**, too. She repeated we all **had to help** Chris. She mentioned Jami **would** also **help**.
Could, might, ought to, should, would, and all perfect modals do *not* change.	"Alex could help." "Ellen could have helped."	Carol said Alex **could help**. Carol said that Ellen **could have helped**.
When *must* expresses probability, it does **not** change.	"Camila must be tired." "She must have a lot to do."	Joe said Camila **must be** tired. Joe said she **must have** a lot to do.

2 **Practice** The Bureau of Labor Statistics compiles numerous statistics on jobs in the United States. The following information comes from a recent study. Change the information from direct statements to reported speech, making necessary changes in tenses. Begin with *This study showed* (*found, noted,* and so on). . . .

Example "White-collar jobs are increasing faster than blue-collar occupations."
This study showed that white-collar jobs were increasing faster than blue-collar jobs.

1. "The trend will continue indefinitely."
2. "Computer-related jobs are becoming more and more popular."
3. "The number of teaching jobs has begun to increase."
4. "Many bank tellers have lost their jobs."
5. "Many clerical workers may be replaced by new office machines."
6. "Some fields of medicine are already overstaffed."
7. "The job market in other areas of medicine, such as nursing and physical therapy, should grow."
8. "A higher percentage of older people are going to work."
9. "A good education has become more important in finding a well-paying job."
10. "Most areas of computer work continue to offer opportunities."

D. Changes in Pronouns, Adjectives, and Adverbials with Reported Speech

Pronouns, time and place expressions, and certain verbs are often changed in reported speech. The changes are made to show the correct relationship between the original information and the reported information. All of these changes must be made consistently.

7.5 Changes in Pronouns, Adjectives, and Adverbials with Reported Speech

Structures	Explanations	Quotations	Reported Speech
Pronouns and Demonstrative Adjectives	In reported speech, some pronouns and demonstrative adjectives (*this, these*) change to show the correct relationship by person, time, and place.	"I would like you to help us." "These pages need to be corrected."	Susan said that **she** would like **me** to help **them**. She said that **those** pages needed to be corrected.
Time and Place Expressions	Time and place expressions may also change. The change depends on when and where the reported speech occurs.	"We need the work now." "We will need the other pages tomorrow."	She said that they needed the work **then**. She added that they would need the other pages **the following day**.
Verbs	Some verbs are directional or time-related: *come / go, bring / take*. These verbs often change according to where and when the reported speech occurs.	"You should bring them here when you come to work."	She said that I should **take** them **there** when I **went** to work.

E. Changing Commands to Reported Speech

Commands are often changed into noun clauses in reported speech.

7.6 Changing Commands to Reported Speech

	Explanations	Commands	Reported Speech
Should	To change a command, an appropriate subject and a modal verb must be added to the command. *Should* is a very common choice for the modal.	"Finish your report by 10:00." "Be sure to proofread it."	My manager told me that **I should finish** my report by 10:00. My manager said that **I should be** sure to proofread it.
Other Modals	*Should* is often used in reported commands, but *must, need to, have to,* and *ought to* can also be added, depending on the strength of the command.	"Make ten copies." "Put it in a binder." "Get it to me by 10:05."	He said that I **had to give** it to him by 10:05.

Note: Commands can also be reduced to infinitive phrases. This is discussed in detail in Part 5.

3 Practice Part of a boss's job is to tell new employees what they have to do. Imagine that you are beginning a job. Your new boss told you many of the following things. Change the commands to reported speech. Use *said* or *told* and a variety of modals in your new sentences.

Example Be on time every day.

> *My boss told me that I had to be on time every day.*

1. Be at your desk by 9:00.
2. Do not arrive late except for emergencies.
3. Call me in case of an emergency.
4. Do not take more than 15 minutes for your breaks.
5. Leave for lunch at the scheduled time.
6. Do not make personal phone calls while you are working.
7. Do not send personal emails.
8. Limit your time on the Internet.
9. Call as early as possible if you are sick.
10. Schedule your vacations as far in advance as possible.

4 Practice Like work, school is often a world of rules and regulations. Teachers often tell students what they *have to, should, shouldn't, must not,* or *can* do. Make at least six sentences beginning with *Teachers tell students (us) that . . .* or *Teachers say that. . . .*

Example Teachers say that we must not chew gum in class.

5 Practice Change the following quotations to reported speech. Pay close attention to changes in verb tenses and in pronouns. Remember to add a reporting clause (*He said . . . , She added. . . .*) before each sentence.

Example Molly told me that she was a computer programmer around San Francisco, but that she had grown up in India. She said that she had helped design several new Web sites. She added that. . . .

1. "I'm a computer programmer around San Francisco. I grew up in India. I helped design several new Web sites. There's a lot of pressure in this type of work. Shopping and playing golf seem to relieve some of the tension."

2. "I've been moving furniture for five years. Yesterday we made a local delivery. Tonight we'll be working on a job about 20 miles from here. Next week I might be halfway across the country. I don't think I could ever sit at a desk all day."

3. "I started delivering newspapers when I was seven. The work was hard and I didn't make very much money. Now I work in a coal mine, and my wife works, too. We still don't make enough money. The more things change, the more they stay the same."

4. "I'm a tennis instructor, and I love my job. I can really help people play better when they listen to me. I may do something else in a few years. Maybe I should join an organization and do some volunteer work."

Using What You've Learned

6 **Telling about Jobs and Work Experience** In pairs, take turns asking each other the following questions and add some of your own. Then report briefly to the class on the information your partner gave you. Begin each sentence of your report with *X said . . . , X told me . . . , X remarked . . . , X mentioned . . . ,* etc.

Example *Nestor told me that he had had several different jobs.*

1. Have you ever had a job?

2. If so, what kinds of jobs have you had? What were your duties, your hours, and so forth?

3. Did you enjoy your work?

4. What was the most unusual thing that ever happened to you while you were working?

5. If you haven't worked, what jobs would you be interested in trying?

6. Are you preparing for a career now? What will your duties be in that type of job?

7 **Doing an Interview** Interview a friend, roommate, or someone in your community who is working full time. Ask them what they do, what their job is like, and what they like and dislike about it. Then report the information to the class.

Part 2 Clauses with Embedded Questions

Setting the Context

Previewing the Passage Discuss the questions with a group.

Have you ever interviewed for a job? What types of questions did the interviewer ask you?

Reading Read the passage.

Job Interviewing

Susan: Hi, Ellen. How was the job interview? How did it go?

Ellen: I think that it went well, but I'm not sure whether I've got the job. They're still interviewing a few more candidates. There are so many people looking for jobs these days.

Susan: Well, tell me about the interview. Who did you talk to? What kinds of questions did they ask?

5

Ellen:	I talked with Mrs. Harris. Of course, she asked me how much experience I'd had and why I wanted to work there. I told her about my work in Boston and Toronto. Then she wanted to know why I was quitting my job in Toronto.	
Susan:	What did you tell her?	10
Ellen:	I didn't know what to say. I finally said that I was tired of living in a city and that I'd like to move to a smaller town. I couldn't tell her what had really happened. She would never hire me then!	

 Discussing Ideas Discuss the questions with a partner.

Which of the following requests for information seems more polite? Why? Why are you quitting your job in Toronto? I'd like to know why you are quitting your job in Toronto. Why do you think that Ellen is quitting her job? Give at least three possibilities.

Grammar Structures and Practice

A. Clauses with Embedded Questions

Information questions may be changed to noun clauses. Question words such as *when, why, what,* and *who(m)* are used to introduce these embedded questions.

7.7 Clauses with Embedded Questions

Explanations	Information Questions	Noun Clauses with Question Words
Use question words—such as *when, why, what*—to introduce embedded questions.	When will you start your new job?	She wanted to know *when* I would start my new job.
When the question is changed to a noun clause, the subject must come *before* the verb, as it does in statements.	How much will you make?	She wondered *how much* I'll make.
	Who is going to be my supervisor?	Could you tell me *who* my supervisor is going to be?
Auxiliary verbs used to make questions are *not* used in the noun clause.	Why did you leave your last job?	She asked me *why* I had left my last job.

1 Practice The following are typical questions asked on a job application or in a job interview. Change them from direct questions to noun clauses with question words. Use the examples as models.

Examples   application / What is your name?
On an application, you will be asked what your name is.
interview / Why will you be an asset to the company?
During an interview, you may (might, could) be asked why you will be an asset to the company.

1. application / Where did you go to school?

2. application / Where do you live?

3. application / What work experience do you have?

4. application / Why do you want to work here?

5. interview / What coursework or special training have you had?

6. interview / How will your training and experience help you in this job?

7. interview / What are your strengths and weaknesses?

8. interview / Why should we hire you?

9. interview / How would you describe yourself? What kind of a person are you?

10. interview / How much money do you hope to earn?

B. Clauses with *If* and *Whether*

Yes / no questions may be changed to noun clauses by using *if* or *whether (or not)* to introduce them. Remember that the subject must come *before* the verb in the noun clause.

7.8   Clauses with *If* and *Whether*

Structures	Explanations	Yes/No Questions	Noun Clauses with *if, whether*
If	*If* is used in conversational English and in formal English. It often implies there is a *yes / no* answer.	Do you have any job openings? Is the manager here now?	I asked **if** they had any job openings. Do you know **if** the manager is here now?
Whether	*Whether* is preferred in formal English. It implies choice among alternatives rather than a strict *yes / no* decision.	Should I talk to the manager? Do I need an appointment?	I would like to know **whether (or not)** I should talk to the manager **(or not)**. I would like to know **whether (or not)** I need an appointment.

2 Practice Jobs are not the only situations that require interviews. Colleges and universities often use interviews to help in admissions and placement, especially with non native English speakers. The following list includes some typical questions used in academic interviews. Change them from direct questions to noun clauses with *if* or *whether*. Use the example as a model.

Example Are you applying to several schools?
I will (may, might) be asked if I am applying to several schools.
OR
I will (may, might) be asked whether I am applying to several schools.

1. Do you have your high school (or college) transcripts?

2. Do you have letters of recommendation?

3. Is your family supporting you? Do you have a scholarship? Will you need financial aid?

4. Have you taken the TOEFL® test? Did you find certain sections more difficult than others?

5. Did you take the admissions test (SAT, ACT, GRE, etc.)? Have you received your scores?

6. Are you planning to live with your parents? Have you ever lived on your own before?

3 Practice The following are typical questions asked during job interviews in specific careers. Imagine that you interviewed for one of these jobs. Tell about the questions you were asked. Change the direct questions to embedded questions. Pay close attention to the type of questions being asked (information questions or *yes / no* questions). Use the question words to begin your clauses or add *if* or *whether* when necessary. Pay close attention to shifts in verb tenses in the noun clauses.

Example executive secretary
How fast do you type?
The interviewer asked (wanted to know, inquired about) how fast I typed and whether I could.... Then she wanted to know....

1. executive secretary
   a. Can you use a fax machine?
   b. What other office machines do you know how to use?
   c. Which office software are you familiar with?
   d. Are you comfortable with the Internet?

2. truck driver
   a. Do you have a license for driving trucks?
   b. Have you ever hauled a load of over ten tons?
   c. Do you have a good driving record?
   d. Where did you last work?

3. graphic artist
   a. Who have you worked for?
   b. Which design software programs have you used?
   c. Have you had any experience with digital imaging?
   d. Do you have a portfolio?

4. restaurant manager
   a. How many people have you supervised?
   b. What kinds of restaurants have you worked in?
   c. How many meals did the restaurant serve per day?
   d. What hours was the restaurant open?

4 **Practice** After you return to your office from lunch, your assistant hands you a message from Janet. You know several women named Janet. In pairs, use the following cues to ask and answer questions about this message. One of you is the assistant, and one of you is Janet's friend.

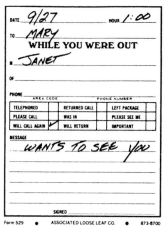

DATE 9/27   HOUR 1:00
TO MARY
WHILE YOU WERE OUT
■ JANET
OF
PHONE
AREA CODE   PHONE NUMBER

TELEPHONED		RETURNED CALL		LEFT PACKAGE	
PLEASE CALL		WAS IN		PLEASE SEE ME	
WILL CALL AGAIN	✓	WILL RETURN		IMPORTANT	

MESSAGE
WANTS TO SEE YOU

SIGNED
Form 529   •   ASSOCIATED LOOSE LEAF CO.   •   873-8700

Examples what / last name

    A: Did she tell you what her last name was?

    B: Sorry, she didn't tell me.

    where / call her

    A: Did she say where I could call her?

    B: No, she didn't leave her number.

1. what / want

2. if (whether) / call back

3. when / call back

4. how long / be in town

5. where / call from

6. if (whether) / be important

7. how / get my number

8. if (whether) / be free tomorrow

 5 Practice A coworker has just told you that your boss is angry and wants to see you immediately. With a partner, complete the following list of questions to ask the coworker. Then find a different partner. Your second partner will play the part of coworker.

Example Did she say who _she was angry with_?

    Did she mention whether ____ _I was involved_ ____?

1. Did she tell you why _____?

2. Do you know whether _____?

3. I need to know when _____.

4. Did she mention where _____?

5. Could you tell me what _____?

6. She must have told you who _____.

6 Practice Do you plan to work after you have finished your studies? Will you be looking for a job in the near future? What are some of your concerns? Complete the following sentences in your own words, telling about your hopes, fears, and goals. Use a question word (*how much, how often, where, when, why, if, whether,* etc.) to begin each clause that you add.

Example Everything depends on *when I finish school.*

1. I'm concerned about. . . .

2. I'm interested in. . . .

3. I don't really care about. . . .

4. I'm (not) worried about. . . .

5. I've been thinking about. . . .

6. So far, I haven't paid attention to. . . .

7. Sometimes I'm nervous about. . . .

8. Right now, I'm tired of. . . .

Using What You've Learned

7 **Role-playing Job Interviews** Whether you have worked or not, you have probably been interviewed at one time or another. Sharpen your skills by role-playing interviews for various jobs. You will probably not have tried these jobs, so be sure to use your imagination as you ask and answer job-related questions. Interview for three of these jobs or think of your own.

Jobs

auto mechanic	carpenter	jet pilot
ballet dancer	computer hacker	lead singer in a rock group
bartender	ESL teacher	model
beautician	florist	smuggler
brain surgeon	genetic engineer	taxi driver

Be sure to ask for the following information.

Interviewers

1. personal data: name, address, and so on
2. previous work experience in general and previous experience in this area
3. reasons for leaving last job
4. hopes, plans, career goals

Interviewees

1. hours and salary
2. vacation time
3. benefits
4. working conditions
5. job security

Useful Expressions

I would like to know (if, whether, when, how much, etc.). . . .

Could (Would) you explain (describe, tell me, etc.). . . ?

Would you mind explaining (telling me, etc.). . . ?

It's important for me to know when (how, how often, etc.). . . .

When you are finished, report to the class about which job your partner was seeking, whether you hired him or her, and why or why not.

Previewing the Passage Discuss the questions with a group.

When the economy is growing, does everyone benefit?

Reading Read the passage.

Equality for All?

In many ways, the U.S. economy is the envy of the world. However, all the news is not good. One very troubling aspect of the "miracle economy" is the difference in income between rich and poor. In the last 30 years, the money made by wealthier Americans has increased dramatically. At the same time, when adjusted for inflation, the income of the poorest 20 percent has dropped. Some economists say that differences in income levels are an essential part of the capitalist economic system. They believe that higher incomes are the reward of harder work and more important contributions to the economy. Other experts argue that such a great difference in wealth is harmful to society. They say that it undermines the ideas of opportunity and equality and thus it leads to increases in violence and crime. In their opinion, it is essential that the government close the income gap between rich and poor.

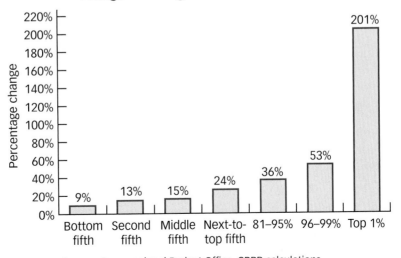

Change in Average After-Tax Income: 1979–2000

Source: Congressional Budget Office, CBPP calculations

Discussing Ideas Discuss the questions with a partner.

What reasons can you give for the gap in income in a wealthy nation such as the United States? Do you think something should be done to close this gap between the rich and the poor? If so, what?

Grammar Structures and Practice

A. Statements of Urgency with *That*

A special form can be used to soften a command. This form is called the subjunctive.

7.9 Statements of Urgency with *That*		
Explanations	**Adjectives**	**Examples**
The subjunctive form is the same as the simple form of the verb (*be, go, have*, etc.). *Not* comes before the verb in the negative. These statements are similar to commands but less direct and thus "softer." Compare: *Be on time! It's crucial that you be on time.*	advisable imperative best important crucial necessary desirable urgent essential vital	It is **essential** that he **be** on time. It is **important** that you not **arrive** late. It was **urgent** that they **discuss** the matter. It was **vital** that she **make** a decision immediately.

Note: Modal verbs are not used in the noun clause with this type of construction. Correct: It was desirable that they *talk*. Incorrect: *It was desirable that they *should talk*.

1 Practice Rephrase these sentences to begin with *It is important* (*essential, urgent,* etc.). . . . Make any other necessary changes.

In a recent speech, an activist for economic change demanded the following:

Example People must be made aware of employment issues.

It is essential that people be made aware of employment issues.

1. The gap between rich and poor must be closed.

2. Sex or race must not be used to judge workers.

3. Employers must not discriminate against women or minorities.

4. Every qualified person must have equal opportunity for employment.

5. Every person in the country must have access to a quality education.

6. The company should try to hire people from all parts of the population.

7. There should be more minorities in management positions.

8. There must be more economic development in poorer areas.

9. More affordable housing should be built.

10. All children must have the opportunity to attend quality schools.

B. Urgent Requests with *That*

The subjunctive is also used in noun clauses with *that,* which follow certain verbs of request. This form of request is formal and polite yet fairly strong.

7.10	Urgent Requests with *That*	
Verbs	**Explanations**	**Examples**
advise **ask** **command** **require** **urge**	The verb in the main clause may be in any tense. The simple form is used for the verb in the noun clause. In conversational English, infinitives are normally used after the verbs *advise, ask, command, require,* and *urge,* rather than clauses with *that.*	We **asked** that the manager **attend** the meeting. We **asked** the manager **to attend** the meeting.
demand **insist** **desire** **propose** **recommend** **request** **suggest**	For these verbs also, the verb in the main clause may be in any tense. The simple form is used for the verb in the noun clause. With the verbs *demand, insist, desire, propose, recommend, request,* and *suggest,* infinitives are not normally substituted.	We were going to **request** that the vice president **participate**. We **demand** that something **be** done about these problems. We **desire** that everyone **be** aware of the problems.

Note: As with statements of urgency, modal verbs are not used in noun clauses with this type of construction.

---

2 **Practice** Every workplace has rules that employees are required to follow. "Soften" the following commands by changing them to strong requests. Begin each request with *My boss asks that . . . , requests that . . . , insists that . . . , requires that . . . ,* and so forth. Make any other necessary changes.

Example Be on time.
> *My boss requires that I be on time.*

1. Don't make personal calls.

2. Keep your breaks to 15 minutes.

3. Don't leave before five o'clock.

4. Work fast but try not to make mistakes.

5. Plan your vacations in advance.

6. Be friendly but efficient.

7. Stay off the Internet.

8. Come to me if you have any problems.

3 **Practice** Unions traditionally have tried to bring better salaries and working conditions to workers at lower income levels. The following is a list of issues that a union has brought to a software corporation named Macrohard. Change the list so that each item includes a noun clause with *that*.

Example The union asked Macrohard to improve the salaries of the lowest-paid workers.

The union asked that Macrohard improve the salaries of the lowest-paid workers.

1. The union asked Macrohard to provide health insurance to all employees.
2. The union asked the company to provide child care.
3. The workers demanded to be given equal pay for equal work.
4. The union requested the company to publicize all job openings.
5. The workers demanded to be given equal consideration for promotions.
6. The union urged the company to forbid all forms of sexual harassment.
7. The workers asked the company to allow job sharing.
8. The union advised Macrohard to allow flexible schedules.
9. The union urged the company to give one-month vacations.
10. The workers urged the union representative to negotiate the best possible contract.

4 **Practice** Imagine that you are a union representative for one of the groups listed below. You are concerned with the health, safety, pay, and benefits of your union members. What are some of the "demands" that you will make to the workers' employers? Use your own ideas to complete each sentence.

Unions

Truck Drivers' Local 441 [1]
Farm Workers' Local 70
Nuclear Power Plant Workers' Local 10
Textile Workers' Local 55
Restaurant Workers' Local 12
Brain Surgeons' Local 617
Secret Agents' Local 007

1. I (will) ask that. . . .
2. I (will) demand that. . . .
3. In my opinion, it's necessary that. . . .
4. In fact, it's vital that. . . .
5. Because of . . . , it's urgent that. . . .
6. In conclusion, I request that. . . .

---

[1] A *local* is a local union group, often a branch of an intermediate or national group. The number is the "designation number" for the particular local union.

5 Practice Mrs. Jones is the manager of a large insurance office. Her assistant, Bill Thomas, has just arrived late. It is 9:45. As you read the following conversation, imagine that you are Bill Thomas. Using reported speech, pretend that you are retelling this conversation to a friend later in the day. Make all necessary changes in verbs, pronouns, and adverbs.

Example I really had some problems this morning. First, Mrs. Jones told me that I was late and that I. . . .

Mrs. Jones:	You're late! You were late yesterday, too. I hope that you won't continue this.
Bill:	I'm sorry, Mrs. Jones. The bus broke down today.
Mrs. Jones:	What happened yesterday?
Bill:	I'm really sorry. I forgot to tell you that I had a doctor's appointment. The appointment was for 7:45, but the doctor ran late with the patient before me. I wasn't able to get in to see him until 8:15.
Mrs. Jones:	That's understandable. However, I ask that you tell me these things. I also ask that you come on time. It is essential that we run on schedule here.
Bill:	Sorry again, Mrs. Jones. I hope that you'll forgive me.
Mrs. Jones:	All right, but don't let it happen again. Now, where is that report that you promised me? When will you be finished with the Weir account? Have you found all the information that you need?

Using What You've Learned

 6 Role-playing Labor Negotiations In pairs, role-play some of the following situations involving problems between an employer and employee or add a few original situations. Take turns role-playing the boss and the employee. Try to use these expressions in your role-plays:

It's vital that. . . .
I (We) demand that. . . .
It's urgent that. . . .
We insist that. . . .
It is essential that. . . .
I (We) request that. . . .
I (We) ask that. . . .
I wonder why (how, etc.). . . .
I would like to know if (why, when, etc.). . . .
Could you tell me why (how, who, etc.) . . . ?

Problems

1. X works full time but doesn't make enough money to support his / her family. X wants a significant raise.

2. W is late to work more often than he / she is on time.

3. J's boss often requires that J stay after 5:00 P.M. to do extra work. J feels he / she is being taken advantage of.

4. Y's knowledge of computers is very important to the business, but he / she spends a lot of time surfing the Internet while at work. Other employees believe he / she doesn't work as hard as they do.

5. Z gossips about fellow employees and has created some serious problems. Many of the other employees are upset and are threatening to quit.

6. T's wife is about to give birth. T wants to take three months off work because he is about to be a father.

Part 4   Clauses as Subjects of Sentences

Setting the Context

Previewing the Passage Discuss the questions with a group.

In your opinion, do most people like their jobs? Explain your answers.

Reading Read the passage.

Job Satisfaction

While Studs Terkel was writing his book *Working*, he asked 135 people, from elevator operators to company presidents, "How do you like your job?" The overwhelming majority answered, "I don't!"

Why people dislike their jobs is often obvious. In today's world of mass production and division of labor, few people are doing a job that is unique. Most workers perform tasks just like thousands or millions of other workers. As a result, few workers feel truly necessary or important. They seldom get the feeling of satisfaction that comes from accomplishing something.

5

That job satisfaction is related to productivity is also obvious. What seems to give most people satisfaction is to complete an entire project. Yet the organization of business today rarely allows workers that opportunity. Although workers today have better pay and benefits, safer working conditions, and more job security, their productivity level has fallen throughout the world. Dissatisfied workers do not perform as well as those who are satisfied.

10

 Discussing Ideas Discuss the questions with a partner.

What are some of the most boring jobs you can think of? What are the most interesting? Can you do a good job if you hate what you are doing?

Grammar Structures and Practice

A. Clauses as Subjects of Sentences

A noun clause may be used as the subject of a sentence. In this case, the noun clause *must* begin with a connecting word and take a singular verb.

7.11 Clauses as Subjects of Sentences		
Explanations	**Words or Phrases as Subjects**	**Noun Clauses as Subjects**
The noun clause *must* begin with a connecting word.	**Their job** is difficult.	**What they do** is difficult.
	His mistakes are numerous.	**What he is known for** is his mistakes.
The noun clause takes a singular verb.	**Something** is certain.	**That he is a troublemaker** is certain.

1 Practice English speakers will often answer a question by beginning with a noun clause formed from the question. This is particularly common when the person is trying to avoid answering the question. Change the following questions to noun clauses and use the clauses as subjects to complete the phrases. *Note:* With *yes / no* questions, only *whether* is used.

Example Why is Harry always late?   . . . is a mystery to me.
Why Harry is always late is a mystery to me.

1. Where is Harry today?   . . . is a mystery to me.

2. Why isn't he at work?   . . . is not important.

3. Is he sick again?   . . . is none of our business.

4. Why does he have so many days off?   . . . doesn't concern us.

5. How does he get any work done?　　　. . . doesn't really matter.

6. Has the boss decided to fire him?　　　. . . is irrelevant.

7. How much does he make?　　　. . . is his business.

8. Does he have a company car?　　　. . . is confidential.

2 **Practice** English speakers will also begin sentences with noun clauses formed from questions in order to stall. Rephrasing the original question into a clause allows the person a little time to think over the answer. In pairs, take turns asking and answering the questions that follow. You may want to talk about work and experiences with jobs, or you may answer more generally about your schoolwork, hobbies, and so forth. Begin your responses with noun clauses.

Example What do you like to do the most?

What I like to do most is to talk with people.
OR
What I like to do most is to spend time outdoors.

1. What do you like to do the most?

2. Why do you like to do this?

3. What do you least like to do?

4. How do you work best (slowly, under pressure, etc.)?

5. Where do you work best (at home, in an office, etc.)? Why?

6. When do you work best (in the morning, on rainy days, etc.)? Why?

7. What do you like to wear to work (casual clothes, a suit and tie, etc.)?

8. When do you take breaks (when you finish a project, when you feel like it, etc.)?

B. Anticipatory *It* + Clauses with *That*

In conversational English, *it* is often used to begin sentences rather than placing the noun clause in subject position.

7.12	Anticipatory *It* + Clauses with *That*	
Explanations	**Noun Clauses as Subjects**	**Anticipatory *It***
Anticipatory *it* + noun clause is common in conversational English. Remember that sentences with *it* + adjectives of urgency (*vital, urgent, necessary*, etc.) are followed by verbs in the subjunctive mood.	**That he is a corporate spy** is now certain. **That we arrest him** is necessary.	It is certain **that he is a corporate spy.** It is necessary **that we arrest him.**

3 Practice Change the following sentences to begin with *it* instead of noun clauses.

Example   That Harry dislikes his job so much is a shame.
   It's a shame that Harry dislikes his job so much.

1. That Harry is unhappy in his job is obvious.
2. That he hasn't already quit is surprising.
3. That he has stayed at this job so long amazes me.
4. That he will quit soon is almost certain.
5. That he find a better-paying job is essential.
6. That he might not make enough to support his family worries us.

4 Practice Do you intend to work? What are your job prospects? Will you be able to find a job that you like and that pays well? Form at least six sentences on this topic. Begin them with *It's (un)likely (fairly certain, doubtful, too bad, lucky,* etc.) *that. . . .*

5 Practice Many factors are involved in job satisfaction, but not everyone places the same value on each factor. Whether you have worked, are working now, or may work in the future, consider the following list of concerns. In your opinion, what is or is not important in thinking about working and the job market? Form noun clauses from the information and use them to complete the following sentences. Then rephrase your sentences to use anticipatory *it.*

amount of job security	number of sick days
amount of money	place of employment
amount of responsibility	type of benefits
amount of vacation time	type of work
hours of work per day	type of working conditions

Example   place of employment
   Where I work isn't really important to me because I can live almost anywhere.
   It isn't really important to me where I work because. . . .
   OR
   Where I work concerns me because I don't want to live in a large city.
   It concerns me where I work because. . . .

1. . . . concerns me because. . . .
2. . . . worries me. . . .
3. . . . matters to me. . . .
4. . . . is important to me. . . .

5. . . . doesn't concern me. . . .
6. . . . doesn't worry me. . . .
7. . . . doesn't matter to me. . . .
8. . . . isn't important to me. . . .

6 **Error Analysis** Exploitco, Inc., has decided to cut its costs. It plans to lay off workers, and the workers, obviously, are not happy about this. The following sentences have errors in their use of noun clauses. Find and correct the errors.

announced
Example Exploitco ~~announces~~ that it was going to lay off 50 workers.

1. The workers asked why was the company going to do this.
2. The management said them that the company was losing money.
3. The workers asked to the management if the company had considered alternatives.
4. According to the management, it was necessary that workers were laid off.
5. The workers told to the management that they would like to discuss the situation.
6. The workers suggested that everyone took pay cuts.
7. What would that do was to save all the jobs.
8. Working together, the workers and management decided how would they solve the problem.

Using What You've Learned

7 **Role-playing Complaints** Do you have some complaints about your home, school, or job? Choose one of the following combinations. In pairs, role-play your complaints.

two roommates
a teacher and a student
a student and a person in the school administration
a parent and a child
a boss and an employee

Useful Expressions

What bothers (irks, irritates) me is. . . .
What drives me crazy is. . . .
What I can't stand is. . . .
What I don't like is. . . .
Why I get angry (upset, etc.) is. . . .

8 **Giving an Interview** Imagine that you are a gossip columnist and your job is to get as much information as possible during an interview. Your interviewees are often upset by your questions and do their best to avoid answering. Work in pairs and role-play your interviews.

Interviewees

Bill Gates	a rock star	the president
your teacher	a sports figure	a movie star

Useful Expressions

. . . is none of your business.

. . . is private.

. . . doesn't (shouldn't) concern you.

. . . is irrelevant.

. . . is top secret.

. . . is not something I can discuss.

. . . must be kept confidential.

Part 5   Reduction of Noun Clauses to Infinitive Phrases

Setting the Context

Previewing the Passage Discuss the questions with a group.

How would you define stress? When do you feel stress? What jobs do you consider the most stressful?

Reading Read the passage.

Job Stress

All jobs create some type of stress. Perhaps your boss asks you to work overtime to complete a report by a certain deadline. Maybe it is necessary for you to stand in the same spot at an assembly line eight hours a day, five days a week. There could be days when you are forced to sit at your desk with nothing to do, watching the clock, but you must not leave because you are at work.   5
Each of these situations creates stress.

Through many years of evolution, your body has learned how to respond to stress based on its instinct for survival. Just as if you were in the wilderness facing a wild animal, your body reacts to stress by preparing for fight or flight. Your muscles tense. Your blood vessels constrict. Your pulse rate shoots up, and your   10
blood pressure soars.

Learning how to cope with stress is of primary importance in today's work world. Stress affects job performance, relationships, and the personal well-being of millions of people. The U.S. Clearinghouse for Mental Health Information claims that American businesses lose billions of dollars annually because of em-   15
ployees' stress-related disabilities. Health authorities estimate that as many as 60 percent of all doctor visits in the United States are due to psychological stress rather than specific illnesses.

Discussing Ideas Discuss the questions with a partner.

Do you believe that 60 percent of all doctor visits in the United States are due to stress? What are some physical and emotional reactions that you have when you are under stress? Some people perform better under moderate stress. Are you one of these?

Grammar Structures and Practice

A. Reduction of *That* Clauses in the Subjunctive Mood

Noun clauses in the subjunctive mood are commonly reduced to infinitive phrases. All adjectives of urgency preceded by *it* (*it is important, vital,* etc.) can be reduced as in the following chart.

7.13 Reduction of *That* Clauses in the Subjunctive Mood

Explanations	Noun Clauses	Infinitive Phrases
Sentences with anticipatory *it* + adjective + noun clause can be reduced to infinitive phrases.	It's **important** that you **call**. It was **essential** that he **have** the money.	It's **important for you to call**. It was **essential for him to have** the money.
Sentences with the following verbs of request can also be reduced to infinitives: *advise, ask, command, require, urge*.	I'll **advise** that he **call** right away. He **urged** that I **see** a lawyer.	I'll **advise him to call** right away. He **urged me to see** a lawyer.

1 Practice Working conditions are often a source of stress on the job. As Japanese manufacturers have shown, improvements in working conditions can often make a tremendous difference in employee productivity. The recommendations that follow are based on Japanese methods. Change the noun clauses to infinitive phrases.

Example To reduce stress, it is important that a person take periodic breaks to relax.

To reduce stress, it is important (for a person) to take periodic breaks to relax.

1. It is best that workers have a pleasant place to relax.

2. It is advisable that workers get regular exercise time on the job.

3. It is crucial that people work in a healthy environment.

4. It is essential that a worker have proper lighting.

5. It is vital that workers breathe clean air.

6. It is imperative that workers feel safe.

7. It is necessary that management provide training on new equipment.

8. It is important that management and workers have regular safety reviews.

2 Practice Decision making is another area where many Japanese companies have used effective strategies. Through participating in decision making, workers feel more responsibility for their work. This, in turn, reduces the stress that comes from feeling insecure in a position. In the following sentences, change the noun clauses to infinitive phrases. Include an indirect object when necessary.

Example Workers around the world are asking that their employers give them more power.

Workers around the world are asking their employers to give them more power.

1. Workers have asked that management allow them to participate in major decisions.

2. Negotiators have advised that management give workers more responsibility.

3. Workers have urged that companies reward employees for suggesting improvements.

4. Workers have asked that management allow them to do more of their work at home.

5. Workers have urged that management meet regularly with employees.

6. Negotiators have advised that management treat employees with respect.

7. Workers have asked that management consider dramatic changes.

8. Management has asked that workers be patient.

3 **Practice** Imagine that you are in the following situations. What can you do to promote the health, well-being, and productivity of everyone on the job? Express your ideas by completing the following sentences in your own words. Use infinitive phrases.

1. You are a manager in a large insurance office. Most of your workers spend eight hours a day at a desk, working on computers, meeting customers, or answering phones. What do you feel is important for maximum efficiency in the office?

   a. In my opinion, it's important. . . .
   b. It's also necessary. . . .
   c. In fact, it's essential. . . .
   d. It's best. . . .

2. You are an assembly-line worker in an automobile manufacturing plant. Each person on the line adds, checks, or paints one part of the automobile. You work with heavy machines that can be dangerous. What would you request of the management to make your work safer, more productive, or more pleasant?

   a. I would ask. . . .
   b. In fact, I have advised. . . .
   c. The government should require. . . .
   d. I strongly urge. . . .

B. Reduction of Indirect Commands, Requests, and Embedded Questions

Commands can be reduced to infinitive phrases in reported speech. The infinitive phrase expresses the same meaning as *should* + verb.

7.14 Reductions of Commands

Explanations	Commands	Reported Speech	Infinitive Phrases*
The verb *say* does not take a noun or pronoun before either a noun clause or an infinitive.	Stop it!	She said that we should stop it.	She said to stop it.
The verb *tell* must be followed by a noun or pronoun (as an indirect object). The direct object (a noun clause or an infinitive) follows the indirect object.	Finish the work. Do a good job.	She told us that we should finish the work. She told us that we should do a good job.	She told us to finish the work. She told us to do a good job.

* With infinitive phrases, the verbs *advise, beg, command, direct, encourage, order, urge,* and *warn* follow the same pattern as *tell*. A noun or pronoun (the indirect object) must be included before the infinitive.

Requests with *Will you . . . , Would you . . . ,* and *Could you . . .* can be reduced to infinitive phrases.

7.15 Reduction of Requests for Action and for Permission

Explanations	Requests	Reported Speech	Infinitive Phrases
Requests for Action			
The indirect object *must* be used with the infinitive phrase.	Will you help me? Could you lend me $5?	She asked (me) if I could help her. She asked (me) whether I could lend her $5.	She asked me to help her. She asked me to lend her $5.
Requests for Permission			
Requests with *May I . . . , Could I . . . ,* and *Can I . . . ,* can also be reduced to infinitive phrases, but *no* indirect object is used.	Could I leave early?	John asked (me) if he could leave early.	John asked to leave early.

Yes / no and information questions with modal auxiliaries may be reduced to infinitive phrases. With both types of questions, the speaker and the subject of the question *must* be the same person(s).

7.16 Reduction of Embedded Questions

Explanations	Questions	Embedded Questions	Infinitive Phrases
Yes / No **Questions**			
In reduced *yes / no* questions, *whether (or not)* is always used in an infinitive phrase.	Should I come early?	Jay asked if he should come early.	Jay asked whether to come early.
Information Questions			
With embedded information questions, a question word (*what, when, which,* etc.) is always used with the infinitive phrase.	Which pages should I read?	I asked (her) which pages I should read.	I asked (her) which pages to read.

4 **Practice** Losing a job is difficult, both psychologically and financially. Imagine that you have been laid off from your job. The following are things you would like to know. Rephrase the questions to use infinitive phrases.

Example How can I find a new job?
  I would like to know how to find a new job.

1. How long should I wait before applying for another job?
2. What kind of job should I look for?
3. How much money can I expect?
4. Where should I look?
5. What should I write on my résumé?
6. What can I do with so much free time?
7. How can I avoid becoming depressed?
8. How can I qualify for unemployment benefits?

5 **Practice** Losing a job and being unemployed presents a number of dilemmas. Rephrase the following questions to use infinitive phrases.

Example Should I borrow money to pay my bills?
  I don't know whether to borrow money to pay my bills.

1. Should I go back to school?
2. Should I wait for a good job?

3. Should I take a low-paying job?

4. Should I ask my family for help?

5. Should I give up my apartment?

6. Should I move in with my parents?

7. Should I get a roommate?

8. Should I go to an employment agency?

6 Practice Finding a job can be difficult, and sometimes you have to be very resourceful to come up with good possibilities. Imagine that a friend of yours is looking for a job. Give him or her some advice. Change the following commands to statements with infinitive phrases. Use the example as a model.

Example Go to the city employment office.

I would tell (urge, advise) my friend to go to the city employment office.

1. Read the want ads.

2. Ask everyone you know about possible jobs.

3. Don't wait for people to call you.

4. Visit all the major businesses in the area.

5. Talk to the counselors at your school.

6. Put an ad in the paper under "Positions Wanted."

7. Don't give up.

8. Try every possible method.

7 Practice Do you have any other suggestions for someone who is job hunting? Make a list of at least five sentences with infinitive phrases.

Using What You've Learned

8 Negotiating You and your classmates are employed in an automobile assembly plant. Several years ago, your company borrowed heavily from a bank, and the loan has come due. Unfortunately, your company has been losing money and cannot repay the loan. The bank has agreed not to demand its money immediately if your company reduces its budget by 25 percent.

Divide into two groups: one, the management, and the other, the employees. In your groups, decide what areas you would like to see the 25 percent reduction come from.

Be sure to adopt a hard-line bargaining position as well as a more moderate position. For example, even though you are willing to accept a 5 percent salary decrease, you might begin by demanding that your salary stay the same.

Finally, meet with members of the other group and try to negotiate a new contract. If you don't reach a compromise by the end of the class, the bank will foreclose and all of you will lose your jobs. Use the following data as you plan your strategy and negotiate.

EXPLOITCO, INC.
Management: 10 people
Workers: 200

PERCENTAGE OF BUDGET

Production costs	20%
Research and development	15%
Company psychiatrist	3%
Recreational facilities	3%
Campaign contributions	5%

	EMPLOYEES	MANAGEMENT
Salaries	15%	15%
Pensions	5%	5%
Health insurance	4%	4%
Paid vacation	1%	1%
Free lunches	2%	2%

As you negotiate, you might want to use the following expressions:

I (We) would like to know. . . .

Could you explain (tell us, etc.). . . .

I (We) don't understand. . . .

What we want is. . . .

What we are trying to do is. . . .

Why we are . . . is. . . .

How we. . . .

We demand (insist, ask, etc.). . . .

It is necessary (essential, crucial, advisable, etc.). . . .

Noun Clauses and Noun Clause Reductions

Problem area with noun clauses often appear on standardized English proficiency exams. Check your understanding of these structures by completing the sample items that follow.

Remember that . . .

✓ With reported speech, you must be consistent in changes in verb tenses, modal auxiliaries, pronouns, and adverbials.

✓ The word order of a question changes when it is placed within a noun clause.

✓ The simple form of the verb is used in noun clauses following statements of urgency or urgent requests.

✓ Many noun clauses can be reduced to infinitive phrases.

Part 1 Circle the best completion for the following.

Example   Susan said _____ would like to help.

   Ⓐ that   Ⓑ then

   Ⓒ she   Ⓓ if

1. Mr. Saffian promised that he _____ arrive yesterday.

   Ⓐ will   Ⓑ can

   Ⓒ would   Ⓓ had

2. The supervisor wanted to reach a consensus about _____ the work.

   Ⓐ if to finish   Ⓑ when she should finished

   Ⓒ whether to finish   Ⓓ finished

3. The interviewer was interested in how _____ process the new information.

   Ⓐ rapid I could   Ⓑ rapidly could I

   Ⓒ could I   Ⓓ rapidly I could

4. It is important that a person _____ ways to reduce stress on the job.

   Ⓐ finds   Ⓑ find

   Ⓒ is finding   Ⓓ will find

5. Mrs. Jones asked _____ fulfillment from a hard day's work.

   Ⓐ do you gain   Ⓑ did I gain

   Ⓒ whether I gained or not   Ⓓ whether or not I gained

Part 2 Each sentence has one error. Circle the letter below the word(s) containing the error.

Example   We <u>were going</u> to <u>request</u> <u>that</u> the president also <u>participates</u>.
                        A   B   C   Ⓓ

1. <u>It</u> is essential that everyone <u>is</u> on time to the meeting and that everyone <u>be</u>
   A   B   C

   <u>well prepared</u>.
      D

2. The official <u>demanded</u> that we <u>terminated</u> our involvement in the project
               A   B

   before she <u>returned</u> from her <u>furlough</u> in South America.
              C   D

3. Exactly <u>where is</u> Roberto today <u>is</u> something that the boss <u>insists</u> that she
              A   B   C

   <u>ascertain</u> immediately.
   D

4. <u>The</u> author Studs Terkel once <u>told</u> that the overwhelming majority of people
   A   B

   he <u>had interviewed</u> <u>did not</u> like their jobs.
        C   D

5. What did the lawyer <u>advise</u> the couple was <u>to confer</u> with a trained and
               A   B

   licensed marriage counselor before <u>the two</u> even contemplated
                                      C

   <u>getting</u> a divorce.
     D

Self-Assessment Log

Check the things you did in this chapter. How well can you do each one?

	Not Very Well	Fairly Well	Very Well
I can use noun clauses appropriately in a variety of positions in sentences.	❏	❏	❏
I can use embedded questions appropriately.	❏	❏	❏
I can use verb tenses appropriately in reported speech.	❏	❏	❏
I can use adjectives, adverbs, and pronouns appropriately in reported speech	❏	❏	❏
I can use appropriate verb forms with statements and requests of urgency.	❏	❏	❏
I can use infinitive reductions of noun clauses.	❏	❏	❏
I can take a test about noun clauses and related structures.	❏	❏	❏
I understand new information about trends in work in the United States, and I can use new structures and vocabulary to talk and write about related topics.	❏	❏	❏

Breakthroughs

❝If I have seen further than others, it is by standing upon the shoulders of giants.**❞**

—Sir Isaac Newton

Connecting to the Topic

1 What is a breakthrough?

2 How and when do you think breakthroughs occur?

3 Can you give some examples of breakthroughs in engineering, medicine, or art?

In this chapter, you will study the forms and uses of verbs in the passive voice. The time frame of a passive verb may be the same as that of an active verb, but the focus of the passive sentence is quite different. As you study the chapter, pay careful attention to the focus of the passive constructions.

Reading Read the following passage. It introduces the chapter theme "Breakthroughs" and raises some of the topics and issues you will cover in the chapter.

The Gifts of History

If the last 100 years is associated with anything, it is technological change. In transportation, for example, we have gone from the horse and buggy to the space shuttle. In medicine, diseases that could not even have been recognized a few years ago are now being diagnosed with sophisticated equipment and treated with genetic therapy, laser surgery, or newly synthesized drugs. How has so much been done in such a short time? The answer is that it hasn't. Not in such a short time, that is.   5

Of course, it is true that countless great advances have been made in our lifetimes. Yet, it is just as true that today's technological "miracles" are based on concepts of engineering, biology, physics, and chemistry that were discovered hundreds, if not thousands, of years ago. Thus, today's "unprecedented" achievements should not be viewed in isolation. They are the fruit of our technological inheritance that has been accumulated over centuries.   10

As Albert Einstein wrote when reflecting on his lifetime of work, "My inner and outer life is built upon the labors of my fellow men, both living and dead."   15

Discussing Ideas Discuss the questions with a partner.

What does the expression *the fruit of our technological inheritance* mean? Can you think of examples where current advances are directly based on years of inherited knowledge?

Setting the Context

Previewing the Passage Discuss the questions with a group.

How important is technology to our lives? Have we become accustomed to too many machines?

Reading Read the passage.

Technology: It's Everywhere!

How important is technology? Take a moment and look around. It hardly matters what time it is or where you are. Almost everything that you own, use, or even touch in the course of a normal day was created through technology.

In the morning, your toast is made and the coffee is brewed by electronic machines. You are transported to school or work by bus, train, car, or bike. During the day, you receive messages that are transmitted via phone, fax, or the Internet. Back home, dinner is prepared in a microwave, and programs are delivered to your television via antenna, cable, or satellite dish. And these are only a few examples.

You may like technology or hate it, but one thing is certain. In today's world, technology is almost impossible to escape.

 Discussing Ideas Discuss the questions with a partner.

Which machines are most important to you? Could you live without machines? Why or why not?

Grammar Structures and Practice

A. Introduction to the Passive Voice

All verbs have active voice forms, but only transitive verbs (verbs that take an object) can appear in either the active or the passive voice. The voice (active or passive) does not normally affect meaning but it *does* change the focus of the sentence.

8.1 The Passive Voice

Structures	Examples	Focus
Active	SUBJECT · VERB · OBJECT My dog bit the mailman.	In the active voice, the focus is on the agent or doer of the action (*my dog*).
Passive	The mailman was bitten by my dog. SUBJECT · VERB · AGENT	In the passive voice, the focus is shifted to the receiver of the action (*the mailman*).

1 **Practice** In each of the following sets of sentences, underline the verb(s) and indicate which verbs are passive and which are active. Then circle the noun that has the main focus in each sentence.

Example _passive_ (The telephone) was invented by Alexander Graham Bell in 1876.

active (Alexander Graham Bell) invented the telephone in 1876.

1. _____ Since 1876, many advances have been made in the field of communications.

_____ Since 1876, we have made many advances in the field of communications.

2. _____ Several companies began to produce personal computers in the 1970s.

_____ Personal computers began to be produced by several companies in the 1970s.

3. _____ By the late 1970s, portable cellular phones had been introduced and were being tested in both the U.S. and Japan.

_____ By the late 1970s, companies in both the U.S. and Japan had introduced and were testing portable cellular phones.

4. _____ By the early 1990s, the Internet was being used to communicate all over the world.

_____ By the early 1990s, people were using the Internet to communicate all over the world.

5. _____ By last year, technicians should have connected most colleges in the United States to the Internet.

_____ By last year, most colleges in the United States should have been connected to the Internet.

6. _____ Now, millions of students are doing research electronically.

_____ Now, research is being done electronically by millions of students.

7. _____ Today people can make phone calls, pay bills, produce movies, design buildings, and teach classes with computers.

_____ Today phone calls can be made, bills can be paid, movies can be produced, buildings can be designed, and classes can be taught with computers.

8. _____ How will our lives be changed by this technology?

_____ How will this technology change our lives?

B. The Simple Tenses

Passive forms of verbs have the same general meanings and time frames as verbs in the active voice.

- The passive voice of verbs in simple tenses is formed in this way: *will be, am, is, are, was, were* + past participle (+ *by* + agent).
- Adverbs of frequency usually come after the first auxiliary verb.

8.2 The Simple Tenses

	Active	Passive
Past Focus	Samuel Morse **invented** the Morse Code. Samuel Morse	The Morse Code **was invented** by Samuel Morse. The Morse Code
Present Focus	Inventors **make** new discoveries every day. Inventors	New discoveries **are made** by inventors every day. New discoveries
Future Focus	Technology **will control** our lives. Technology	Our lives **will be controlled** by technology. Our lives

2 Practice Underline all uses of the passive voice in the passage "Technology: It's Everywhere!" on page 335. Give the tense and time frame of each.

3 Practice Which of the following sentences can be changed to the passive voice? First, underline the subject(s) and double underline the verb(s) in each and circle any direct objects. Then change the sentences to the passive voice if possible.

Example   Scientists discover new technological advances every day.

New technological advances are discovered by scientists every day.

1. New technological advances usually arrive in major cities first.
2. Satellites transmit overseas telephone calls.
3. Computers design cars.
4. Athletes use computers to monitor their workouts.
5. Laser scanners read food prices in supermarkets.
6. Scientists compete to be the first to develop new products.
7. Hundreds of new products flood the market each year.
8. Some technologies spread very quickly.

C. By + Agent

By + noun (or pronoun) can be used in passive sentences to tell who or what performed the action of the verb. Note that most passive sentences in English do not contain these phrases, however. Use by + agent *only if* the phrase gives the following information:

8.3 By + Agent	
Uses of *By* + Agent	**Examples**
Information that is necessary to the meaning of the sentence	Houses **will be run** *by computers.*
A particular name or idea that is important in the context	Nine magnificent symphonies **were composed** *by Beethoven.*
New or unusual information	The telephone **was invented** *by Alexander Graham Bell.* It **was invented** in the 1870s.

4 **Practice** Read the following sentences and cross out *by + agent* where it is not necessary.

Example   Today, television is transmitted ~~by people and machines~~ to and from almost every part of the globe.

1. Television was originally created by people purely for entertainment.

2. Today, television is used by people for all types of purposes.

3. Television was made possible by researchers through a variety of technological breakthroughs.

4. In 1884, a scanner disk was developed by a German, Paul Nipkow.

5. Using this disk, an image was broken down into thousands of dots by Nipkow.

6. Later, a device was created by V. K. Zworykin that was used by him to scan and duplicate images using electron beams.

7. The cathode-ray picture tube was perfected and the first TV sets were produced by Allen B. DuMont in 1939.

8. On February 1, 1940, the first official program was broadcast in the United States by the National Broadcasting Company (NBC).

9. Soon, a variety of programs were being broadcast by different companies around the United States.

10. These early programs were all transmitted by the companies in black and white.

11. Later, color transmissions were achieved by researchers.

12. Today, very clear color transmissions are sent by companies across the globe in a matter of seconds.

5 **Practice** Change the sentences to the passive. Include *by* + agent when appropriate.

Example From about 1850 to 1910, many technological advances altered day-to-day life.

From about 1850 to 1910, day-to-day life was altered by many technological advances.

1. Elisha Otis exhibited the first modern elevator at the New York World's Fair in 1853.

2. From the 1850s to the 1880s, many inventors improved the steel-making process.

3. Cheap production of steel made stronger and taller buildings possible.

4. Using steel construction and elevators, builders soon built structures with more than five or six stories.

5. Thomas Edison of the United States and Joseph Swan of Great Britain simultaneously produced the first electric lamps in the late 1870s.

6. Willis Carrier invented air conditioning in 1911.

7. Air conditioning opened up entire new parts of the United States and the world for habitation.

8. People built hundreds of new houses in hot places like Houston, Texas, and Phoenix, Arizona.

▲ Thomas Edison

D. Common Expressions in the Passive Voice

There are many common expressions in English that use the passive voice. Notice the variety of prepositions that follow these expressions; *by* is also used, depending on the context.

8.4 Common Expressions in the Passive Voice		
be accustomed to	be equipped with	be made of (from)
be based on	be filled with (by)	be made up of
be composed of	be formed of (from, by)	be noted for
be connected to	be involved in (with)	be related to
be covered with	be known for (as)	be shown in (at, on)
be derived from	be known to + *verb*	be suited for
be designed for	be linked to	be used for (as, with)
be developed for (with)	be located in (at, on)	be used to + *verb*

Note: Verbs of emotion such as *amaze, bore,* and *interest* are often used in passive constructions. (*He's interested in sports. I'm amazed at her progress.*) For more on verbs of emotion, see Part 5.

6 **Practice** Use appropriate expressions from the preceding list to complete the following sentences. Use present or future tenses.

Example In the future, even powerful computers _____*will be made*_____ of portable components.

1. Today, most people _____ (still) to using paper, pencil, and their hands to do many chores.

2. Much of our work _____ up of manual tasks, such as opening and closing things, lifting and carrying things, and writing and typing things.

3. In the future, our houses and apartments _____ with amazing devices to help us communicate, do our work and shopping, and manage our homes.

4. Many of the devices _____ to a central house computer.

5. Some of these futuristic devices _____ to control the lighting and temperature in the house.

6. Other robot-like devices _____ for cleaning the house, doing laundry, and cooking.

7. Computer monitors _____ in the kitchen, the home office, and other important areas.

8. Your desk _____ (not) with papers; instead, it will have only a computer.

E. *Get* + Adjective or Past Participle

Another common English expression is *to get* + adjective / past participle.

8.5 *Get* + Adjective or Past Participle		
Explanations	**Structures**	**Examples**
In idiomatic expressions, *get* frequently takes the place of the more formal verb "become." *Get* (meaning *become*) + adjective or past participle is a form of the passive that is seldom used in writing but frequently used in conversation.	***get* + adjective** ***get* + past participle**	I **got angry** about the situation. I **got upset** about the situation. I **got worried** about the situation.

7 **Practice** Use *get* + adjective or past participle to complete the following to make true statements.

1. I get frustrated when. . . .
2. I always get sick when. . . .
3. When I'm late for class, I get. . . .
4. Before difficult exams, I get. . . .
5. If I don't sleep well, I get. . . .
6. I get bored when. . . .
7. I get really excited (about). . . .
8. I get confused. . . .

F. Anticipatory *It*

The passive voice is often used with *it* to avoid mentioning the agent or source. *By* + agent is rarely used with these constructions.

8.6 Anticipatory *It*		
Explanations	**Structures**	**Examples**
It is often used with the passive form of verbs such as *believe, confirm, deny, estimate, fear, hope, mention, report, say,* and *think.* Past expressions like *it was believed* indicate that these ideas have changed.	**Active** **Passive**	**People said, "The Earth is flat."** **It was said,** "The Earth is flat." **It was said** that the Earth was flat.*

That is added when a direct quote is changed to reported speech. In reported speech, verbs often shift to past tenses. See Chapter 7 for more on reported speech.

8 Practice As we learn more about our world, many beliefs change. Expressions such as *it was believed, it was felt,* or *it was said* are followed by noun clauses to indicate past beliefs that have changed. In these cases, the verbs in the noun clauses normally take past forms. For example, *are* becomes *were,* and *will* becomes *would.* Rephrase the quotations by using *It was believed, said, felt, thought,* or *feared.*

Example "Telephones will ruin the postal service."

It was believed that telephones would ruin the postal service.

1. "A telephone will always be too expensive for most people to have."
2. "Television will eliminate the movie industry."
3. "Faxes are useful only in large businesses."
4. "Computers are too complicated for ordinary people to use."
5. "All employees need to work in the office every day."
6. "It is too dangerous to have automatic tellers."
7. "Most people don't want to have a lot of electronic gadgets in their homes."
8. "Videotape is useful only for advertising firms."

9 Practice Complete the following passage with active or passive forms of the verbs in parentheses. Use simple verb tenses and add negatives and adverbs when indicated.

Electronic Mail Networks

Email __is commonly used__ on many university campuses by faculty and
          (use / commonly)

students who wish to communicate more easily and frequently among them-

selves. In an English as a Second Language course last semester, for example,

class discussions _____ place by email. During that course,
                          1 (take)

homework assignments _____ out over the network, and
                          2 (give / sometimes)

"chat lines" _____ so that the students could practice their
                  3 (organize)

language skills by email. Some students _____ by today's
                                              4 (overwhelm)

communication technology. However, most universities _____
                                                            5 (offer)

workshops for those who want to learn about email. Once email learners

_____ with the basic knowledge of how to use the network,
      6 (equip)

they _____ into not only a local but also a global network.
          7 (link)

And that global network _____ to expand daily.
                              8 (continue)

10 Practice Across college campuses, text messaging is a very popular way of communicating, and a "new language" has developed to make IM (Internet text messaging) faster and more efficient. Use the following abbreviations and their "translations" to make complete sentences. Then share any common IM abbreviations used in your native language and explain their meanings.

Example *"Are you okay?" is abbreviated as RUOK.*

Are you okay?	RUOK	Just in case	JIC
Be right back	BRB	No problem	NP
But I could be wrong	BICBW	Oh, I see. . . .	OIC
By the way	BTW	See you	CU
Got to go	G2G	See you later	CUL8R
I don't know. . . .	IDK	Talk to you later. . . .	TTUL
I'm sorry	IMS	What?	?
Just kidding. . . .	JK	You there?	UT?

Using What You've Learned

11 Describing Processes Many of you have developed hobbies or have worked in a particular field or career. Consider some of the processes involved in your hobby or your work and how you can explain one or two of them step by step. Then in pairs or small groups, give a clear, but fairly detailed, explanation of the process to your classmates.

For example, if you are a civil engineer, you may want to describe how a road is built, how land is surveyed, or how a bridge is constructed. If you have a hobby such as photography, perhaps you could talk about how film is developed or how pictures are enlarged.

Setting the Context

Previewing the Passage Discuss the questions with a group.

What changes have occurred in medicine in the last 150 years? What break-throughs have taken place in our knowledge of medical care and treatments?

Reading Read the passage.

Miracles in Medicine

Just imagine that you were alive 150 years ago and that you were in a serious accident or had a serious illness. What were your chances of survival?

At that time, only a few truly effective medicinal remedies had been developed. For example, cinchona bark (quinine) was used to fight malaria, and digitalis was used to treat heart failure. Other infections or diseases simply had to 5 run their course, and the patient either died or recovered, with little medical help.

Since those days, medicine has been completely transformed by a large number of discoveries. An amazing array of "wonder drugs" have been developed, and today they are commonly used worldwide. Antibiotics, for example, 10 have made it possible to treat bacterial infections; the development of anti-malarial drugs has been a very important factor in allowing people to live productively in the tropics; and vaccines have been effective in preventing many diseases. In fact, smallpox has been virtually eliminated from the face of the Earth. 15

As a result of these medical miracles, your chances of surviving both a very bad accident and a serious illness have increased dramatically—thank goodness!

Discussing Ideas Discuss the questions with a partner.

What serious infectious diseases, which were formerly common, have now become rare? Can you name other important therapeutic drug discoveries?

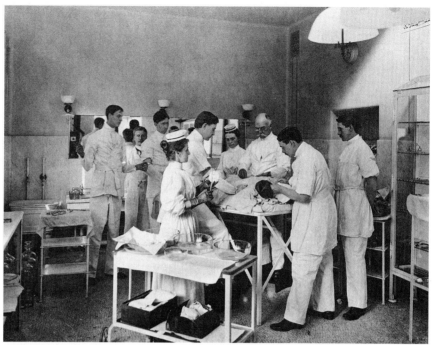

▲ A 1923 operating room

Grammar Structures and Practice

A. The Perfect Tenses

The passive voice of verbs in the perfect tenses is formed in this way: *have (will have, has, had)* + *been* + past participle (+ *by* + agent). Adverbs of frequency generally come after the first auxiliary verb.

8.7 The Perfect Tenses		
	Active	**Passive**
Present Perfect	Drug companies **have developed** many new antibiotics since the 1950s. **Focus:** Drug companies	Many new antibiotics **have been developed** since the 1950s. Many new antibiotics
Past Perfect	Until the 1950s, scientists **had developed** few antibiotics. **Focus:** Scientists	Until the 1950s, few antibiotics **had been developed**. Few antibiotics
Future Perfect	Within the next few years, companies **will have developed** several new drugs. **Focus:** Companies	Within the next few years, several new drugs **will have been developed**. Several new drugs

Note: The perfect continuous tenses (*will have, have, has,* or *had been* + verb + *ing*) are not used in the passive voice.

1 **Practice** Quickly reread the passage "Miracles in Medicine" on page 345. Find all sentences in the passive voice and tell the subject and verb in each. Do any of the passive sentences include an agent?

2 **Practice** Which of the following sentences are in the active voice, and which are in the passive voice? Label each. Then label the subject (S), verb (V), object (O), and / or agent (A) in the sentence.

<blockquote>

                                                         S   V   O

Example _active_ Throughout most of history, humans had known little about the causes of and cures for disease.

                                                  S   V

       passive Throughout most of history, little had been known about the causes of and cures for disease. _no agent_

</blockquote>

1. _____ Until the end of the 19th century, the idea of microbes had been regarded as "nonsense."

2. _____ Lacking an understanding of infection, most doctors had believed diseases to be "imbalances" in a person's body fluids.

3. _____ Sick patients had been viewed as "overexcited" or "exhausted."

4. _____ Bloodletting[1] had been seen as the best way to rebalance an overexcited patient.

5. _____ Until the discovery of "laughing gas" (nitrous oxide) in 1844, tooth extractions and surgeries had been performed without anesthesia.

6. _____ After Pasteur had proposed his theory of germs as the source of infections, Joseph Lister developed antiseptics to clean instruments and treat wounds.

7. _____ Since Alexander Fleming's discovery of the healing properties of penicillin in 1928, antibiotics have become second only to aspirin as the most commonly used drugs in the world.

8. _____ In modern times, many diseases have been eradicated through immunizations, better hygiene, and better nutrition.

9. _____ Postsurgical infections have declined ever since doctors began washing their hands between patients.

10. _____ Pure drinking water and pasteurized milk have helped to eliminate cholera, typhoid, and typhus in many parts of the world.

11. _____ In recent years, a great deal of research has been devoted to controlling or curing diseases such as cancer and AIDS.

12. _____ By the end of this decade, more breakthroughs will have been made in laser surgery, electronic imaging, and organ transplants.

---

[1]_bloodletting_ the intentional opening of blood vessels and removal of blood

3 Practice Using the example as a model, form complete sentences from the following cues. Use the past perfect passive in your sentences. Begin each sentence with *Before antibiotics. . . .*

Example cinchona bark / use / malaria
Before antibiotics, cinchona bark had been used to treat malaria.

1. sulfa drugs / prescribe for infections
2. brandy, cold water, and castor oil / use to treat pneumonia
3. bloodletting / recommend for almost any disease
4. whisky / give for exhaustion
5. opium / use for many ailments
6. small doses of mercury / prescribe to treat syphilis
7. raw cabbage juice / take for ulcers
8. honey / put on open wounds

4 Practice Older remedies are not necessarily bad remedies. In fact, many excellent remedies have been passed down through the centuries. Chinese remedies are some of the most interesting and best tested. Tell about some of them by forming complete sentences from the ten cues that follow. Use the present perfect tense of the passive voice.

Example some of these remedies / test in laboratories, but others have not
Some of these remedies have been tested in laboratories, but others have not.

1. all of these remedies / test "clinically" in China over centuries
2. the gingko tree / use in Chinese medicine for almost 4,000 years
3. asthma, bronchitis, and tuberculosis / treat with ginkgo seeds and fruit for hundreds of years
4. gingko leaves / prescribe in Europe for strokes and blocked arteries
5. dried sea horse / use to treat swollen thyroid glands for thousands of years
6. ulcers / treat with licorice root
7. licorice root / find to soothe and reduce inflammation
8. orange rind / burn to keep mosquitoes away for over a thousand years
9. orange rind / use as a cure for digestive ailments for many centuries
10. sweet wormwood / successfully prescribe for malaria for over 1,500 years

Cultural Note

Complementary and Alternative Medicine

Alternative medicines, medical practices that fall outside conventional western medical protocol, are becoming increasingly popular. In developed nations, close to 50 percent of the population use some type of alternative-medicine care. This percentage is likely much higher in developing countries, where access to conventional medicine is more limited. There are thousands of alternative medical treatments including acupuncture, chiropractic, meditation, prayer, reflexology, and other therapies.

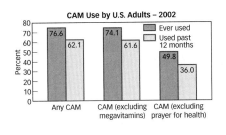

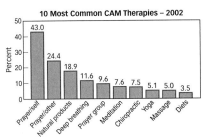

Source: Barnes P. Powell-Griner E. McFann K. Nahin R. CDC Advance Data Report #343.
Complementary and Alternative Medicine Use Among Adults: United States, 2002. May 27, 2004

5 **Practice** Imagine that you work in a hospital emergency room, and a patient who had been in a car accident has just been admitted. In pairs, go over the following checklist. Ask questions using the present perfect tense of the passive voice. Give short answers using the past participle.

Example notify the patient's family
A: Has the patient's family been notified?
B: Notified.

1. take the patient's temperature
2. check his blood pressure
3. take the patient's pulse
4. treat the patient for shock
5. draw blood samples
6. order X-rays
7. bandage his wounds
8. give the patient plasma

6 **Practice** What medical breakthroughs will occur during the next 50 years? The following are a few that doctors expect. Complete each of the eight sentences with the future perfect passive form of the verbs in parentheses.

Example Within the upcoming years, several important medical research projects _will have been completed_ (complete).

1. By the year 2050, medicine as we know it today _____ (transform / completely).

2. Within the upcoming years, much more _____ (learn) about human genetics.

3. Within the next 50 years, many new drugs _____ (develop) to fight bacteria that have become resistant to antibiotics.

4. New types of sutures[1] _____ (create) for closing wounds.

5. By the year 2050, hundreds of thousands of organ transplants _____ (perform).

6. New drugs _____ (develop) to counteract the body's rejection of transplanted organs.

7. Within the next 50 years, new forms of laser surgery _____ (perfect).

8. By the time we reach old age, incredible advances _____ (make) in medicine.

_____

[1]_suture_ fiber used to sew parts of the living body

7 **Practice** Use present forms—simple or perfect—of the verbs in parentheses to complete the following passage. Choose between active and passive forms. Note any cases where more than one tense may be appropriate.

The Healing Power of Plants

We ____ _often think_ ____ of medicine as human-made capsules or tablets.

(think / often)
Yet, the truth _____ that over 25 percent of the drugs that

1 (be)
_____ yearly in the United States _____ from

2 (sell)   3 (derive)
plants. Birth control pills, aspirin, digitoxin, and morphine

_____ from plants. When we _____ these

4 (make)   5 (buy)
drugs, however, their original appearance _____ completely.

6 (alter)
The active chemicals _____ from the plants, and they

7 (extract / already)
_____ into pills or _____ into capsules along

8 (press)   9 (place)
with inactive substances. Thus, despite the "antiseptic" appearance of these

drugs, they _____ very "earthy" origins. They

10 (have)
_____ from bark, dried leaves, flowers, or roots.

11 (derive)

8 **Practice** Use simple or perfect forms of the verbs in parentheses to complete the following passage. Choose between active and passive forms. Note any case where more than one tense may be appropriate.

Aspirin

For centuries, many cultures ___*have recognized*___ the healing power of
(recognize)

the willow tree. Long before the beginnings of modern medicine, willow bark

_____ to treat fever and inflammation. The ancient Greeks
1 (use)

_____ a very creative explanation for its success. They
2 (have)

_____ that even though this tree _____ along
3 (notice)   4 (grow)

river banks and its "feet" _____ damp, it _____
5 (be)   6 (remain)

healthy. The Greeks _____ that the tree _____
7 (reason)   8 (protect)

by its bark.

The active ingredient in willow bark, salicin, _____ ex-
9 (be)

tremely bitter and _____ many patients. As a result, until this
10 (irritate)

century, the bark _____ by doctors but _____
11 (prescribe / often)   12 (not take / always)

by their patients, who _____ that the cure _____
13 (feel)   14 (be)

worse than the disease.

Then, in 1897, _____ a major breakthrough. Felix Hoff-
15 (come)

man, who _____ for Bayer of Germany, _____
16 (work)   17 (discover)

a derivative of salicin, acetylsalicylic acid, and aspirin was born.

Of all the wonder drugs, aspirin _____ the most remark-
18 (be / perhaps)

able. In history, no other drug _____ so widely and for so many
19 (use)

purposes. Since its discovery, aspirin _____ the pain of millions of
20 (ease)

people, especially those who _____ from arthritis.
21 (suffer)

▲ Before aspirin, bark from willow trees was used to treat illness.

Using What You've Learned

9 **Describing Home Remedies** What do you know about home remedies? Work together in small groups, and share your knowledge of these cures. What have they been used for? Which are effective, and which are not? Finally, add at least one cure that has been used in your culture and answer the same questions about it.

castor oil	copper bracelets	ginseng
celery juice	garlic and garlic juice	moldy bread

10 **Giving a Report on a Medical Breakthrough** In the past 150 years, a complete transformation has occurred in medicine and health care. Prepare a brief report for your class on a breakthrough in medicine of particular interest to you. Use one of these topics, or choose one of your own. Be sure to include the following: What is it? When was it developed? By whom? How is it used? What had been used before its development? Do an Internet search or visit your library to get more information.

antibiotics	insulin	PET
burn treatment	kidney dialysis	radiation therapy
cancer treatment	laser surgery	steroids
contact lenses	MRI	ultrasound
diagnostic X-ray	organ transplants	vaccines
the human genome	pasteurization	vitamins

Setting the Context

Previewing the Passage Discuss the questions with a group.

How has farming changed during the last 200 to 300 years? Can you give any specific examples?

Reading Read the passage.

Food for Thought

In the history of the Earth, settled agriculture is a relatively recent phenomenon. It was only about 10,000 years ago that animals were first being domesticated and crops were being cultivated and harvested. Before that time, humans had fed themselves through fishing, hunting birds and animals, and gathering wild food.   5

During most of the past 10,000 years, agricultural development progressed slowly. Cultivation began with crops such as rice, corn, and gourds. By the time of the ancient Greeks, some products were actually being imported and exported, especially grains from Egypt. By the fall of the Roman Empire, new farming methods were being introduced all over Western Europe.   10

It wasn't until the 19th century, however, that major changes in agriculture took place. Migration to the American plains led to the development of both tools and techniques for higher production. At the present time, the United States has achieved such efficiency that a large surplus of food is being produced.   15

Discussing Ideas Discuss the questions with a partner.

What do you think are the most important crops for a society to grow? Why? What climate is required for these crops?

Grammar Structures and Practice

The Continuous Tenses

The passive voice of verbs in the present and past continuous tenses is formed in this way: *be (am, is, are, was, were) + being +* past participle *(+ by +* agent). Adverbs of frequency generally come after the first auxiliary verb.

8.8	The Continuous Tenses	
	Active	**Passive**
Present Continuous	Today, farmers **are using** sophisticated machinery to plant and cultivate their farms. **Focus:** Farmers	Today, sophisticated machinery **is being used** to plant and cultivate farms. **Focus:** Sophisticated machinery
Past Continuous	A century ago, farmers **were using** oxen to pull cultivators. **Focus:** Farmers	A century ago, oxen **were being used** to pull cultivators. **Focus:** Oxen

Note: The future continuous tense (*will be +* verb *+ ing*) and the present and past perfect continuous tense (*have, has,* or *had been +* verb *+ ing*) are not used in the passive voice.

---

1 Practice Quickly reread the passage "Food for Thought" on page 353 and underline all passive voice verbs. What is the tense and time frame of each? Do any of the passive sentences have agents?

2 Practice Complete the following sentences using the past continuous tense in the passive voice of the verbs in parentheses.

Example For thousands of years, agricultural development techniques changed very slowly. However, beginning in the Middle Ages, change became much more rapid. By the Middle Ages, oxen __*were being bred*__ (breed) for farm work, crops __*were being rotated*__ (rotate), and some irrigation __*was being used*__ (use).

1. By the Middle Ages, a wide variety of crops _____ (produce) throughout Europe.

2. In Spain, sugar cane _____ (grow) and merino sheep _____ (raise) for their wool.

3. In Italy, silk from silkworms _____ (harvest) and rice _____ (cultivate).

4. By the 1800s, many new farming techniques _____ (use), but most work _____ (do / still) by hand or by animals.

5. By 1850, horse-drawn reaping machines[1] _____ (use).

6. Soon after, steam engines _____ (attach) to a variety of farm equipment.

7. A hundred years later, however, most farming worldwide _____ (do / still) using human and animal power.

8. Between 1950 and 1970, major changes occurred in mechanization, and by 1970, tractors _____ (use) in most parts of the world.

_____

[1]*reaping machines* machines that helped harvest crops

3 **Practice** Throughout history, humans have tried to breed better plants and animals. Today, with our increasing knowledge of plant genetics, amazing changes are taking place. Form complete sentences from the following cues. Use the present continuous tense of the passive voice.

Example Many new techniques / develop in agriculture and plant genetics.
Many new techniques are being developed in agriculture and plant genetics.

1. New techniques / develop to allow for direct planting of rice.
2. Soybeans / use to make a variety of new high-protein food products.
3. Stronger wheat plants / develop to withstand damage from storms.
4. Strawberries / breed to resist damage from frost.
5. Beans / engineer to create their own fertilizer.
6. Gene banks / establish in many countries to preserve important seed material.
7. Freeze-drying / perfect to allow for rapid, economical preservation of many vegetables.
8. Potatoes / breed to grow in a much wider variety of climates.

4 **Review** Complete the following with active or passive forms of the verbs in parentheses. Use appropriate verb tenses and add negatives and adverbs when indicated.

The Webs that Scientists Want to Weave

During the 18th century, French scientists _____*filled*_____ barns
(fill)

with spiders in hopes of harvesting their webs to spin into thread. Millions of

spiders _____ because it _____ several thou-
1 (need)   2 (take)

sand just to make enough thread for a single dress! Unfortunately, though, the

spiders _____ with the French scientists, and the experiment
3 (not cooperate)

_____ a disaster. The scientists _____ to colo-
4 (consider)   5 (try)

nize spiders in the same way as silkworms, which _____ for
6 (colonize / successfully)

centuries. Why _____ this experiment _____?
7   8 (fail)

When the spiders _____ together in large numbers, they
9 (group)

_____ fiercely or _____
10 (fight)   11 (eat)

each other. The French experiment _____,
12 (fail)

but over the years, interest in spider silk

_____ because of its unique properties. It
13 (persist)

_____ the strongest material that
14 (be)

_____ on Earth—five times stronger than
15 (find)

steel. At the same time, it _____ 30 percent
16 (be)

more flexible than nylon and _____ able to absorb three times
17 (be)

the impact force of materials that _____ to make bulletproof
18 (use / currently)

vests.

Today, many researchers _____ to search for the keys to
19 (continue)

spider silk, and one group _____ to study the gene that
20 (begin)

_____ spider silk formation. In the future, it is possible that
21 (determine)

spider silk _____ for a multitude of purposes, such as sutures,
22 (use)

suspension bridges, and "improved" bulletproof vests!

Using What You've Learned

5 **Doing Research** Use the resources in your library (encyclopedias, newspaper articles, journals, etc.) or from the Internet to gather information about a breakthrough or significant change in a field that you are interested in. It may even be your own research or the research of a colleague. After you have gathered your information, write a brief composition explaining the work. Later, in pairs or small groups, take turns telling (not reading) about this research. If your topic is specialized, do your best to explain in language that everyone will understand.

Part 4 | The Modal Auxiliaries

Setting the Context

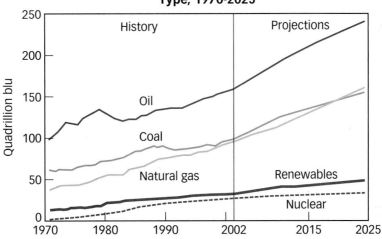

World Marketed Energy Use by Fuel Type, 1970-2025

Previewing the Passage Discuss the questions with a group.

How long do you think the world's oil supplies will last? What would happen if we ran out tomorrow?

Reading Read the passage.

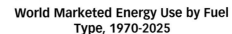

Low on Energy

It is difficult to overstate the importance of coal, oil, and natural gas—the so-called fossil fuels.

Without them, most industries could never have mechanized, and industrialization might not have occurred. Without them, virtually every engine would die, and the vast majority of lights would suddenly be extinguished. 5

Nowadays the question is no longer if we will ever run out of these precious resources; the question is when. It took perhaps 500 million years for fossil fuels to develop. Fifty years from now, supplies may well be exhausted. At that point, anything could happen. We might even plunge into a pre-industrial world in which millions would die of hunger and the rule of law would collapse. 10

As we begin the new millennium, it is clear that much time has been lost. Policies encouraging conservation and alternative energy sources should have been started decades ago. Still, the situation is far from hopeless. With the world's best minds working on the problem, a practical alternative to fossil fuels could certainly be found. But do we have the resolve necessary to search for 15 the solution, and is there enough time?

 Discussing Ideas Discuss the questions with a partner.

What alternatives to fossil fuels do you know of? Which do you think is the most important? What steps do you think should be taken concerning our energy needs?

Grammar Structures and Practice

The Modal Auxiliaries

The simple passive voice of modal auxiliaries is formed in this way: modal (*can, could, may, might, must, ought to, shall, should, will, would*) + *be* + past participle (+ *by* + agent). The perfect passive form follows this pattern: modal + *have been* + past participle.

8.9 The Modal Auxiliaries

	Modals		Active	Passive
Simple Modals	can could may might must	ought to shall should will would	We **could conserve** more oil today. **Focus:** We	More oil **could be conserved** today. **Focus:** More oil
Perfect Modals	can have could have may have might have must have*	ought to have shall have should have will have would have	We **could have conserved** more oil in the past. **Focus:** We	More oil **could have been conserved** in the past. **Focus:** More oil

*Note: The perfect form of *must* gives the meaning of probability only; it does not express need. Compare: *The work must be finished* (probability or need, depending on the context). *The work must have been finished* (probability only).

1 Practice In the following sentences, change the verbs from the active voice to the passive voice whenever possible. Omit the agent unless it is important to the meaning of the sentence.

Example We should recycle bottles and cans.
Bottles and cans should be recycled.

1. We should have developed solar power sooner.

2. We might use methane now instead of other fuels.

3. We ought to develop new biodegradable plastics.

4. We should carpool as much as possible.

5. We must educate people about energy.

6. We ought to have researched alternative energy sources a long time ago.

7. We should have put more money into energy research.

8. We could have tried different types of generators and engines.

2 Practice Complete these sentences with the active or passive forms of the modals and verbs in parentheses.

Example Oil ___*may be replaced*___ (may / replace) by other forms of energy.

1. Most experts agree that solar power _____ (will / become) an important energy source, but there is little agreement on when this _____ (can / accomplish).

2. Today, the world is almost completely dependent on oil, so a long transition period _____ (will / need) before solar power _____ (can / replace) oil.

3. Which fuel _____ (should / use) until solar energy _____ (can / produce) in sufficient quantities? Clearly, the choice _____ (must / come) from fossil fuels. Our entire industrial capacity depends on fossil fuels.

4. Thus, fossil fuels _____ (cannot / abandon). But which of the fossil fuels _____ (should / use) during the transition to solar power?

5. Coal and oil are such heavy polluters that they _____ (should / avoid). Natural gas is clean burning, but it _____ (cannot / find) in necessary quantities.

6. What we need is an energy source that is nonpolluting and one that we
_____ (can / find) in unlimited quantities.

7. The incredible truth is that such a fuel has existed for millions of years. This
fuel _____ (can / recover) easily, and no new technology
_____ (will / require) to use it.

8. This seemingly magical substance is methane. We _____ (can /
find) this highly efficient fuel almost anywhere. Methane is a natural by-
product of decomposing organic matter.

9. Whenever leaves, bits of food, or dead animals decay and return to the soil,
methane _____ (produce). This process _____
(can / control), and the gas _____ (can / collect).

10. It _____ (can / put) to many uses. For example, it
_____ (might / replace) natural gas for cooking.

3 Practice The following passage is written entirely in the active voice. It contains
sentences that could be improved by using the passive voice. Rewrite the selection
using sentences in the passive voice when appropriate. Omit the agent if it is not
necessary to the meaning of the sentence.

Energy Planning

Since the 1800s, when oil first became an important resource, we have
known that the supply could not last forever. Today, it is obvious that we should
not use these supplies freely. In fact, it is clear that governments ought to regulate them.

We should have created a general energy plan decades ago. Just when the   5
government could have enacted such a plan is debatable. However, surely after
World War II, the direction of our industrial development was clear, and people
could have done something.

Today, with the size and complexity of our industrial system, it would be extremely difficult to begin a strict energy plan. However, if people had developed   10
a plan in the 1940s, we probably could have enforced it. In this way, we might
manage our resources in a more efficient way.

4 Practice The process of refining oil is explained in the following passage, which is
written entirely in the active voice. First, read the passage for meaning. Then improve it
stylistically by changing some of the sentences to the passive voice. Remember to omit
the agent when appropriate. Finally, in small groups, compare the changes you made
and explain why you made them.

Refineries

People can use a variety of techniques to refine oil, but the most common is separation. The separation process has several steps. First, technicians heat the oil in a large furnace, and from there they send it into a fractionating tower. This tower is a steel cylinder about 130 feet (40 meters) high. When the hot oil enters the tower, it turns into vapor. This vapor rises naturally. As it rises, its tempera- 5 ture begins to fall, and the components of the oil separate according to their weight. At this time, workers take the heavy oil from the bottom of the tower. During the process, workers must also remove lubricating oil, kerosene, and gasoline from higher points. Uncondensed gas rises to the top of the tower, where a mechanism releases it through a pipe. Another mechanism recycles 10 this gas into the tower for further separation.

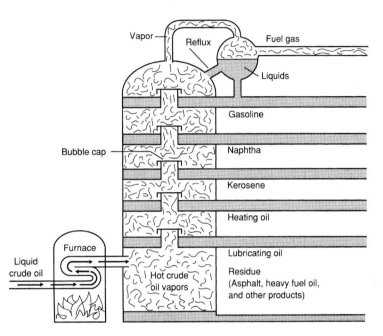

5 **Error Analysis** Many of the following sentences have errors in their use of the active or passive voice. Find and correct all errors. Note that there may be more than one way of correcting each error.

Example In the 1890s, several industries were developed pedal-powered machines.

Correction: In the 1890s, several industries developed pedal-powered machines.
OR
Pedal-powered machines were developed by several industries in the 1890s.

1. Three times as much power can delivered by the legs as by the arms.

2. By the late 1890s, tools such as saws and grinding wheels was being powered by bicycle-like machines.

3. Pedal power was abandoned soon after the development of gasoline engines.

4. However, it has "rediscovered" recently.

5. Today "people-powered" tools are making several different manufacturers.

6. These tools are been used by some craftspeople and farmers.

7. A number of tasks may be performed by "people-powered" tools.

8. For example, grain can ground, water can pumped, and land can cleared, plowed, and cultivated.

6 **Review** Complete the following with the active or passive voice of the verbs in parentheses. Use any of the verb tenses and / or modals covered in this chapter.

Geothermal Power

One energy source that ____*has been used*____ for hundreds of years is ge-
(use)

othermal power. Geothermal power is simply the heat that

_____ by volcanic activity below the Earth's surface. This nat-
1 (produce)

ural energy source _____ to use in many ways. In Iceland, for
2 (put)

example, geothermally heated water _____ since 1930. Today,
3 (use)

a large majority of homes there _____ geothermally. Electricity
4 (heat)

_____ by turbines that _____ by naturally
5 (generate / also)   6 (power)

heated water. In fact, geothermal power _____ to such an ex-
7 (develop)

tent in Iceland that dependence on fossil fuels _____. Plus, this
8 (reduce)

use of geothermal power _____ a tremendous side benefit; air
9 (bring)

pollution _____.
10 (cut / drastically)

Unfortunately, up until now, few countries _____ Iceland's
11 (follow)

example. Nations such as the United States and Canada _____
12 (bless)

with numerous geothermal areas that _____ safely and easily.
13 (exploit)

Both hot water and electricity _____ at low prices. Yet, neither
14 (provide)

country _____ advantage of its geothermal resources. Cur-
15 (take)

rently, only a small number of hot springs _____ to provide hot
16 (use)

water, and many fewer _____ electricity.
17 (produce)

7 **Review** Complete the following with the active or passive voice of the verbs in the parentheses. Use any of the verb tenses or modals covered in this chapter.

Hydroelectric Energy

The world relies heavily on fossil fuels, yet other excellent sources of energy _have already been developed_ . Hydroelectricity, for example, is a very
(already / develop)

attractive form of energy. Its power source _____ by rain and
1 (renew / regularly)

snow. And, obviously, hydroelectricity _____ the atmosphere.
2 (not pollute)

Because of these advantages, hydroelectric sites _____ in
3 (exploit)

many parts of the world. In Sweden, for example, over 75 percent of their energy needs _____ by hydroelectricity.
4 (provide)

Unfortunately, however, most of the untapped hydroelectric sites

_____ in parts of the world where people _____
5 (find)   6 (not need)

a large amount of energy. Sites with great promise _____ in
7 (exist)

Canada, Latin America, India, and Russia, yet they _____.
8 (not exploit)

Sadly, despite its great potential as a source of clean, renewable energy, only a

few countries are making hydroelectricity a top priority.

▲ Itaipu dam on the borders of Brazil and Argentina

8 **Review** Complete the following passage by using either the active or passive forms of the verbs and modals in parentheses. Use any of the tenses and modals covered in this chapter.

Chasing Windmills

During the 1970s, a wind-power industry began to emerge in the United States. It _____*grew*_____ out of the search for alternatives to oil as en-
(grow)

ergy sources. A major project _____ by the U.S. government to
1 (fund)

construct a wide variety of large wind turbines. At the time, it

_____ that wind power _____ a globally-used, pol-
2 (believe)   3 (become)

lution-free, renewable source of energy. But, by the 1980s, the United States' in-

terest in wind power _____, except in California.
4 (disappear / almost)

In California, wind-power projects _____. Both individuals
5 (not abandon)

and power companies _____ the idea. Today, wind power
6 (pursue)

_____ to produce almost two percent of the entire state's elec-
7 (use)

tricity. The same amount of energy _____ by wind as
8 (can / produce)

_____ by one nuclear reactor.
9 (produce)

In Europe, wind power never lost favor as it did in the United States. Sev-

eral countries _____ in conducting research and development.
10 (persist)

In order for wind power to become truly workable for the future, many im-

provements _____. Better turbines _____, and af-
11 (must / make)   12 (must / build)

fordable ways of harnessing the wind _____. Today, numerous
13 (must / design)

wind-power projects _____, especially in offshore wind farms,
14 (plan)

where strong winds _____ most reliable.
15 (be)

▲ In the U.S., wind power has increased an average of over 25% per year since 1990.

Using What You've Learned

9 **Describing Processes and Giving Recommendations** In small groups, talk about a practice in a field with which you are familiar—for example, engineering, construction, cooking, teaching chemistry (English, etc.). First, give a careful description of how the practice is currently done. Then give your opinion on ways this practice could be improved. State your recommendations on what *must, has to, should,* or *ought to* be done.

10 **Describing Problems and Giving Possible Solutions** In pairs, examine a problem your country or the world is facing today. Examples include inflation, unemployment, foreign debt, pollution, crime, and drug use. After you have described the problem, examine its roots and discuss what exactly caused this problem. Then offer your opinions on what *could, should,* or *ought to* have been done five, ten, or 20 years ago to avoid the current situation. Finally, tell your group what you believe *should, ought to,* or *must* be done now.

Setting the Context

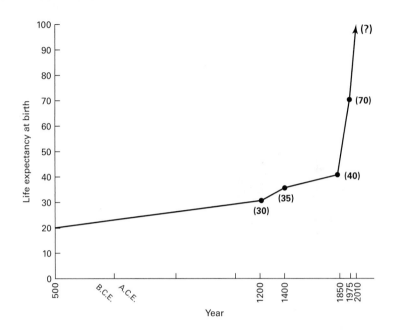

Previewing the Passage Discuss the questions with a group.

One tremendous benefit of the breakthroughs of the last 100–150 years is a greatly increased lifespan. Humans are living longer, and as a result, the definition of old age is changing. What comes to mind when you think of the word *old*? In your opinion, at what age does old age begin? How do or should old people act?

Reading Read the passage.

Living Longer and Enjoying Life More

Aging is one of the few things assured in this changeable world. When we think of getting older, we see ourselves graying, balding, and sagging . . . suffering a progression of indignities associated with our years. In the words of one old-timer, "Old age is like living on an island steadily shrinking in size."

But no matter how much we may be worried or frightened about aging, 5 many seniors are very satisfied with the golden years of their lives. Over the past several decades, all the positive changes in health and well-being have transformed what it means to become old. With modern breakthroughs in nutrition and health care, we now see senior citizens living longer and enjoying their

lives more. In addition, the improvements in transportation and the revolution 10
in Internet communication allow even the oldest among us to actively participate in the world.

Then there are also the traditional benefits of aging. The elderly are often
the heads of large families, enjoying the love and respect of the younger members of their clans. Being grandparents allows them to love and cherish the new 15
children in the family while avoiding the burdens of parenthood.

And, finally, as actor Maurice Chevalier noted, old age does not seem so
bad, "Not if I consider the alternative."

 Discussing Ideas Discuss the questions with a partner.

In your culture, are people treated with more respect as they get older? What is the
alternative to old age that Maurice Chevalier alludes to?

Grammar Structures and Practice

A. Participles with Verbs of Emotions and Sensations

Be + the past participle of many verbs can be used to express emotions or sensations
that we feel.
- *By* may be used with the past participle of all of these verbs. Other prepositions may
  also be used.
- *Be* + the present participle of many of these verbs can be used to describe the effect
  of something on us.
- A phrase with *to* can be used with the present participle (*to me, to them, to Mary*).

8.10 Participles with Verbs of Emotions and Sensations

Past Participles			Examples
amazed (at)	excited (about)	satisfied	The test **confused** them.
astonished (about)	exhausted (from)	(with) (about)	They **were confused by (about)** the test.
bewildered (about)	fascinated (with)	scared (of)*	The test **was confusing to** them.
bored (with)	frightened (about)	shocked (about)	The test results **surprised** me.
concerned (about)*	frustrated (with)	stimulated (by)	I **was surprised about (by)** the results.
confused (about)	interested (in)	stunned (about)	The results **were surprising to** me.
convinced (about)	intrigued (with)	surprised (about)	The news **worried** him.
determined (to)*	perplexed (with)	tired (of)	He **was worried about** the news.*
disappointed (about)	pleased (with)*	upset (about)	
disgusted (about)	reassured (by)	worried (about)*	
encourage (about)	saddened		

* The present participle of these verbs is seldom used in this way. Correct: *The movie scared me. I was scared
by the movie.* Incorrect: **The movie was scaring to me.*

1 **Practice** Use your own ideas and information to complete the following. Make sentences with both present and past participles.

Example _____ frustrates me. It is _____
because. . . . I am _____ when . . . .
English frustrates me. It is frustrating to me because I don't
know enough vocabulary. I am especially frustrated when I have
to write essays.

1. _____ interests me.

   It is _____ because. . . .

   I am _____ when. . . .

2. _____ confuses me.

   It is _____ because. . . .

   I get _____ when. . . .

3. _____ fascinates me.

   It is _____ because. . . .

   I feel _____ when. . . .

4. _____ amuses me.

   It is _____ because. . . .

   I am _____ when. . . .

5. _____ frustrates me.

   It is _____ because. . . .

   I feel _____ when. . . .

6. _____ intrigues me.

   It is _____ because. . . .

   I feel _____ when. . . .

7. _____ bores me.

   It is _____ because. . . .

   I get _____ when. . . .

8. _____ exhausts me.

   It is _____ because. . . .

   I get _____ when. . . .

9. _____ frightens me.

   It is _____ because. . . .

   I get _____ when. . . .

10. _____ amazes me.

It is _____ because. . . .

I get _____ when. . . .

B. Causative and Structurally Related Verbs

Several verbs in English use special constructions with the simple form, the infinitive, or the past participle of the second verb.

8.11	Causative and Structurally Related Verbs	
Active Forms		
	Explanations	**Examples**
Help *	_Help_ uses (pro)noun + simple form of a second verb or (pro)noun + infinitive.	We **helped him (to) enter** the pool.
Let **Allow**	_Let_ uses a (pro)noun + simple form. _Allow_ is followed by (pro)noun + infinitive.	We **let him enter** the pool. We **allowed him to enter** the pool.
Have	_Have_ is similar in meaning to _arrange for._ Have may be followed by (pro)noun + simple verb. (You have someone _do_ something for you.)	She **had the servant bring** a drink to her. John **had a lab test** the water.
Make **Force**	_Make_ is similar in meaning to _force_, although _force_ can be stronger. _Make_ is followed by (pro)noun + simple form. _Force_ is followed by (pro)noun + infinitive.	She **made them leave** after ten minutes. She **forced them to take** some food home.
Passive Forms		
Let	Let may be followed by a passive construction: _Let_ + (pro)noun + _be_ + past participle.	She **let her car be washed**.
Get **Have** **Need** **Want** **Would like**	_Get, have, like, need, want,_ and _would like_ may be followed by a passive construction: verb + (pro)noun + past participle. (You _have, get, need, want,_ or _would like_ something _done_.)	He **got the water tested** (by a lab). He **had the water tested** (by a lab). She **needs the drink brought** to her (by a servant). She **wants the snack brought** to her (by a servant). She **would like a snack brought** to her (by a servant).

Note: See Chapter 9 for more information on infinitives.

2 Practice For thousands of years, people have believed that certain waters could stop or reverse the aging process. Complete the following sentences about such treatments by forming a phrase from the words in parentheses.

Example   Can some substances make (age / disappear)?
Can some substances make age disappear?

1. In Greek mythology, Zeus's wife Hera visited a spring that made (the signs of age / vanish).

2. Hera forced (other beautiful women / stay away) from this spring.

3. The Roman god Jupiter let (certain people / enter) the special waters of Juventas.

4. Jupiter allowed (these lucky bathers / regain) their youth.

5. Of course, these waters helped (the bathers / feel) young again.

6. The Bible mentions the "fountain of life" from which the Lord let (Adam and Eve / drink).

7. In search of the "fountain of youth," Ponce de Leon had (native guides / take) him to present-day Florida in 1512. (Unfortunately, Ponce de Leon found an Indian arrow instead and died at age 61.)

8. In the 1930s, patients began coming to the Swiss clinic, La Prairie, to have (Dr. Paul Niehans / give) them his rejuvenating "cell therapy" injections.

9. Today, many people have (doctors / inject) their facial skin with special chemicals.

10. These chemical can make (wrinkles / disappear), but they can also make (people / lose) some movement in their facial muscles.

11. Americans spend millions of dollars each year on lotions and creams that help (reduce / the effects) of aging.

12. Such creams supposedly make (your skin / look) years younger.

3 Practice Change the following sentences from the active to the passive voice. Delete the nouns.

Example   Many older people are having doctors replace their hips.
Many older people are having their hips replaced.

1. Because of the medical advances of the last several decades, people can have doctors replace many joints.

2. They can have doctors rebuild their knees or their hips.

3. Both men and women are getting technicians to inject them with substances to reduce wrinkles.

4. People are getting plastic surgeons to reconstruct their faces, stomachs, and hips.

5. I would like a surgeon to remove all my wrinkles.

6. I need to have a doctor shrink my stomach.

7. I want to have a doctor change my nose.

8. I have to have a technician reduce my waist this afternoon so that I can wear a size 7 tonight.

C. Verbs with Two-Part Objects

Catch, find, keep, leave, and *send* can be followed by a (pro)noun and a second verb.

8.12	Verbs with Two-Part Objects	
Structures	**Explanations**	**Examples**
Verb + Past Participle	The past participle describes a completed activity. The past participle rarely follows *catch* or *send*.	We **found** the key **hidden** in a chest. He **kept** the horse **tied** to a tree.
Verb + Present Participle	The present participle is used for the second verb to describe an activity in progress.	They **caught** him **cheating** on his taxes. We **left** her **working** in the field.

D. Verbs of Perception

The verbs *feel, hear, listen, look at, notice, observe, perceive, see, smell, taste,* and *witness* can be followed by a noun or object pronoun + a second verb.

- The second verb can be either a present participle or a simple form, usually with little difference in meaning.
- With certain verbs of "finality" (*complete, die, end, finish,* and so on), there is a difference in meaning in the two forms.

8.13	Verbs of Perception	
Active Forms		
	Explanations	**Examples**
Simple Form	The simple form implies the completion of an action (the action of the second verb).	We watched the sun **go down**. We saw the man **die**.
Present Participle	The present participle refers to an action in progress.	I watched the sun **going down**. I saw the man **dying**.
Passive Form		
***Being* + Past Participle**	Only *being* + past participle can be used with passive constructions. These constructions can imply either completed actions or actions in progress.	I noticed him **being helped** into a car. We saw him **being rushed** to the hospital.

4 Practice Form participial phrases from the words in parentheses.

Example We saw (the old man / sleep) in his rocker.
We saw the old man sleeping in his rocker.

1. With today's more active lifestyles, you won't find (all senior citizens / sit) in rocking chairs.

2. You may never catch (they / knit).

3. You may never see (they / rest) quietly.

4. Where will you find many of today's seniors and what will you see (they / do)?

5. Stop by a fitness center and you can observe 70, 80, and even 90-year olds (do / aerobics) or (use / exercise machines).

6. The pain of arthritis is more likely to send some (seniors / run to) a yoga class than to a doctor.

7. You can watch (seniors / stretch and bend) as if they were 30 years old.

8. Visit local trails and you may observe ("the elderly" / jog or bicycle).

9. During bad weather, you can find (seniors / spend) time in shopping malls.

10. You won't find (these active seniors / seat) on a bench.

11. You'll see (them / power-walk) to stay in shape.

12. Some seniors are so fit that they can leave (younger people / stand) far behind them.

13. You may find (the younger people / leave) far behind.

14. Of course, even today's active seniors feel (their energy / lag) from time to time.

15. Quiet pursuits are important, too, and you will see many seniors (enjoy / museums), (visit / the library), and (take classes) on college campuses.

16. In the years to come, you will see (the United States / transform) by the energy of its active seniors.

▲ Today's seniors enjoy active lifestyles.

5 Practice Complete the following passage with the appropriate form of the verbs in parentheses. Choose from the simple form or present or past participle.

The Reinvention of Retirement

If you look into the not-too-distant future, you may see many great advances ___developing___. But what do demographics[1] experts see
(develop)

_____ shape in the near future? Many see a major crisis
1 (take)

_____ on the world's horizon. These experts are
2 (loom)

_____ about a shift in world population, and they are genuinely _____.
3 (concern)

uinely _____.
4 (worry)

What is this crisis that much of the world may soon find itself

_____? For the first time in human history, there will most
5 (face)

likely be a shortage of young workers and an abundance of retirees in many

parts of the world. In Japan, for example, almost 20 percent of the population

is already over age 65, and the percentage is _____ to increase
6 (expect)

steadily. With so many _____ workers about to retire, compa-
7 (age)

nies worldwide may be _____ _____ qualified
8 (catch)   9 (lack)

employees. When people retire, they often take their knowledge with them be-

cause few companies have _____ for systematic transfer of
10 (prepare)

knowledge from the old to the young. Of course, systematic transfer of knowl-

edge should help any company _____ better, and it is
11 (perform)

_____ that companies do not already have such systems in place.
12 (surprise)

Nevertheless, even if knowledge is _____ within a company,
13 (transfer)

who will do the work? This shift in demographics will most likely make many

countries _____ their rules about retirement. Today, most
14 (change)

countries make workers _____ at a certain age, often 65. What
15 (retire)

changes can be _____? First of all, countries could let older
16 (make)

workers _____ at their jobs with no penalties and loss of
17 (continue)

benefits. Or, they could use tax incentives to keep the elderly

_____ longer.
18 (work)

Flexible scheduling and job sharing would also help older people

_____ at their jobs longer. Such changes could obviously bene-
19 (continue)

fit younger workers, too. So, today's _____ demographics may
20 (shift)

bring about a major reinvention of workplace organization—for the better of

all workers.

The Graying of the Factory Floor
U.S. workforce by age group,
% change 2000–10

Sources: Conference Board; Bureau of Labour

Different Departure Times
Exit ages and employment
rates, 2004

Employment rates of older workers
(% of age group 55–64)

Source: Adecco

_____

[1] *demographics* the study of population and population trends

6 Review Complete the following with active or passive forms of the verbs in parentheses. Use appropriate verb tenses, simple form, present or past participle, and forms of modal auxiliaries. Add negatives or adverbs when indicated.

My name _____ *is* _____ Harry. I _____ *have seen* _____ many
(be)   (see)

things in my life. You see, I _____ almost 100 years ago. When I
1 (bear)

_____ in upstate New York, our family _____
2 (grow up)   3 (not have)

a lot of the conveniences that we _____ today.
4 (have)

_____ there hot water in the house? Ha! There
5 (be)

_____ any water at all except the water that _____
6 (not be)   7 (carry)

into the house in a pail. There _____ any electricity either. We
8 (not be)

_____ (9 light) the house with gas lamps and candles. Our meals _____ (10 cook) on a wood stove. Every morning, the cows _____ (11 milk) and during the day, the crops _____ (12 tend).

You see, we _____ (13 not have) things _____ (14 do) for us. We _____ (15 do) them ourselves. We _____ (16 help) the cows _____ (17 give) birth. If the roof _____ (18 need) _____ (19 fix), we fixed it. If one of us _____ (20 get) sick, we couldn't have him _____ (21 examine) by a doctor. There was no doctor near us, so we were the "doctors." We _____ (22 see) the sun _____ (23 rise), and for entertainment, we _____ (24 watch) the sun _____ (25 set). Yes, it _____ (26 be) hard sometimes, but back then, nobody _____ (27 know) any different life than the one we _____ (28 lead).

Today, everything _____ (29 change). We _____ (30 have) so many modern conveniences that we _____ (31 have / rarely) to get our hands dirty. Our food _____ (32 produce) for us. We _____ (33 walk / rarely) anywhere. We _____ (34 have) our hair _____ (35 cut), our nails _____ (36 manicure), our cars _____ (37 wash), and our houses _____ (38 clean). When we _____ (39 get) sick, we _____ (40 care) for not just by qualified doctors but by medical specialists. We _____ (41 go / even) to doctors to make us _____ (42 look) and _____ (43 feel) younger than we are. Yes, I _____ (44 see) many breakthroughs in these last one hundred years, and life _____ (45 be) a lot easier. But, we _____ (46 be / also) much more dependent on our technology and the services that _____ (47 provide) to us by others. Sometimes, I _____ (48 think) back on the way things were when I _____ (49 grow) up, and I _____ (50 wonder) if life wasn't better back then.

7 **Making Cross-Cultural Observations** Every culture is unique. Mention some of the differences between two cultures you are familiar with or know well. Work in small groups and share observations about cultural similarities and differences. Use *hear, listen to, notice, observe, see, watch,* and *witness* as you talk.

Example *I've noticed many differences between my native culture and this culture. I've noticed people being more assertive here, and sometimes, I've even seen people being very aggressive. . . .*

8 **Describing a Place** Imagine that you have had the opportunity to travel to a very unusual place, the place of your dreams. You did, saw, heard, and experienced many fascinating things. Use your imagination to envision your trip. Then in small groups, give a description of your "experiences," using as much detail as possible. Finally, write a short composition describing what you saw, heard, felt, witnessed, or noticed.

Example *I visited the fascinating country of Yemen. Located at the edge of the Arabian Peninsula, Yemen was for centuries isolated from other cultures and visitors were not allowed. Now visitors are welcomed, and I took full advantage. I saw the wondrous architecture in places such as the Palace of Wadi Dhar. In the "suk,¹" I smelled spices being ground and watched tradesmen pounding copper into bowls. I even witnessed men chewing a mild drug called qat².. . .*

---

¹*suk* marketplace in Arabic
²*qat* mild narcotic leaves chewed during socializing in Yemen and parts of Eastern Africa

▲ The Palace of Wadi Dhar outside of Sanaa, Yemen

Use of the Passive Voice and Related Structures

Verbs in the passive voice are frequently tested on standardized English proficiency exams. Review these commonly tested structures and check your understanding by completing the sample items that follow.

Remember that . . .

✓ The passive is formed in this way: (modal auxiliary) + *be* + past participle.

✓ The verb *be* is singular or plural depending on the subject of the passive sentence.

✓ The verb *be* gives the appropriate tense and time frame for the sentence.

✓ Passive verb constructions may be followed by a variety of prepositions.

✓ Certain verbs may be followed by the past participle, present participle, or simple form of a second verb.

Part 1 Circle the best completion for the following.

Example   Morse code _____ by Samuel Morse.

      (A) invented   (B) was invent

      (C) was invented   (D) did invent

1. Do you know if Mary _____ the Smiths?

      (A) be related to   (B) be related with

      (C) is related with   (D) is related to

2. Several countries may institute tax incentives to keep elderly people _____ longer.

      (A) work   (B) worked

      (C) working   (D) to work

3. Robot-like machines _____ to do a variety of household tasks.

      (A) can now be used   (B) can be now used

      (C) can now use   (D) can now be using

4. Aspirin _____ the bark of the willow tree.

      (A) is derived to   (B) are derived from

      (C) is derived from   (D) are deriving from

5. Potatoes, now a major source of food worldwide, _____ brought to Europe by Spaniards in the 16th century.

      (A) was   (B) were

      (C) had been   (D) was being

Part 2 Each sentence has one error. Circle the letter below the word(s) containing the error.

Example   Email <u>commonly</u> <u>is used</u> on many university campuses <u>by faculty</u> and
                        (A)   B   C
              students who wish <u>to communicate</u> more easily and frequently.
                                        D

1. In <u>humankind's</u> thousands of years on Earth, <u>many resources</u>, including wood,
         A   B
   wind, water, and coal, <u>have been using</u> to <u>produce</u> energy.
                                  C   D

2. Measures <u>should be taken</u> decades ago <u>to decrease</u> <u>the</u> world's dependence
                    A   B   C
   on oil; amazingly, such measures <u>are still being debated</u>.
                                            D

3. It <u>was assumed</u> that fossil fuels <u>will last</u> forever and that as technology
           A   B
   <u>developed</u>, it <u>would simply become</u> easier to extract these precious resources.
        C   D

4. Dr. Drissi is <u>particularly</u> <u>interesting</u> in <u>doing</u> research on the effect of aging on
                      A   B   C
   <u>workplace</u> performance.
        D

5. Natural gas <u>is</u> a <u>much</u> cleaner source of energy than coal or oil but unfortunately
                   A   B
   <u>are not found</u> in sufficient quantities <u>to be used</u> extensively worldwide.
         C   D

Self-Assessment Log

Check the things you did in this chapter. How well can you do each one?

	Not Very Well	Fairly Well	Very Well
I can use a variety of tenses in the passive voice.	❏	❏	❏
I can omit the *by* + agent phrases after passive voice verbs when appropriate.	❏	❏	❏
I can use singular verbs with singular nouns and plural verbs with plural nouns.	❏	❏	❏
I can use appropriate prepositions after passive voice verbs.	❏	❏	❏
I can use appropriate prepositions after verbs of emotions and sensations.	❏	❏	❏
I can use appropriate verb forms after causative verbs.	❏	❏	❏
I can use appropriate verb forms after verbs with two-part objects.	❏	❏	❏
I can use appropriate verb forms after verbs of perception.	❏	❏	❏
I can take a test reviewing problem areas with sentences, verbs, modals, and the passive voice.	❏	❏	❏
I understand new information about breakthroughs in human knowledge and development, and I can use new structures and vocabulary to talk and write about related topics.	❏	❏	❏

Art and Entertainment

❝Every artist dips his brush in his own soul, and paints his own nature into his pictures.**❞**

—Henry Ward Beecher

Connecting to the Topic

1 What is art?

2 What makes a person an artist?

3 Where do artists get their inspiration?

Introduction

In this chapter, you will study some of the forms and uses of infinitives and gerunds. As you study, pay close attention to which verbs are followed by infinitives and which are followed by gerunds. Also, note any difference in meaning when both an infinitive and a gerund may be used.

Reading Read the following passage. It introduces the chapter theme "Art and Entertainment" and raises some of the topics and issues you will cover in the chapter.

What Is Art?

Trying to define art is almost impossible because each individual has an opinion on what is or is not art. For some, art is only certain types of music or painting or sculpture, while for others, art includes any creative act. The best way, then, to define art may be to consider what it does rather than what it is.

For most people, the function of art is to be pleasing to the eye or ear. In fact, art has served as decoration since prehistoric times. Yet, does something have to be beautiful to be art? Can a disturbing or distasteful piece be considered art? Does the definition of art as beauty exclude works like Picasso's *Guernica*, shown on page 381, which portrays the destruction of an entire town? 5

According to some critics, art goes beyond beauty. It involves making the world understandable by bringing order to the chaos of human experience. But can this definition be appropriate when one considers the chaos in works such as Michelangelo's *Last Judgment* or Erik Satie's *Through the Looking Glass*? 10

Perhaps we can define art only by giving a more general explanation of its function. Art historian John Canaday expresses this idea by saying that art is meant to clarify, intensify, or otherwise enlarge our experience of life. 15

 Discussing Ideas Discuss the questions with a partner.

How many types of art can you name? Do you believe all creative work qualifies as art?

Part 1   Gerunds

Setting the Context

Previewing the Passage Discuss the questions with a group.

Many people say that jazz is the only truly American art form. What do you know about jazz? Do you like jazz music?

Reading Read the passage.

Jazz

Jazz musicians are unique as creative artists. Many poets, painters, and novelists are accustomed to working alone, but this is often impossible for jazz musicians. Because of the nature of jazz, most of their playing and practicing must be with other musicians. They need each other's sounds and impulses to become inspired.   5

To develop their own styles, jazz musicians must be ingenious and versatile. Playing jazz involves remembering hundreds of musical phrases and improvising on them during a solo. Each musician's personal style develops through various ways of improvising.

Some jazz musicians are so skillful at improvising that they can even impro-   10 vise on their mistakes. The late trumpeter Dizzy Gillespie was famous for using any mistake to begin a new improvisation. By using a mistake to begin a new melody, he created a whole new piece of music.

▲ Dizzy Gillespie

 Discussing Ideas Discuss the questions with a partner.

What does it mean to improvise? There is so much improvisation in jazz that every time musicians play a particular song, they change it. Do you know of any type of music other than jazz in which improvisation is so important?

Grammar Structures and Practice

A. Gerunds

Gerunds may be used in place of nouns or pronouns. They can function as the subject or the complement of a sentence. They may also be used as the object of a verb or preposition.

9.1 Functions of Gerunds

Explanations	Structures	Examples
A gerund is verb + *ing*.	**Subject**	**Singing** is a lot of fun.
Gerunds can be negative, and they can have subjects and objects.	**Complement**	My favorite pastime is **listening** to music.
	Object of a Verb	I enjoy **dancing**.
Not is used before the gerund to form the negative.	**Object of a Preposition**	I often relax by **playing** the guitar.
	Negative Gerund	**Not owning** a guitar makes it difficult for me to practice.
A possessive noun or adjective can precede it as the subject of the gerund. In conversational English, however, object forms (rather than possessive forms) are also used as subjects of the gerund.	**Subjects of Gerunds**	I always enjoy **Michael's (his) guitar playing**. He's used to **my sitting and listening** for hours. *He's used to **me sitting and listening** for hours.
	Objects of Gerunds	**Playing flamenco guitar** can be difficult. **The playing of flamenco guitar** can be difficult.

*This form is incorrect but is frequently used in conversational English.

If a verb form is used after a preposition, it must be the gerund form. Gerunds commonly follow the expressions in the table below:

9.2 Gerunds as Objects of Prepositions

Expressions Often Followed by Gerunds		Examples
be afraid of	insist on	We're excited **about going** to the concert.
be excited about	plan on	Let's plan **on leaving** early.
be (get) tired of	succeed at (in)	I'm thinking **about getting** season tickets.
be good at (in)	think of (about)	Good musicians improve **by practicing** every day.
be interested in		He was tired **after practicing** for five hours.

To is used as a preposition in the following expressions. These expressions *must* be followed by a gerund if a verb form is used.

9.3 *To* + Gerund

Expressions Often Followed by Gerunds		Examples
be accustomed to	look forward to	I **am accustomed to spending a lot of time outdoors.**
be given to	object to	I **am used to spending** a lot of time outdoors.*
be used to	plead innocent (guilt) to	I'm **looking forward to going** to the beach.

*Do not confuse *used to* (habitual past) with *be used to* (*be accustomed to*).

1 **Practice** What kinds of music do you like? Do you play any instruments? Would you like to learn any? Using your own ideas, complete the following sentences with appropriate prepositions and gerunds or gerund phrases.

Example I am (I wish I were) good _____*at playing*_____ the flute.

1. I'm interested _____ more (about) music.

2. I'd like to be better _____ different kinds of music.

3. I'm planning _____ some new records this week.

4. I get tired _____ the same kinds of music.

5. I'm accustomed _____ a wide variety of music.

6. Instead _____ to a ball game, I'd much rather go to a concert.

7. I'm looking forward _____ to a concert soon.

8. I'm also thinking _____ . . . .

2 **Practice** Add at least six of your own comments on different instruments, music, or musicians. Use gerunds or gerund phrases with the following cues.

Example *I'm really interested in learning more about jazz.*

(not) be interested in	instead of
(not) be used to	look forward to
(not) be successful at	object to
(not) care about	plan on
in spite of	take advantage of

3 **Practice** The following sentences use infinitives of purpose to explain how someone did something. Rephrase each sentence to use *by* + a gerund. Use the example as a model.

Miles Davis, a brilliant trumpeter, was a high-school student in St. Louis in the early 1950s when he met jazz greats Charlie Parker and Dizzy Gillespie. He moved to New York City at age 18, began playing with Parker and Gillespie, and became a star.

Example Miles Davis came to New York to learn more about jazz music.
Miles Davis learned more about jazz music by coming to New York.

1. At first in New York, he worked several odd jobs to make money.

2. Miles played with jazz greats Dizzy Gillespie and Charlie Parker to learn more about a new movement in jazz called *bebop.*

▲ Miles Davis

3. Eventually, he started his own band to give himself more musical freedom.

4. In the following years, Miles blended many types of jazz to create his own special sound.

5. While playing, he often turned his back to the audience to keep his concentration.

6. In the 1950s, he used illegal drugs to try to escape loneliness.

7. He gave up drugs in the 1960s to improve his health.

8. Throughout most of his career, Miles traveled around the world to give his music a wide audience.

B. Gerunds as Objects of Verbs

If a verb form is used after the following verbs, it must be the gerund form

9.4 Gerunds as Objects of Verbs

Verbs Often Followed by Gerunds			Examples
admit	discuss	miss	We **appreciate your helping** us.
anticipate	dread	postpone	I **can't help getting** nervous.
appreciate	enjoy	prevent	We **discussed taking** a trip.
avoid	escape	recall	He **dreads taking** tests.
be worth	excuse	recommend	They **finished washing** the dishes.
can't help	finish	resent	I **forgive your being** late.
complete	forgive	resist	We **miss seeing** our families.
consider	imagine	risk	He **postponed going** home.
defer	involve	spend time	He **suggested taking** a break.
delay	mention	suggest	She **spent a lot of time studying**.
deny	mind (meaning	tolerate	I **don't understand your not preparing** for the test.
detest	dislike)	understand	

4 **Practice** Imagine that you have gone to a concert. Tell about it by completing the following sentences with gerunds or gerund phrases formed from the cues in parentheses. Use subjects with the gerunds when indicated.

Example We all enjoyed (go / to the concert).

We all enjoyed going to the concert.

1. The concert certainly was worth (see).

2. I wouldn't mind (see / that group again).

3. I admit (not like / all the music).

4. We certainly appreciated (your / give / us the tickets).

5. We are considering (go / to another concert).

6. It will involve (make plans / well in advance).

7. I'd recommend (your / buy / tickets soon).

8. I suggest (call / the box office today).

9. Don't postpone (buy / tickets).

10. We anticipate (the concert's / be sold out).

5 **Practice** Using your own words, form complete sentences from the following cues.

Example mention / go

Jack mentioned going skiing this weekend.

1. appreciate / take	6. don't mind / drive
2. consider / return	7. recommend / see
3. discuss / return	8. spend time / visit
4. imagine / see	9. suggest / go
5. involve / plan	10. can't help / wonder

6 **Practice** In pairs, take turns asking and answering the following questions.

1. Do you spend a lot of time listening to music?

2. What types of music do you enjoy? Are there any types you dislike?

3. Do you enjoy going to concerts? What types of concerts do you enjoy most?

4. Whom would you recommend seeing in concert?

5. Name some musicians that you think are worth paying a lot of money to see.

6. Would it be worth driving an hour to see these musicians?

7. Would it be worth spending a lot of time waiting in lines for tickets or for a performance?

8. Do you anticipating going to a concert any time soon?

C. Subjects of Gerunds

A possessive noun or adjective is often used as the subject of a gerund. However, if the subject is a long noun phrase or if it is not a person, *the* + [gerund] + *of* + [subject] can be used.

9.5 Subjects of Gerunds	
Structures	**Examples**
Gerund Without a Subject	**Singing** is something I enjoy very much. Beautiful **singing** is something I always enjoy.
Possessive as Subject	**Ella's singing** has thrilled countless audiences. I will never forget **Ella Fitzgerald's singing**. **Her singing** was truly magnificent.
The **+ Gerund +** *of*	I will never forget the **singing of the jazz great, Ella Fitzgerald**. I will never forget the sound of **the shattering of glass**.

7 Practice Rephrase the following sentences to include gerund forms of the verbs in parentheses. Include the subject of the gerund with each sentence. In cases where possessives and phrases with *of* are possible, show both.

▲ Louis Armstrong

1. There is only one "Mr. Jazz." <u>Louis Armstrong's playing</u> (Louis Armstrong / play) has influenced jazz ever since the 1920s. Through _____ (he / improvise), "Satchmo" actually changed the art of trumpet playing. He made the trumpet do things that were supposed to be impossible.

_____ (he / "bend") of trumpet sounds astonished musicians everywhere.

2. _____ (represent) the legacy of Louis Armstrong, Dizzy Gillespie, and Miles Davis among modern jazz trumpet players is Wynton Marsalis. _____ (He / understand) of the major trends in the history of jazz are evident in his distinctive performances. _____ (complement) this is his technical brilliance. _____ (train) for years as a classical musician has given his _____ (play) a distinctive refined sound. For years, Marsalis considered _____ (dedicate) himself to classical music. Today, he is primarily involved in _____ (perform) jazz. However, he still enjoys _____ (appear) in some classical concerts.

3. It is not difficult to name great jazz vocalists of the past. _____ (Billie Holiday / sing) was the personification of swing. _____ (Joe Williams / sing) personified blues, and _____ (Ella Fitzgerald / sing) represents the essence of modern jazz.

D. Direct Objects of Gerunds

Like verbs, gerunds may have direct objects. Gerunds that have direct objects may be phrased in two ways, as shown in the table below.

9.6 Direct Objects of Gerunds		
Structures	**Explanations**	**Examples**
Gerund + Object	Gerunds are commonly followed by noun or pronoun direct objects.	**Arranging music** can be difficult. **Teaching music** is enjoyable.
The + Gerund + _of_ + Object	Using _the_ with the gerund and _of_ with the object places stronger emphasis on the gerund in its use as a noun.	**The arranging of music** is a major focus of the graduate program. **The teaching of music** can be very enjoyable.

8 Practice Complete the following sentences by forming gerund phrases that use *the* and *of*.

Example Jazz developed through *the combining of many styles* (combine / many styles) of music.

1. Jazz was born through _____ (mix / different races, cultures, and music).

2. The earliest forms of jazz began in New Orleans with _____ (blend / work songs, spirituals, blues, folk, and traditional music).

3. Jazz involved _____ (combine / traditional styles and new rhythms).

4. Some early jazz began with _____ (change / the rhythm of traditional marches and waltzes).

5. New Orleans provided the right atmosphere for _____ (interweave / black and white music).

6. Jazz always involves much more than _____ (play / musical notes).

7. It is _____ (express / one's individuality) through music.

8. For the musician, the heart of jazz is _____ (release / tension and emotion) through music.

Using What You've Learned

9 Role-playing Do you plan on going to a concert soon? In pairs, role-play a phone call or a visit to a theater box office to get information about tickets. Use as many of the following as possible in your role-play.

I'm interested in. . . .	I suggest. . . .
Would you mind . . . ?	I'd recommend. . . .
I (would) appreciate. . . .	I hope that you'll enjoy. . . .
Is it worth . . . ?	If you don't mind. . . .

10 Discussing Music Longfellow said, "Music is the universal language of mankind." In small groups, discuss whether all music is, in fact, a language that everyone can understand. As you talk, share your own ideas on music. What is music? Is everything that we hear today really music? What kinds of music do you prefer? What kinds of music are popular today?

11 **Describing How to Play an Instrument** How can you become a good musician? How do you learn to play a guitar, a piano, a flute, a harp, a violin, or a saxophone? If you know about an instrument, give a brief description of the basic steps in learning to play it. For example, "You can become a good musician by practicing every day. . . ." Or, "If you're interested in playing the piano, you start by learning the scales. . . ." If you don't play an instrument, tell about another art form such as dance or acting, or a hobby or sport that you enjoy.

Part 2 | Infinitives

Setting the Context

Previewing the Passage Discuss the questions with a group.

Today, artists use everything from blowtorches to computers in their work. Yet some of the most beautiful work is still done by hand. Which tools did (do) traditional artists from your culture use?

▲ "El Dorado" gold work from Colombia, was created before the arrival of the Europeans.

Reading Read the passage.

Pre-Columbian Gold Work

Using gold for trade was rare among the Indians in ancient America because gold was sacred. Symbolic of great power, gold was believed to have a direct link to the gods, especially the sun god. Thus, it was too precious to use as money. Instead, gold was an offering. It was a special tribute for an individual to give to the gods or to a patron. Above all, gold was important in funeral practices. Exquisite ornaments were used to decorate important graves, and most of the pre-Columbian gold work still in existence comes from such burial sites.

Unfortunately, much of the gold work that European explorers acquired was melted down to send to Europe. As a result, the gold work that remains has been found, for the most part, in more recently discovered graves.

 Discussing Ideas Discuss the questions with a partner.

What happened to the gold work that the European explorers found? Can you think of other examples of art that has been taken or destroyed by outsiders?

Grammar Structures and Practice

A. Functions of Infinitives

An infinitive may replace a noun or pronoun. Infinitives can be used in these ways:

9.7 Functions of Infinitives		
Explanations	**Structures**	**Examples**
The infinitive is *to* + verb. Infinitives may be used in place of a noun or pronoun as the subject or complement of a sentence, as the subject after "anticipatory" *it*, or as the object of a verb.	**Subject** **Complement** **With Anticipatory *It*** **Object of a Verb**	**To visit** South America is one of my goals. One of my goals is **to visit** South America. It's one of my goals **to visit** South America. I would like **to visit** South America.
Not is used before the infinitive to form the negative.	**Negative Infinitive**	It would be a shame **not to go**.
For + a noun or object pronoun can precede an infinitive as its subject.	**Subjects of Infinitives**	It would be a shame **for him not to go**.
Infinitives may also be used in a phrase showing purpose. These infinitive phrases may be used at various points within a sentence. *In order* can be used before an infinitive of purpose, but it is not necessary and is often omitted.	**Infinitives of Purpose**	**In order to see** everything, plan to stay several months. You should plan to stay several months **in order to see** everything. **To see** everything, you should stay several months.

B. Infinitives as Objects of Verbs

Infinitives may be used as objects of the following verbs. If a verb form is used after these verbs, it must be the infinitive form.

9.8 Infinitives as Objects of Verbs

Verbs Often Followed by Infinitives			Examples
agree	deserve	pretend	They **agreed to help**.
appear	endeavor	proceed	We **can't afford to move** now.
arrange	fail	prove	**Do** you **care to have** some coffee?
be	forget	refuse	We **decided to leave** early.
be about	happen	seem	She **deserves to be paid** more.
be supposed	hesitate	serve	I **failed to recognize** the problem.
(can't) afford	hope	struggle	He **forgot to call**.
care	learn	swear	We **prepared to leave** at dawn.
claim	manage	tend	He **pretended to be sleeping**.
come	mean	threaten	She **refused to help**.
consent	offer	volunteer	You **seem to be** upset.
decide	plan	wait	I **volunteered to help** after school.
demand	prepare		We **waited to say** good-bye.

1 **Practice** Imagine that you went to the Gold Museum in Bogotá, Colombia. Tell about your visit by completing the following sentences, using appropriate infinitive forms. Be sure to include negatives when indicated.

Example We planned / go / to the Gold Museum
We planned to go to the Gold Museum.

1. Everyone agreed / meet / at the museum

2. There appeared / be / hundreds of people at the museum

3. We happened / choose / a busy day

4. We had hoped / go / when it wasn't crowded

5. We waited for the crowds / leave

6. We decided / not / stay

7. We agreed / come back / later

8. We plan / never / go / there on a holiday again

2 **Practice** Working with a partner, create a story of approximately 20 sentences. You can tell about a visit somewhere, as in Exercise 1. Or, you can choose another topic entirely. Form sentences from each of the following cues and include these sentences in your story. When you are finished, present your story to the class.

1. agree / wait

2. decide / not go

3. hope / return

4. learn / ask

5. offer / help

6. prepare / leave

7. seem / not want

8. manage / understand

C. Verbs that May Be Followed by (Pro)Nouns and Infinitives

The following list of verbs may use an infinitive object or a (pro)noun object and an infinitive.

9.9 Verbs that May Be Followed by (Pro)Nouns and Infinitives	
Verb + Infinitive	**Verb + (Pro)noun + Infinitive**
I asked **to go**. I would like **to go**.	I asked **Camila to go**. I would like **her to go**.

Verbs + (Optional Object) + Infinitive				
ask beg choose	dare expect help[1]	intend need[2] prefer[3]	promise want	wish would like[3]

[1]*Help* may be followed by an infinitive or by the simple form of a verb. Compare: *I helped her to do it. I helped her do it.*

[2]In certain cases, *need* may be followed by a gerund. Compare: *I need to wash my car. My car needs washing.*

[3]See Part 3 for more information on these verbs.

D. Verbs That Must Be Followed by a (Pro)noun Object Before an Infinitive

In the active voice, the following verbs *must* have a (pro)noun object before an infinitive. In the passive voice, the infinitive may follow the verb directly.

9.10 Verbs That Must Be Followed by a (Pro)Noun Object Before an Infinitive

Active Verb + (Pro)Noun + Infinitive	Passive Verb + Infinitive
We hired **him to do** the work. We told **him to do** the work.	He **was hired to do** the work. He **was told to do** the work.

Verbs + Object + Infinitive				
allow	command	forbid	motivate	show . . . how
appoint	compel	force	oblige	teach
believe	convince	get[1]	order	tell
cause	direct	hire	permit	urge
caution	enable	implore	persuade	use
challenge	encourage	instruct	remind	warn
			require	

[1]*Get* is not used in the passive voice. In the active voice, it normally uses a (pro)noun object. In some idiomatic expressions, however, it is directly followed by an infinitive: *I get to go.* (I am allowed or permitted to go.) *I've got to go.* (I must go.)

---

3 **Practice** Complete the following by using appropriate infinitive forms. Add a noun or pronoun object when necessary and include negatives when indicated.

Example We asked / stay
We asked to stay. No (pro)noun object is necessary.
We convinced / not / stay
We convinced her not to stay. A (pro)noun object is necessary.

1. He was asked / stay

2. He chose / not / stay

3. They told / stay

4. We were told / stay

5. They were encouraged / help

6. We encouraged / help

7. She was convinced / take a trip

8. We convinced / take a trip

9. The extra money enabled / pay for the trip

10. The extra money allowed / pay for the trip

4 Practice South America has a wealth of material for anyone interested in arts or crafts: music, dance, poetry, novels, painting, sculpture, architecture, and beautiful and varied craft work.

Imagine that you have the opportunity to go anywhere in South America. In pairs, take turns completing, asking, and answering these questions about your travels.

1. Where would you choose to . . . ?

2. Why would you like to . . . ?

3. How would you plan to . . . ?

4. Would you decide to . . . ?

5. What do you hope to . . . ?

6. Do you intend to . . . ?

7. Whom would you ask to . . . ?

8. Would you prefer to . . . ?

9. Who(m) would you want to . . . ?

10. What would you expect to . . . ?

E. Adverbs, Adjectives, and Nouns Followed by Infinitives

Adverbs, adjectives, and nouns may also be followed by infinitives. These structures can take special forms as shown below.

9.11 Adverbs, Adjectives, and Nouns Followed by Infinitives

Explanations	Structures	Examples
Too and *enough* are often used with infinitives. *When, where,* and *how* can also be followed by infinitives. These phrases are reduced forms of noun clauses.	**Adverbs + Infinitives**	Pure gold is **too** soft **to use** in jewelry. Pure gold is not hard **enough to use** in jewelry. Can you tell me **where to buy** nice jewelry? (Can you tell me where I can buy some?)
Adjectives such as *excited, happy, pleased,* and *sad* are frequently followed by infinitives. Present participles such as *boring* and *interesting* are also followed by infinitives. *To* or *for* are often used to include a subject with the participle. Infinitives can also follow ordinals or superlatives (*first, last*) and *it* + adjective. *Of* (not *for*) is used with these.	**Adjectives + Infinitives**	It was **wonderful to visit** the museum. I was **happy to go** there. It was **great to be able to go** there. It was **fascinating to see** the exhibit. It was **fascinating to learn** about gold. It was **fascinating to me to see** that. I was the **last person to leave**. I was the **last to leave**. It was **nice of you to join me**.
Infinitives may be used after nouns as reduced forms of adjective clauses.	**Nouns + Infinitives**	There are so many **things to see**. (There are so many things that we can see.)

5 Practice Consider these examples of pre-Colombian workmanship. Imagine the tools and the working conditions involved in making them. What are your reactions to them? Complete the following sentences, using appropriate infinitives as you express your opinions.

Example It is amazing *to see the quality of workmanship in these pieces.*

1. I wonder if it was difficult. . . .

2. How did the artists get enough . . . ?

3. How were they able . . . ?

4. These pieces seem too. . . .

5. The artists must have worked hard. . . .

6. I wonder who was the first. . . .

7. I wonder if it was easy. . . .

8. I would enjoy learning how. . . .

9. It would be nice. . . .

10. I would like to know where. . . .

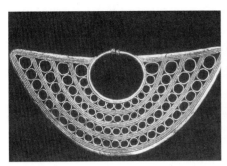

▲ Necklace

▲ Earrings

▲ Figure

6 **Practice** Complete the passage by using appropriate infinitive or gerund forms of the verbs in parentheses.

Example Craftsmen in Colombia and Peru had known how __*to work*__ (work) with gold well before 400 B.C.E.

1. Despite the primitive quality of their tools, they were able _____ (master) almost every technique for _____ (work) with gold known today.

2. These craftsmen learned how _____ (heat) gold until it was soft.

3. This allowed artists _____ (stretch) and _____ (hammer) the gold without _____ (break) it.

4. Normally, gold tends _____ (break) easily.

5. Later, these craftsmen developed the lost wax technique, which involved _____ (melt) gold and _____ (pour) it into molds.

6. In order _____ (use) this technique, the artist had _____ (be) skillful at _____ (work) with gold.

7. Some artists were so highly regarded that they were not permitted _____ (do) any other form of work.

8. These ancient smiths were so advanced that only a few of today's methods of _____ (work) with gold were unknown to them.

7 **Practice** Complete the following by using appropriate infinitive or gerund forms of the verbs in parentheses.

White Gold

It is soft, yet tough enough _____*to pull*_____ and _____
_____(pull)_____1 (pound)
into almost any shape. It can be melted down _____ again. It
_____2 (use)
gleams in the sun and is better at _____ light than anything else.
_____3 (reflect)

It is silver—a metal people have treasured for at least 5,000 years. During

that time, they have managed _____ up nearly one million tons
_____4 (dig)
of it, almost enough _____ three solid columns each the size of
_____5 (make)
the Washington Monument, which is 555 feet high.

Much of the world's silver has been used _____ coins. The
_____6 (make)
first silver coins are believed _____ from around 600 B.C.E.
_____7 (date)
People had used chunks of silver for _____ long before that
_____8 (trade)
time, but _____ became easier with the use of coins.
_____9 (trade)

Like gold, pure silver is malleable; a good silversmith knows how

_____ or _____ it into shape without
_____10 (pound)_____11 (beat)
_____ it. Objects made of pure silver are normally too soft
_____12 (break)
_____, though. A silversmith needs _____
_____13 (use)_____14 (add)
other metals _____ the silver. Sterling silver, for example, con-
_____15 (strengthen)
sists of 925 parts silver mixed with 75 parts copper.

8 Practice Complete the following passage by using appropriate infinitive or gerund forms of the verbs in parentheses.

Precious Metals in the Americas

Silver played almost as big a part as gold in _____bringing_____ many
                                              (bring)

Europeans to the Americas. The Incas and the Aztecs had mined both of these

precious metals, and word of their riches was enough _____ thou-
                                                       1 (bring)

sands of Europeans who hoped _____ rich in the Americas.
                               2 (become)

For 200 years after _____ the Americas, Spain was the wealthi-
                      3 (discover)

est nation in the world, and merchants in many places refused

_____ any form of money other than the Spanish silver dollar.
4 (accept)

Since the early days of the Americas, silver has brought a different sort of

wealth as people have learned _____ it in a variety of impor-
                               5 (employ)

tant ways. _____ mirrors, X-rays, and photographic film and
           6 (coat)

_____ electricity are only a few of its uses. In fact, silver is
7 (conduct)

even used for _____ rain; pilots seed clouds with crystals of
               8 (make)

silver salts, which causes rain _____.
                                 9 (form)

9 Error Analysis All of the following sentences contain errors in the use of infinitives or gerunds. Find the errors and make the necessary corrections.

                                        e
Example Pure gold is soft to using in jewelry.

1. I would enjoy to learn how to make jewelry.
2. She asked me going with her to South America.
3. Everyone agreed meeting me at the steps in front of the concert hall.
4. Marguerite refused helping me with the painting.
5. Miles Davis' play is beautiful.
6. The playing jazz is a difficult art form.
7. I can't help to go to at least once a week.
8. The students are very excited about to visit the Louvre Museum.
9. Marina isn't used to practice the piano yet.
10. I like to relax by paint with oil.

Using What You've Learned

 10 Discussing Hobbies and Pastimes What artistic activities do you participate in during your free time? Are you interested in painting or drawing? Taking photographs? Playing music? Do you like to go to concerts and museums? What kinds of art or artistic activities do you dislike? Which do you avoid? Discuss your interests with a partner, using as many of the words and expressions from the following list as possible. Remember which are followed by gerunds and which are followed by infinitives.

It's fun . . .	avoid	enjoy
It's boring . . .	be accustomed to	expect
It's enjoyable . . .	be interested in	plan
It's interesting . . .	encourage (someone)	plan on
It's relaxing . . .		

11 Playing a Guessing Game Think of all the tools or materials that you work with on a daily basis: pencils, erasers, notebooks, rulers, dictionaries, bicycles, cars, spoons, knives, faucets, chairs, and so forth. Choose one item, exotic or ordinary, and write at least a six-sentence description of how and why it is used. Later, read your description to the class, but do not tell your classmates what the item is. Let them guess, based on your description of it.

12 Describing Artisanry from Your Culture Cultures around the world have special crafts. The Chinese are famous for their porcelain, brush paintings, and carpets. Middle Easterners are famous for their rugs as well as ceramics and ironwork. Central and South American groups are noted for weaving, pottery, and basketry. Africans are renowned for wood carving.

Is there a highly developed craft that is typical in your culture? Or perhaps there is another art form, such as music or dance, that is a cultural specialty. Individually or in small groups, prepare a brief presentation (five to ten minutes) on an art or craft in your culture. Try to bring examples to help illustrate your presentation. As you prepare, use as many infinitives and gerunds as possible.

Setting the Context

▲ *Impression, Sunrise* by Claude Monet

Previewing the Passage Discuss the questions with a group.

Are you familiar with impressionist art? Who are some of the more famous impressionist painters? Have you seen any of their works? Where?

Reading Read the passage.

The Impressionists

On April 15, 1874, a small group of artists including, Pissarro, Degas, Cézanne, Sisley, Monet, Morisot, and Renoir, held their first exhibition in Paris. The paintings that they displayed are recognized today as masterpieces. However, at that time, this artwork caused the public to react with disappointment and disgust. It seemed for a moment as though all of Paris had stopped to criti-   5
cize the radical style of these artists.

Art critics were virtually unanimous in their panning[1] of the exhibition. Some even advised burning all of the paintings. One critic sarcastically labeled the group's technique "impressionist," after seeing *Impression, Sunrise,*[2] a painting by Claude Monet. The critic had meant to ridicule[3] the techniques of the group,   10
yet it was this name that the group adopted. The group had already been trying to define their technique for some time. After hearing these remarks, the painters stopped looking for definitions and began to call themselves impressionists.

---

[1]*pan* strongly criticize
[2]*impression* in this sense, an idea or memory that is not distinct, precise, or well defined
[3]*ridicule* make fun of

Discussing Ideas Discuss the questions with a partner.

Though impressionist art was ridiculed in the beginning, today it is appreciated around the world. Are people always resistant to new trends or revolutionary ideas? What are some current trends in art, music, or fashion that some people cannot accept? Do you think any of these trends will one day become as popular as the impressionist paintings?

Grammar Structures and Practice

A. Verbs Followed by Either Gerunds or Infinitives with Little or No Change in Meaning

These verbs may be followed by either a gerund or an infinitive with little or no change in meaning.

9.12	Verbs with Little or No Difference in Meaning When Followed Either by a Gerund or an Infinitive	
Verbs	**Explanations**	**Examples**
Begin **Can(not) bear** **Can(not) stand** **Continue** **Start**	These verbs are commonly followed by either infinitives or gerunds with little difference in meaning.	I **began studying** art several years ago. I **began to study** art several years ago. I **continue studying** art today. I **continue to study** art today.
Attempt **Intend** **Neglect** **Hate**	With these verbs, both forms are correct, but infinitives are used more often after them.	I've **attempted to do** several oil paintings. I've **attempted doing** several oil paintings.
(Dis)like **Love** **Prefer**	With these verbs, both forms are often used. However, *only* infinitives are used when the verbs are in the conditional.	I **like to go** to museums. I **like going** to museums. I **would like to go** to that museum.

B. Verbs Followed by Either Gerunds or Infinitives, But with a Change in Meaning

These verbs can be followed by either gerunds or infinitives, but the sentences can have completely different meanings, depending on which is used.

9.13	Verbs That Have Different Meanings When Followed Either by a Gerund or an Infinitive	
Verbs	**Explanations**	**Examples**
Infinitives with Forget, Regret, and Remember	Infinitives follow *forget, regret,* and *remember* when these verbs express a first (or earlier) action. The infinitive expresses the second (or later) action. *To inform, to say,* or *to tell* are the most common infinitives used after *regret.* Other verbs normally use the gerund form after *regret.*	I **forgot to tell** you what happened. (I didn't tell you.) I **regret to give** you this news. (I am sorry about the news that I'm about to give you.) Did you **remember to tell** him the story? (Did you tell him?)
Gerunds with Forget, Regret, and Remember	Gerunds follow these verbs when the verb expresses the second action. The gerund expresses the first action.	Have you **forgotten** (about) **telling** him that? (You told him.) I **regret not giving** him more advice. (I didn't give him more advice.) Do you **remember promising** me that you would tell him? (You promised me.)
Infinitives with Try	When *try* means *attempt,* it is followed by an infinitive.	I **tried to talk** to him, but he was too busy. (I didn't talk to him.)
Gerunds with Try	*Try* can also mean *experiment* (with different alternatives). In this case, it is followed by a gerund.	I **tried talking to him**, but he wouldn't change his mind. (I talked to him.)
Infinitives with Quit and Stop	When an infinitive follows *quit* or *stop,* it tells the reason or purpose for stopping.	We **stopped to take** a break. (We stopped our work in order to take a break.)
Gerunds with Quit and Stop	When a gerund follows these verbs, it tells *who* or *what* was stopped.	We **stopped taking** long breaks. (We used to take long breaks, but we don't anymore.)
Infinitives with Mean	*Mean* followed by an infinitive means *intend* or *plan.*	Did you **mean to spend** so much?
Gerunds with Mean	*Mean* followed by a gerund means *involve* or *signify.* An impersonal subject (*this, that, it,* etc.) is normally used with *mean* + a gerund.	It **means not having** enough money for the rest of the month.
Infinitives with Propose	*Propose* followed by an infinitive means *intend.*	I **propose to nominate** John at the next meeting.
Gerunds with Propose	*Propose* followed by a gerund means *suggest.*	I **propose asking** him first before you nominate him.

C. Verbs Followed by Either Gerunds or Infinitives

With these verbs, use of the gerund or infinitive depends on several things:

- These verbs may be followed by gerunds if no (pro)noun object is used.
- If a (pro)noun object is used, it is followed by an infinitive.
- Infinitives are also used when these verbs are in the passive voice.

9.14	Verbs That Are Followed by Gerunds or Infinitives, Depending on the Use of a (Pro)Noun Object	
Verbs	**Structures**	**Examples**
advise allow encourage forbid permit teach	**Verb + Gerund** **Active Verb + (Pro)Noun + Infinitive** **Passive Verb + Infinitive**	I advise **taking** your digital camera. We **do not permit using** a flash. They **advised** me **to take** my digital camera. They **won't permit us to use** a flash. I **was advised to take** my digital camera. It **is not permitted to use** a flash.

Note: In certain cases, a gerund is used after *teach* + object. This most often occurs with common school subjects such as reading, painting, and singing. (*I teach [children] reading and writing.*)

---

1 **Practice** Many of the sentences in the following conversation may be completed by using either infinitives or gerunds. In cases where only one form is possible, explain why.

Anne: I can't believe this: I'm leaving for Europe tomorrow, and I haven't even

started ___*to pack / packing*___ yet! Talk about disorganized. I'm sure I'll

           (pack)

forget _____ my passport, or my tickets, or something.

         1 (take)

Joan: I'd love _____ with you, especially to Paris. How long

         2 (go)

will you be there?

Anne: I'll be there for five or six days. I'd prefer _____ a year

                      3 (spend)

or two in Paris, but even a few days is fine with me. I'm going to try

_____ as many museums as I can—the Louvre, the

    4 (visit)

Musée Rodin . . .

Joan: Remember _____ the Musée Marmottan. It has some of

        5 (visit)

Claude Monet's most beautiful paintings, including many of the *Water*

Lilies series. Try _____ at least an afternoon there. I

        6 (spend)

meant _____ a day there myself, but I wasn't able to. It

7 (spend)

would have meant _____ our plans.

8 (change)

Anne: I remember _____ me about that. Didn't you try

9 (you / tell)

_____ several times, but the museum was closed?

10 (go)

Joan: I'd tell you the story again, but you should stop _____

11 (talk)

and start _____.

12 (pack)

2 **Practice** Form complete sentences from the following.

Example That museum forbids / take backpacks inside

That museum forbids taking backpacks inside.

1. That museum does not permit you / take pictures

2. At least, they do not permit / use a flash

3. People are not permitted / use a flash here

4. You are forbidden / use a flash

5. The museum forbids / use a flash

6. My friend teaches people / take pictures without a flash

7. She could teach you / take good pictures without your flash

8. Flash cameras can cause the colors / fade

9. The museum encourages people / buy prints there instead

10. The prints are very good. I advise / buy several

3 **Practice** Complete the following passage by using infinitive or gerund forms of the verbs in parentheses.

Impressionism

Before Monet painted *Impression, Sunrise,* art critics had used the word

Impressionism to _____suggest_____ incompleteness or a superficial vision

(suggest)

of the subject. The impressionists decided _____ the name and

1 (adopt)

wished _____ a suitable definition for it. One suggestion was

2 (find)

_____ in terms of light rather than in terms of physical shape.

3 (paint)

In order _____ impressionism, one must remember

4 (define)

_____ the impressionists' concern for light rather than form.
5 (consider)

Instead of _____ the form of an object, the impressionists
6 (analyze)

allowed themselves _____ only the light reflected from the
7 (see)

object. This is because they were interested in _____ the
8 (reproduce)

effect of the light alone. Thus, flowers in the distance that appeared

_____ blurs of color were painted as blurs, even if the artist
9 (be)

happened _____ the flowers well enough _____
10 (know)   11 (reproduce)

them exactly from memory.

4 **Practice** Complete the following passage by using infinitive or gerund forms of
the verbs in parentheses.

Édouard Manet

A witty, kind, and handsome Parisian gentleman, Édouard Manet
(1832–1883) was an unlikely revolutionary. He seemed _____*to stand*_____
(stand)

apart from the controversy surrounding him. He wanted only

_____ recognition for his art. Manet appeared _____
1 (gain)   2 (not understand)

why his work stimulated such a storm of criticism.

Yet Manet was a revolutionary. His paintings *Déjeuner sur l'herbe* and

Olympia caused the entire Parisian art world _____ with
3 (shake)

amazement. Manet was the first _____ the new trends of mod-
4 (begin)

ernism. A great innovator, he disliked _____ old styles.
5 (follow)

_____ of form, color, and light shows a completely modern way
6 (he / handle)

of _____. He was the first in the Parisian art world
7 (think)

_____, Is art simply a recording of reality? Does it have
8 (ask)

_____ the past? Are artists forbidden _____
9 (imitate)   10 (create)

their own interpretations?

The importance of Manet's work goes beyond the quality of his painting. It

anticipated many trends _____. He borrowed from the old mas-
11 (come)

ters but avoided _____ them. In essence, Manet was successful
                        12 (imitate)

at _____ ideas from old art and _____ these
        13 (take)   14 (redefine)

ideas in terms of the new. His struggle _____ his vision encour-
                                              15 (define)

aged a generation of young artists _____ their own vision of art.
                                        16 (explore)

Using What You've Learned

5 Describing a Piece of Artwork The pieces of art that follow were considered revolutionary and in some cases "crude," "simplistic," "distasteful," or "disgusting" when they were first shown. The appearance of each, however, prompted irreversible changes in the art world of the time. In small groups, discuss your own opinions of these particular works of art. Which do you like or dislike? Can you imagine why they were considered outrageous? In your discussion, try to use as many of these words or phrases as possible.

avoid	be successful at	imagine	object to
be accustomed to	be used to	know (how)	prefer
be fascinated with	can't help	(not) approve of	tend
be / get tired of	can't stand	(not) care for	understand
be interested in	enjoy	(not) mind	(would) like

▲ *The Scream* by Edvard Munch

▲ *The Little White girl: Symphony in White, No. 2* by James Whistler

▲ *The Starry Night* (1889) by Vincent van Gogh

6 **Writing About Art and Artists** An old Chinese proverb says, "There are pictures in poems and poems in pictures." What do you think is meant by this? Write a short composition explaining this proverb.

Part 4 | Continuous and Perfect Forms of Gerunds and Infinitives

Setting the Context

 Previewing the Passage Discuss the questions with a group.

Gardens can be forms of art. Where do you think the garden in this picture is located? Have you ever visited such a garden? If so, where?

Reading Reading a passage.

The Gardens of East Asia

Gardens in Asia are magical places. They have existed as art forms for many centuries. Oriental gardens are a blend of man-made landscaping and natural scenery. Horticulture is combined with architecture, painting, literature, and calligraphy to recreate the beauty of larger landscapes and to create a sense of peace.   5

Even in ancient times, garden designers appear to have mastered the art of imitating nature. Gardens seem not to have been planned, yet in reality every detail was considered and every element was chosen with care. After having been selected carefully and thoughtfully, plants, trees, rocks, stones, and sand were all placed in ways that imitated famous vistas or simply conveyed peace   10
and tranquility.

Of course, most ancient gardens have gone through significant changes over the centuries. Much of what we now know about their original forms comes from paintings and scenes on ceramics. However, some gardens of East Asia appear to have been preserved relatively well. Today, these gardens are   15
among the most favored tourist destinations in China, Japan, and Korea.

Discussing Ideas Discuss the questions with a group.

Gardens are obviously very changeable. They depend on the weather, and they need on-going maintenance. In your opinion, can art be something ever-changing? Or, must art forms be relatively permanent?

Grammar Structures and Practice

A. Continuous and Perfect Forms of Infinitives

Continuous infinitives emphasize the idea of an action in progress. Perfect infinitives emphasize the completion of an action.

9.15 Continuous and Perfect Forms of Infinitives		
Structures	**Explanations**	**Examples**
		(not) to be + past participle
CONTINUOUS INFINITIVES	Continuous infinitives often occur after the verbs *agree, appear, arrange, happen, hope, expect, plan, pretend, promise,* and *seem.* They are also common after passive constructions with verbs such as *say, think,* and *believe.*	We plan **to be working** on the garden by 9:00 A.M. tomorrow. We expect **to be planting** flowers and shrubs later in the day. We expect **not to be working** late. They are thought **to be working** today.
		(not) to have + past participle
PERFECT ACTIVE INFINITIVES	Perfect infinitives often occur after *appear, claim, expect, happen, hope, pretend,* and *seem.*	We hope **to have finished** the garden by 5:00 P.M. today. They claim **to have finished** the project already.
		(not) to have been + past participle
PERFECT PASSIVE INFINITIVES	They are also common after passive constructions with verbs such as *say, think,* and *believe.*	Mr. Smith expects the garden **to have been finished** by 5:00 P.M. We expect it **not to have been completed** yet.

1 Practice Complete the following sentences using the active or passive infinitive forms of the words in parentheses. Note the cases where both the simple and the perfect forms can be used.

Example The tourists plan ___*to be spending*___ (spend) the entire day visiting gardens.

1. Hangzhou and Suzhou appear _____ (know) for their beauty for many centuries.

2. There is a Chinese expression, which seems _____ (repeat) since ancient times: "Above there is Heaven, below there is Hangzhou and Suzhou."

3. The Lion Grove garden in Suzhuo is believed _____ (build) in the 1340s by the monk Tianru.

4. Monk Tianru and other disciples are believed _____ (create) the garden in memory of their teacher, the monk Zhongfeng.

5. The garden is famous for its rockery, which appears _____ (make) of limestone taken from Taihu Lake.

6. The name "Lion Grove" came from a Buddhist story in which lions seem _____ (sit) peacefully in a bamboo forest.

7. Rocks in the Lion Grove garden appear _____ (pile up) in a way that resembled real lions.

8. After the death of Monk Tianru, the garden is believed _____ (own) by many different people who used it as a retreat for painters and calligraphers.

9. Emperor Qianlong (18th century) is said _____ (visit) the site six times and _____ (write) the word Zhenqu, meaning "true delight," in a pavilion.

10. The emperor is thought _____ (delight) with the beauty of the Lion Grove garden.

▲ The Lion Grove garden in Suzhou, China, which dates to around 1342

B. Perfect Forms of Gerunds

In many sentences, the simple gerund and the perfect gerund may be used, but perfect gerunds emphasize the completion of one action before another.

9.16	Perfect Forms of Gerunds	
Structures	**Explanations**	**Examples**
		(not) having + **past participle**
PERFECT ACTIVE GERUNDS	In the examples, both the simple gerund and the perfect gerund are correct. The perfect form emphasizes the sequence of events. The action in the gerund phrase occurred earlier than the action of the main verb.	After **having planted** the garden, you must water it regularly. After **planting** the garden, you must water it regularly. I'm angry about not **having won** the award. I'm angry about not **winning** the award.
		(not) having been + **past participle**
PERFECT PASSIVE GERUNDS	Passive gerunds follow the same guidelines as active gerunds. In many cases, either the simple or the perfect gerund may be used.	After **having been planted**, the garden will need daily care. After **being planted**, the garden will need daily care. I am angry about **having been beaten**. I am angry about **being beaten**.

2 **Practice** In the following sentences, change the form of the gerund from simple to perfect.

Example After working on the project for several hours, I had a backache.
After having worked on the project for several hours, I had a backache.

1. The teacher was upset about the student's lying to her.

2. I appreciate your helping me with my math homework.

3. I regret not going to college when I had the chance.

4. Ana was pleased about being chosen for the scholarship.

5. My husband was angry at me for not giving him an important message.

6. I don't remember hearing that man's name before.

7. I can't forgive your taking my car without permission.

8. John's failing the entrance exam makes him ineligible to attend the college.

9. She felt hurt about not being invited to the party.

10. Not finishing college did not stop Arthur from becoming a millionaire.

3 **Practice** Complete the following sentences using simple or perfect gerund forms (active or passive) of the words in parentheses. Note the cases where either the simple or the perfect form could be used.

▲ Japanese tea ceremony

Japanese Tea Gardens

1. Over the centuries, Japanese gardens have been a way of

   _____*bringing*_____ (bring) the harmony and peace of nature into daily life.

   In fact, the tea garden was created as a way of _____

   (escape) the busy world and of _____ (leave) worries and

   cares behind. It was designed to give a feeling of _____

   (transport) to a place far from the world's hustle and bustle.

2. Today's version of the tea garden and tea ceremony originated with a Zen

   monk, Shuko. Shuko was fortunate in _____ (live) a long life:

   from 1423 to 1502. The idea of the tea garden came from Shuko's concerns

   about _____ (have) a quiet space in the midst of urban life.

   Shuko imagined a peaceful place where a small group of people might spend

   time _____ (talk) quietly.

3. A later tea master, Sen no Rikyu (1521–91) appears _____

   (refine) both the ceremony itself and the setting. Sen no Rikyu recommended

   _____ (make) tea houses as rustic[1] as possible while

   _____ (highlight) the beauty of the materials

   _____ (use) in the construction.

4. To Rikyu, the tea garden represented the transition between the distraction of

   the world and the serenity of the tea house. The garden was the path to a place

where people could escape _____ (catch) up in the world.
After _____ (spend) quiet moments _____
(walk) slowly down the "dewy path" of the garden, visitors would arrive at the
tea house.

5. The tea ceremony itself involved _____ (follow) very specific
steps. The host was responsible for _____ (make) the tea,
which was done slowly and gracefully. While _____ (serve)
tea, the group would sit in silence. After _____ (serve) the
tea, the host would begin _____ (converse). After
_____ (serve), the guests would discuss Zen philosophy and
art. Painting, drawing, and other art forms were always important topics while
_____ (sip) tea. After _____ (complete) the
ceremony, the guests and the hosts relax, and ceremonial dignity would change
to friendly conversation.

---

[1]*rustic* charmingly simple and unsophisticated; plain or with a rough quality

4 **Review** Complete the following passage by using infinitive or gerund forms of the
verbs in parentheses. Choose from simple, continuous, and perfect forms in either the
active or passive voice. Show any cases where more than one form is appropriate.

Korean Gardens

Throughout East Asia, gardening has been an art form for centuries. With
many ideas *having / been exchanged* among countries, it is not surprising
                    (exchange)
_____ similarities in gardens across the region. However,
        1 (see)
differences   exist,   and   it   is   fascinating   _____   and
                                                              2 (notice)
_____ the unique characteristics of gardens from country to
        3 (study)
country.

One of the most beautiful gardens _____ in the Orient is
                                            4 (create)
the Huwon Garden of the Palace in Seoul, South Korea. The palace itself is said
_____ around 1400, and it served as a royal palace until 1910.
        5 (build)
The Huwon garden covers an area of about 300,000 square meters. The highest
point of the gardens is almost 100 meters above sea level, and 17 pavilions were

constructed there. Because of _____ in harmony with the land-
6 (they / place)
scape, these pavilions do not seem _____ the hillside. Rather,
7 (dominate)
they blend in quite naturally.

In fact, though Huwon is man-made, the entire garden appears
_____ by nature. That is, the garden gives a feeling of
8 (form)
_____ completely natural. Each rock seems _____
9 (be)   10 (sit)
in a place where Nature herself might have put it. Plants, shrubs, and trees appear _____ there, it would appear, by Nature, not by humans.
11 (place)
Overall, the natural beauty of this setting is magnificent.

The beauty of the garden has a tremendous effect on visitors. While
_____ the two-kilometer path through the garden, people begin
12 (walk)
_____ in harmony with nature. Their thoughts seem clearer
13 (feel)
and their ideas more peaceful as they continue _____ through
14 (stroll)
the gardens. This effect appears _____ true over many cen-
15 (be)
turies, as ancient stories relate that Korean kings would often visit the garden
_____ with their confidants before _____ deci-
16 (consult)   17 (make)
sions on important matters.

Using What You've Learned

5 **Discussing Gardens and Natural Settings** Gardening serves different
purposes throughout the world. Where food is all-important, gardens are strictly for
growing vegetables or fruit. In other parts of the wor1d, gardens are art forms, and their
purpose is not to feed but rather to please or decorate. In small groups, compare
gardens in your own region or country. After discussing the gardens, give a brief
summary of your opinions to the entire class.

In your discussion, use as many of the following verbs and expressions as possible:

appear	enjoy	suggest	be accustomed to
appreciate	imagine	understand	be used to
can't help	mention	want	be curious about
detest	miss	wish	be interested in
dislike	seem	would like	be famous for

Previewing the Passage Discuss the questions with a group.

Are you familiar with traditional African art? What materials have Africans traditionally used to create art forms? Do you like these art forms?

Reading Read the passage.

African Art

For many people, to create art is to express the moral and religious beliefs that form the basis of their lives. This has been particularly true in the case of African art. African sculpting, dancing, storytelling, and music all developed from religion. Because of this religious influence, African art had two chief characteristics: variety in form and similarity in style. Different areas of Africa   5 specialized in different forms—statues, drums, dances, masks—because the rituals of African religion were varied. Yet the basic art styles throughout Africa were remarkably similar because everything was a variation on traditional religious themes. Most of African art has had this consciously religious function. The sculpting, dancing, singing, and drum music have all been designed to rein-   10 force the creative energy of life. Far from being primitive, African art is a highly stylized expression of spirituality.

Discussing Ideas Discuss the questions with a partner.

In the early 1900s, many revolutionary artists such as Picasso, Braque, and Matisse looked to African art as a source of inspiration. Much of today's popular music has its roots in African music. In which kinds of music can you see the strongest evidence of African influence?

Grammar Structures and Practice

A. Gerunds and Infinitives as Subjects and Complements

Both infinitives and gerunds may be used as subjects and complements of sentences.

- Gerunds are more commonly used as subjects.
- Infinitives often follow *it* as the subject of a sentence.
- Both gerunds and infinitives appear as complements, although infinitives are more common.

9.17 Gerunds and Infinitives as Subjects and Complements

Structures	Explanations	Examples
Gerund Subject	Gerunds are often used as subjects to express a process or an action inprogress.	**Sculpting** is one of the important types of art from Africa. **Sculpting** in Africa has been dated to ancient times. **Working** with bronze was a specialty of artists from Benin.
Gerund Complement	Gerunds may be used as complements after *be*, but infinitives are used as complements after other linking verbs. See below.	A specialty in Benin was **working** with bronze. (Artists appear **to have had** a special place in the society of Benin.)
Infinitive Subject	Infinitives are occasionally used as subjects to refer to a goal, purpose, or intention.	**To produce** (or **producing**) a detailed figure may take anywhere from a few hours to several weeks.
Infinitive with Anticipatory *It*	An infinitive often follows the verb when the "anticipatory" it is the subject of the sentence.	**It** can take several weeks **to produce** a detailed figure.
Infinitive Complement	Infinitives are often used as complements with the linking verbs *be*, *seem*, and *appear*.	A difficult part of the task is **to select** the best type of wood for a particular carving. Artists appear **to have had** a special place in the society of Benin.

1 Practice Today, machines do much of our work for us. As a result, some of the qualities associated with handmade items have been lost. Our clothing may be cheaper, but it is no longer unique. Most of the fabrics are synthetic. Our food is processed from start to finish. Even much of our music is electronic.

Do you think we have sacrificed quality by relying so heavily on machines? Have we already lost the skills to make things carefully by hand? Do you believe that it is important to protect folk or traditional arts and crafts? Give your own opinions on this subject by completing the following with infinitive phrases.

Example *It's (not) important to preserve traditional arts and crafts.*

1. It would be a shame. . . .
2. It's difficult. . . .
3. It's much more interesting. . . .
4. It's better. . . .
5. It would also be fascinating. . . .
6. It's hard. . . .
7. It's necessary. . . .
8. It's (im)possible. . . .

Now rephrase your sentences to begin with gerunds.

Example *Preserving traditional arts and crafts is (not) important.*

B. Parallelism

Parallelism involves preferences in style. When several structures are grammatically correct, style dictates which to choose. Generally, parallelism means using the same structures for the same function in a sentence. When a choice is possible, use gerunds only, or infinitives only. In a list, for example, do not mix gerunds and infinitives.

- Sentences with more than one infinitive or gerund should use the same form (either infinitive or gerund, not both) whenever possible.
- Parallelism is especially important when coordinating conjunctions are used or when a series of items is listed.

9.18 Parallelism	
Parallel Structures	Traditional art in Africa includes **sculpting, dancing,** and **storytelling**.
Lack of Parallel Structures (poor style)	*Traditional art in Africa includes **sculpting, dancing,** and **to tell** stories. *Traditional art includes **sculpture, dancing,** and **storytelling**. *Traditional art includes **sculpting, dance,** and **to tell stories**.

2 Practice Complete the following eight sentences with appropriate infinitive or gerund forms of the verbs in parentheses. In some cases, either form will be appropriate, so be sure to use parallel structures in your sentences.

Example Non-Africans often consider _____*sculpting*_____ (sculpt) as the greatest traditional African art, but to Africans, _____*dancing*_____ (dance) is perhaps their most important art form.

African Dance

1. _____ (dance) is a way of _____ (unite) two important parts of African life: religion and community life.

2. African dance can be a part of a ceremony for _____ (mark) the start of a hunt or _____ (give) thanks for a successful harvest.

3. It is often used _____ (commemorate) a birth or death or _____ (celebrate) a marriage.

4. Often, dance is festive, a time _____ (honor) special spirits, or it is purely recreational, a time for people _____ (enjoy) themselves.

5. For Africans, _____ (dance) is _____ (move) spontaneously to the rhythm of the drums.

6. African _____ (drum) involves _____ (create) an individual rhythm, _____ (follow) the other drummers, and _____ (respond) to their rhythms.

7. African drums are constructed _____ (produce) dozens of sounds, and every drummer attempts _____ (make) new combinations of sounds.

8. Frequently, it is impossible for Westerners _____ (duplicate) or even _____ (follow) complex African rhythms.

3 **Practice** Complete the following sentences by using infinitive or gerund forms of the verbs in parentheses. If you believe that either may be appropriate, explain why.

Example An African woodcarver's main function was _____*to create*_____ (creating) sculpture for religious purposes.

1. _____ (attract) and _____ (keep) specific spirits inside a carving was a way to protect the village from harm.

2. _____ (express) energy or life force in physical form is still the goal of African woodcarvers.

3. It must have been important _____ (combine) art and practicality because household items such as cups, spoons, and stools have shown amazing workmanship.

4. _____ (wear) carved wooden masks was a part of many religious dances, and the mask itself was believed to have special powers.

5. _____ (collect) African sculpture became a favorite pastime of Europeans and Americans; as a result, few original pieces remain in Africa today.

6. Today, _____ (carve) religious or household items has been replaced by _____ (produce) souvenirs for tourists.

7. Now it is almost impossible _____ (find) carvings of the same quality as in the past.

4 **Practice Error Analysis** Many of these sentences contain errors in the use of infinitives and gerunds. Find any errors and make the necessary corrections.

Example The nation of Benin had been a powerful center of commerce in west Africa for centuries when Europeans began ̮explore the region.

to explore OR exploring

1. Long before Europeans came for to explore tropical Africa, the powerful nation of Benin had been flourishing in what is now southern Nigeria.

2. Benin society was dignified and well ordered; it was headed by a king, or *Oba*, who was all powerful yet tolerant enough to allow a good deal of personal freedom in his kingdom.

3. In spite of not to have create a written language, the Beninese left beautiful bronze plaques and figures as records of their civilization.

4. The *Oba* hired artists to design the plaques in order to decorate his palace.

5. These plaques recorded numerous scenes of life in Benin, and many showed two important aspects of the culture: hunting and to trade.

6. Only the strongest Beninese men could become hunters and then only after to have completed rigorous training.

7. Young hunters had to learn how to track animals, moving quickly and quietly, and surviving in the forest for days without food.

8. When European explorers arrived, they couldn't help to be amazed at the amount of commerce in Benin.

9. Benin was the commercial center of western Africa, and Beninese merchants were clever enough outthinking the Europeans, who had expected dealing with simple natives.

10. Beninese merchants had an elaborate money system, and they dealt in the buying and to sell of ironwork, weapons, farm tools, wood carvings, and food.

Using What You've Learned

5 **Storytelling** Oral tradition and the art of storytelling are important aspects of African life. A storyteller may be able to recount the 500-year history of his or her family or village.

In small groups, take turns telling stories about your family, town, or region. Your story may be a favorite from childhood: *When my great-grandfather was a young boy, Native Americans in northern Wisconsin took care of him and helped raise him. . . .* Or it may be a story from your town: *In San Joaquin, they tell the story of La Llorona. La Llorona is a ghost who is often heard crying for her lost baby. . . .*

As you tell your story, try to talk continuously for at least four minutes. Do your best to include as many infinitives and gerunds as you can.

Focus on Testing

Use of Infinitives and Gerunds
Problem areas with infinitives and gerunds often appear on standardized English proficiency exams. Check your understanding of these structures by completing the sample items that follow.

Remember that . . .
✓ Certain verbs can be followed by gerunds, others by infinitives, and some verbs by either.
✓ Gerunds (not infinitives) are used after prepositions.
✓ A possessive noun or adjective is often used as the subject of a gerund.
✓ Some verbs must be followed by a (pro)noun object before an infinitive.

Part 1 Circle the best completion for the following.

Example   We convinced her not _____.

    Ⓐ she stay   Ⓑ stayed

    Ⓒ to stay   Ⓓ stay

1. Mrs. Morris is interested _____ to the store.

    Ⓐ in go   Ⓑ at going

    Ⓒ in going   Ⓓ with going

2. The teacher expected the students _____ the assignment the day before.

    Ⓐ to finished   Ⓑ that they finished

    Ⓒ to have finished   Ⓓ finish

3. She took that class _____ her English.

    Ⓐ in order improve   Ⓑ to improve

    Ⓒ in order improving   Ⓓ improve

4. _____ Ella Fitzgerald entertained audiences everywhere.

    Ⓐ Singing of   Ⓑ Singing

    Ⓒ The singing   Ⓓ The singing of

5. We agreed _____ at the theater.

    Ⓐ to meet   Ⓑ meeting

    Ⓒ in order to meeting   Ⓓ for meeting

Part 2 Each sentence has one error. Circle the letter below the word(s) containing the error.

Example   Dance <u>can be</u> a festive time <u>for honor</u> special spirits or it <u>can be</u> a
                   A   Ⓑ   C

    purely recreational time for people <u>to enjoy</u> themselves.
                                  D

1. Jack and Mary were forced <u>to</u> <u>selling</u> their home <u>because</u> they couldn't <u>make</u>
                          A B   C   D

    the house payments.

2. The lab director was upset because of the <u>experiment's</u> <u>having</u> been <u>started</u>
                                      A   B   C

    but not <u>finishing</u>.
            D

3. They <u>expected</u> <u>for her</u> <u>to go</u> to that restaurant because she always liked <u>trying</u>
           A   B   C   D

    different kinds of food.

4. The job was <u>tiring</u>, so the workers stopped <u>taking a break</u> and <u>relaxed</u> on <u>a</u>
                 A   B   C   D

    bench in the sun.

5. We advised <u>Frank and Julie</u> <u>seeing</u> a marriage counselor <u>before</u> their
                A   B   C

    relationship actually started <u>to deteriorate</u>.
                             D

Self-Assessment Log

Check the things you did in this chapter. How well can you do each one?

	Not Very Well	Fairly Well	Very Well
I can use gerunds and infinitives in a variety of locations in a sentence.	❑	❑	❑
I can use gerunds with prepositions and certain verbs.	❑	❑	❑
I can use infinitives with nouns, adjectives, adverbs, and certain verbs.	❑	❑	❑
I can use subjects and negatives with gerunds and infinitives.	❑	❑	❑
I can use continuous infinitives appropriately.	❑	❑	❑
I can use perfect gerunds and infinitives appropriately.	❑	❑	❑
I can use perfect passive gerunds and infinitives appropriately.	❑	❑	❑
I can take a test about gerunds and infinitives.	❑	❑	❑
I understand new information about the arts and individual artists, and I can use new structures and vocabulary to talk and write about related topics.	❑	❑	❑

Conflict and Reconciliation

❝Our Earth is but a small star in a great universe. Yet of it we can make, if we choose, a planet unvexed by war, untroubled by hunger or fear, undivided by senseless distinctions of race, color, or theory.❞

—Stephen Vicent Benét

Connecting to the Topic

1 What kind of a world would you like to live in?

2 If you could make major changes in our world, what changes would you make?

3 What do you think are the best things about our world at the present time?

Introduction

In this chapter, you will look at ways to express hopes and wishes, and you will study conditional sentences. With these, you will study more about the subjunctive mood and about modal auxiliaries.

Reading Read the following passage. It introduces the chapter theme "Conflict and Reconciliation" and raises some of the topics and issues you will cover in the chapter.

Humans and the Environment: Conflict or Coexistence?

"We have forgotten the earth, forgotten it in the sense that we fail to regard it as the source of our life." —Fairfield Osborn

Humans have a history of trying to control the environment. We have learned to produce a constant food supply through farming, to regulate our temperature through use of clothing and heating and cooling systems, and to build 5 shelters that can withstand even the greatest extremes in weather.

Our history has been a constant struggle to survive the rigors of our environment. Because of this struggle, we often look at the world as an opponent to be conquered, dominated, and exploited. But as we change the environment to fit our needs and desires, we damage the fragile balance of nature, sometimes 10 irreparably. Unfortunately, there are too many people for us to continue this battle with our earth. If the population were small, our impact would not be significant. But the impact of over 5 billion people is tremendous.

Today, the world is at a crossroads. Many plants and animals are near extinction, and the all-important food chain is in jeopardy. If we had tried to live 15 with our environment instead of fighting it, we would not have caused such widespread damage, and the environment would not be in danger today. If we continue to abuse our world, we will almost certainly destroy it.

 Discussing Ideas Discuss the questions with a partner.

In what ways does the environment of an area change when a large population moves into it? From your experience, are people generally careful to respect their environment? How can humans reconcile their conflicts with the environment?

Part 1 | *Hope* Versus *Wish*

Setting the Context

Previewing the Passage Discuss the questions with a group.

Think again about the major problems we face today. Which ones do you think are the most serious? Can one person do anything to help solve these problems?

Reading Read the passage.

Taking Responsibility

What kind of country do you want? What kind of world? What can you, the average person, do to help achieve this kind of world?

There are many who believe that it is impossible for an individual to have an effect on the world situation. These people often wish that the situation were different and that our problems had never developed. Still, they do nothing. 5
They may hope that solutions are possible or that the problems will disappear, but they think that the solutions are completely out of their control.

Others feel that giving up and withdrawing from the world is the worst possible decision. They believe in activism and personal involvement. They hope that through their activities they will be able to effect changes and thus to 10
influence leaders and policies.

Discussing Ideas Discuss the questions with a partner.

Where do you stand? Are you someone who tries hard to make changes and to find solutions, even for major problems? Can you think of individuals who have had a profound effect on major world problems?

Grammar Structures and Practice

A. *Hope* Versus *Wish*

Hope and *wish* are used to express desires.

- The verb *hope* is generally used to express optimism, that something is possible.
- The verb *wish* is often used to express impossibility or improbability, that the speaker wants reality to be other than it is.
- Both *hope* and *wish* are often followed by noun clauses. Compare the following:

10.1 Hope Versus Wish

Time Frame	Verbs	Examples	Implied Meanings
Future	hope wish	I **hope** that our team **will win** tonight. I **wish** that our team **could win** tonight. I **wish** that our team **were going** to win tonight.	I think that they have a chance to win. I doubt that they can win.
Present	hope wish	I **hope** that he **has** some money now. I **wish** that he **had** some money now.	He may have some money. He doesn't have any money.
Past	hope wish	I **hope** the team **won** last night. I **wish** the team **had won** last night.	I don't know if they won, but it's possible. I know the team lost last night.

Notes: Wish has an optimistic meaning in certain expressions: We wish you a happy birthday! I wish you a merry Christmas. Wish has the same meaning as want when it is followed by an infinitive: I wish to work here.

---

1 **Practice** What can you do to help make changes? One possibility is writing petitions to local, regional, or even world leaders. The following petition was written to the United Nations by middle-school students. Underline the verbs in the noun clauses. Indicate whether the verbs express past, present, or future time frames.

Example We hope that you <u>will read</u> our proposals carefully. future

1. We hope that you, as world leaders, are concerned about the survival of all humans. _____

2. We hope that you recognize the seriousness of today's problems.
_____

3. We wish that we were in the position to do something about the serious problems of today: war, disease, environmental damage and catastrophe, and more. _____

4. We wish that all countries had begun long ago to work on the problems of the world. _____

5. We wish that people everywhere had more concern for the world around them.
_____

6. We wish that governments had faced the problems of drugs and arms trafficking long ago. _____

7. We wish that people had cared more about the environment many decades ago.
_____

8. We wish there were a way to end all civil wars. _____

9. We wish that all countries were working together to create a better world.
_____

10. We wish that all nations could live in peace. _____

11. We hope that future generations will have a peaceful, healthy environment. _____

12. We hope that the leaders of the world will face these problems so that today's young people will have a world in the future. _____

B. Subjunctive Forms with *Wish*

When followed by a noun clause, the verb *wish* is often used to express impossibility or improbability, that the speaker wants reality to be other than it is.

- When a noun clause follows *wish*, the verb in the noun clause is in the subjunctive mood.
- Modal auxiliaries are sometimes used with present and future forms.
- *That* is optional in sentences with *wish* and *hope*.

10.2	Subjunctive Forms with *Wish*	
Structures	**Explanations**	**Examples**
Wishes About the Future **Wishes About the Present**	Present and future wishes are expressed by using *would*, *could*, or a subjunctive verb form. In most cases, this form is the same as the simple past tense. In formal English, *were* is used for all forms of the verb *be*. In informal English, *was* is often used with *I*, *he*, *she*, and *it*.	I **wish** that the situation **were going** to change. I **wish** the situation **would (could)** change. Tony **wishes** he **were** still young. I **wish** I **could leave** right now. I **wish** that we saw them more often.
Wishes About the Past	Past wishes use the past subjunctive. The past form is the same as the past perfect (*had* + past participle). In conversation, perfect modals are sometimes used.	I **wish** they **had arrived** earlier. I **wish** that they **hadn't stayed** so late. She **wishes** she **could have gone**.

2 **Practice** Quickly reread the passage "Taking Responsibility" on page 429. Then do the following:

1. Find the two clauses that follow *wish* in the second paragraph. Underline the verb(s) in each of these clauses. What is the time frame in the first clause? What about the second?

2. Find the two clauses that follow *hope* in the second paragraph. Underline the verbs and identify the time frame in each.

3 **Practice** Read the following statements about issues affecting the quality of life on earth. Then add correct verb forms to the personal statements that follow.

■ **Overpopulation:** Projections of current growth rates suggest that the Earth's population will increase to eight billion before the year 2030.

Debbie L., Westwood, California: "I wish that more people <u>realized / would realize</u> the dangers of the population explosion. I wish we
_(realize)
_____ to control our growth long ago. I hope that we
_{1 (begin)}
_____ able to do something before it's too late."
_{2 (be)}

■ **Nuclear Power and Nuclear Weapons:** The greatest danger to human survival is the splitting of the atom, even when this is done for peaceful purposes.

Gunter N., Heidelberg, Germany: "I hope that people _____ to
_{3 (begin)}
realize how dangerous our situation is. I hope they _____ our
_{4 (understand)}
present capability to destroy ourselves. I wish everyone _____
_{5 (know)}
how much radiation escapes from nuclear power plants every day. We must stop nuclear development now! I wish that we _____ how to
_{6 (learn / never)}
split the atom."

Luis G., Caracas, Venezuela: "I'm an engineer, and I believe that use of nuclear power is necessary. I wish that people _____ more about our
_{7 (understand)}
energy situation worldwide. I wish they _____ how soon we'll
_{8 (realize)}
run out of oil. We need other sources of energy. I hope that attitudes about nuclear power _____."
_{9 (change)}

■ **Pollution of the Oceans:** The oceans could be dead within a decade or two unless our neglect and abuse of them is swiftly reversed. . . . Pollution is not the only immediate threat to the seas. . . . Overfishing has depleted many fish species to the point where their recovery is in doubt.

Rodney U., Gloucester, Massachusetts: "I'm a deep-sea fisherman. . . . I wish our world leaders _____ me on a fishing trip. I wish they
10 (join)

_____ the damage we've already done to our oceans. Pollution
11 (see)

spreads far out to sea now. So many areas are overfished. I hope that countries around the world _____ to cooperate before it's too late. We've
12 (start)

got to work together to save our oceans."

▲ According to the World Wildlife Fund, more than 70% of the world's fisheries are overexploited. Overfishing threatens the economy and traditional livelihoods of communities across the world.

4 **Practice** Life is a constant series of choices. Unfortunately, many decisions are based on temporary needs or desires rather than on long-term goals. Can you think of any examples of this from your society? Choose two of the five points listed below that are relevant to your region or country. Then give a detailed description based on these four questions.

- What exactly happened?
- What do you wish had happened instead?
- What is happening now, as a result?
- What do you wish were happening?

1. a period of social change (changes in family structure, roles, education, mobility, etc.)

2. economic changes

3. a period of political change (a revolution, elections, a political scandal)

4. an environmental crisis (pollution, overcrowding, destruction of a particular area, the loss of human, animal, or plant life)

5. a natural disaster and/or the preparation for it (an earthquake, a tidal wave, a volcanic eruption)

Example economic changes

> a. *Venezuela is an oil-producing country. In the early 1970s, the rise in oil prices caused drastic changes in our society. We began to import most of our food, clothing, medicine, and machinery. We relied on oil money.*
>
> b. *I wish we had realized the effect of this. I wish we had planned for the future instead of spending all our income so quickly.*
>
> c. *Today, Venezuela has a very different economic and political situation, but there are still many social problems.*
>
> d. *I wish we produced more of our own products. I wish we were saving our oil for the future. I wish we could solve our social problems, too.*

Using What You've Learned

5 **Expressing Hopes and Wishes** What are your opinions on the problems raised in Activities 3 and 4? Do you view them as solvable? Or do you believe that the opportunity for solutions has passed? Give your reactions by making at least two statements about each issue. Use *hope* or *wish* in your statements.

6 **Writing a Petition** In small groups, write a petition to the United Nations or to world leaders. It may be about one particular issue, such as population or environmental concerns, or it may be a more general statement of your hopes and wishes. Include at least six statements using *wish* and *hope*.

7 **Researching Environmental Organizations** Do some research on the Internet. Visit the Web sites of several environmental organizations, and then choose one that particularly interests you. Find out what the primary focus of the organization is-that is, activities such as camping and canoeing, land preservation, or political action, for example. Then find out what the organization is doing in your area or country. Finally, give a brief report to the class on what you've learned.

Setting the Context

Previewing the Passage Discuss the questions with a group.

Are there any societies in existence today that are virtually free of conflict? Could such a society ever exist? Why or why not?

Reading Read the passage.

Model Societies

The last 100 years have witnessed some of the most amazing and most rapid changes in history. Many of these changes have helped humans immensely, but others have created a number of complex problems that threaten our very existence.

Yet these problems are not unsolvable. Both individuals and groups are ac- 5
tively searching for solutions.   Some people are even designing model societies
that would not suffer from many of today's ills.

As we are beginning the 21st century, think about the type of society you
would like to live in. Then imagine that you had the opportunity to create it. If
you actually had the opportunity, could you plan a new society? Should you 10
have this chance, you would first have to recognize the shortcomings of societies today. Next, you would be faced with the monumental task of designing a
society that would not develop similar or worse problems. How would you accomplish this?

Discussing Ideas Discuss the questions with a partner.

What are *shortcomings*? In your opinion, what are some of the major shortcomings
in modern societies?

A. *Otherwise:* Present Time

Otherwise is a transition that is used to contrast reality with wishes and dreams.

10.3 *Otherwise*	
Explanations	**Examples**
Otherwise means "if not" or "if the situation were different." The auxiliaries *would*, *could*, and *might* are frequently used after *otherwise*. Like other transitions, *otherwise* is often used after a semicolon.	That city has terrible smog; — **otherwise**, the summers **would be** nice. **otherwise**, I **could enjoy** living there. — **otherwise**, we **might move** there.

1 Practice Sahelia is an imaginary developing country. Read each of Sahelia's problems. Then use *otherwise* to complete the sentences that follow.

Example *Problem:* few schools. The minister of education steals 50 percent of the education budget; otherwise, *Sahelia might have more schools.*

1. *Problem:* few qualified teachers. Sahelia pays its teachers one dollar a week; otherwise, . . .

2. *Problem:* underdeveloped economy. Sahelia exports 90 percent of its natural resources; otherwise, . . .

3. *Problem:* few industries. The military budget consumes 75 percent of the country's G.N.P. (gross national product); otherwise, . . .

4. *Problem:* shortage of skilled workers. Most of the skilled workers are in the military; otherwise, . . .

5. *Problem:* hunger. Sahelia exports most of its food; otherwise, . . .

6. *Problem:* disease. There are few doctors in Sahelia; otherwise, . . .

B. Imaginary Conditions: Present and Unspecified Time

Imaginary conditional sentences express conditions that are hypothetical or that the speaker thinks of as untrue, contrary to fact. They may be wishes and dreams, or they may express advice.

10.4 Imaginary Conditions: Present and Unspecified Time

Explanations	Examples	Implied Meanings
In these conditional sentences, a subjunctive form of the verb is used in the *if* clause. It is the same as the simple past except that *were*, not *was*, is used for the verb *be*.	**If** Sahelia **had** more doctors, there **would be** less disease.	Sahelia has few doctors. Because of this, disease is a serious problem.
	If the educational system **were** better, they **could train** more doctors.	The educational system is not adequate, and, as a result, Sahelia cannot train many doctors.
	If developed countries **gave** more aid, Sahelia might **develop** more industries.	Developed countries do not give Sahelia much aid, so Sahelia hasn't been able to develop many industries.

2 Practice Imagine that you are a citizen of Technologica, an imaginary country with a set of problems quite different from Sahelia's. Study Technologica's list of problems. Then form sentences with *if* that explain what *would, could,* or *might* happen if the wishes that follow came true.

Problems

pollution (air, water, land are unsafe)

lack of energy (all oil is imported)

lack of food (almost all food is imported)

high unemployment and inflation rates

high crime rate

negative trade balance

lack of open space

Example *I wish fewer people drove cars. If fewer people drove, the air would be cleaner.*

1. I wish the industries were more concerned about pollution. If. . . .
2. I wish Technologica had its own source of energy. If. . . .
3. I wish the government managed the economy better. If. . . .
4. I wish the wealth of the country were distributed more equally. If. . . .
5. I wish Technologica produced more of its own food. If. . . .
6. I wish we had more natural resources. If. . . .

3 **Practice** Consider the following situation. The United Nations has chosen you to develop the plans for a model society. Choose one of the statements in each of the following sets. Then make one or more sentences using *if* to explain the reasons for your choice.

Example   There would be free medical care.
Everyone would pay for medical care.
In my model society, there would be free medical care. If there were free medical care, we could eliminate many common diseases. If we were able to eliminate most diseases, . . .

In my model society, . . .

1. There would be only one ethnic group.
All ethnic groups would be welcome.

2. There would be complete freedom of religion.
Only one religion would be allowed.

3. The government would control the press.
There would be no control of the press.

4. The military would be small.
The military would be large.

5. All people could own and carry guns.
There would be strict gun-control laws.

6. There would be free housing.
Housing would not be free.

4 **Practice** In Activity 3, you discussed some ideas about a model society. Now consider some more fundamental issues. In small groups, discuss the following questions. Look up words you don't understand. Then write notes on the advantages and disadvantages of each option. Finally, use these notes to create sentences with *if*.

1. What type of economy would you set up?

	Advantages	Disadvantages
capitalist	*economy develops quickly*	*a large class of poor people*
	some people very rich	*inflation, unemployment*
	_____	_____
	_____	_____
socialist	_____	_____
	_____	_____
	_____	_____
	_____	_____

Example *If we had a capitalist economy, the economy would develop quickly and some people would become very rich. However, a large class of poor people might form, and inflation and unemployment would be constant problems. If we had a socialist system, there might be . . . However, . . .*

2. What would the most important economic activity be?

	Advantages	**Disadvantages**
heavy industry	_____	_____
	_____	_____
	_____	_____
	_____	_____
high tech	_____	_____
	_____	_____
	_____	_____
agriculture	_____	_____
	_____	_____
	_____	_____
services	_____	_____
	_____	_____
	_____	_____
	_____	_____
	_____	_____

3. What type of government would you establish?

	Advantages	**Disadvantages**
religious	_____	_____
	_____	_____
	_____	_____
	_____	_____
secular	_____	_____
	_____	_____
	_____	_____
	_____	_____
	_____	_____

4. Who would make important decisions?

	Advantages	Disadvantages
supreme	_____	_____
leader	_____	_____
	_____	_____
	_____	_____
	_____	_____
	_____	_____
parliament	_____	_____
	_____	_____
	_____	_____
	_____	_____
	_____	_____
computer	_____	_____
	_____	_____
	_____	_____
	_____	_____

5 **Practice** Answer one of the questions from Activity 4 in writing. Begin your composition with a statement about which option you would select. (*In my model society, there would be a capitalist economy. . . .*) Then support this opinion by listing the advantages of this option over the other(s). Use *if* clauses whenever possible.

C. Imaginary Conditionals with *Should* or *Were* + Infinitive

Should or *were* + infinitive is sometimes used instead of *if*. In this case, *should* or *were* comes before the subject.
- With *should*, delete *if* and use the simple form of the main verb.
- With *were,* delete *if* and use the infinitive form of the main verb.

10.5 Imaginary Conditionals with *Should* or *Were* + Infinitive

Structures	Examples
With *if* Without *if*	If our military **became** weak, **Should** our military **become** weak, — our country might be invaded. **Were** our military **to become** weak,
With *if* Without *if*	If a world war started, Should **a world war start**, — it would be terrible. **Were** a world war **to start**,

Note: Should and *were* + infinitive are occasionally used without deleting *if.* Compare:

If I — came / were to leave / should leave — soon, there would be trouble.

---

6 Practice One of the most important problems any society must face is crime. In your model society, what would happen to people who broke the law? Use *should* and *were . . . to* and suggest penalties for the following crimes.

Example robbing a bank

Should you rob a bank, you would go to prison for two years.
Were you to rob a bank, you could spend two years in jail.

1. stealing a car

2. rioting

3. trying to overthrow the government

4. throwing a tomato at the supreme leader

5. spying for a hostile country

6. buying goods on the black market

7 Practice Complete the following by adding the correct forms of the verbs in parentheses.

Arcosanti

Architect and visionary Paolo Soleri _____*believes*_____ that it
                                                    (believe)
_____ possible to create model communities. According to So-
  1 (be / still)
leri, if all buildings in Arcosanti, Pablo Soleri's model community in Arizona,

_____ constructed in a small area, large tracts of open space
    2 (be)

_____ the community. If all the buildings _____
  3 (surround)   4 (be)

close together, people _____ little need for cars. They
5 (have)
_____ to their destinations. In this way, people
6 (walk)
_____ daily exercise, which _____ them stay
7 (get)   8 (help)
in better health. They _____ their neighbors much better.
9 (know / also)
Should this _____ true, it _____ down on
10 (be)   11 (cut)
crime.

To prove his point, in 1970, Soleri _____ to build a town
12 (begin)
called Arcosanti in the desert near Phoenix, Arizona, in the southwest region of
the United States. He _____ Arcosanti using his ideas for a
13 (design)
model community. Now, over 30 years later, thousands of city planners and
other visitors _____ to Arcosanti each year to experience its
14 (flock)
unique environment.

Many of us wish the world _____ a more livable place.
15 (be)
Soleri and other planners _____ something about it!
16 (do)

Using What You've Learned

8 **Making Wishes** An old saying is that if you wish upon the first star of the night, your wish will come true. Practice five wishes now, and then later, look for the first star of the evening to wish *for real!*

Your five wishes may be for anything or anyone—for yourself, your family, a friend, your country. Write your wishes and follow each with an explanation using *if.* Then share your wishes with your classmates.

Example *I wish we didn't have finals in a few weeks. If we didn't have finals, I could go out tonight instead of studying for them.*

 9 **Discussing Crimes and Possible Punishments** What are some of the penalties for crimes in your hometown or country? For example, what is the penalty for speeding? For running a red light? For using a weapon? Share your information in pairs or small groups. Take turns telling about crimes and justice in different places. In your examples, try to use clauses with *if, should,* or *were* + infinitive.

Example *In my country, should you run a red light, probably nothing would happen because nobody pays attention to the traffic signals.*

10 **Giving Advice** Is the situation in your community similar in some ways to that in Sahelia or Technologica? Does it have a different set of problems? In pairs, pretend that you are the newly appointed chief adviser to the leader of your country. It is your job to suggest solutions to the country's problems. After your partner (the leader) explains a problem, suggest a possible solution, using *If I were you*. Then explain what *would, could,* or *might* happen if the leader followed your advice.

Example **Leader:** We have a terrible problem with air pollution.

Adviser: If I were you, I'd outlaw all private cars, and the air pollution problem would be solved. On the other hand, were you to outlaw cars, there might be a revolution!

11 **Planning a New Society** Imagine that volcanoes have just formed a new island in the Pacific Ocean. It is over 1,000 miles from the nearest land, so it does not belong to any country. Although there is no vegetation at present, the island has rich soil, beautiful beaches, and an ample supply of natural resources.

In small groups, design the ideal society for this island. You might begin by naming the island and drawing a map to show its size, shape, and position in the world. Next, consider the questions mentioned earlier concerning the economy, political system, judicial system, and the ethnic background of the people. Give as much specific information as possible. For example, if the society were industrial, which industries would you establish and how would the island feed itself? If it were agricultural, which crops would it grow, and how would it get industrial goods?

Would the island export any of its products? If so, to where? Would the island form any alliances with other nations? If so, which nations? How large would the population be?

When you are finished, have one member of your group give a brief presentation summarizing the most important characteristics of your ideal society.

Setting the Context

Previewing the Passage Discuss the questions with a group.

What is the largest city that you know of? What is its population? What are conditions like in this city? Is the situation improving or getting worse?

Reading Read the passage.

Too Late?

Many of the world's large urban areas are suffering from multiple problems that have resulted from massive growth without careful planning. Shortages of safe drinking water, severe air pollution, poorly developed public transportation systems, and high crime rates are common features of population centers around the globe.

With proper planning, we could have avoided many of these problems. For example, governments might have managed growth. They could have provided systems of transportation and sanitation so important to quality of life. They should have limited the use of automobiles and developed clean energy sources.

They might have, they could have, they should have done all these things. The unfortunate truth is that they didn't. That is, we didn't. Now it's too late.

Or is it?

5

10

Discussing Ideas Discuss the questions with a partner.

Does your city have the problems mentioned in the passage? Do you think the problems could have been avoided? How? The writer seems to think it is really too late to make basic improvements in our environment. Do you agree?

Grammar Structures and Practice

Perfect Modal Auxiliaries

Perfect modal auxiliaries can be used to express activities or situations in the past that were not real or that did *not* occur.

- Perfect modal auxiliaries often express our wishes in hindsight.
- Perfect modal auxiliaries follow this pattern: modal + *(not) have* + past participle.

10.6 Perfect Modal Auxiliaries

Structures	Explanations	Examples
Unfulfilled Intentions and Preferences **Would (not) have**	*Would have* refers to past intentions that were not fulfilled.	We **would have moved**, but we couldn't find another place.
Would rather (not) have	*Would rather have* refers to past preferences that were not fulfilled. *Than* + simple form is often added for comparisons of wishes with reality.	We **would rather have moved** to the country than have stayed in the city.
Unfulfilled Advice **Should (not) have** **Ought (not) to have**	*Should have* and *ought to have* refer to actions that were advisable but that did *not* take place. *Ought to have* is less common than *should have*.	We **should have sold** our house before the company built the factory across the road.
Past Possibilities **Could (not) have** **Might (not) have** **May (not) have**	*Could have, might have,* and *may have* refer to past possibilities. In some cases, these express alternatives that were not taken. In others, the speaker or writer is uncertain whether the action took place. In some contexts, *could have* also refers to past abilities.	We **could have protested** the building of the factory. He **might have listened** to our complaints. Some of the neighbors **may have spoken** to the owners.
Past Probabilities **Must (not) have**	*Must have* refers to past probabilities. The speaker or writer is fairly certain of the accuracy of the statement.	The company **must not have been concerned** about our health and well-being. They **must have cared** more about making money.

Note: In rapid speech, perfect modals are seldom pronounced clearly. *Have* is often pronounced as *a* or *of*, as in *shudda* or *shudduv.*

1 Practice Quickly reread the passage "Too Late?" on page 444. Then do the following:

1. Underline the modal auxiliaries in the second and third paragraphs. Do these modal auxiliaries refer to real events or situations? If not, what do they refer to?

2. What form of the main verb is used after these auxiliaries?

2 Rapid Oral Practice Go around the class in a chain, changing the following to include perfect modal auxiliaries.

Example A: I wouldn't do that.
           B: *I wouldn't have done that.*
           B: She could help us.
           C: *She could have helped us.*

1. We should leave.
2. They couldn't help us.
3. It must be right.
4. He may have a problem.
5. I ought to go.
6. It might not work.
7. She may call.
8. I wouldn't try that.
9. He'd rather stay home.
10. We might go there.
11. It couldn't be true.
12. We'd like to discuss it.
13. I'd rather not tell you.
14. She could do it.
15. We ought to tell him.
16. They might stop him.

3 Practice Use your imagination to give at least two answers to the following questions. Use *would have* or *would not have* + *but* or *except that*.

Example Why didn't you move to Rio last year?
         I would have moved there, but (except that) I didn't have the money.
         I would have moved there, but (except that) I got an excellent job in New York.

         Why did you stay here all summer?
         I would not have stayed, but I couldn't get any time off work.
         I would not have stayed, but I met someone wonderful.

1. Santiago has a terrible air-pollution problem. Why haven't city officials done something to clean the air?

2. Your parents moved to Santiago 20 years ago. Why did they originally move there?

3. They left Santiago and bought a small farm in the country. Why didn't you go with them?

4. You have had a terrible cough for over a week. Why haven't you been to a doctor?

5. You are a month overdue in paying your rent. Why haven't you paid it?

6. You haven't called your parents for weeks. Why haven't you called them?

7. You missed class. Why were you absent?

8. You haven't handed in your last homework assignment. Why not?

4 **Practice** Complete the thought in the following statements by using *would rather have* or *would rather not have.*

Example Today, Sam went to work early.
He would rather have stayed home.
He would rather not have gone to work.

1. Yesterday afternoon at 5:00, Sam was in downtown Dreckville.

2. There was a terrible traffic jam, so he decided to park his car and wait.

3. Sam had to sit on the side of the expressway for hours.

4. Sam listened to the radio for a long time.

5. He got out of his car and began to walk.

6. After a while, he found a fast-food restaurant.

7. He ate a hamburger.

8. The traffic jam never cleared up, so he slept in his car.

5 Practice Dreckville, an imaginary city in the center of the United States, has many problems. Make suggestions on what Dreckville *could have, might have,* or *should have done* to avoid the following problems. Give at least four suggestions for each problem.

Example Dreckville has little greenery. There is one major park area, but it is in a financial and industrial district. Most residential areas have no green space. Two-thirds of Dreckville's population live in dense apartment complexes. Children play in the street for lack of other areas to play in. *Dreckville could have planned a park system. Dreckville should have designed small squares or plazas in the center of each neighborhood.*

1. Dreckville has no real city center. Its businesses and industries are spread out over a large area. They are connected by a complicated network of freeways. The average commute to work by car takes 35 minutes; some commuters travel over an hour and a half each way.

2. Dreckville has a limited bus service but no subway system. Most of the suburbs are not on bus lines. The average fare is $4.45. Most of the bus lines do not have frequent service. The average time between buses is 30 minutes. Only ten percent of the population uses the system.

3. A river runs through Dreckville. Its water is highly polluted. Most of the industry around Dreckville is located just outside the city limits, along the river. Several factories dump their wastes into the river.

4. Dreckville has an average of 150 smog-alert days per year (days when children and older people should stay indoors because the air quality is so poor).

6 Practice Read the statements and use *must have, could have, may have,* and *might have* to suggest answers to the questions. Give at least two answers for each.

Example There are no birds left in Dreckville. What happened to them?
The pollution must have killed them. The birds could have died from a disease. They might have moved south and never come back!

1. Yesterday at 7:30 A.M., an empty bus was parked in the middle of Dreckville's largest street. What was wrong with the bus? Where was the bus driver?

2. Francesca waited for 30 minutes for the bus to come. Finally, she gave up. How did she get to work?

3. She went by the river on the way to work and noticed that several dead fish were floating on top of the water. What killed the fish?

4. She arrived at work 45 minutes later. Her boss was angry. What did he say to her?

5. At lunchtime, Francesca went to the bank, but there was no money in her account. What happened to her money?

6. After work, Francesca was supposed to meet friends for coffee. She went to the café, but her friends weren't there. What happened?

7. When she returned home, she found a window broken and all of her clothes thrown on the floor. What had happened while she was at work?

8. Francesca looked at the mess in her house. What did she do?

Using What You've Learned

7 **Making Excuses** Are you good at making up excuses for things you haven't done? Who in your class is the best at making up excuses? First, make a list of five things that you haven't done but that you should have done. Then, think up your excuses and take turns telling them to the class. If you wish, take a vote on whose excuses are the best, worst, or most creative.

Example *I haven't written to my parents. Well, I would have written them last week, but I lost all of my pens and my dog ate all my stationery.*

8 **Investigating a Crime** The mayor of Dreckville disappeared mysteriously two months ago. At first, most people thought that he had been kidnapped. However, in the last few days, the following information has been leaked to the press.

- The mayor is living in a mansion in Rio de Janeiro.
- More than $5 million is missing from the city treasury.
- The mayor has a Swiss bank account containing $20 million.
- He accepted bribes from chemical companies that were polluting the river and from an oil company.
- He used his money and influence to block the development of mass transportation.
- Just before the last three elections, he tampered with the computers that count votes.
- The police have been investigating the mayor for over a year, and they were about to arrest him.

Separate into groups of three or four. Pretend that you are members of a special task force to fight corruption in government and that you must give a report to the city council of Dreckville. First, use modals of probability / possibility to speculate on what exactly the mayor did and why he did these things. Then draw up a list of actions that the police and the city council *should have, could have,* or *might have taken* to prevent this scandal. Finally, make a set of recommendations for the future. Be sure to address how the mayor can be brought to justice and how the government could or should prevent this type of corruption in the future. Remember, the mayor may not be the only corrupt official in the government. When you are finished, have one member of your task force report your findings and recommendations to the class.

Setting the Context

▲ Is "progress" always desirable?

 Previewing the Passage Discuss the questions with a group.

What are some of the technological changes of the last century? Has the advancement of technology usually had a beneficial effect? Give reasons to support your answer.

Reading Read the passage.

Progress?

The tremendous impact of change in our lives constantly presents us with new issues, new challenges, new questions to resolve. As our technological awareness grows, we develop new and "better" systems for controlling our world. Yet, are these systems really better? Is technology really a key to solving our problems? 5

As we look at past accomplishments, we can say that much of our technological progress is associated with a few great people. If the minds like those of Galileo, Watt, Edison, and Einstein hadn't existed, our technology would not have advanced as quickly, and the world would be a much different place. But would it be a worse place to live in, or might it in some ways be better? 10

Discussing Ideas Discuss the questions with a partner.

Think about the final question in the passage and imagine our world without the technological progress of the past 200 years. Without such progress, how would our world be worse? How might it be better?

Grammar Structures and Practice

A. *Otherwise:* Past Time

Otherwise is a transition that is used to contrast reality with wishes and dreams.

10.7 *Otherwise:* Past Time	
Explanations	**Examples**
In past time, *otherwise* means "if the situation had been different." *Would have, could have,* and *might have* + past participle are commonly used with *otherwise*.	James Watt invented the steam engine in the 1700s; **otherwise**, the Industrial Revolution **might not have begun** then. The Wright brothers invented the first airplane. **Otherwise**, they **wouldn't have become** famous.

1 Practice The advent of agriculture led to radical changes in human society. In the following sentences, substitute *otherwise* for the connecting word and make all necessary changes.

Example Humans began cultivating food about 10,000 years ago; in this way, they developed a stable food source.

Humans began cultivating food about 10,000 years ago; otherwise, they wouldn't (couldn't) have developed a stable food source.

1. Humans learned a great deal about plants, so they were able to develop methods of farming.

2. People began to grow crops; because of this, they had fairly dependable supplies of food.

3. Tribes no longer had to follow herds of animals, so they settled in permanent villages.

4. People had more than enough food; therefore, they had time to develop new technologies.

5. People had more free time, so they devoted themselves to music, art, and other creative efforts.

6. Some areas were naturally suited for agriculture; thus, tribes fought over these areas.

7. War became a common occurrence, so people developed new and more sophisticated weapons.

8. Humans learned how to use metal; hence, they were able to fabricate spears, knives, and later, guns.

B. Imaginary Conditions: Past Time

Conditional sentences with *if* can be used to speculate about past situations or events that did *not* take place.

10.8 Imaginary Conditions: Past Time		
Explanations	**Examples**	**Implied Meanings**
In these conditional sentences, the verb in the *if* clause is *had* + the past participle. Sometimes *if* is deleted and the auxiliary *had* is placed before the subject. In negative sentences where *if* is deleted, *not* follows the subject. In either case, the verb in the main clause is usually *would have*, *could have*, or *might have* + past participle.	If humans **had not learned** to use metal, they **would** never **have invented** guns. **Had** humans **not learned** to use metal, they **would** never **have invented** guns. People **could not have grown** crops in many areas if they **hadn't learned** how irrigate. People **could not have grown** crops in many areas **had** they **not learned** how to irrigate.	Humans learned to use metal, and one result was the invention of guns. People were able to grow crops in many areas because they learned how to irrigate.

2 **Practice** The following is a list of some of the early historical events that led to improved weaponry. Use *if* to connect each event with its results. Create at least eight new sentences.

Example The Greeks learned to bend and laminate wood. They created new farming tools. They invented the bow and arrow.
If the Greeks hadn't learned to bend and laminate wood, they wouldn't have created new farming tools or invented the bow and arrow.

1. The Chinese invented gunpowder. They invented fireworks.

2. Ancient Egyptians needed a sharp, durable tool for harvesting wheat. They made the first metal sword.

3. Ancient East Africans developed an iron industry. They made new and more effective spears and knives.

4. The East Africans were able to defeat invaders. They became successful traders.

5. Europeans traveled to China in the 13th century. They started to import spices. They found new ways to preserve meat.

6. The Europeans learned about gunpowder. They developed firearms.

3 Practice Complete the following sentences by adding the correct forms of the verbs in parentheses. Use the modal auxiliaries *would, could,* and *might.*

Example If Otto Lilienthal _____*hadn't died*_____ (not die) in a gliding accident, he *might have invented* (invent) the first "powered" aircraft.

1. The Wright brothers built and flew the first airplane. If the Wright brothers _____ (not be) wealthy, they _____ (not afford) to work on this project.

2. Had they _____ (not study) the design of earlier German gliders, it _____ (take) them years to design their own.

3. Consistent strong winds were necessary for the first flights. The Wrights _____ (not move) to Kitty Hawk, North Carolina, if it _____ (not have) the best wind conditions for test flights.

4. On December 17, 1903, they made the world's first powered flight. Flier 1 _____ (not fly) if the Wrights _____ (not develop) a lightweight gasoline engine.

5. A number of French and German inventors were working on planes at the same time. Someone else _____ (develop) the first plane in a few months if the Wrights _____ (not succeed).

6. Aircraft didn't become important until World War I. Had the war _____ (not break out), the development of the airplane _____ (take) much longer.

▲ The Wright brothers with one of their early airplanes

4 **Practice** Read the following historical events. List some of the things that happened at that time because of the event. Then form sentences with *if* that show how the results were connected. Use the example as a model.

Example   People learned to farm.
They didn't have to hunt for all of their food. They built cities. . . . If people hadn't learned to farm, they would have had to hunt for all of their food. If they had had to hunt for all of their food, they wouldn't have built cities.

1. People learned to use metal.

2. People developed ocean-going boats.

3. Columbus discovered the "New World."

4. James Watt invented an efficient and inexpensive engine.

5. Gregor Mendel did landmark work in understanding genetics.

6. Alexander Fleming discovered penicillin.

7. Marie Curie learned the properties of radium.

8. Einstein developed theories about the atom.

C. Imaginary Conditionals: Past and Present Time

Conditional sentences with *if* can be used to describe past actions or situations that have affected the present.

10.9 Imaginary Conditionals: Past and Present Time		
Explanations	**Examples**	**Implied Meanings**
The verb in the *if* clause is *had* + a past participle. The verb in the main clause is usually *would*, *could*, or *might* + a simple or continuous verb. If can be deleted and the subject and verb (auxiliary) inverted.	If Columbus **hadn't claimed** the "New World" for Spain, most South Americans **might speak** Portuguese today. **Had** Einstein **not lived**, we **would have** a much different world.	Columbus claimed the "New World" for Spain, and therefore, most of South America is Spanish-speaking today. Einstein and his work played a major role in developments that affect our lives today.

5 Practice Complete the following sentences, giving at least two imaginary present results for each *if* clause.

Example If the car hadn't been invented, *we might still be using horses as a major means of transportation.*
. . . we might not have so much air pollution.

1. If humans hadn't developed systems for writing. . . .
2. If people hadn't learned about growing plants for food. . . .
3. Had the gun been banned 50 years ago. . . .
4. If aircraft had never been developed. . . .
5. If penicillin hadn't been discovered. . . .
6. If elevators hadn't been invented. . . .
7. If satellites had never been launched. . . .
8. If computers had never been invented. . . .
9. Had cell phones never been developed. . . .
10. If a nuclear war had started five years ago. . . .

6 Practice Technological advances have led to both great achievements and disasters. Read the following four summaries and react to each by writing at least three sentences using *if* clauses. Include both past and present conditional clauses in your sentences.

Example Because of political problems in the mid-1970s, Portugal postponed planting new cork oaks. People cut the existing forests for cork or for firewood, and no new plantings were started. The result was a worldwide shortage of cork for use in wine bottles. Today, manufacturers use half-plastic, half-cork stoppers even for vintage wines.
If Portugal hadn't been having political problems, this situation might not have occurred.
If Portugal had replanted the trees, there wouldn't have been a cork shortage. If there hadn't been a cork shortage, manufacturers might not be using plastic corks.

1. The extensive nuclear testing in Nevada in the 1950s spread deadly radiation throughout the area. After one explosion in 1953, 4,300 sheep died. Today, hundreds of residents living near the testing area have developed cancer. They sued the government and won millions of dollars.

2. A farmer near Newburgh, New York, fertilized his field too early in the spring of 1979; as a result, he killed thousands of birds. Approximately 10,000 birds of varying species were found dead. They died because they ate the powerful fertilizer pellets. Because the ground was still hard, the pellets did not sink in, and the birds mistook the pellets for food.

3. In the early morning of December 3, 1984 there was a tragic gas leak at the Union Carbide pesticide plant in Bhopal, India. The plant had not produced pesticide for some years, and its safety systems had not been maintained. It is estimated that 20,000 people eventually died because of the gas leak and that hundreds of thousands were made seriously ill.

4. In 1989, 11 million gallons of crude oil spilled into Prince William Sound in Alaska when the oil tanker *Exxon Valdez* hit a reef. Prior to the crash, the captain of the *Valdez*, who had been drinking, went to sleep, leaving a junior officer in command of the vessel. Exxon ultimately spent $2.1 billion on the cleanup, but enormous environmental damage had already been done before the cleanup began. More than 15 years after the spill, Prince William Sound looks clean enough; however, oil still lies a few inches under the surface of the water in some areas.

▲ The 1989 oil spill from Exxon's tanker *Valdez* was one of the worst human-created ecological disasters of all time.

5. Cod fishing off Canada expanded massively during the 1980s, and the seas off the East Coast were very heavily fished. After several years, fisherman found their nets empty and their economic futures very shaky. The disappearance of cod devasted villages and towns throughout the eastern provinces of Canada. By 2003, Canada was forced to announce the complete closure of fishing for cod in Newfoundland, the Maritime Provinces, and Quebec.

6. In December 2004, a massive earthquake in the Indian Ocean caused a series of tsunamis that killed approximately 310,000 people—220,000 in Indonesia alone. One reason for the size of the disaster is that there hadn't been a major tsunami in this area since 1883; therefore, most people had no idea that this could happen. Also, there was no tsunami alert system in the region; as a result, there was no warning before the tsunamis hit. Another problem is that there is a lack of infrastructure in many of the countries in this area, so reconstruction has been slow.

Using What You've Learned

7 **Looking at Causes and Effects** Choose one political, social, economic, or technical development that has significantly affected our lives. Research your topic and prepare a brief presentation. Include a summary of the history of the development and a short list of its positive and negative effects. Finally, speculate on what would (not) have happened and how our lives would be different had this development not taken place.

8 **Describing Turning Points** Think about some turning points in your own life. Think about some of the choices that you have made and the events or changes that have occurred because of them. Then write a short composition about one of these. Describe how your life changed because of the decision, and then describe how it might have been or might be if you had done things differently. You can choose from the following ideas or create some of your own. Finally, share your thoughts in a small group discussion with your classmates.

- If you had chosen a different language to study, what might it have been? How would this have affected your current work or studies?

- If you had chosen a different career, what might you have studied? Why?

- If you had grown up in a different place, where might it have been? How would your life be different today because of it?

- What if you had gotten married at age 16? How would your life have been different? What would you be doing today?

Setting the Context

▲ Statue of Chief Seattle in
Seattle, Washington

Previewing the Passage Discuss the following in a group.

Chief Seattle was an Indian leader from the Puget Sound area near Seattle, Washington, which grew from a small village bearing his name to the large urban center of today. Seattle and many Native Americans regarded the Earth in a special way. The words below are an excerpt from a speech attributed to Seattle. Though the origin of the speech is in question, the ideas remain profound. What do you know about the differences between the traditional Native American views of the Earth and the ways societies treat the Earth today.

Reading Read the passage.

Protecting Our Earth

If man does not learn, he will destroy the Earth and leave behind only a desert. You must teach your children that the ground beneath your feet is the ashes of our grandfathers. If you tell your children that the Earth is rich with the lives of our kin, they will respect the land. Teach your children that the Earth is our mother. Whatever befalls the Earth, befalls the sons of the Earth. If men spit upon the ground, they spit upon themselves.

5

—Chief Seattle, 1854

Discussing Ideas Discuss the questions with a partner.

What did Seattle want people to learn? What are some of the things that have happened to our Earth since Chief Seattle's time?

Grammar Practice

1 **Review** Complete the passage with the appropriate forms of the verbs in parentheses. Choose either active or passive voice. Add negatives, adverbs, and modal auxiliaries when appropriate.

Acid Rain

Since the 1930s, industrial plants and automobiles around the world _have released / have been releasing_ (release) larger and larger quantities of chemicals into the air. Whenever certain chemicals _____ in the atmosphere, acids _____. If certain wind patterns _____, these acids _____ in the upper atmosphere. The acid _____ thousands of miles before it _____ to the Earth as rain, snow, or fog. Although the phenomenon _____ many scientific terms, it _____ as acid rain. Worldwide, environmental damage _____ by acid rain.

      1 (combine)
      2 (produce)
      3 (exist)
      4 (stay)
      5 (travel)
      6 (return)
      7 (have)
      8 (know / generally)
      9 (cause / already)

For decades, acid rain _____ buildings and monuments in many parts of the world. It _____ through both stone and metal. It _____ changes in the chemistry of soil and lake water across the globe. As rainwater and soil _____ more acidic, young trees _____. Likewise, lakes that _____ with fish in the past _____ beautifully blue but totally empty of fish because of the change in their acidity. It _____ that acid rain _____ human health through the water that we _____ and the air that we _____.

      10 (damage)
      11 (eat)
      12 (produce / also)
      13 (become)
      14 (die)
      15 (fill / once)
      16 (be / now)
      17 (suspect / also)
      18 (affect)
      19 (drink)
      20 (breathe)

▲ The effects of acid rain on a sculpture

2 **Review** Read the information on pesticides and use it to complete the exercise that follows. Use a variety of connecting words to rephrase and combine the following sentences. Then put your new sentences into paragraph form.

Example Farmers use pesticides. According to farmers, harvests increase dramatically. Crop losses during storage decrease.

Farmers use pesticides in order to increase their harvests dramatically and decrease their crop losses during storage.
OR
Farmers use pesticides; otherwise, they believe their harvests would decrease dramatically and their crop losses would increase during storage.

1. We use pesticides. We affect more than just the pest.

2. We use pesticides. We also affect birds and animals. These birds and animals feed on the pests.

3. A chain reaction exists from the poison in pesticides. One insect, bird, or animal eats another.

4. For example, aphids eat crops. These crops have been sprayed. The poison enters the aphids' systems.

5. A ladybug eats aphids. These aphids have been poisoned. The poison accumulates in the ladybug.

6. A sparrow eats the ladybug. The ladybug had accumulated poison. The sparrow absorbs the poison.

7. A larger bird such as a hawk eats the sparrow. The bird also eats the accumulated poison from thousands of insects.

8. A hawk consumes large amounts of the poison. The poison affects the hawk in serious ways.

9. The poison damages the hawk's internal organs. The hawk is not able to reproduce.

10. All of these creatures form a food chain. The damage began long before with the spraying of an aphid. This damage occurred to the hawk.

3 **Review** Complete the following with the appropriate form of the verbs in parentheses. Choose from gerunds, infinitives, present and past participles, and simple forms. Add subjects or negatives when indicated.

Deforestation

According to *National Geographic*, the world is facing an ___alarming___ (alarm) disaster: deforestation, the loss of our forests. Scientists worldwide are _____ 1 (alarm) because forests continue _____ 2 (disappear) at a _____ 3 (frighten) rate. In some places, our green Earth is turning into desert.

Fires _____ 4 (cause) by lightning and other natural phenomena account for some forest loss. Nevertheless, humans are responsible for the majority. Human crimes such as arson and human activities such as _____ 5 (log) and _____ 6 (land-clear) for _____ 7 (farm) and _____ 8 (graze) account for most of the loss. The statistics certainly are _____ 9 (frighten):

- Since the end of the last ice age, approximately half the world's forests have been destroyed, mostly because of _____ 10 (humans / expand) their activities and settlements.

- Humans have managed _____ 11 (damage) or _____ 12 (destroy) almost 90 percent of West Africa's coastal rain forests.

- The world's two largest surviving regions of rain forest, in Brazil and

Indonesia, are being stripped very rapidly as humans use fire, bulldoz-ers, and even bombs _____ forests for agriculture or
13 (clear)
_____. When a forest is destroyed, the first thing
14 (mine)
_____ is living space. Seventy percent of the Earth's
15 (lose)
land animals and plants live in forests.

When a forest is cut, animals are forced _____, and some
16 (move)
are able _____ quickly enough to newly _____
17 (adapt)   18 (find)
environments. But for most animals and plants, the change is too rapid
_____. Without their natural habitats, hundreds of species risk
19 (they / survive)
_____ extinct.
20 (become)

Loss of natural habitats is compounded by weather change. Rain forests
help _____ rainfall, not only locally but also regionally and
21 (generate)
globally. Studies have shown that _____ rain forests in West
22 (destroy)
Africa may have caused two decades of droughts in the interior of the continent.

Worst of all, perhaps, is that deforestation leads to desertification. And, de-sertification tends _____ what scientists call a "runaway phe-
23 (be)
nomenon." Once it begins _____ in a particular area, it rapidly
24 (occur)
starts _____ and is almost impossible _____.
25 (spread)   26 (stop)
Generally, desertification cannot be reversed within a human lifetime.

If we let the deforestation and subsequent desertification _____,
27 (continue)
we risk _____ our own habitat. While governments and conser-
28 (damage / permanently)
vation groups around the world are committed to _____
29 (protect)
forests, to date their efforts have not been enough _____ the
30 (slow)
rate of _____, much less _____ it. Perhaps the
31 (cut)   32 (stop)
most important step toward _____ the destruction of forests
33 (halt)
and other green areas is _____ public awareness. Until more
34 (heighten)
people know about the threats, the trees will keep on _____.
35 (fall)

———————————

Adapted from *National Geographic*, "Eye in the Sky"

▲ Scientists estimate that 80 percent of the Earth's forest cover has already been destroyed.

Cultural Note

Julia Butterfly Hill: Eco-hero or Eco-terrorist?

Julia Butterfly Hill is an environmentalist who doesn't just write articles or attend rallies. She takes direct, nonviolent action. For 738 days, from December 10, 1997, to December 18, 1999, Hill lived high above the ground in a tree, which she named "Luna," in northern California. She did this in order to prevent a lumber company from cutting this majestic 600-year-old redwood down. Despite numerous attempts by the lumber company to physically force her out of the tree, Hill stayed for more than two years until lumber executives finally agreed to let Luna and all other trees within three acres grow in peace.

4 Review Working with a partner, complete the following sentences in at least two different ways. In each case, use the *-ing*, *-ed*, infinitive, or simple form of a verb.

Example: *I'm afraid of losing my hair.*
I'm afraid of big business damaging the environment.

1. I'm afraid of
2. It's fascinating
3. I appreciate
4. It's difficult
5. My parents refuse
6. I like . . . instead of. . . .
7. My brother advised me
8. I don't mind
9. My fiancé(e) is looking forward to
10. My professor appreciates
11. It's wonderful
12. I enjoy . . ., but my wife prefers. . . .
13. I remember . . . when I was young.
14. Did you remember . . . before you went to bed?
15. My best friend asked
16. The police caught the thief
17. We watched the sun
18. Yesterday, I had my car
19. We left the old couple
20. I saw the young man being

5 Review Acid rain, pesticide poisoning, and other forms of pollution are tremendous threats to the environment. However, these pollutants seem almost insignificant when compared to the ultimate man-made ecological disaster—a nuclear war or a nuclear accident. Examine the chart and then answer the questions, using complete sentences.

1. If there were a nuclear explosion in your city,

    a. how high would the temperature climb?

    b. how many people living within 20 miles would survive?

    c. approximately how many people would die instantly?

2. If you are 50 miles from a nuclear explosion,

    a. will you die instantly?

    b. will you get sick?

    c. where will you find food that is safe to eat and water that is safe to drink?

3. If you lived 1,000 miles from the nearest explosion,

    a. would you be safe?

    b. what problems would you probably have?

    c. what might be the effect on your future children?

4. If you think a nuclear war is about to start,

    a. whom will you contact?

    b. what plans will you make?

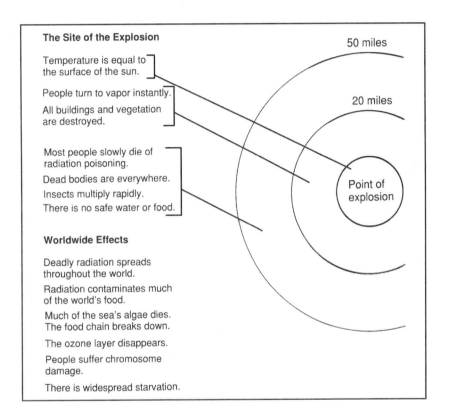

The Site of the Explosion

50 miles

Temperature is equal to the surface of the sun.

People turn to vapor instantly.

All buildings and vegetation are destroyed.

20 miles

Most people slowly die of radiation poisoning.

Dead bodies are everywhere.

Insects multiply rapidly.

There is no safe water or food.

Point of explosion

Worldwide Effects

Deadly radiation spreads throughout the world.

Radiation contaminates much of the world's food.

Much of the sea's algae dies. The food chain breaks down.

The ozone layer disappears.

People suffer chromosome damage.

There is widespread starvation.

---

6 **Review** Imagine that it is now the year 2099. Your home is Earth, and it is a very pleasant place. As the 22nd century approaches, you are looking back and imagining what might have or might not have happened during the 21st century. Use past subjunctive forms of the verbs in parentheses or add perfect modal auxiliaries to complete the following passage.

Looking Back at the Years 2000–2098

Life in the 21st century has been very pleasant, thanks to a memorable event in the year 2019. In that year, the entire world decided to work together. The 21st century _would (might) have been_ very different if that event
(be)

_____.
1 (happen / never)

If we _____ to work together, there _____
2 (not decide)   3 (be)

a total disaster. Our environment _____ beyond repair if we
4 (damage)

_____ pollution, use of resources, and farming and fishing
5 (not control)

methods. The population of the world _____ to grow, and more
6 (continue)

and more people _____ to the cities.
7 (move)

If the Earth's population _____ to grow, we _____
8 (continue)   9 (not provide)

free medical care and education for everyone. There _____
10 (be)

problems with jobs. And of course, there _____ enough food to
11 (not be)

go around.

Fortunately, though, at the beginning of the 21st century, our governments were very wise. As a result, we have a healthy environment, sufficient food and medical care, free education, and safe, interesting jobs for everyone. By working together, we _____ a very nice place for all the citizens of
12 (create)

the Earth.

7 **Review** The following passage was written many years ago by the noted anthropologist Margaret Mead (1901–1978), yet its message holds true today. First read the passage for meaning. Then follow the instructions below.

Margaret Mead Speaking on the Future of Humanity

I am optimistic by nature. I am glad that I am alive. I am glad that I am living at this particular, very difficult, very dangerous, and very crucial period in human history.

To this extent, my viewpoint about the future reflects a personal temperamental bent—something that must always be taken into account. But, of course, unsupported optimism is not enough.

I support my optimism with my knowledge of how far mankind has come. Throughout the hundreds of thousands of years that human life has evolved, at first physically and later culturally, human beings have withstood tremendous changes and have adjusted to radically new demands. What we have to realize, I believe, is that human ingenuity, imagination, and faith in life itself have been crucial both in initiating changes and in meeting new demands imposed by change.

As an anthropologist, I also have seen how a living generation of men born into a Stone Age culture has moved into a modern world all at once, skipping the many small steps by which mankind as a whole moved from the distant past into the present.

I find these things encouraging. An earlier generation invented the idea of invention. Now we have invented the industrialization of invention—a way of meeting a recognized problem by setting hundreds of trained persons together to work out solutions and, equally important, to work out the means of putting solutions into practice.

This is what made it possible to send men to the moon and to begin the exploration of outer space. This should give us reason to believe also that we can meet the interlocking problems of runaway populations, war, and the pollution of the Earth on which we depend for life. None of these problems is as insoluble.

What we need is the will to demand solutions and the patience to learn how to carry them out.

—Margaret Mead

Instructions Here are cues to help you paraphrase Margaret Mead's ideas. First complete the exercise by creating sentences with reporting clauses. Then rework and combine these ideas to write a six- to eight-sentence summary of Mead's essay.

Margaret Mead said. . . .   She told us. . . .

She mentioned. . . .   She believed. . . .

Example optimistic by nature
    Margaret Mead said that she was optimistic by nature.

1. glad to be alive

2. glad / live

3. support / optimism

4. human beings / withstand tremendous changes

5. human ingenuity, imagination, and faith in life / crucial to change

6. see Stone Age cultures / move into the modern world in one generation

7. mankind as a whole / move by small steps into the present

8. be encouraged by these things

9. people / can solve the problems of population, war, and pollution

10. need the will and patience to find and carry out solutions

Using What You've Learned

8 **Discussing Problems and Possible Solutions** Reread the opening passage "Humans and the Environment: Conflict or Coexistence?" on page 428. Then consider all of the problems raised in this chapter, along with other issues not raised here. In small groups, discuss the various issues that seem most critical to you. Talk about what the current situation is, how it developed, how it might have developed differently, and what its impact on the future might or will be. As you discuss, make some notes and begin to organize your ideas.

After your discussion, choose the one issue that you believe needs the most urgent attention. Use your notes and any additional ideas as the basis for a composition. In your composition, look at both reality and unreality. First, describe the current situation. Then, hypothesize about the past, present, and future—if things had been done differently. Finally, work again in the same groups and share your compositions.

- abortion
- AIDS
- air and water pollution
- cancer
- disposal of nuclear waste
- extinction of species

- global weather changes
- hazardous waste disposal
- population growth and control
- storage or elimination of nuclear weapons
- urban migration

9 **Writing a Poem** Have you ever written a poem in your native language? Have you ever written poetry in English? You may be surprised to discover that writing poetry in a second language can be an enjoyable and liberating experience. Since poetry is based on images and not grammar, it offers writers an unparalleled opportunity to be creative. Because poetry is an art form, poets don't have to follow every grammatical rule. They only need to be sure that their messages can be understood.

As a final activity, write an eight- to ten-line poem about your vision of the future. You can do this individually, in small groups, or as a class. You may also like to write a poem about a notable family member, classmate, or place. Use the instructions on page 469 to guide you, or feel free to change them.

Line 1: Give a four- to five-word sentence with a subject and a verb.

Line 2: Add three modifiers to describe a noun in Line 1.

Line 3: Compare the noun to something. Use the word *like*.

Line 4: Add a participial phrase that gives motion to the noun(s) in Line 3.

Line 5: Add two or three adverbs or adjectives to describe the motion in Line 4.

Line 6: Use a metaphor to make this action either very great or very small.

Line 7: Give nouns and adjectives that refer to your idea in Line 1.

Lines 8 (9, 10): Give your opinion or final comment on the idea from Line 1.

Here is a sample poem.

Space

Will there be a time when there won't be space anymore—
Open space, free space, space to move around?
Space is like a huge ocean wave.
Moving outward, upward, roaring toward the edge.
Completely free,
More freedom than cars on a freeway or apartments in a city.
So little space that everything seems airtight, can't breathe, no light,
Too many things crowded together,
Not enough space for clear skies, sunlight, or me.

Review of Problem Areas from Chapters 6–10

A variety of problem areas are included in this test. Check your understanding by completing the sample items that follow.

Part 1 Circle the best completion for the following.

Example   If Ned _____ the train, he would have been late for work.

    (A) has missed   (B) missed

    (C) had missed   (D) had been missing

1. It is imperative _____ to the meeting.

    (A) that he comes   (B) that he come

    (C) he comes   (D) he must come

2. Around the world, copper cables _____ glass fibers used to transmit electronic messages.

    (A) are been replaced by   (B) are being replaced

    (C) are replacing by   (D) are being replaced by

3. She remarked _____ to play tennis.

    (A) what it was a beautiful day   (B) was it a beautiful day

    (C) what a beautiful day was it   (D) what a beautiful day it was

4. Fossil fuels, such as oil and natural gas, _____ plant and animal material deposited on the sea floor millions of years ago.

    (A) are formed to   (B) is formed from

    (C) are formed from   (D) is formed to

5. The researcher explained that a child's brain was one mass, whereas an adult's brain _____ into two hemispheres.

    (A) was separated   (B) is separated

    (C) was separate   (D) is separate

6. _____ the nonviolent means that Mohandas K. Gandhi advocated, his followers often resorted to violence.

    (A) Despite of   (B) In spite

    (C) In spite of   (D) Despite the fact that

7. Were she _____ there, she could pick up the package for us.

  (A) to going   (B) went

  (C) going   (D) go

8. The universe is known _____.

  (A) to have expand   (B) to be expanding

  (C) expanding   (D) having expanded

9. I hope the team _____ last night.

  (A) win   (B) had won

  (C) won   (D) will win

10. Much of the world's silver has been used _____ coins.

  (A) to making   (B) made

  (C) make   (D) to make

Part 2 Each sentence has one error. Circle the letter below the word(s) containing the error.

Example The 20th century <u>might have been</u> different <u>than</u> it <u>was</u> if that event
                                      A   B   C

       <u>has never happened</u>.
           (D)

1. If English <u>didn't have</u> <u>so many</u> vocabulary words, it <u>might</u> <u>have seemed</u> easier
             A   B   C   D

    to learn.

2. <u>The</u> Russian physiologist I. P. Pavlov conducted experiments with dogs
    A

    <u>in order to</u> he <u>could learn</u> more about responses to <u>a variety of stimuli</u>.
        B   C   D

3. When <u>questioned</u> by the police, the young woman said <u>that</u> she <u>has left</u> the
            A   B   C

    store before the robbery <u>took</u> place.
                         D

4. If they <u>had had</u> more time, they <u>could had</u> visited the Statue of Liberty,
    A   B   C

    <u>along with</u> the United Nations.
       D

5. If Orville and Wilbur Wright <u>hadn't</u> <u>went to</u> Kitty Hawk, North Carolina, to test

                                  A   B

their flying machines, they might not <u>have encountered</u> the right winds to

                                          C

<u>make the launch possible.</u>

          D

6. <u>The</u> first <u>major</u> oil fields in Saudi Arabia <u>was discovered</u> in 1923 by Socal, <u>a</u>

    A   B   C   D

United States oil company.

7. <u>That</u> elderly, gray-haired man <u>must have been</u> <u>confuse</u> about the time of his

     A   B   C

appointment because he arrived two hours <u>ahead of schedule.</u>

                                                        D

8. A reporter's job consists <u>of</u> <u>gathering</u> information and <u>to write</u> <u>news</u> stories.

                              A   B   C   D

9. Galileo <u>put</u> in prison <u>because of</u> his public statements <u>regarding</u> <u>the rotation</u>

          A   B   C   D

of the Earth around the sun.

10. Should the Prime Minister <u>to receive</u> <u>another vote</u> of no confidence, she

                                        A   B

<u>would</u> be forced <u>to dissolve</u> her government.

   C   D

Self-Assessment Log

Check the things you did in this chapter. How well did you do each one?

	Not Very Well	Fairly Well	Very Well
I can use appropriate verb and modal auxiliary forms in noun clauses after *hope* and *wish*.	❑	❑	❑
I can use the transition *otherwise* appropriately.	❑	❑	❑
I can use appropriate verb forms in conditional sentences with *if*.	❑	❑	❑
I can use appropriate forms of modal auxiliaries in conditional sentences with *if*.	❑	❑	❑
I can use appropriate punctuation.	❑	❑	❑
I can take a test about adverb clauses, noun clauses, a variety of verb forms and tenses, modal auxiliaries, gerunds, and infinitives.	❑	❑	❑
I understand new information about past, present, and future environmental, political, and economic concerns, and I can use new structures and vocabulary to talk and write about related topics.	❑	❑	❑

Appendix 1

Irregular Verbs

Simple Form	Past	Past Participle	Simple Form	Past	Past Participle
arise	arose	arisen	flee	fled	fled
awake	awoke / awaked	awaked / awoken	fly	flew	flown
be	was / were	been	forbid	forbade	forbidden
bear	bore	borne / born	forget	forgot	forgotten
beat	beat	beat	forsake	forsook	forsaken
become	became	become	freeze	froze	frozen
begin	began	begun	get	got	got / gotten
bend	bent	bent	give	gave	given
bet	bet	bet	go	went	gone
bite	bit	bitten	grind	ground	ground
bleed	bled	bled	grow	grew	grown
blow	blew	blown	hang	hung / hanged	hung / hanged
break	broke	broken	have	had	had
breed	bred	bred	hear	heard	heard
bring	brought	brought	hide	hid	hidden
broadcast	broadcast	broadcast	hit	hit	hit
build	built	built	hold	held	held
burst	burst	burst	hurt	hurt	hurt
buy	bought	bought	keep	kept	kept
cast	cast	cast	know	knew	known
catch	caught	caught	lay	laid	laid
choose	chose	chosen	lead	led	led
cling	clung	clung	leap	leapt	leapt
come	came	come	leave	left	left
cost	cost	cost	lend	lent	lent
creep	crept	crept	let	let	let
cut	cut	cut	lie	lay	lain
deal	dealt	dealt	light	lit / lighted	lit / lighted
dig	dug	dug	lose	lost	lost
do	did	done	make	made	made
draw	drew	drawn	mean	meant	meant
drink	drank	drunk	meet	met	met
drive	drove	driven	overcome	overcame	overcome
eat	ate	eaten	pay	paid	paid
fall	fell	fallen	prove	proved	proved / proven*
feed	fed	fed	put	put	put
feel	felt	felt	quit	quit	quit
fight	fought	fought	read	read	read
find	found	found	ride	rode	ridden

Irregular Verbs

Simple Form	Past	Past Participle	Simple Form	Past	Past Participle
ring	rang	rung	stand	stood	stood
rise	rose	risen	steal	stole	stolen
run	ran	run	stick	stuck	stuck
say	said	said	sting	stung	stung
see	saw	seen	strike	struck	struck / stricken*
seek	sought	sought	strive	strove	striven
sell	sold	sold	swear	swore	sworn
send	sent	sent	sweep	swept	swept
set	set	set	swim	swam	swum
shake	shook	shaken	swing	swung	swung
shoot	shot	shot	take	took	taken
show	showed	showed / shown*	teach	taught	taught
shut	shut	shut	tear	tore	torn
sing	sang	sung	tell	told	told
sink	sank	sunk	think	thought	thought
sit	sat	sat	throw	threw	thrown
sleep	slept	slept	thrust	thrust	thrust
slide	slid	slid	understand	understood	understood
slit	slit	slit	upset	upset	upset
speak	spoke	spoken	wake	woke / waked	woken / waked
spend	spent	spent	wear	wore	worn
spin	spun	spun	weave	wove	woven
split	split	split	wind	wound	wound
spread	spread	spread	withdraw	withdrew	withdrawn
spring	sprang	sprung	write	wrote	written

*These participles are most often used with the passive voice.

Appendix 2

Spelling Rules and Irregular Noun Plurals

Spelling Rules for *-s*, *-ed*, *-er*, *-est*, and *-ing* Endings

This chart summarizes the basic spelling rules for endings with verbs, nouns, adjectives, and adverbs.

Rule	Word	*-s*	*-ed*	*-er*	*-est*	*-ing*
For most words, simply add *-s*, *-ed*, *-er*, *-est*, or *-ing* without making any other changes.	clean cool	cleans cools	cleaned cooled	cleaner cooler	cleanest coolest	cleaning cooling

Spelling changes occur with the following:

Rule	Word	*-s*	*-ed*	*-er*	*-est*	*-ing*
For words ending in a consonant + *y*, change the *y* to *i* before adding *-s*, *-ed*, *-er*, or *-est*. Do *not* change or drop the *y* before adding *-ing*.	carry happy lonely study worry	carries studies worries	carried studied worried	carrier happier lonelier worrier	happiest loneliest	carrying studying worrying
For most words ending in *e*, drop the *e* before adding *-ed*, *-er*, *-est*, or *-ing*. *Exceptions:*	dance late nice save write agree canoe		danced saved	dancer later nicer saver writer	latest nicest	dancing saving writing agreeing canoeing
For many words ending in one vowel and one consonant, double the final consonant before adding *-ed*, *-er*, *-est*, or *-ing*. These include one-syllable words and words with stress on the final syllable.	begin hot mad plan occur refer run shop win		planned occurred referred shopped	beginner hotter madder planner runner shopper winner	hottest maddest	beginning planning occurring referring running shopping winning

Spelling changes occur with the following:

Rule	Word	-s	-ed	-er	-est	-ing
In words ending in one vowel and one consonant, do *not* double the final consonant if the last syllable is not stressed. *Exceptions:* including words ending in *w*, *x*, or *y*	enter happen open travel visit bus fix play sew	buses	entered happened opened traveled visited bused fixed played sewed	opener traveler fixer player sewer		entering happening opening traveling visiting busing fixing playing sewing
For most words ending in *f* or *lf*, change the *f* to *v* and add -*es*. *Exceptions:*	half loaf shelf belief chief proof roof safe	halves loaves shelves beliefs chiefs proofs roofs safes	halved shelved	shelver		halving shelving
For words ending in *ch*, *sh*, *s*, *x*, *z*, and sometimes *o*, add -*es*. *Exceptions:*	church wash class fix quiz tomato zero dynamo ghetto monarch piano portfolio radio studio	churches washes classes fixes quizzes tomatoes zeroes dynamos ghettos monarchs pianos portfolios radios studios				

Irregular Noun Plurals

person	people	foot	feet	deer	deer	series	series
child	children	tooth	teeth	fish	fish	species	species
man	men		goose	geese			
woman	women		ox	oxen			

Irregular Noun Plurals with Foreign Origins

alumnus	alumni	analysis	analyses	basis	bases	crisis	crises
criterion	criteria	curriculum	curricula	hypothesis	hypotheses	oasis	oases
memorandum	memoranda	synthesis	syntheses	thesis	theses	radius	radii
phenomenon	phenomena	nucleus	nuclei	stimulus	stimuli		
syllabus	syllabi or syllabuses						
index	indices or indexes						

477

Appendix 3

The with Proper Nouns

The has specific uses with proper nouns, especially with geographical locations. Because proper nouns identify specific places, *the* is often used. There are few exceptions to the rules. Study the following chart and use it for reference.

With *the*		Without *the*	
The is used when the class of noun (continent, country, etc.) comes before the name: *the* + class + *of* + name.	the continent of Asia the United States of America the U.S.A.	*The* is not used with names of planets, continents, countries, states, provinces, cities, and streets.	Mars Africa Antarctica Russia Ohio Quebec
The is used with most names of regions.	the West the Midwest the equator		Austin State Street
Exceptions:	New England southern (northern, etc.)	*Exceptions:*	(the) earth the world the Netherlands
The is used with plural islands, lakes, and mountains.	the Hawaiian Islands the Great Lakes the Alps	*The* is not used with singular islands, lakes, and mountains.	Oahu Fiji Lake Superior Mt. Whitney
The is used with oceans, seas, rivers, canals, deserts, jungles, forests, and bridges.*	the Pacific Ocean the Persian Gulf the Mississippi River the Suez Canal the Sahara Desert the Black Forest the Golden Gate Bridge	*Exceptions:*	the Isle of Wight the Matterhorn (and other mountains with German names that are used in English)
The is generally used when the word *college*, *university*, or *school* comes before the name: *the* + ... + *of* + name.	the University of California the Rhode Island School of Design	*The* is not used when the name of a college or university comes before the word *college* or *university*. *Exception:*	Boston University Amherst College the Sorbonne
The is used with adjectives of nationality and other adjectives that function as nouns.	the Germans the Japanese the rich the poor the strong	*The* is not used with names of languages. *Note: The* is used with the word *language*: *the German language.*	German Japanese

* The class name is often omitted with well-known oceans, deserts, and rivers: *the Atlantic*, *the Nile*.

With *the*		Without *the*	
The is used in dates when the number comes before the month.	the twenty-eighth of March	*The* is not used in dates when the month begins the phrase.	March 28
The is used with decades, centuries, and eras.	the 1800s the 1990s the Dark Ages	*The* is not used with specific years.	1890 1951
The is used with names of museums and libraries.	the Museum of Modern Art the Chicago Public Library		

Appendix 4

Verbs not Normally Used in the Continuous Tenses

The following verbs are seldom used in the continuous tenses. In some cases, the continuous form is used in certain idiomatic expressions or in descriptions of the definite action.

Thoughts or Feelings		Examples	Notes
appear	mean*	We **need** to discuss the situation.	These verbs are rarely used in
appreciate	mind	We **think** that this is a serious issue.	a continuous tense; the verbs
be	miss	We **consider** it to be a problem.	with an asterisk (*), however,
believe	need	We **want** to make several improvements.	sometimes appear in a
consider*	prefer		continuous tense (especially
desire	realize	*Compare:*	the present perfect continuous).
dislike	recognize	Bob **is thinking** about his problems.	
doubt	remember	He **has been considering** a variety of solutions	The verbs *think* and *consider*
feel*	seem	He **has been meaning** to talk to you about it.	occasionally appear in the
hate	think*		present continuous tense, also.
know	understand		
like	want*		
love			

Perceptions		Examples	Notes
feel	smell	The ocean **looks** cold today.	These verbs sometimes appear
hear	sound	The wind **feels** very cold and damp.	in a continuous tense in the
look	taste		description of a specific action
see		*Compare:*	or in certain idioms.
		I **am looking** at the ocean now.	
		I **am feeling** a little seasick.	

Possession		Examples	Notes
belong to	own	We **own** a house.	These verbs almost never
cost	possess	It **belongs** to my sister and me.	appear in continuous tenses,
have		The house **has** four bedrooms.	except for the verb *have*. In
			idiomatic use, *be having* has
		Compare:	several meanings, including "be
		We've **been having** fun lately.	experiencing" or "be eating,
		We're **having** a party next weekend.	drinking."

Appendix 5

Modal Auxiliaries and Related Structures

Modal Auxiliaries		
Auxiliary	Function and Time Frame	Examples
can	present ability present impossibility informal present request	I **can** swim very well. I **cannot** finish this exercise. **Can** you help me?
could	present ability	I **could** speak French when I was younger.
could have	past ability (unfulfilled)	With some help, I **could have** finished earlier.
may	present request or permission present possibility	**May** I help you? He **may** be sleeping now.
may have	past possibility	He **may have** gone out somewhere.
might	present possibility present advice or suggestion	I **might** go to the movies, or I might stay home. You **might** see a doctor if your cold doesn't improve.
might have	past possibility	She **might have** gone to the library.
must	present need present probability	Everyone **must** pay his taxes. He's not eating. He **must** not be hungry.
must not	present prohibition	Students **must not** cheat on tests.
must have	past probability	You **must have** been tired after the game.
ought to	present advice present expectation	You **ought to** work faster. The check **ought to** come tomorrow.
ought to have	past advice (not taken) past expectation	We **ought to have** finished this long ago. She **ought to have** gotten the check yesterday.
should	present advice present expectation	You **should** be very careful if you go there. The mail **should** arrive soon.
should have	past advice (not taken) past expectation	We **should have** started this weeks ago. He **should have** arrived an hour ago.
will	present requests future intentions	**Will** you please help us? He**'ll** help us if he can.
would	present request past habits	**Would** you please help? **Would** you mind helping me? As a child, I **would** play outside everyday after school

481

Related Structures

Related Structures	Function and Time Frame	Examples
be able to	present ability past ability	We **aren't able to** leave now. We **weren't able to** see the play.
didn't have to	past lack of need	I **didn't have to** work last Sunday.
had better	present advice	You **had better not** eat that.
have got to	present need	She **has got to** leave now.
have to	present need	She **has to** leave now.
not have to had to	present lack of need past need	It's early. We **don't have to** leave yet. I **had to** work last Saturday.
used to	past habits	We **used to** relax on the weekend, but now we work.

Appendix 6

Summary of Gerunds and Infinitives

Verbs Often Followed by Gerunds

admit	She **admitted** stealing the money.	involve	This job **involves** meeting a lot of people.
anticipate	We **anticipate** arriving late.	keep (on)	**Keep on** working until I tell you to stop.
appreciate	I really **appreciated** getting your card.	mention	Did she **mention** quitting her job?
avoid	She **avoids** stepping on cracks—a superstition.	miss	I **miss** hearing your voice.
be worth	I am sure it **is worth** waiting.	postpone	Will they **postpone** calling a meeting?
can't help	He **can't help** getting upset about that.	practice	A good tennis player has to **practice** serving.
consider	Have you **considered** moving?	recommend	I **recommend** taking some aspirin.
delay	They **delayed** starting the game because of the rain.	regret	I **regret** saying that.
deny	He **denied** speeding.	risk	She **risked** losing all her money in that deal.
dislike	He really **dislikes** getting up early.	spend (time)	Do you **spend** much **time** doing your homework?
dread	She **dreads** going to the dentist.	suggest	They **suggested** having a picnic.
enjoy	We always **enjoy** traveling.	tolerate	I can't **tolerate** listening to rock music.
escape	We narrowly **escaped** hitting the other car.	understand	Do you **understand** his not calling?
finish	Have you **finished** writing that paper?		
forgive	I can **forgive** his cheating, but I can't forgive his lying.		
imagine	Can you **imagine** living in Bogotá?		

Verbs Often Followed by Infinitives

afford	We can't **afford** to go.	know how	Do you **know how** to play squash?
agree	They **agreed** to help.	learn	She is **learning** to play tennis.
appear	She **appeared** to be calm.	manage	Somehow he **managed** to finish the race.
be	We **were** to do the homework in Chapter 3.	offer	They **offered** to help us.
be able	**Were** you **able** to finish the work?	plan	We **planned** to leave earlier.
be supposed	You **were supposed** to do it yesterday.	prepare	They **prepared** to get on board the plane.
care	I don't **care** to go.	pretend	He **pretended** not to notice us.
decide	He **decided** to stay.	refuse	I **refuse** to get up at 5:00 A.M.!
deserve	She **deserves** to get a high grade.	seem	He **seems** to be upset.
fail	They **failed** to make the announcement.	tend	She **tends** to forget things.
forget	I **forgot** to buy eggs.	threaten	The employee **threatened** to quit.
happen	Did he **happen** to stop by?	volunteer	Several people **volunteered** to help us.
have	I **have** to leave.	wait	She **waited** for the letter carrier to come.
hesitate	Don't **hesitate** to call!	wish	We **wished** to go, but we couldn't.
hope	We **hope** to visit Rome next spring.		
intend	I **intend** to stop there for several days.		

Subject + Verb + (Optional Noun or Pronoun) + infinitive

ask	We **asked** to come. We **asked** them to come.	**promise**	She **promised** to help. She **promised** her mother to help.
beg	He **begged** to go. He **begged** us to go.	**want**	They **want** to leave. They **want** us to leave.
dare	I **dare** to go. I **dared** him to go.	**would like**	He **would like** to stay. He **would like** you to stay.
expect	I **expect** to finish soon. I **expect** them to finish soon.	**use**	They **used** to live there. (habitual past) They **used** a hammer to fix the table. (method)
need	I **need** to go. I **need** you to go.		

Subject + Verb + Noun or Pronoun + infinitive

advise*	The doctor **advised** me to rest.	**permit***	Will they **permit** us to camp here?
allow*	He won't **allow** you to swim.	**persuade**	Perhaps we can **persuade** them to let us go.
cause*	The accident **caused** me to faint.		
convince	She **convinced** us to try again.	**remind**	Did you **remind** her to buy milk?
encourage*	I **encourage** you to study languages.	**require**	The school **required** us to wear uniforms.
force	The hijacker **forced** them to land the plane.	**teach***	He **taught** me to play tennis.
get	He **got** them to pay ransom.	**tell**	I **told** him not to come.
hire	We **hired** you to do the job.	**urge**	We **urge** you to change your mind.
invite	They **invited** us to come.	**warn**	I am **warning** you to stop!
order	I am **ordering** you to stop!		

* These verbs are followed by gerunds if no noun or pronoun object is used after the main verb.

Verb + Gerund or Infinitive (Same Meaning)

begin	She **began** to work (working) on the project.	**hate**	He **hates** to play (playing) golf.
		like	I **like** to play (playing) tennis.
can't bear	I **can't bear** to see (seeing) her work so much.	**love**	Mary **loves** to read (reading) novels.
		neglect	We **neglected** to tell (telling) her about that.
can't stand	She **can't stand** to stay (staying) alone at night.		
		prefer	I **prefer** to go (going) alone.
continue	They'll **continue** to practice (practicing) several days more.	**start**	We **started** to worry (worrying) about the situation.

Verb + Gerund or Infinitive (Different Meanings)

mean	I **meant** to finish the project sooner. This **means** delaying the project.	**remember**	Did you **remember** to tell her? I **remember** telling her about it, but she forgot.
quit (stop)	He **quit (stopped)** to take a long break. We **quit (stopped)** taking breaks in order to leave work.	**try**	We **tried** to call you, but the phone was out of order. I **tried** calling, and then I decided to write you a note.

Photo Credits

Page 3: (c) image100 Ltd; 11: (c) Todd Gipstein/CORBIS; 14: Susan Kuklin/Photo Researchers; 21: (c) Bettmann/CORBIS; 25: (c) BananaStock/JupiterImages; 32: (c) Eric Lessing/Art Resource, NY; 47: (c) Ryan McVay/Getty Images; 65, 70: (c) Bettmann/ CORBIS; 77: (c) Royalty-Free/CORBIS; 79: (c) William Whitehurst/CORBIS; 85: (c) Bettmann/CORBIS; 88: (c) Tom McHugh/PhotoResearchers; 103: Underwood & Underwood/CORBIS; 104: (c) DPA/The Image Works; 107: (c) UPI/Bettmann/CORBIS; 115: (c) Comstock/PunchStock; 121: (c) image100 Ltd; 130: (c) Sandra Baker/Getty Images; 136 (top): (c) Digital Vision; 136 (bottom): (c) PhotoAlto/PunchStock; 153: (c) Hisham F. Ibrahim /Getty Images; 155: (c) Royalty-Free/CORBIS; 156: (c) Gian Berto Vanni/ CORBIS; 160: (c) Bettmann/CORBIS; 164: (c) Jan Butchofsky-Houser/CORBIS; 166 (left): (c) James Gritz/Getty Images; 166 (middle): (c) Brand X Pictures/PunchStock; 166 (right): (c) Comstock/PunchStock; 168: (c) Adalberto Rios Szalay/Sexto Sol/Getty Images; 169: (c) Macduff Everton/CORBIS; 170, 174: (c) Royalty-Free/CORBIS; 177, 183: (c) George Holton/Photo Researchers; 185 (left): (c) Ingo Jezierski/Getty Images; 185 (right): (c) John Wang/Getty Images; 187: (c) Royalty-Free/ CORBIS; 189: (c) Glen Allison/Getty Images; 191: (c) MedioImages/Getty Images; 194: (c) PhotoLink/PhotoDisc/Getty Images; 199: (c) Patrick Ward/CORBISL 201: (c) Digital Vision/PunchStock; 203: Courtesy Lea Monaghan; 207, 218: (c) Bettmann/CORBIS; 221: Culver Pictures; 224, 226, 230, 242: (c) Bettmann/CORBIS; 249: (c) M. Freeman/PhotoLink/Getty Images; 251: (c) Scott Bodell/Getty Images; 254: Relativity by M. C. Escher, National Galley of Art, Washington, D.C. Gift of Mrs. C. V. Roosevelt; 268: (c) Christopher Briscoe/Photo Researchers; 270: (c) Bettmann/CORBIS; 293: (c) Rob Crandall/Stock Boston; 333: (c) Michael Grecco/Stock Boston; 335: (c) PhotoDisc; 340: Library of Congress; 346: (c) Bettmann/CORBIS; 352: (c) Mark C. Burnett/Stock Boston; 353 (left): (c) Sean Sprague/Stock Boston; 353 (right): (c) Bob Daemmrich/Stock Boston; 363: (c) Digital Vision/PunchStock; 365: (c) Russell D. Curtis; 372: (c) Royalty-Free/CORBIS; 376: (c) Wolfgang Kaehler/CORBIS; 381: (c) Art Resource, NY; 384: (c) Bettmann/CORBIS; 387: (c) Lynn Goldsmith/CORBIS; 389: (c) Ted Streshinsky/CORBIS; 392: (c) Victor Englebert/Photo Researchers; 399 (left): (c) Robert Frerck/Woodfin Camp & Associates; 399 (middle): (c) Loren McIntyre/Woodfin Camp & Associates; 399 (right): (c) Victor Englebert/Photo Researchers; 403: (c) Giraudon/Art Resource, NY; 409 (left): (c) Scala/Art Resource, NY; 409 (right): (c) Tate Gallery, London/Art Resource, NY; 410: (c) The Museum of Modern Art; 411: (c) M. Freeman/PhotoLink/Getty Images; 413: (c) Yann Layma/Getty Images; 415: (c) PhotoLink/Getty Images; 418: (c) Stephenie Dinkins/Photo Researchers; 427: AP/Wide World Photos; 433: (c) M. Freeman/ PhotoLink/Getty Images; 450: (c) Royalty-Free/CORBIS; 456: (c) Natalie Fobes/CORBIS; 458: (c) Richard Cummins/CORBIS; 460: (c) Bob Kramer/Stock Boston; 463: (c) Pat Powers and Cherryl Schafer/Getty Images; 469: (c) Digital Vision.

Text Credits

Page 2 © Charles Howard-Bury and George Leigh Mallory. *Everest Reconnaissance: The First Expedition of 1921*. London: Hodder & Stoughton, 1991. **Page 10** © Rhoda Metraux. *Margaret Mead, Some Personal Views*. New York: Walker & Co., 1979.

Skills Index